THE CRAFT OF WARGAMING

A DETAILED PLANNING GUIDE FOR DEFENSE PLANNERS AND ANALYSTS

THE CRAFT OF WARGAMING

A DETAILED PLANNING GUIDE FOR DEFENSE PLANNERS AND ANALYSTS

COL. JEFF APPLEGET, USA (RET.), COL. ROBERT BURKS, USA (RET.), AND FRED CAMERON

NAVAL INSTITUTE PRESS
ANNAPOLIS, MARYLAND

Naval Institute Press
291 Wood Road
Annapolis, MD 21402

© 2020 by Jeff Appleget, Robert Burks, Fred Cameron
All rights reserved. No part of this book may be reproduced or utilized in any form or by any means, electronic or mechanical, including photocopying and recording, or by any information storage and retrieval system, without permission in writing from the publisher.

First Naval Institute Press paperback edition published in 2025.
ISBN: 978-1-68247-978-0 (paperback)

The Library of Congress has cataloged the hardcover edition as follows:
Names: Appleget, Jeff, author. | Burks, Robert, author. | Cameron, Fred, author.
Title: The craft of wargaming : a detailed planning guide for defense planners and analysts / Jeff Appleget, Robert Burks, Fred Cameron.
Other titles: Detailed planning guide for defense planners and analysts
Description: Annapolis, MD : Naval Institute Press, [2020] | Includes bibliographical references and index
Identifiers: LCCN 2020016797 (print) | LCCN 2020016798 (ebook) | ISBN 9781682473764 (hardback) | ISBN 9781682473771 (epub) | ISBN 9781682473771 (ebook)
Subjects: LCSH: War games. | Simulation games. | Military art and science.
Classification: LCC U310 .A66 2020 (print) | LCC U310 (ebook) | DDC 355.4/8 — dc23
LC record available at https://lccn.loc.gov/2020016797
LC ebook record available at https://lccn.loc.gov/2020016798

♾ Print editions meet the requirements of ANSI/NISO z39.48-1992 (Permanence of Paper).
Printed in the United States of America.

9 8 7 6 5 4 3 2 1

CONTENTS

LIST OF FIGURES	x
INTRODUCTION	**1**
PART I. FOUNDATIONS	**13**
Chapter 1. Analytic Wargaming	**15**
Chapter 2. Craft of Wargaming	**21**
Who Needs Wargaming?	27
Building a Cadre of Uniformed Wargamers	30
The Education of a Wargaming Apprentice	31
Learning from Previous Wargaming Education	32
Chapter 3. Wargaming Characteristics	**36**
Elements of Wargaming	37
Information Structure	43
Player Engagement Structure	45
Relationship between Information and Player Engagement	48
Wargame Adjudication	49
Chapter 4. Wargaming History	**51**
History of Kriegsspiel	52
Plan Orange at the Naval War College	54
Admiral Yarnell and Pearl Harbor	55
Battle of Midway	56
World War II Outcome for Japan	57
Desert Crossing	58

Chapter 5. Analytic Wargaming Fundamentals — 61
- The Cycle of Communications — 62
- The Five Phases of Wargame Construction — 63
- The Troubled Nation of Zefra — 68

PART II. FUNDAMENTALS — 75

Chapter 6. Initiate — 77
- Sponsor Engagement — 78
- Initial Engagement — 81
- Clarification Engagement — 82
- Scoping Engagement — 87
- Sponsor Agreement — 90
- Data Collection and Management Plan — 91
- Wargame Practical Exercises 1–4 — 97

Chapter 7. Design — 101
- Measurement Space — 103
- Scenario — 106
- Data — 107
- Methods, Models, and Tools — 111
- Players — 115
- Assumptions — 116
- Measurement Space: Idealized and Reality — 116
- Wargame Practical Exercise 5 — 118

Chapter 8. Development — 120
- Play-testing — 122
- Play-testing the Data Collection Management Plan — 124
- Contingencies — 126
- Rules and Procedures — 129
- Wargame Practical Exercises 6–7 — 130

Chapter 9. Conduct — 132
- Preparation for Execution — 132
- Execution — 134
- Wargame Practical Exercise 8 — 137

Chapter 10. Analysis — 139
- Beginning the Analysis — 139
- Post-Wargame Analysis — 140
- Characterizing Wargame Analysis Findings — 141
- Observations, Insights, and Results — 141
- Finalizing Wargaming Findings — 143
- Future Work — 144
- Wargame Practical Exercises 9–10 — 145

PART III. PLANNING AND MANAGEMENT — 149

Chapter 11. Planning and Managing an Analytic Wargame — 151
- Scheduling the Wargame — 151
- Data Collection — 152
- Wargame Plan — 155

Chapter 12. Course of Action Wargaming — 156
- Doctrinal Wargaming Framework — 158
- Free-Thinking Adversary — 162
- Facilitating More Wargaming — 165

Chapter 13. Special Considerations for Less Structured Wargames — 168
- BOGGSAT versus Seminar Wargames — 169
- Facilitation of Seminar and Less Structured Wargames — 170
- Adjudication Techniques for Less Structured Wargames — 172
- Seminar and Less Structured Wargame Analysis — 175

Chapter 14. Educational and Experiential Wargames — 176
- Experiential Wargames — 177
- Educational Wargaming — 180
- Play-testing Educational and Experiential Wargames — 181
- Series of Wargames for the DoD Planning Process — 182
- Training Exercises: Wargames or Not? — 183

Chapter 15. Best and Worst Practices — 186
- Initiate Phase — 186
- Design Phase — 192

Develop Phase	198
Conduct Phase	202
Analysis Phase	207

Appendix 1. Practical Exercise Zefra Brief — 210

Appendix 2. Zefra Scenario — 214

Background: Situation	218
Background: Attitudes and Goals—The Factions within Zefra	224
Desired End States	234
Player Objectives	237

Appendix 3. Practical Exercise Solutions — 253

Chapter 6 Practical Exercise 1 Solution	253
Chapter 6 Practical Exercise 2: Preparing for the Second Sponsor Interaction Solution	255
Practical Exercise 3 Solution	256
Practical Exercise 4 CLA Solution	257
Chapter 7 Practical Exercise 5: Designing the Measurement Space Solution	258
Chapter 8 Practical Exercise 6: Play-Test Solution	261
Practical Exercise 7: Final Rehearsal, Large Wargame Solution	262
Chapter 9 Practical Exercise 8: Game Director Managing Crises	263
Chapter 10 Practical Exercise 9: Quick-Look Report	265
Practical Exercise 10: Analysis	266

Appendix 4. Wargaming Gateway Exam — 268

Part 1: Wargaming Fundamentals	268
Part 2: Wargaming Fundamentals—Seven Elements	269
Part 3: Design and Development of Wargames	270
Part 4: Conducting Wargames	272
Part 5: Analysis of Wargames	273
Part 6: Analysis Methods	274
Part 7: Sponsors	274
Part 8: Constraints, Limitations, and Assumptions	275
Part 9: Seminar Wargames	276

Appendix 5. Case Studies in Wargaming Design — **278**

- Case Study 1: South China Sea Confrontation 2030 — 279
- Case Study 2: Employment of Non-Lethal Capabilities for Visit, Board, Search, and Seizure Operations — 283
- Case Study 3: Fleet Design and Expeditionary Advanced Basing Operations in the Baltic Sea — 289
- Case Study 4: Distributed Lethality—Eastern Mediterranean — 292
- Case Study 5: Carrier Presence Wargame — 296
- Case Study 6: LITMUS Wargaming in the South China Sea — 302
- Case Study 7: High North — 306
- Case Study 8: Trident Delphi — 310

Appendix 6. The Crisis in Zefra: A Matrix Game — **314**

- Aim — 314
- How to Play — 315
- Notes about Arguments — 317
- Turn Length — 317
- Inter-Turn Negotiations — 319
- Elections — 319
- Secret Arguments — 319
- Measure of Success — 320
- Killing Arguments — 320
- Big Projects — 321
- Method, Models, and Tools — 321
- The Crisis in Zefra Matrix Wargame — 323
- Roles — 325

NOTES — 333
BIBLIOGRAPHY — 343
INDEX — 349

FIGURES

Five Phases of Wargame Construction	63
The Zefran Timeline to War	70
The Core Elements of the DCMP	95
Applying Wargaming Principles	166
The Island of Capricornia	218
Crisis in Zefra Cards	318
Crisis in Zefra Game Board	324

INTRODUCTION

Now the great secret of its power lies in the existence of the enemy, a live, vigorous enemy in the next room waiting feverishly to take advantage of any of our mistakes, ever ready to puncture any visionary scheme, to haul us down to earth.

—CAPTAIN WILLIAM MCCARTY LITTLE,
U.S. NAVY, 1912[1]

"This is not a game at all! It's training for war! I shall recommend it enthusiastically to the whole army."[2] These statements, attributed to General Karl von Muffling after watching a demonstration of Georg von Reisswitz's now famous *Kriegsspiel* (wargame), ushered in the modern age of wargaming. The nineteenth century was a period of intellectual curiosity, which enabled the merging of the sciences, mathematical theory, and military strategy to develop a series of unprecedented military simulations of war. These simulations were designed to immerse players in the realities of war with representative terrain, models, and the latest mathematical and scientific theories. What followed von Reisswitz's Kriegsspiel was a century of further development and adoption by the world's great powers of the use of wargaming as a method to train and educate military leaders.[3] Von Reisswitz's wargames came to be known as "rigid Kriegsspiel" for the extensive number of rules and the amount of calculations required for their conduct. Eventually, the wargame became so complex that military leaders sought alternatives to them. Kriegsspiel clearly demonstrated the value of wargaming, but it was time for a change, and the Prussian army developed "free Kriegsspiel" as an easier alternative to the rigid game. This version of wargaming was used extensively by the Prussian army and was a common technique as part of a staff ride with combat-experienced senior officers posing military problems for their juniors to solve. Typically, senior officers acted as the final authority for the solutions proposed by the junior officers, thus replacing the great volume of adjudication rules of rigid Kriegsspiel with a facilitator.[4]

Wargaming practitioners can see that free Kriegsspiel, with its focus on humans making decisions, is the ancestor of what is today referred to as wargaming. Rigid Kriegsspiel, with its extensive rules and calculations, is actually more akin to the computer-augmented wargames and computer-based combat simulations that became the go-to analysis solution for defense organizations around the world since the late twentieth century. Both wargames and combat simulations address the study of warfare, human decisionmaking, and the calculation and quantification of combat outcomes, respectively, but neither provide a stand-alone analysis capability to be used in exclusion of the other.

This book is designed to support defense planners and analysts on their journey from wargaming apprentices to journeymen in the craft of wargaming. Our focus is on providing these individuals a window into wargaming, which is a part of their professional development. Despite the book's focus on wargaming apprentices, we believe that professional wargamers, senior leaders, and all decisionmakers in government and industry will gain something from the principles covered in this book. Hopefully, these individuals will acquire new insights or wargaming techniques to augment their capabilities or simply a better understanding of what wargaming can do for them. Despite our focus on the Department of Defense (DoD), the topics covered in this book will apply to the whole of government and any groups or individuals wrestling to gain insights into complex or wicked problems. We also believe that hobby or commercial wargamers will find part II of the book, with its focus on designing the wargame, of particular interest in the design and development of their own wargames.

Before we can begin our journey, we require a solid foundation upon which to build a study of wargaming, and this starts with a clear and concise definition of the term. The definition of wargaming has evolved over the last century and is slowly moving toward a basic consensus among practitioners, but today a shared common definition still does not exist. U.S. doctrine contains a couple of similar but slightly different definitions of a wargame. One common definition found throughout U.S. doctrine is "a simulation, by whatever means, of a military operation involving two or more opposing forces, using rules, data, and procedures designed to depict an actual or assumed real-life situation."[5] This was an update of Peter Perla's 1990 definition of a wargame as "a warfare model or simulation, using rules, data, and procedures, not involving actual military forces, and in which the flow of events is affected by, and in turn affects, decisions made during the course of those events by players representing the opposing sides."[6] These definitions capture many of the necessary elements of wargaming, but they also capture most military activities short of actual operations, to include the use of closed-loop computer-based combat simulations. In short, the definition is too broad to serve as a starting foundation.

The use of the terms "model" and "simulation," while accurate, unfortunately coincided with the rise of computer-based combat simulations in defense organizations in the 1990s, and these simulations were grouped under the general term "modeling and simulation" or "M&S."[7] This nomenclature muddied the waters, and many analysts and military leaders saw computer-based combat simulations as a replacement for wargaming, misunderstanding that these combat simulations had no way of actually replicating the complex human decisionmaking process required to employ forces in combat. Perla's deliberate inclusion of the phrase "not involving actual military forces" had the additional implications of excluding exercises and experiments—events that do involve the use of actual military forces—as venues that could also be leveraged to investigate human decisionmaking. Finally, the phrase "the opposing sides" highlighted a Red versus Blue construct—entirely understandable, since for more than four decades following the end of World War II, the Western world focused on a North Atlantic Treaty Organization (NATO)–Warsaw Pact kinetic engagement in Europe. However, the collapse of the Warsaw Pact began to force organizations to focus on more than just the Red versus Blue construct.

An updated version of Peter Perla's definition, and one that has been adopted by U.S. doctrine writers, that addresses the critical changes since

1990 is: "A dynamic representation of conflict or competition in a synthetic environment, in which people make decisions and respond to the consequences of those decisions."[8] This definition is becoming widely accepted among wargame practitioners, and the 2017 update to Joint Publication 5-0, *Joint Planning*, captured this updated definition for a wargame.[9]

The replacement of "models or simulations" with "dynamic representation" helps to dispel the notion that wargames must be instantiated on a computer. The omission of the caveat "not involving actual military forces" is also a welcome change. One of the clear benefits of wargaming is the ability to investigate human decisionmaking without conducting an expensive large-scale exercise that exposes personnel and equipment to risk. However, if a large-scale exercise is to be conducted and it does not detract from the exercise's purpose to integrate an investigation of decisionmaking, then that opportunity should be seized. The human decisionmaking portion of the exercise would actually be a wargame, and it should be designed and developed with the rigor necessary to make the event a worthwhile investment of resources. This integration is how wargaming fits within the cycle of research, which will be discussed in chapter 4. One historic example of this comes from World War II, where the Nazis actually wargamed as they were fighting a battle in the Ardennes. The wargame was designed to simulate an Allied attack in the sector the wargaming units were defending, and the Allies actually attacked as the wargame was being played. Field marshal Walter Model had everyone but the commanders whose units were in contact continue to play the wargame as the battle unfolded.[10]

Finally, "people make decisions" opens the way for the complex world that we face in the twenty-first century where most operations have elements of a whole of government framework and hybrid war constructs that involve much more than the engagement of two military forces in a kinetic exchange.

One goal of all wargames is to immerse the players in an environment with the required level of realism to permit the investigation of the human decisionmaking process. Wargaming is often used in analytic organizations to gain insights into challenges that involve future force structures and force design. Large analytic studies, sometimes called campaign analyses, may use both wargaming and computer-based combat simulations to assess current or future capabilities and concepts. Wargaming is part of the U.S.

joint planning process as it is used to assess U.S., joint, or coalition forces' courses of action (COAs) against an adversary's most likely and most dangerous courses of action.[11] In addition, there are many other DoD planning activities that are similar to wargames. Command post exercises, tactical exercises without troops, and rehearsal of concept drills are but a few of these activities that share many similarities with wargaming and may actually be considered wargames under the definition we use. Once we have established a good wargaming foundation, chapter 12 will cover these wargame-like activities in more detail, to include addressing when you should use them and what you can expect to gain from them.

When wargaming practitioners from around the globe meet, there is often a fundamental disconnect about the utilization of wargames that occurs when people from different organizations talk about their efforts. This disconnect is natural and expected because different organizations have different purposes for conducting wargames. While no two wargames, by their nature, are the same, they do possess an identifiable primary purpose for being conducted. We distinguish between three different major purposes for wargames: educational, experiential, and analytical. In this discussion, we have consciously left out entertainment as a primary purpose despite the fact that games for entertainment dwarf all other types, in terms of dollars spent on them.[12] We recognize that the utilization of entertainment games—such as "Railroad Tycoon," which has sold millions of copies—is increasing within many organizations and education programs.[13] Our intent of only including the three purposes of educational, experiential, and analytical is to keep the focus on the most likely wargames that young planners and analysts will encounter or utilize in their profession.

The three purposes for wargaming really depend on one major component related to the desire of the designer to either convey knowledge or create knowledge. The purpose of an educational wargame is to educate its players. It is designed to convey knowledge of some subject to the participants. Most of DoD's professional military education institutions use educational wargames to reinforce learning objectives, while exposing their students to historic or future scenarios. The intent is to present the students with situations that they are likely to encounter during the course of their professional careers and to reinforce the knowledge they gained in the classroom. One of the U.S. Navy's most famous series of wargames, the Plan Orange (war against Japan) wargames conducted at the U.S. Naval War College (NWC) from 1919 to 1940, were run as educational wargames (chart maneuvers) for the college's students.[14] The U.S. Marine Corps War College has used modified off-the-shelf hobby games as capstone events to drive home the concepts taught in the classroom and to help the students understand "the range of strategies and options."[15]

The focus of an experiential wargame is to provide the players with experience that will better prepare them to do specific jobs or tasks, and this category does include training wargames. In many cases, it is designed to convey knowledge of their roles and responsibilities in the organization. The U.S. Army Command and General Staff College conducts a division exercise as part of the curriculum to give the students experience in developing orders to maneuver the division,[16] preparing them to assume positions on a division staff upon graduation. Command post exercises are a common training exercise conducted throughout the U.S. Army for battalion, brigade, and division staffs that allow them to exercise their staff functions during a wargame.[17] Doing so provides them with useful training experiences that they can leverage when their organizations go to war. In both educational and experiential wargames, the focus of the wargame is on the players, and the primary product of the wargame is better educated or better trained players.

An analytic or analytical wargame focuses not on educating the players but on extracting knowledge or information from the game to support a sponsor who is seeking answers or insights to a particular problem. The primary products of an analytic wargame are the insights and findings that address the sponsor's problem, usually communicated with a written analysis report. Planning wargames, many of which seek to assess different COAs as part of the U.S. Armed Forces' formal planning process,[18] are arguably the most important type of analytic wargame as they seek to identify risks and vulnerabilities, enabling the organization to produce viable, executable plans for future military operations.

Analytic wargames also have an important role building future force structures or operational concepts. These wargames may focus on examining future technologies or concepts, where the sponsor is asking for help deciding on future research investments for the armed forces. Once technologies are mature enough to consider integrating them into the fighting force, an acquisition study called an analysis of alternatives is conducted by DoD analytic organizations in conjunction with their services. New concepts of operations, concepts of employment, and tactics, techniques, and procedures should be explored when DoD is considering integrating new weapons systems or technologies into its formations. This is the "how to fight" component of the study, which is perfectly suited for the use of analytic wargames. Once the analysts understand how each alternative will fight, they can then turn to the computer-based combat simulations to assess *how well* each formation fights when equipped with a particular alternative. Studies that combine both wargaming and computer-based combat simulations are often called campaign analyses.

The experimentation and test and evaluation communities of many countries also use analytic wargames. Live experiments and tests of weapons systems are always expensive endeavors, and conducting wargames to help plan and shape these experiments and tests is an important part of the cycle of research. Pre-event wargames often lead to a better understanding of how the event needs to be shaped and planned, and focus the event on the most productive use of resources to inform the program being investigated.

Analytic wargames are often used to investigate potential solutions to wartime challenges. Wargaming was one of the first techniques used by the original operations research analysts as the discipline was born in the early stages of World War II. Teams of experts sought answers to such challenging questions as how to use radar effectively to guide the interception of Nazi bombers attacking Britain and to mitigate the Luftwaffe's ability to strike maritime convoys, and whether placing additional armor on the B-17 bomber would help lessen their losses during the strategic bombing campaign. For example, in 1942, the Royal Navy was attempting to counter the successes of the German U-boats in the North Atlantic. The Western Approaches Tactical Unit (WATU) conducted a series of wargames to understand what tactics U-boats were employing to attack Allied convoys. Initial wargaming enabled the WATU to develop an understanding of the tactics. They then developed convoy escort tactics to counter U-boat operations, testing and refining those tactics in subsequent wargames.[19]

Although an analytic wargame is not developed with the primary purpose of educating or training its players, choosing players with the appropriate experience is critical for a successful wargame because the players make the decisions that underpin the insights and answers that address the sponsor's problem. The WATU wargames had the advantage of using both junior and senior convoy escort officers as players. In this case, the analytic wargames actually served as educational wargames, as the convoy escort officers serving as players helped develop, refine, and thus learn the new convoy escort tactics that they would then employ in future operations. We will discuss the importance of players more in chapter 7.

As we have just demonstrated, all wargames do not neatly fit into only one of the three wargame purposes. It is entirely possible to have some benefits from overlapping purposes in a wargame. Player learning may indeed occur during an analytic wargame, and an educational wargame might produce analytic insights of interest to senior leaders. Educational wargames can also provide experiential benefits to the players. As the chief of the general staff for the Prussian army, Helmuth von Moltke utilized wargames as part of the education of future operational commanders. He personally conducted annual exercise rides, combining wargames with on-site staff rides to enhance the operational thinking of his future commanders, experience that they could leverage as they commanded their units.[20] Moltke's *Tactical Problems from 1858–1882* represents an early example of this process to educate the Prussian general staff.[21] The NWC Plan Orange wargames provide another example of the potential blending of purposes. It was fortunate that the NWC faculty had the foresight to document and catalog the results of each of the more than three hundred Plan Orange wargames conducted to educate NWC students.[22] At the time of their execution, the wargames had provided a significant learning opportunity for the young Navy officers involved in them, and in the years leading up to World War II, the NWC faculty sought to ensure their capstone Plan Orange wargame continued to challenge their students. To do this, the faculty changed the strengths and weaknesses of the Japanese in the capstone wargame each year. This was done not with analysis in mind, but to preclude the graduating class from telling the incoming students how to win the capstone wargame against the Japanese![23] A few months into the war, Admiral Chester Nimitz sent two lieutenant commanders back to the NWC to see if the faculty had happened to stumble upon Japanese strengths and weaknesses in their quest to keep the capstone a viable educational wargame. Two of the

NWC wargames did indeed have Japanese attributes that were similar to what current intelligence was reporting, so those NWC wargaming results were dusted off and reexamined for analytic purposes.[24] Admiral Nimitz captured the importance of the Plan Orange wargaming efforts and their apparent success in supporting planning during the war in his 1960 speech to the Naval War College. The speech contained the well-known quote that "the war with Japan had been re-enacted in the game rooms by so many people and in so many different ways that nothing that happened during the war was a surprise—absolutely nothing except the kamikaze tactics towards the end of the war."[25] His confidence in the games provides an endorsement of some analytical games' ability to provide insight into future operations and to educate future officers.

This book is divided into three parts. Part I, "Foundations," offers relevant highlights from the history of wargaming, addresses the status of wargaming today, and provides an overview of the many characteristics of wargaming that distinguish one wargame from another. This part of the book establishes the foundation for understanding wargaming and is necessary for anyone who supervises wargaming teams as well as for team members, as both the examination of recent wargaming history and the discussion of wargaming characteristics will provide an understanding of the realm of the possible when deciding the type of wargame that will best address a particular problem or study. Chapter 1 provides a broader discussion of analytic wargaming and why it is important. Chapter 2 establishes why we believe wargaming is a craft that should be practiced by doing versus just observing for anyone to get better at designing and executing wargames. Chapter 3 lays the foundation of wargaming characteristics for the reader. While we argue that these characteristics are common in educational, experiential, and analytic wargames, we will focus on analytical wargames in this book. Chapter 4 provides a wave-top view of prominent wargaming in recent history. Chapter 5 introduces the concept of analytical wargaming that we will cover in greater detail in part II of the book.

Part II, "Fundamentals," consists of six chapters that get to the heart of understanding how to initiate, design, develop, conduct, and analyze a wargame. These chapters describe the basic wargaming fundamentals that are necessary for a team to create an analytic wargame. This section of the book breaks the wargame creation process into five distinct phases: initiate (chapter 6), design (chapter 7), develop (chapter 8), conduct (chapter 9), and analyze (chapter 10). For each phase, we will discuss the key tasks that a wargaming team should address if it is to have a reasonable chance at designing, developing, conducting, and analyzing a successful wargame. These five chapters are critical in the process of constructing an analytical wargame. However, as discussed in chapter 2, wargaming is a craft that is learned through active participation, not by reading or watching. To help with this learning process, this section of the book will introduce the reader to the troubled nation of "Zefra" on the Pacific island of "Capricornia." As readers learn the fundamental concepts of wargaming, they will have the opportunity to develop the components of a wargame addressing the issues in Zefra. We advise the reader to take advantage of the practical exercises presented in the book. The craft of wargaming should be practiced as part of the learning process, and these practical exercises provide an opportunity to experience the construction of an analytical wargame.

Part III, "Planning and Management," is for those who will supervise or lead a wargame processing effort. While part II addresses the principles and key tasks a design group should complete to create an analytical wargame, there are several other key tasks that will need to be managed to enable the wargaming team's efforts to ultimately succeed. While the wargaming team is focused on the design and development of the wargame, supervisors need to be setting conditions for the wargame to be a success (best practices) as well as being aware of the pitfalls that may set it up to fail (worst practices). Chapter 12 demonstrates using the analytical wargaming framework to create relevant and useful planning wargames. Chapter 13 reinforces using the analytical wargaming framework for seminar wargames, which, without rigor, are useless. Chapter 14 will demonstrate the benefits of using the analytical wargaming process to design both educational and experiential games. The final chapter of the book provides an examination of the worst practices observed in U.S. DoD wargaming today and why they tend to occur, and suggests the best practices that will allow wargaming practitioners to be successful in their efforts.

Wargaming is a critical skill set for any planner and analyst. All operational analysis and planning assume some type of rational value model for measures of effectiveness, measures of performance, and critical planning factors and assumptions. Effective wargaming provides a demonstrated technique to help the planner or analyst determine if and when any of these are appropriate. Through the contents of this book, planners and analysts will gain a better understanding of how analytical wargames are able to support research efforts. In addition, analytic wargaming is a critical element for any planner or analyst who is attempting to understand today's complex operational environment filled with wicked problems. In many of these situations, analytic wargaming will provide an excellent opportunity to explore the nature of the problem and to support the development of hypotheses for additional research. Completing this book will not mark the end of your wargaming education but instead will represent the first step in becoming a wargaming practitioner. It should be followed by a hands-on attitude of getting involved in wargaming and seeking out those experienced wargaming practitioners who can pass on the best practices that they have garnered throughout their long careers. Wargaming is a craft that requires its practitioners to plan, initiate, design, conduct, analyze, and play wargames. We hope that this book inspires both novices and professional and hobby wargamers alike to continue their journeys to become better wargamers.

PART I
FOUNDATIONS

CHAPTER 1

Analytic Wargaming

■ ■ ■ ■

Analytic wargames have one key difference from educational and training wargames: analytic wargames are product-focused, not player-focused. Typically, analytic wargames focus on extracting information from the players—not only their decisions, but the "why" behind them—to inform a product sought by an analyst, study sponsor, or decisionmaker. These products can range from a critical assessment of the opportunities and risks a new plan has to a concept of operations to be instantiated in a closed-loop combat simulation, and a well-designed analytic wargame will bring its players to decisions that will inform those products. The level and type of information extracted from the wargame will depend on the type of game and where it sits on the wargame continuum. We will discuss these types of wargames in more detail in chapter 3. In contrast, training and educational wargames are not usually considered analytic games, as the product of these games is better trained or educated players. For completeness, entertainment-focused wargames are intended for the entertainment or enjoyment of the players. But what is an analytic or analytical wargame? The definition tends to vary slightly depending on the organization or individual point of view. Several examples include: "a wargame conducted for the purpose of deriving information which may be used to assist military commanders and executives in reaching decisions";[1] "a game conducted for the purpose of deriving information that may be used to assist the sponsor in reaching decisions";[2] and "the act of competitive, contextualized decisionmaking within predefined constraints for the purpose of insights into complex, adaptive, interactive, and cognitive systems."[3]

Each of these definitions captures the basic essence that analytic wargames are focused on the product of information or insights gained from the wargame to support answering a bigger question or problem for an individual or organization. For this book, we use a version of Jon Compton's definition and see analytic wargames as designed to collect and analyze information from wargame play, with the results feeding directly into a decision, being used to develop additional analytic products, or helping to create additional research hypotheses or theories of victory for additional analysis. As an example, outputs of analytic wargames such as concepts of operation, courses of action, and operations plans are commonly used to "feed" other analytic activities or serve as the operational foundation for computer-based combat simulation analysis. Analysts and planners should not treat an analytical wargame as a single stand-alone event designed in isolation to address any particular set of questions or issues. As Compton has pointed out on several occasions, its power comes from being used to "gain insight into complex questions in order to generate a better analytical focus, be it at the strategic, operational, tactical, or some other level of analysis."[4]

Unfortunately, in the last half of the twentieth century, two events served to relegate the craft of wargaming to the sidelines in the U.S. Department of Defense. The first was Secretary of Defense Robert McNamara's embracing of operations research techniques, which led to the thinking that every important defense process or procurement program required quantification. Some believe that the undue focus on attrition models during the Vietnam War era contributed to McNamara's introduction of systems analysis.[5] The second was the incorporation of the computer into this systems analysis approach to defense planning.[6] As computers became available, defense wargamers realized they could perform some useful bookkeeping functions much more easily and quickly than humans. Relying on a computer for time/distance calculations and tracking ammunition expenditures could lessen the burden on wargaming staffs and free them to focus on more vital aspects of wargaming while restricting players to physically realistic moves. In the beginning, these computer systems were used in support of analytical wargaming to help with bookkeeping, accounting for vehicle movement and logistics, and adjudicating engagements.[7] The Battle Analyzer and Tactical Trainer for Local Engagements utilized a Wang 2200 computer to handle the complex and time-consuming computation, recording, and management requirements of the wargame, allowing players the freedom to focus on their tactical decisions.[8]

As computing capability increased, the additional functionality and memory allowed computers to approximate more of the processes of combat, and the closed-loop combat simulation was born. After analysts developed, collected, and entered all the appropriate input data, terrain, sensor, and weapons system performance, orders of battle, and concepts of operations into the computer, the closed-loop combat simulation could run through days or months of combat using entirely automated decision-making processes. This approach allowed the simulation to determine the final outcome of the engagement, documented by reams of output data, most of it quantitative. It is easy to see why this process was first thought of as "computer wargaming" and why several combatant commands adopted the Joint Staff's combat simulation Tactical Warfare Model.[9]

The conjunction of systems thinking and computing power happened as the Cold War (1945–89) was building toward having the largest two opposing armed forces in the history of the world stare at each other across the inter-German border. The battlefield for this future war was Western Europe. The opponents would be NATO and the Warsaw Pact. The invasion corridor Warsaw Pact forces would come through narrowed at the Fulda Gap and opened up into the north German plain. By the time of the rise of the computer, the two would-be opponents had been studying each other and the upcoming battle for Europe for well over two decades. The opponents knew each other well, had identified the others' leaders, studied their war plans, and created their own. The arms race sought to ensure neither side could obtain a technological edge that would shift the delicate balance of power. Quantifying the technological capabilities of forces became the focus of the analysis that underpinned U.S. defense acquisition decisions, and this played perfectly into the strength of closed-loop combat simulations. It became common for organizations to embrace the closed-loop combat simulation as their flagship tool of analysis and let their analytical wargaming capability atrophy. However, several analytic organizations, such as the U.S. Army Training and Doctrine Command Analysis Center and the Center for Army Analysis, quickly figured out that wargaming and computer-based combat simulations could be cleverly leveraged together, where wargaming informed the concepts of operation, schemes of maneuver, and tactics, techniques, and procedures that were then instantiated into the combat simulation to adjudicate the force-on-force engagements.[10]

Fortunately, wargaming did not die during the Cold War, and some analytic organizations maintained a level of their wargaming capability. Schoolhouses, such as the U.S. service war colleges and staff schools, continued to do some educational wargaming, although the pressure to insert computer simulations into the process was pervasive. Trainers often conducted wargames to train commanders and staffs, leveraging combat simulations to adjudicate battle outcomes. The use of wargames in the defense planning process continued to grow and gave rise to the series of wargames to address national defense requirements under Title 10 of the U.S. Code. These wargames grew out of the success of the U.S. Navy's global wargame series, which began in 1979, and are used today by all U.S services as a means to develop insights into organizing, training, and equipping future forces.[11] During the 1990s, these wargames included the Air Force's Global Engagement and the Army's Army After Next.[12] Over the years, the execution of Title 10 wargames morphed, many incorporating suites of combat simulations, drastically changing their focus and often "training" the participants to learn the nuances of the combat simulations, or gaming the simulation, in order to "win" the war.

As the Berlin Wall crumbled and the U.S. focus began to slowly shift from large-scale kinetic operations, so too did the foundational reliance on combat simulations for some analytic organizations. After September 11, as the Iraq and Afghanistan conflicts entrenched the U.S armed forces in counterinsurgency campaigns, Unified Quest, the Army's Title 10 wargame, shifted its focus on whole of government approaches to counterinsurgency, and the kinetic operations of previous years were not the primary focus of the wargame.[13] While the closed-loop combat simulation will continue to be a useful and necessary analytic tool, it is not the "Swiss Army knife" of analysis. Protracted major combat operations against a major foe where two combatants focus solely on kinetic engagements are only one of the many operations armed forces are likely to face in the future. Future wars are far more likely to share many of the characteristics of the current conflicts in Iraq, Afghanistan, Syria, Ukraine, Yemen, and Libya: state and non-state actors fighting to establish order over poorly governed regions of the world, using conventional military force along with insurgency, terrorism, and other elements, sometimes collectively labeled as irregular warfare, to exert influence on the civilian populations. Tribal alliances, religion, economics, and culture have much more impact on these battles than the technological capabilities of a large, uniformed armed force. In fact, these irregular warfare (IW) techniques are not new and were developed for the expressed purpose of negating the advantages of a large, technologically superior armed force in a disputed region.

As the United States fought IW campaigns in Afghanistan and Iraq, combat modelers worked to update their combat simulations to accommodate IW. Some added a third side to their simulation. Others added civilians on the battlefield, so kinetic engagements between two uniformed armed forces would cause "collateral damage" among the populace. At the time, these efforts were falling short in keeping up with the rapidly changing operational environment. The whole dynamic of warfare changes when the center of gravity shifts from defeating a military to influencing a civilian population, and kinetic engagements between armed combatants were infrequent, small, sporadic, and often counterproductive.[14] General David Petraeus, USA, and the counterinsurgency doctrine presented in Field Manual 3-24, *Counterinsurgency*, said it best: "You can't kill your way out of a counterinsurgency."[15] Whole of government approaches and modeling civilian populations' attitudes and behaviors were required, and even the cleverest of the combat modelers found these to present significant challenges in closed-loop models—thus the re-emergence of analytic wargaming.

Analytic wargames re-emerged in the 2010 timeframe and began to enjoy a renaissance as a method to develop insights and address complex problems in the defense community. However, for the analysis and planning community raised on closed-loop simulations and little practical experience in the diverse nature of wargames, there were some critical concerns with placing more emphasis on analytic wargames. As an example, many in the analytical community view analysis as a scientific method of providing decisionmakers with a quantitative basis for decisions.[16] Wargaming is about the players and decisions, not about science and mathematics, although there are definitely elements of science and mathematics in many wargames. This distinction makes it difficult for young analysts and planners to see how analytic wargaming fits within analysis. Analysts who have been educated on models and simulations recognize wargames as "a simulation of one replication" or a "sample size of one," noting that you could not run a particular wargame thirty times, altering random variables to generate reams of quantitative output for statistical analysis. While they are correct that traditional statistical methods are often not useful to analyze the output of wargames, they miss the larger picture—a wargame's focus is typically on qualitative data, human behavior, interactions, and decisions produced by the human players. The purpose of an analytical wargame is not to answer any specific question with a point solution. Analytical wargaming really begins to shine when it is used as a method for discovering the "topography of complex, wicked problems that involve human cognitive competitions in complex environments."[17] These wargames help planners and analysts to gain insights into the true nature of the problem, focus their research questions, and, in many cases, support establishing hypotheses for additional research.

This book's focus on analytic wargaming is a conscious one, although we believe the five phases needed to create an analytic wargame are easily adapted to other wargaming purposes such as education and training, and we will address this later in the book. Our intent is to outline a structured process that allows a planner or analyst to design, develop, conduct, and analyze their own viable analytic wargame. As with any book on a craft, our process is designed to embrace best practices learned by wargaming practitioners, as well as to avoid those worst practices that set the stage for failed or poor wargames. The following chapters will discuss the five phases in detail and support the neophyte's journey to better wargaming.

CHAPTER 2

Craft of Wargaming

■ ■ ■ ■

An organizational focus on modeling and simulation, at the expense of wargaming, comes with a potential lost opportunity in terms of organizational learning. The benefits of conducting a wargame versus a pure focus on modeling and simulation go beyond just the ability for an organization to augment analysis efforts and gain insights into complex wicked problems. The complexity of modeling and simulation typically means that the individual who gains the most during the process is the modeler who is tasked to instantiate the scenario and concept of operations within the model or simulation. However, in a wargame, all participants, designers, players, and analysts can viscerally learn from the wargaming process, execution, and any mistakes they make during the process. As more organizations begin reengaging in the wargaming process, we believe they will start to discover this additional learning opportunity.

In 2015, as wargaming began to enjoy a renaissance of sorts in the U.S. Department of Defense, wargamers were already organizing communities of practice to exchange ideas and best practices. One of the best venues has been the series of annual Connections conferences. The first was stood up in the United States in 1993, followed by the United Kingdom (2013), Australia and the Netherlands (both 2014), and Canada (2016).[1] The attendees come from a variety of backgrounds, from hobbyists to defense wargamers and from business to government professionals. One of the benefits of having such a diverse crowd exchange wargaming ideas is the awareness that organizations are using wargames for a variety of purposes around the world and that there is no one-size-fits-all checklist, template, or process that will provide a suitable repeatable methodology that fits all purposes for designing a wargame.

Awareness is growing in the wargaming community that the first step in the design process is to have a clear understanding of the wargame's purpose and how it impacts the ideas that practitioners present and exchange. One reason for establishing this common understanding is simple: when an experienced wargamer is lecturing about a best practice that applies to their wargaming domain, this practice may be specific to the purpose of that wargame. That is, a best practice for an educational wargame may not apply to an analytic wargame and vice versa. This means that the development of any formal or even informal wargaming education should include cognizance of the basic purposes of wargaming.

We can see some of the differences between wargame purposes by examining the practices of organizations that conduct wargames. Because of the nature of wargaming, many organizations have developed their own sets of procedures, methods, and processes, learned through years of experience in designing and developing wargames. Examples include wargaming handbooks created by the U.S. Naval War College[2] and the U.S. Army War College[3]—institutions that conduct both educational and analytic wargames—and the United Kingdom Ministry of Defence,[4] which focuses more on experiential and analytical wargames. There are many common elements of the wargame design process across these organizations as well as some significant differences that are unique to each organization. Although there may be discussions over methodology between wargaming practitioners, most now recognize that there is no one right way to create and conduct a wargame. In addition, the renewed emphasis on wargaming has reenergized discussion and debate in the wargaming community about wargaming design being either an art or a science. We will not attempt to make the case that wargaming is either an art or a science or something entirely different. Our intention in bringing up the debate at this point is for the neophyte and novice wargamer to understand that discussion in the wargaming community is ongoing. At this point, we again remind you that in our experience, the only absolute in wargaming is that there are no absolutes. The challenge of any design approach, be it art or science or something else, is ensuring that the wargame achieves the organization's purpose and objective.

Some practitioners call wargaming an art, and it could be argued that Peter Perla's book, *The Art of Wargaming*, may have established the foundation for this approach. A dictionary definition of art is "the expression or application of human creative skill and imagination ... producing works to be appreciated primarily for their beauty or emotional power."[5] Clearly, a wargame is an application of creative skill, a thought that Perla expresses in his book.[6] We believe that, in most good wargames, creative skill and imagination are applied to ensure that the wargame resonates with the players, suspends their disbelief, and facilitates their immersion in the wargame. In addition, Perla described the artistic view as "stimulating the players to experience" the narrative of the wargame.[7] This design point tends to focus on exploring/exploiting the natural tensions between relationships, both individual and organizations, to tease out and discover potential conflicts between individuals and adversaries. This artistry might be found in a clever game mechanic that brings out the benefits of a new technology or concept or in an innovative way to communicate changes or updates to the scenario, such as the use of prerecorded television news bulletins broadcast in the wargaming venue as if they were coming from a cable television news service. Can wargames be designed and conducted without any creativity and imagination? Probably not; you may have seen a wargame that has little to no creativity apparent to the players, and you may have noticed that it seems to be a chore for the players to maintain their focus. A wargame designed with creativity and imagination usually has a much better chance of achieving its purpose.

The flip side of the art and science coin is the approach where a fair amount of science is used to design a wargame. One aspect of this approach is the tendency to focus on or emphasize capturing elements of the real world, including the players, in the wargame. Typically, science-focused designers produce methods, models, and tools that capture real-world effects in an effort to create as realistic an immersive environment as possible for the players. These methods, models, and tools can take various forms and include algorithmic rule sets and quantitative adjudication methods, such as complex look-up tables or computer simulations. We believe that there are usually components of good wargames that are informed by some scientific processes. A strict view of science or analysis tends to follow stringent protocols, processes, and procedures, where scientists are precise and there is a scientific method that outlines the procedure for scientific inquiry.[8] In fact, here is where the analytical paths of the wargamer and the combat simulator tend to diverge. Closed-loop computer-based combat simulations, derived from defense wargaming in the mid-twentieth century, *do* allow a form of scientific inquiry through a scientific method–like process. An analysis using these simulations will typically start with some identified hypothesis—for example, that a ground combat force equipped with main battle tanks will be more operationally effective when the older tank is replaced with a more capable main battle tank. The analyst can then examine the operational effectiveness of the ground combat force equipped with the current tank in a stochastic closed-loop combat simulation by completing thirty or more replications of a scenario and conducting statistical analysis of the output data, measuring the operational effectiveness of the force using metrics of lethality, survivability, and sustainability. The analyst could then take the same ground combat force but replace the performance data of the current main battle tank with the data from the newer, more capable main battle tank that shoots farther, delivers more accurate fires, and is faster. The analyst will change nothing else in the simulation so that the performance data of the main battle tank is the sole variable changed in this analysis effort. They can then run another thirty replications with this modified force and conduct the same statistical analysis with the same three metrics, providing the basis to compare the difference in operational effectiveness of the original force with the modified force.

This application of the scientific method is using only closed-loop combat simulations to conduct an analytic study; there is no human decisionmaking that influences the outcome of the study, and thus the process of using closed-loop combat simulations to compare operational effectiveness is *not* a wargame. Keep in mind that the results garnered from this approach may not be valid since the simulation is still employing the same doctrine based on the less capable tank. This would have been a great opportunity to conduct a more science-focused wargame, in support of the closed-loop simulation, to help discover if there would be a change in how an organization employs the newer tank. This is why you should be careful in using any single method or approach to develop and conduct wargaming and analytical efforts.

Now let's talk about an analytic wargame that is seeking to develop a new concept of operation, perhaps one for a force equipped with a new main battle tank. First, planners and analysts will likely have some difficulty in crafting a hypothesis or an initial experimental construct that could be used in this situation. In fact, the wargame, as Compton's theory suggests, will likely support the development of the hypothesis for follow-on analytic analysis with potentially closed-loop simulation.[9] In developing this new concept, we will need to analyze different force employment options with the purpose of creating a single concept of operation that best leverages the attributes of this new main battle tank. Experienced force commanders are brought in as players, and a team of players that can accurately represent the adversary is also brought in to provide a dynamic opponent. Each player decision that is made during the wargame is in essence a variable that will affect the wargame's output. Data collectors will collect each player decision and the rationale for it, as well as the context within which the decision was made. Even if you could plot out all the decisions that each player will make in a wargame, imagine trying to trace each finding of the wargame back to a single, specific player's decision. The scientific component to wargaming will attempt to model as much of the reality of the operational environment as possible in order to elicit the player's decision and the accompanying rationale. We believe many wargames will have elements of science, and in fact this book seeks to outline some methods and procedures that, if applied, heighten the chances that the designed wargame will achieve its purpose.

We do not argue that wargame design is either an art or a science, but we do emphasize the purpose and objective of the wargame will drive the design process. In fact, we really believe that wargaming design is probably a mixture or combination of both art and science. Our approach to teaching wargaming is focused on the planner and analyst designing the wargame, and we treat wargaming as a craft—as "an activity involving skill in making things by hand" and the "members of a skilled profession."[10]

Wargaming is a skilled profession, much like the professions of carpentry or masonry. A journeyman carpenter can make useful tables and chairs by following a template; a master carpenter can design a work of beauty that has both form and function. A journeyman mason can build a standard fireplace; a master mason can design and build a cathedral with the beauty of Notre Dame or Westminster Abbey. We believe that the craft of wargaming focuses on elements of both art and science in the design process, and these elements are learned by actually doing wargaming.

The objective of any organized professional craft is to continue to advance the state of the craft by collecting and disseminating best practices, setting standards of experience and education that determine which tasks a craftsman at a certain level should be able to accomplish and when a craftsman advances to the next level. Since 2011, the Connections series of wargaming conferences has been great forums for the open debate and discussion about the craft of wargaming. For example, Connections UK included a working group session focused on building the wargaming profession.

In summary, the members of a craft want to ensure that its good reputation, as witnessed by the public's experience with its craftsmen, is maintained. The craft of wargaming discussion is a great first step, but some work still needs to be done in many organizations. The U.S. Defense Department still spends a considerable amount of professional military education (PME) time to produce better planners and analysts but offers few actual opportunities for students to become better wargamers. As an example, an analyst in the U.S. military, based on undergraduate, postgraduate, PME, and work experience, will spend, conservatively speaking, about 1,800 hours to become a novice analyst, with little to none of that time including actual education, training, or experience in wargaming.[11]

Everyone involved in wargaming started as a novice, where we define novice as new to or inexperienced in wargaming. Many novices to wargaming, in particular planners who are required to create a planning wargame for the first time, look for a checklist that, if followed, will lead to a productive and successful wargame. Unfortunately, there is not a universal set of procedures by which all wargames can be designed. Instead, there are best practices that have been learned by wargaming practitioners through two primary components: education and experience. Most of a wargamer's skill, like any skill, is acquired and internalized through hands-on experience. A novice could read every book written about wargaming, but most would still struggle to translate that book knowledge into a successful wargame without also building a foundation of experience that can be leveraged to design a wargame. The vast majority of this experience is accumulated through the creation and playing of wargames. The benefits of both of these activities can be greatly enhanced when the wargamer is apprenticed to a more experienced craftsman who can guide them with their own experiences and the craft's best practices that they have learned along the way.

So where do novice wargamers turn to start their journey? If you are a novice wargamer, you have chosen wisely—you have picked up a book on wargaming to see what it is all about! After reading our book, we heartily recommend Peter Perla's book, which we reference repeatedly. When you read it, you will no doubt recognize many of the foundations and the tenets that you have seen in this book. But, as we have discussed, book learning alone is only the beginning of the wargaming journey; you will want to seek out a wargaming community of practice and start to play and design your own wargames.

WHO NEEDS WARGAMING?

Since our wargaming focus is within the U.S. Department of Defense, we begin by telling you where wargamers are needed in DoD. First and foremost, every military headquarters responsible for producing plans or developing future operation concepts, especially those flag-level headquarters such as combatant commands, are required to conduct wargames. Every operation or contingency plan requires wargaming to understand the risks associated with the developed courses of action for this plan, and future operational concepts typically require multiple wargames to help develop understanding and insights of the new concepts. At the time of this writing, the wargaming done by our headquarters suffers because most of the wargame designers are still novices with little training or experience. There are still challenges with both planning and analytical organizations recognizing that they have a problem with wargaming, and without that recognition, these organizations will continue to miss the mark in their analysis and planning endeavors. Doctrine and professional military education require planners and analysts to conduct wargaming, but there is little actual education on how to do analytical wargaming. This is beginning to change to some degree, with several schools introducing educational and experiential wargaming into their curricula.

Planning organizations struggle with conducting good consistent wargaming for three primary reasons: lack of adequate resources, so wargaming is hastily done in many cases with a "check the block" mentality; lack of experienced supervisors, so any wargaming that is done is by default; and the lack of experienced wargamers, including players and not just designers, to lead teams that design and conduct quality wargames. Many organizations tend to contract either teams of wargamers to augment their staffs or analytical organizations such as RAND, the Center for Naval Analyses, and Booz Allen Hamilton to design, conduct, and analyze the bigger wargames for their organizations. While these analytical organizations conduct quality wargames, they cannot meet the sheer volume of DoD wargaming requirements. DoD needs to grow its own wargamers. We are not advocating that all members of the defense community become master wargamers; we have a core set of civilian and military individuals who will assume those roles. However, wargaming is clearly part of the planning process, and most planners and analysts are on the path to becoming at least apprentice wargamers. If nothing else, this baseline level of knowledge will enable them to more efficiently engage and interact with outside organizations that will support their wargaming efforts.

The act of wargaming allows the participants to share and build intellectual knowledge about the problem or issue the game is addressing. For example, the wargaming team that designs a noncombatant evacuation operation wargame learns a tremendous amount about the region, the key actors, the applicable doctrine and tactics, techniques, and procedures, and the key challenges that each of the major players will face as the wargame's scenario unfolds. We believe that there is a great organizational learning opportunity if the organization is involved with its own wargaming. Additionally, organizations that do wargames for hire usually have standard tools and formats for designing and conducting games, and some have a limited set of methods, so all wargames that they conduct look fairly similar. Larger analytical organizations may have a suite of tools and models from which to choose, which provides more options. But the bottom line for wargaming design is that it is a best practice to first determine the purpose, objective, and issues that you need to address with the wargame and then design or choose the methods, models, and tools needed to address that unique set of issues.

Many analysts embrace the notion that all analysis must deal with quantification; that is, if no math or statistics is involved, then it is not considered analyst business. This overemphasis on quantification often leads to the follow-on assumption that computer-based combat simulation is the tool of choice for every analytic study. The education of new operations research analysts typically focuses on mathematical programming, statistics, stochastic processes, and computer simulation. What these core disciplines miss is the aspect of human decisionmaking, which is a critical component of the execution of military operations. The best technology in the hands of a poor decisionmaker will have little value. In contrast, decisionmakers who are innovative and creative develop the new tactics and doctrine that best leverage technological advancements in our armed forces. We have talked about using both wargaming and combat simulations in a study. We believe that when possible, the wargaming done for an analytic study should be conducted using the warfighters that own the problem and that analysts from the analytic organization, even if they are military analysts, should be there to support the wargaming effort. These warfighters provide two great benefits to the study: first, the organization that owns the problem has fought a potential solution in the wargame, so the warfighters have been leveraged to provide insight into the problem at hand. Secondly, the warfighters are now engaged in the analytic organization's analysis and can be further leveraged to help ensure any combat simulation runs accurately reflect the warfighters' concepts and tactics, techniques, and procedures. When the results of the study are briefed to senior leadership, the degree of credibility of the results is tremendously enhanced when non-analyst warfighters have their fingerprints on the analysis and are enthusiastic in their support of its findings.

There is still much work to be done in both planning and analytic organizations with respect to the proper utilization of wargaming and wargamers. A critical and difficult first step in this process is to establish a pipeline for DoD that can provide educated planners and analysts who can wargame.

BUILDING A CADRE OF UNIFORMED WARGAMERS

Those few wargamers who can design an entire, complex defense-focused wargame without the help of a team are rare indeed, but as Malcolm Gladwell pointed out in his book *Outliers*,[12] those individuals have typically spent over 10,000 hours acquiring that knowledge—in other words, they have loads of experience. In our craft of wargaming, we would call these few individuals *master* wargamers. But we should be clear here: we are not proposing the creation of an educational path to produce master wargamers. Just as most military officers will never make flag rank, most wargamers will never be master wargamers. First and foremost, we need competent wargamers. As with most crafts, we seek to distinguish between the members of the craft based on their level of education and experience, and we offer these categories we have developed from multiple discussions with the Connections community:[13]

- *Neophyte*: a person who is new to wargaming
- *Novice*: a person who has a general understanding of wargaming and has participated in a small number of games but is still inexperienced
- *Apprentice*: a person who demonstrates an understanding of wargaming, its intellectual underpinnings, definitions, and concepts and who has some experience playing, designing, and conducting wargames. Most have completed an apprentice certification program to obtain the required wargaming education.
- *Journeyman*: a person capable of leading a wargaming team. A journeyman has spent time as an apprentice, has the requisite education, and has participated in the design, development, execution, and analysis of several wargames as an apprentice, and should have some experience as the deputy team lead for several wargames.
- *Master*: a person who has led many successful wargames, is widely recognized by the wargaming community as a "go-to" person when you have challenging questions or issues, and is a frequent contributor to wargaming conferences and communities of interest

THE EDUCATION OF A WARGAMING APPRENTICE

This book is designed to put you on the path to becoming an apprentice. Wargaming apprentices need to learn their tradecraft through a combination of education and experience. The first part can be done through certificate programs or through wargaming courses, which we will discuss shortly. However, the knowledge that certificates and diplomas attest to begins to degrade the day the document is awarded; the experience component brings the most value to a craftsman, or any professional, for that matter. As a thought exercise, would you be happy to be treated by a doctor who received a medical degree from an Ivy League school ten years ago but has never seen a patient and never conducted any continuing education, such as reading medical journals or going to conferences? The way an apprentice obtains the requisite experience is by *doing* wargaming, which includes designing and playing wargames, both professional and commercial. There is great value in terms of learning game mechanics in playing commercial off-the-shelf wargames. It is critical that the apprentice work with a more experienced wargaming craftsman to guide them with best practices.

Most of the mandatory wargaming education that uniformed personnel receive in DoD today does not teach students how to create wargames, focusing instead on participation in them. Playing wargames is essential, but if uniformed leaders never receive an education on wargaming design, who designs these wargames? There needs to be a program of wargaming design education for all uniformed leaders that spans from novice through journeyman, including an executive course for senior leaders.

Junior leaders (novices) should be exposed to playing wargames and be encouraged to do so early in their career. These wargames should be chosen so these young leaders learn decisionmaking in a competitive environment. The *Marine Corps Gazette* reintroduced Tactical Decision Games in 2009 to do just this for the Marine Corps. Wargaming should be encouraged by leaders across the services, and the best way to do this is for subordinates to see their leaders wargaming. Wargaming novices should seek to become apprentices as they move up the ranks of leadership. Mid-career leaders will need wargaming education that teaches them the basic tenets of wargaming and the fundamentals of wargaming design. This will provide them the opportunity to convert their hard-won knowledge into teaching points by creating wargames that their junior leaders can play once the design has been fleshed out and tested. This also provides these leaders with the ability to design analytic wargames for planning and other purposes. Playing more wargames is essential to the process. Playing new wargames exposes the players to new design philosophies and techniques. Once a mid-career leader has learned wargaming design, has participated in designing a wargame, and has passed an apprentice certification exam (testing the education piece), that leader will now be a wargaming apprentice. Wargaming apprentices become journeymen by doing—experiencing designing, developing, conducting, and analyzing wargames. They will need to acquire education on advanced wargaming techniques, experience leading wargaming design teams, and learn about wargaming management. More game play is needed to keep their knowledge of design philosophies and techniques current. Wargaming journeymen who become senior leaders will have the education and experience needed to ensure DoD does good wargaming and planning and will likely need only a refresher course. It is possible that some will become masters, but that is not our focus. However, today's senior leaders have had little, if any, wargaming experience or education. Few know anything about wargaming and don't even have the requisite minimal understanding of it to ensure quality wargaming is being conducted. As a stopgap, today's senior leaders need executive education that is more than just a refresher. This education needs to cover supervision of a wargaming design team, wargaming management, sponsor interactions, and analysis and reporting. Additionally, senior leaders whose organizations contract out wargaming support need to be able to ensure the product their organization receives is of value.

LEARNING FROM PREVIOUS WARGAMING EDUCATION

At the Naval Postgraduate School (NPS), we are firm believers that you learn wargaming best by doing it; reading our book and whatever others you can find is not the best substitute for practical experience. We will provide practical exercises throughout this book for those of you trying to learn on your own, but we strongly encourage you to seek out experienced wargamers, get involved in playing and designing wargames, and join the wargaming community, either on line or in person at events such as Connections.

We feel so strongly about the importance of incorporating both designing and playing in the educational process of future wargamers that we have implemented this in the NPS wargaming curricula. We have designed several wargaming courses, covering both analytical and educational wargaming that build the foundation for budding wargaming craftsmen using the concept of learning by doing to reinforce the principles of wargaming design. Our "Wargaming Applications" course is a core requirement for operations research students. Before we restructured this course in 2009, the focus was on students *participating* in wargames. This was a good introduction, but it did nothing to prepare these soon-to-be operations research analysts for the task of *designing* wargames, so we made the decision in 2009 to focus the course on an educational experience that included wargame design.

We started the students off by playing the board game *Risk*,[14] with a twist thrown in. They were to collect data during game play and report on what the best strategies were, as underpinned by their analysis of the collected data. *Risk* also provided them with an example of what a system wargame looks like. We knew the course needed another hands-on component, a capstone event to demonstrate everything they had learned in the course, so the very first offering allowed the students three weeks (twelve hours of classroom time) to design, develop, conduct, and then analyze the wargame they had designed. An NPS colleague linked us with a DoD sponsor who needed wargaming results quickly, so the students knew they needed to produce results; this was not an academic exercise where failure was an option. We also recognized that you need a team to design and conduct a wargame, so the initial class of seven students formed the first NPS student wargaming team that designed a wargame for a defense sponsor. The big student complaint from this first offering was the need for more time to design, develop, conduct, and analyze the wargame, so we went back to the drawing board to redesign the course for the next offering. We discarded some lectures and combined and condensed others to allow more time for hands-on design experience. We kept *Risk* and added a seminar wargame called "Zefra" adapted from the Canadian Forces' "Army of Tomorrow" study.[15] The students each played one of the player roles in this seminar game. This gave the students a second example of a wargame to experience that they could compare and contrast with the system game

Risk. Additionally, the students also experienced being a player, so they had a better idea when they designed a wargame what information players needed to make their decisions and what players felt like when they had to make a critical decision under the pressure of time. We then conducted the second offering.

We ended the five weeks of lectures with a Wargaming Apprentice Certification Exam. The student teams still had real-world sponsors, but we introduced them to these sponsors after the exam, providing them five weeks (about twenty hours of classroom time, which they still felt was not enough) to complete the sponsored wargame. After several more iterations and course redesigns, we learned two things: first, the students need every hour we could give them for the sponsored wargame. Second, our lectures were not a very effective use of the students' class time. Because the NPS students have two to three other courses they are taking during the eleven-week quarter and may also be deep into researching and writing their theses, there is not much time outside of class for the students to meet as wargaming teams. Thus, giving the students the hour of class time to work in teams to play wargames or work on the sponsored wargame requirements (learn by doing) was a much more effective use of their time than hearing an instructor lecture.

The third design iteration of the course was the charm. We first changed the course offering from four one-hour class meetings in a week to five hours, adding an extra hour to meet each week. We observed that the student teams often needed more than one hour to accomplish meaningful group work, so we provided the teams with two uninterrupted two-hour blocks per week. We recorded all the lectures and put them on the course's website and had the students view those as individual homework assignments. We introduced an online weekly quiz to motivate the students to view the online lectures but also provided a second motivation. We designed hands-on activities for the students to complete during class time as teams, and the weekly online lectures the students viewed before class were aligned with the in-class activities that the student wargaming teams would complete. We also pared the seven- to ten-student team size down to four to six students. We discovered that most teams of more than six students had one or two students who were only tangentially involved in the team activities and hence learned little about wargaming through the teamwork, which was the primary focus of the course. Teams of four to five students usually provide a good mix of skills and experience, and the wargames these teams design, conduct, and analyze were every bit as good as, if not better than, the wargames designed by larger teams. Finally, we linked the real-world sponsors with their student teams during the *second* week of the course instead of the seventh. This was another great motivator, because the students were then able to apply what they had learned each week via the online lectures to creating the building block products that their sponsored wargame required, and they now had the class time to produce those products as teams.

In short, we learned to apply what we later found out to be called "student-centered methods." These methods have titles such as "problem-based learning" and "project-based learning," and they are designed to allow students to collaborate, work on real-world problems, and engage with a larger community of practice—or, as we call it, "learn by doing."[16]

In 2011, as we underwent the first redesign of the resident course, we were asked to teach wargaming to a mixed group of warfighters and analysts from the Canadian Ministry of National Defence. Since that time, NPS wargaming mobile education teams have conducted more than a dozen wargaming courses throughout the world. The team brings the course to the sponsoring organization with the purpose of training a cadre of wargamers. During those five days, teams of novice wargamers learn the craft of wargaming by doing as they work on a wargame that their organization is sponsoring. It is an ambitious course that consists of about 30 percent lecture and 70 percent hands-on practical exercises, as the student teams learn about and then create the building blocks of an analytic wargame. On day five, the teams demonstrate what they have learned by doing: a wargame sponsored by their organization.

The goal of this book is to provide the key educational component foundations or best practices that a novice wargamer needs to work toward becoming a wargaming journeyman. Like a true craftsman, there should be a hands-on component to help learn the craft. While this book cannot and is not intended to replace apprenticing to an experienced wargamer, it will provide multiple practical exercises to help drive home the best practices presented in the text.

CHAPTER 3

Wargaming Characteristics

In the over two hundred years since von Reisswitz introduced Kriegsspiel for the training of Prussian army officers, military forces of many nations have designed and executed countless training, educational, and analytical wargames of many different forms and sizes, making significant contributions to national security objectives. Well-executed wargames during this period captured the complexities of warfare in an immersive environment. These wargames were simple enough to play, realistic enough to keep the players focused, and robust enough to capture the key dynamics of the conflict. They ranged in nature from the original rigid structure of Kriegsspiel, focused on the mathematics of warfare, to the more open seminar style of free Kriegsspiel examining concepts and operational art, to today's seminar and matrix games designed to explore the range of political, military, economic, social, infrastructure, and information factors present in many of today's multi-faceted conflicts. Despite their outward differences in size, form, and structure, these wargames share a heritage with a common set of identifiable characteristics that enable the creation of an environment within which players make decisions that provide useful insights to players, observers, analysts, and sponsors.

ELEMENTS OF WARGAMING

Several texts exist that offer wargaming guidance for both hobby and professional wargame designers. In this case, we are distinguishing between these two categories of games based on the purpose of the game. We define professional wargames as those wargames not created for the commercial market or the purpose of entertainment but designed for industry or defense purposes, which include games designed for educational, experiential, and analytical purposes. Hobby games cover the large number of wargames produced every year for commercial and entertainment purposes. In his book *The Complete Wargames Handbook: How to Play, Design and Find Them*, James Dunnigan gives us the ten steps of wargame design.[1] They include concept development, research, integration, prototype, rules, development, testing, editing, production, and feedback. Peter Perla outlines his seven elements of a wargame, objectives, scenario, data, models, rules, players, and analysis, in *The Art of Wargaming*.[2] The United Kingdom lists eight elements of wargaming—objectives, scenario, players, simulation, rules, data, supporting personnel, and analysis—in the Ministry of Defence's Wargaming Handbook.[3] Although the three sets have similarities, there are some nuanced differences that have worked for each individual or organization. These lists serve as a great lens to focus the designer, but they should not be viewed as a checklist that, if followed, will guarantee that the designed wargame will be a success and achieve its purpose. At this point, we offer a word of caution and a reminder for the analyst or defense planner reviewing any of these lists of essential wargaming elements or characteristics: The only absolute statement about wargaming is that there are no absolutes. These lists, including ours below, serve as a starting point to understanding the basic elements or components of a wargame, but as you gain more experience, you will begin to understand how and when to make deviations or changes to produce a wargame fit for purpose.

We will use a modified version of Peter Perla's seven elements[4] as the framework for designing analytical wargames and as the backbone of the five-phase process that we use to create an analytic wargame described in part II of this book:

- objective
- scenario
- data
- methods, models, and tools
- rules (and procedures)
- players
- analysis

Objective

Every wargame should have a single objective that serves as its focus and sets the conditions for designing and developing it. Our emphasis on a single objective for any wargame is a slight deviation from other lists that suggest that a wargame can have multiple objectives. In our experience, multiple objectives tend to complicate the design, execution, and analysis of the wargame. There will usually be several or many key issues that a sponsor wants examined, but as the wargaming team begins to organize the sponsor's issues, it should become clear that these issues all fit under a single unifying objective. This objective further specifies the purpose of the wargame. In other words, the objective of an educational game could be "to educate students on the use of Special Operations Forces to support conventional forces against a near-peer adversary." The purpose of the wargame, analytic, educational, or experiential, is specified in the wargame's objective. Unless otherwise noted, we will be discussing analytic wargames throughout the book.

Having a singular objective is not an original concept. Francis McHugh presented it in 1966 with his statement that "in practice, it has been found that it is better to point the wargame towards but one of those objectives, that is to select as the primary objective one of the following: (a) provide military commanders with decisionmaking experience (which would be an educational or experiential wargame), or (b) provide military commanders with decisionmaking information."[5] This singular focus includes all types of wargames—from the simplest hobby wargame to the largest professional wargame. Brian Train's "Shining Path" wargame is a re-creation of the *Sendero Luminoso* insurgency against Peru and is designed for its entertainment value.[6] This is a hobby wargame with the objective of providing one or more players the opportunity to refight the conflict. "The Landpower: GAAT" (Georgia, Armenia, Azerbaijan, Turkey), designed by LTC Patrick Schoof, is a wargame used at the U.S. Army Command and General Staff College to reinforce academic instruction.[7] Both of these wargames focus on providing the players with a decisionmaking experience and are examples of education-oriented wargames. The chosen objective will drive the other elements of wargame design and influence the style and format of the wargame. Analytical wargames are typically created to address a defense sponsor's problem, issue, or question. This objective provides the focus of the wargame and generally aligns with the second objective as described by McHugh. Analytic wargames seek to obtain the decisionmaking information from the players that will provide observations or insights that respond to the wargame's problem, issue, or question.

A well-defined objective is essential for any wargame but is especially critical in an analytical one. The game's sponsor and the wargaming team agree on the objective, which becomes the driving force behind the design and development of the wargame. It is without question the most important of the seven elements. The objective sets the focus for the sponsor, designers, and analysts to ensure the wargame provides the necessary structure and rigor to achieve its objective.

Scenario

The scenario sets the stage for player decisions. The scenario is the common starting point from which the sponsors, players, analysts, and other wargame participants address the objective of the wargame. It serves as the first building block for constructing a believable, immersive environment and is designed to provide players with the strategic situation, geographic region, and background story that capture the political, military, economic, and historical circumstances that have led to the current crisis or conflict. One of the designer's greatest challenges is to develop this immersive environment for the players. It should be robust enough to provide the players the latitude to make decisions about issues important to the sponsor without being too restrictive or too permissive. By defining the setting and scope of player decisions, scenarios can steer the course of the wargame into either narrow or broad avenues of exploration. Wargame designers need to be mindful that the scenario must provide the players enough freedom and flexibility to make useful and relevant decisions that ultimately produce the information the wargame designers are seeking. Players who feel as if they are being forced into decisions by the wargame's design rather than by the circumstances of the simulated conflict will lose interest in playing their roles well, and the wargame's output will suffer. We will discuss the necessary components of a scenario in more detail in chapter 7.

Data

Data is the information the players need to help them make decisions. Generally speaking, data serves as the link between the scenario and the mechanics/structure of the wargame. This includes information required by both the players and the wargame's methods, models, and tools. A large body of data, which we call the initiate data, is required at the start of the wargame. As the wargame progresses, players will also rely on feedback data to inform subsequent decisions. The difficulty in wargame design and development is figuring out how much and what kind of data will be required for the wargame. Unfortunately, some analytical wargames suffer from a massive amount of superfluous information that can easily overwhelm players, causing them to deliberate and agonize over the minute details of a decision as they assume that they must somehow process and leverage all the data they have been given. In order to eliminate confusion about wargaming data, we define three broad categories of data:

- Initiate data: information needed at the start of the wargame. It provides background (scenario) information so that players can understand the crisis or conflict and their role in the wargame, and it may include orders of battle and other information about the forces available for their particular role. Initiate data also includes any data necessary for input into the methods, models, or tools used in the wargame.
- Feedback data: data produced during the wargame that provides information to the players on the outcome of their decisions. Some of this data may update the initiate data. A simple example is the starting strength of the unit a player commands. After the first battle, the player will receive feedback on unit losses, and the starting unit strength will be replaced by the current unit strength that reflects the result of the first battle.

- Analysis data: information needed for the post-game analysis to provide insights and answers into the issues. Feedback data is often analysis data.

Method, Models, and Tools

The execution of all wargames requires some form of methods, models, and tools (MMT) that will be used to adjudicate player decisions. We replaced Perla's term "model" with MMT because of the prominence of computer-based combat simulations in the late twentieth century. These combat simulations are often called combat models, and unfortunately wargaming neophytes tend to conflate the wargaming element "model" with the belief that a wargame is required to have a combat simulation as its adjudication tool. Methods, models, and tools serve to open the aperture on adjudication techniques, from facilitator-determined adjudication to combat results tables to spreadsheet models while still permitting models and simulations. The design of the wargame is critical in determining the appropriate types of MMTs that will be required. They need to be flexible enough to deal with unusual decisions and adaptable to data changes, and they need to deliver realistic outcomes (appropriately stochastic). MMTs need to be well documented so assumptions and algorithms are understandable, especially to the analyst attempting to interpret the output.

Rules

Rules and procedures provide the structure that governs the wargame. Procedures usually specify the flow and conduct of the wargame—for example, there will be two turns per hour, and each turn consists of a maneuver cycle and an engagement cycle. Rules tell the players what they can and cannot do—for example, a player can move a maximum of three units per turn. If not observed, the ambitious player may attempt to break rules to gain an advantage in the wargame.

Players

An analytic wargame's results are only as good as the wargame's collective body of players. It is important to have an in-depth understanding of every one of the sponsor's key issues to ensure that the best players are recruited for the wargame. Players' backgrounds and experiences will dictate the information they need to properly play their assigned roles in the wargame. These players need to be provided the appropriate level of information (data) that is reasonably expected for their roles in the wargame. Typically, the single greatest planning mistake in defense wargaming is the choice of the adversary. In many instances, the adversary is not a dynamic, culturally correct, free-thinking opponent but a symmetric mirror image of the friendly player who will typically react in a scripted manner. Wargames with a poorly represented adversary usually produce little of value.

Analysis

The final element, analysis, involves much more than the simple assessment of the outcome of the wargame. In most analytic wargames, the assessment of what happened, who won, and who lost is much less interesting than the analysis that details *why* the outcome occurred in the wargame. Determining the best way to obtain the data required to conduct the wargame analysis is the driving force behind the entire wargame design process. Designing the game around the data the wargame's analysis requires is the only way to ensure that the information extracted from the wargame will address the sponsor's key issues. The focus of the analysis effort is on not only the player's decisions but also developing an understanding of why the players made their decisions. In-game and immediate post-game analysis are part of the analysis plan. In chapter 6, we introduce the data collection and management plan that serves to translate the sponsor's key issues into the analysis data required to address those issues. This plan is the foundation for the wargame's design.

Wargames come in many shapes, sizes, and forms, and it is common to hear wargaming practitioners say that no two wargames are alike. That said, wargames do share some common characteristics, and understanding those allows designers to more efficiently determine how to create a wargame design that will best address the majority of the sponsor's key issues to the required resolution. In this next section, we will establish additional foundational wargaming design terminology concerning the main components of a wargame's framework—the information structure, the player engagement structure, and the adjudication method.

INFORMATION STRUCTURE

Wargames are all about the information that is provided to and extracted from the players during the conduct of the wargame. A wargame is generally open or closed in terms of the availability of player information. Open format wargames allow all players to see the information available to all other players. Many hobby wargames are open wargames in which both players make their moves on the same wargame board with all available pieces visible to each player. Logistically speaking, open wargames are easier to implement because all players are typically gathered in the same room. The classic board wargame *Risk* has an open format in which every player's troops are visible to every other player. In *Risk*, you are not sure what your opponents are planning, but you do have near-perfect information of the strength and disposition of their forces. The open format is usually not useful for gaining insight into command, control, communications, computers, intelligence, surveillance, and reconnaissance issues.

Closed format wargames, on the other hand, restrict the information available to all players. Each player will only be provided the information that their collection assets could reasonably be expected to obtain and report. Closed wargames usually require separate rooms for each team represented, as well as a white cell or control cell that maintains the "ground truth" view of the operational area, tracking the current status of all assets of each side. The white cell may also include the assessment/adjudication team or contain individuals representing key entities, such as higher headquarters, who are not in the wargame but whose input might be critical to it. Closed wargames provide a better opportunity for the exploration of command and control and decisionmaking under uncertainty, and a cleverly constructed closed wargame can provide the means for players to use deception. The simple wargame *Battleship* has a closed format in which the only information each player receives is the "hit" or "miss" response from the opposing player that documents the result of a round fired into an unobserved grid square on the ten-by-ten grid square game board where the opposing player's ships have been arrayed.[8]

In today's complex world, simple constructs are rarely adequate to meet the wargame's objectives, and we often see wargames where the format is a mixture of both open and closed. The rationale for restricting some information while providing other information to all must align with the wargame's design requirements. An often used hybrid format is called "closed planning, open execution." The closed planning session allows teams of players to create plans that they believe will be effective when executed in the open setting. The players may be members of an alliance, such as NATO, or they may be several unit commanders of the same organization. Each player will be able to take individual actions in the open setting, but the desired result of the amalgamation of the alliance's set of actions has been planned in secret and is hopefully not apparent to the alliance's adversaries until they have achieved their desired effects.

A simpler hybrid format allows all players to see the same gameboard, but the design of some of the wargame's markers allows information to be hidden from observation. Imagine a minesweeper that needs to clear a path in a mined harbor for an amphibious landing force. A gridded gameboard represents the harbor by twenty-five grid squares, and the force that is opposing the landing has a capability to mine fifteen of the harbor's grid squares. Twenty-five markers, identical on one side, are arrayed on each of the harbor's grid squares. On the reverse side of the markers, fifteen have a mine symbol, and the other ten are blank. The opposing force knows which are mines and which are not, but the landing force's minesweeper will not know until it visits one of the harbor squares and "clears" the square by searching for mines. Once the minesweeper has conducted clearing operations—which, if the underside of the marker has a mine symbol, may include unplanned detonation of the mine, damaging or sinking the minesweeper if the game rules dictate—the marker is then turned over so all players can see. The game *Stratego* is a chess-like version of the child's game "capture the flag" played on a ten-by-ten–square game board with two sets of thirty colored game pieces; however, the opponent sees only the identical backside of each piece.[9] The front side indicates which of the twelve different types of pieces it is, where there are ten pieces that can move. They range from the most powerful (the field marshal) to the most expendable (the scout), with only one field marshal but many scouts. The other two types of pieces cannot move—the flag and several bombs. The opponent can only learn the precise identity of an opponent's piece through an attack where each piece's identity is revealed when one player challenges the piece through an attack. However, careful observation will indicate, over time, pieces that have not moved.

PLAYER ENGAGEMENT STRUCTURE

Player engagement captures the essence of player interaction experienced in the wargame. Player interactions and engagements can cover a broad spectrum. There is a general consensus in the community that the continuum of wargame player interactions tends to flow from seminar games on the left, with the potential for more creativity and original thought, through matrix games, free Kriegsspiel, to ultimately rigid Kriegsspiel on the right, with less anticipated creativity to more analytical rigor and precision.[10] Each step in the continuum still defies easy definition; they are typically described by a set of characteristics, but one general recognition is the desire of planners and analysts to move down the continuum. The ends of the spectrum represent the extreme in terms of players' potential creativity and initial data requirements. Seminar wargames are typically more open-ended with players engaged in discussions with each other and the facilitator. These types of wargames tend to require less up-front understanding of the rules, since there are few, and can be great for developing understanding of the problem and for developing original thoughts and concepts. System wargames, as we call both free and rigid, have more indirect player interactions, and players tend to operate in a more structured environment, usually relying on terrain and unit representations and more numerically based adjudication tools.

Seminar Wargames

Seminar wargames are a popular choice for wargame design because of the apparent ease in designing and conducting them, and because the only adjudication MMT necessary is the facilitator. There is no clear, concise, or agreed upon definition for a seminar wargame. However, to support understanding in this book and for discussion, we will define a seminar wargame as one in which a scenario, which may range from military to geopolitical or anything in between, is presented to a group/panel of selected subject matter experts who discuss and support developing insights into the issue(s) presented in the scenario. The size and expertise of this group will depend upon the complexity of the examined issues. A seminar is deliberately designed for ease of execution and flexibility. Seminar wargames tend to be open wargames with direct player interaction and a freer interchange of ideas and civil discourse. Players typically are placed in some situation and asked to make decisions, which generally leads to open discussions among the players as guided by the facilitator. This style of play generally helps the group arrive at consensus or find contrarians. These types of wargames are typically conducted in small groups, and the data is qualitative in nature. Planners and analysts can expect to gain better insights and understanding into the problem, potential weaknesses, and original concepts. Without a carefully constructed analysis plan, seminar wargames have the potential of simply becoming a "bunch of guys and gals sitting around the table" (BOGGSAT) event that will have little analytical value.

Matrix Wargames

Matrix wargames are a step along the continuum from seminar to system games. Matrix wargames are a "free-form narrative gaming method in which the effects of game actions are largely determined through player debate and discussion, rather than umpire adjudication or prewritten rules."[11] Matrix wargames are similar in nature to seminar wargames in that the players propose to take an action that then leads to open discussions among the other players, and there is still a reasonably high level of creativity in these actions.[12] However, matrix wargames bring a little more structure and rigor to the process. They are similar in nature to free Kriegsspiel, if there is an umpire, where players are not constrained by a complicated set of rules, statistics, or combat simulations. One example is when war-experienced Prussian officers served as the wargame facilitators, and the younger, less experienced officers were the role players. In matrix games, player actions tend to be more free-flowing and, if executed properly, can capture a much larger range of potential events in a wargame. Similar to seminar wargames, the data generated by the wargame is generally qualitative in nature, but if the wargame is designed correctly, this data will provide insights into the problem and identify potential weaknesses and unique concepts. One typical aspect of matrix wargames is to allow players that have the potential to be affected by the proposing player's action to offer counterarguments. After all arguments and counters have been made, either a consensus about the success of the action is reached, or a facilitator adjudicates the result of the player's action.

The popularity of the matrix game format has ebbed and flowed over its almost-thirty-year history and is currently experiencing a resurgence in popularity as a method to conduct wargames in many organizations. The matrix game format was created in the United States by Chris Engle and published in 1992.[13] The method was developed out of frustration with the number-riddled, complex-ruled wargame designs of the period. In addition, many of these wargames failed to address the issues of the time. An approach was needed that would allow players and the wargame to consider anything that was considered relevant to the players, including culture, beliefs, and population perceptions, which were not part of the current wargame designs.

The starting point of the initial design effort was the development of a "matrix" of cue words that formed the foundation and framework of the game. This initial design approach also included Georg Hegel's theory that thesis and antithesis (argument and counterargument) lead to the synthesis of ideas. The design approach was accepted by the defense community, and over time the matrix of pre-established cue words was dropped, but the name stuck. The beauty of the system is its simple design and execution concept, with the potential to address any wargame setting or situation. Matrix games have been used by many U.S. DoD organizations, McGill University in Canada, the UK Ministry of Defence, the Australian Defence Force, the UK Air Warfare Centre, as well as multiple other organizations around the world for a multitude of situations.

System Wargames

We have included both free and rigid wargames under the heading of system, but we recognize that there is a potentially large spectrum to the left limits of free, which begins to look like a matrix wargame with an umpire or adjudicator, and the right limits of rigid, which approaches modeling and simulation. These games attempt to find the balance between the "realism" of the wargame and its attempt to capture as much of reality as possible and the playability of the game. System wargames will include the traditional wargame rigid Kriegsspiel, many versions of free Kriegsspiel, and most hobby wargames, such as the aforementioned games of *Risk*, *Battleship*, and *Stratego*, which adjudicate all player interactions through models that are described in the rules of the games. We have decided to group these wargames together because of the tendency for system wargames to provide more indirect player interaction, usually through some MMT and a more formal adjudication process. The MMTs will often be mathematically based models, and they have a more prominent role in the execution of system wargames. Like most wargames, there is not a single definition, but we will work with the definition that a system wargame is one with a set of detailed, nondeviating rules, with the provision for chance and player action events to be adjudicated by some formal method. System wargames have the potential to be more rigorous and predictable in nature. The data coming from these types of games have the tendency to provide more details and will be both qualitative and quantitative in nature.

A Useful Blending

Most of the useful wargames designed in support of defense sponsors turn out to be neither of the two endpoint designs but rather hybrid wargames that employ aspects of both seminar and system wargames. They may have two or more adjudication MMTs, and they may use both closed and open information formats. Planning wargames may have a closed seminar component where each team (Red and Blue) discusses and plans their operation. They could then input their moves into a system wargaming construct where their moves are adjudicated using MMTs without ever meeting their opponent face to face, or both teams could meet in an open seminar game to have their planned moves adjudicated by a facilitator or a panel of subject matter experts.

RELATIONSHIP BETWEEN INFORMATION AND PLAYER ENGAGEMENT

There is no typical relationship between the information structure and the style of the wargame. Both the structure and style of a wargame's design are driven by the objective and key issues of the wargame's sponsor. Many seminar wargames are open, but the closed planning, open execution planning wargame is a useful hybrid. System wargames played over a single game board are typically open, but there are mechanisms that allow some aspects of the games to be closed, either temporarily or permanently. Open system wargames can be easily closed by creating multiple game boards and sequestering the various factions of players in separate rooms, allowing a white cell to track all player actions on its own game board.

WARGAME ADJUDICATION

The final common aspect of wargames is the adjudication process. Adjudicating is simply the process for determining the outcome and consequences of player decisions. The decision of wargame designers on the necessary MMTs and style of a wargame usually determines the adjudication method. Adjudication falls into one of four major categories:[14]

- Free: typically the simplest form, where the professional opinion of a facilitator or subject matter expert determines the consequences (adjudication) of player decisions. One advantage of this form of adjudication is that a qualified referee or umpire can handle situations that were not captured or anticipated during the design of the wargame. However, this is usually offset with a delay as the umpire conducts an analysis of the player's actions. This approach tends to produce a discussion of the success or failure of the player's action that provides an opportunity to learn the why behind the decision. This adjudication technique is frequently seen in free Kriegsspiel and matrix wargames.
- Rigid: the consequences of player decisions are adjudicated through some form of MMT such as a set of rules or a mathematical model. One advantage is the potential for a quick response, assuming a well-designed MMT that is suitable to assess most situations. However, the structure of the rules may not cover all situations that might come up during the game, which can lead to confusion among the players as they try and reason out what the justifiable outcome should be. Rigid Kriegsspiel provides an extreme example of this type of adjudication.
- Semi-rigid: the initial adjudication comes from the MMTs, but the facilitator or subject matter expert has the opportunity to modify the results. This approach attempts to capture the strengths of the rigid and free approaches and is a common approach in many analytical wargames.
- Consensual: the group of players reaches an agreement on the outcome of player decisions. This adjudication is reached through a conversation with all players. This approach can have a facilitator to lead the discussion, or the wargame may have a rules structure that allows the players to work through and reach a consensus. This approach

has an advantage of a fuller discussion of the reasons for the player's decisions but will take the most time to adjudicate. This level of adjudication is typically seen in matrix wargames and potentially seminar wargames, depending on the purpose of the wargame.

Analytical wargaming is a valuable decisionmaking technique for leaders to explore and use to gain insights into issues and problems. These wargames have the power to explore issues at all levels of conflict, from tactical to strategic, and across the full spectrum of military operations from kinetic to counterinsurgency. Their adversarial and dynamic nature enables players to explore future situations. Well-structured analytical wargames will generate insights and information (data) that will enhance the sponsor's understanding of the issues addressed in the wargame. The design, development, and analysis of wargames are the subjects of the chapters in part II of this book.

CHAPTER 4

Wargaming History

■ ■ ■

There are far many more detailed treatments of wargaming history than what we describe in the following pages. This collection would include James Dunnigan's book, which provides a review of wargaming from its origins and a discussion of hobby wargaming.[1] Matt Caffrey provides an excellent overview of the impact of wargaming from the rise of modern wargaming to its resurgence in 2015 and beyond.[2] Peter Perla provides a similar historic review of wargaming, with a more thorough discussion covering educational and "professional wargames," which are more akin to experiential wargames as we classify them in this book.[3] Francis McHugh captures much of the same early history of modern wargaming but quickly moves on to wargaming during World War II and wargaming at the U.S. Naval War College.[4] Milan Vego provides one of the better reviews of the roots and history of Prussian/German educational and experiential wargaming. This review essentially encompasses the roots of modern-day wargaming.[5] Our intention in this book is not to restate the history recounted in the above sources but to illuminate some of the more striking examples of wargaming history that also provide lessons for the wargaming apprentice. The true beginnings of wargaming are lost to the ages, but it is clear that abstract military-themed games such as *Wei Hai* and *Chaturanga* were played centuries ago. Some modern games can trace their lineage to these two games, thought by many to be ancient abstract representations of combat.

Wei Hai is thought to have been developed in China thousands of years ago, with some attributing its origins to Sun Tzu.[6] *Wei Hai*, similar to modern-day *Go*, was played on a gridded board with colored stones to represent the player's forces. The winner attempted to control the majority of the board by outmaneuvering/outflanking his opponent. *Chaturanga* originated in India around the sixth century and is considered to be the forerunner of chess.[7] The original version involved four players maneuvering elaborate pieces representing soldiers, chariots, elephants, and cavalry. At best, both of these games were intended to provide a simple understanding of basic military principles and might be considered some of the first educational wargames.

Societies around the world created and played wargames in an effort to instill the basic principles of war in its practitioners. Societies that could field armies that won battles survived and often thrived, and those that could not either were consigned to being the subjects of those that could or ceased to exist altogether. Rulers of nations recognized that their military generals had a better chance of success if they learned to envision the application of force and embrace the value of planning through wargaming before they actually went to war.

HISTORY OF KRIEGSSPIEL

Modern-day wargaming can be traced to the nineteenth-century Prussians, who turned to wargaming out of necessity to help educate military officers in an attempt to counter the military advantages of France and Napoleon. In 1811 Baron von Reisswitz, the Prussian war counselor in Breslau, created a wargame using a table with a model of actual terrain and blocks to represent the various units. Umpires used complex tables and dice for adjudication and would only reveal to each side the information that they would know on the actual battlefield—a *closed wargame* in modern terms. The baron's wargame was used to educate Prussian officers. As the Prussian army grew, many more officers were needed, and the baron's son, Lieutenant Georg H. R. J. von Reisswitz, realized that his father's wargame could be adapted and used to train this new generation of Prussian officers. In 1824 Lieutenant von Reisswitz replaced the terrain table used by his father with topographical maps, making this new version much more portable. He demonstrated the wargame to the Prussian chief of staff, General Karl von Muffling, who became an advocate, and soon the wargame was a requirement throughout the Prussian army. However, a large portion of the Prussian officer corps resented the time required to conduct these wargames, earning Lieutenant von Reisswitz the ire of his peers, and he took his own life in 1827—perhaps the first known casualty of wargaming.[8] Fortunately, wargaming began to take root among the junior members of the Prussian officer corps. One such advocate was Helmuth von Moltke, who understood the advantages of wargaming and even founded the Magdeburg Wargaming Club, one of many clubs that began to form across Prussia.[9] Of course, years later, General von Moltke, as chief of staff of the Prussian army, was in a position to increase the use of wargaming. Moltke even required war college applications to include a letter from the applicant's commander discussing the applicant's wargame performance.[10] During this period, Moltke also began using wargaming as part of contingency planning, which included staff rides and field exercises. This effort expanded the use of wargaming beyond a purely educational tool for Prussian officers.[11]

In the 1870s Prussia introduced a new variant of wargaming called free Kriegsspiel to remove some of the difficulties that were associated with the original rigid Kriegsspiel. Much of the frustration with rigid Kriegsspiel came from the time-consuming table-based adjudication methods. Free Kriegsspiel replaced the rule-based adjudication process by leveraging battle-hardened senior Prussian officers' combat experience to adjudicate wargame outcomes. While this made the wargames faster, this adjudication method required senior officers with combat experience, a model that could not be sustained over long periods of peace.[12]

Many countries attributed the battlefield success of Moltke and the Prussians to the integration of wargaming in their army. Many Western countries began exploring wargaming concepts from the late 1800s to the beginning of World War I for their own militaries. Typically, most of these explorations began with a translation of German wargaming rules. As an example, Major W. R. Livermore is generally credited with the beginning of modern wargaming in the United States. His efforts started in 1883 with a translation of German rules and quickly updated and expanded to capture the statistics from the American Civil War.[13] Unfortunately, his efforts were stymied by the U.S. Army Chief of Staff, General William T. Sherman, who believed Livermore's wargame failed to capture the emotional, psychological, and leadership aspects of warfare. Fortunately for the United States, the Navy was a little more receptive to the notion of wargaming, which it called "chart maneuvers." William McCarty Little's 1887 lecture on wargaming paved the way for U.S. wargaming, ultimately leading to it becoming a part of both the Army and the Naval War College curriculum. However, it was McCarty Little's 1912 article in the U.S. Naval Institute *Proceedings* called "Strategic Naval War Game or Chart Maneuver" that opened the door for analytical wargaming. He argued that wargaming had shaped and would continue to shape the development of national policy and better military plans.

PLAN ORANGE AT THE NAVAL WAR COLLEGE

In 1919 as World War I concluded, U.S. Naval War College faculty had the foresight to begin a campaign of wargaming focused on potential future adversaries. This campaign included many color-coded plans, with Plan Orange, war against the Japanese, becoming the one most thoroughly examined by the NWC faculty and students. Plan Orange wargames were conducted from 1919 until the U.S. entry into World War II in 1941. The primary purpose of these wargames was to educate the NWC students, naval officers on the path to make admiral and assume command of fleets, on a potential Pacific rival that they might one day face in battle. The decision to record and archive the results of each wargame allowed for the possibility of later analysis, comparing and contrasting results based on the differences in the forces, tactics, and decisions.[14]

Plan Orange wargaming evolved through three distinctive phases:

- 1919–27: The U.S. Navy sails off to single-handedly destroy the Imperial Japanese Navy and relieve the Philippines just weeks after a declaration of war.
- 1928–34: The U.S. Navy realizes such a war may last longer and will require a phased approach necessitating large-scale amphibious operations with significant U.S. ground forces.

- 1935–41: The U.S. Navy realizes that, in addition to the U.S. Army and U.S. Marine Corps, U.S. forces will need help from regional partners.[15]

The knowledge garnered in more than two decades of NWC wargaming Plan Orange led Fleet Admiral Chester Nimitz to famously state, "The war with Japan had been enacted in the game rooms at the War College by so many people and in so many different ways that nothing that happened during the war was a surprise—absolutely nothing except the kamikaze tactics toward the end of the war. We had not visualized these."[16] An even more telling tribute to Plan Orange wargaming came early in 1942 when Nimitz sent two young lieutenant commanders back to the Naval War College in Newport to gather previous wargaming results. Because the NWC had changed Japanese strengths and weaknesses in each year's student-led wargame, Nimitz knew that the NWC had wargaming results from one of its annual wargames that would resemble the actual Japanese status that naval intelligence was now reporting to him.[17]

ADMIRAL YARNELL AND PEARL HARBOR

As the NWC was wargaming Plan Orange, U.S. forces were conducting exercises to better understand force capabilities. As a part of the 1932 Grand Joint Army-Navy Exercises, Rear Admiral Harry Yarnell took command of the Blue force with the goal of testing the defenses of the U.S. forces in Hawaii. Yarnell learned to fly in 1920 and was an advocate of airpower and the Navy's newest capital ship, the aircraft carrier. Yarnell's force included two new aircraft carriers, *Lexington* and *Saratoga*, the carrier Yarnell had earlier commanded upon its christening in 1927. Yarnell's mission for this exercise was to land a combined Army–Marine Corps force on Oahu, but the plan also called for Hawaii to be attacked by air. Most senior leaders believed the attacking carrier fleet would be discovered and sunk by the opposing forces' submarines and land-based aircraft long before it could get close enough to launch an air attack (about one hundred nautical miles).[18]

Yarnell knew this as well and devised a plan with three critical elements. First, his fleet would operate with no lights and employing "radio-listening silence," meaning absolutely no radio message transmissions were allowed from any of his forces for any reason. Second, he would maneuver his fleet to an area about sixty nautical miles off the coast of Oahu, where the winter weather was rainy and had produced a thick cloud cover that stretched from his force's position to just short of Pearl Harbor itself. Third, he would launch his attack in the pre-dawn darkness so his planes would emerge from the clouds early on Sunday morning over a sunny Pearl Harbor.

All 152 of his pre–World War II biplanes, launched off of flight decks rolling in heavy seas, successfully conducted their mock attacks, targeting rows of planes parked on runways, the runways themselves, ships anchored in the harbor, and Fort Shafter, the Army headquarters. His attack was unopposed; the defense was caught napping. Yarnell and a few other "airpower advocate" admirals argued that it was a stunning victory and that naval tactics should be reexamined. The battleship admirals, skeptical of these new aircraft carriers, dismissed their claims. The final report made no mention of Yarnell's success. Although the U.S. Navy gave little credence to Yarnell's tactics, the Japanese took note. Japanese observers forwarded a report of Yarnell's exploits to Tokyo. In 1936 Japan's Naval War College circulated a monograph focused on potential military operations against the United States. Contained within the paper: "In case the enemy's fleet is based at Pearl Harbor, the idea should be to open hostilities by surprise attack from the air."

BATTLE OF MIDWAY

Today, the Battle of Midway is celebrated as the turning point of the war against Japan. U.S. forces repelled an attempted invasion of the island and sank four Japanese aircraft carriers, capital ships that the Japanese could ill afford to lose. What is not as well known but now widely accepted by most naval scholars is that the outcome of the battle was a highly unlikely event. The U.S. forces were lucky to find *any* Japanese carriers, much less find and sink all four.[19]

In the spring of 1942, the Japanese were conducting a series of wargames to examine a number of planned Pacific operations, including Midway. Rear Admiral Matome Ugaki, presiding officer of the Japanese combined fleet, frequently intervened to set aside rulings by the wargame's umpires. One of Ugaki's rulings was to "refloat" two Japanese carriers that had been sunk by land-based U.S. air forces in engagements in the Midway wargame so they could participate in the next wargame, an operation against the islands of New Caledonia and Fiji. Some authors portray Ugaki as a senior official who meddled in wargaming activities, ignoring the Midway wargame's "prediction" of the actual outcome, because those two carriers, plus two more, were sunk in the actual battle. This example is often quoted without the full context, as the Midway wargame Ugaki presided over was only one in a series of wargames to examine the Japanese Pacific campaign.[20]

After the Battle of Midway wargame, Ugaki counseled the players about the possibility of an enemy carrier task force appearing on the Japanese forces' flank, which is exactly what did happen, and he also took steps to downgrade the B-17s' effectiveness in attacking ships, another insight that was borne out by actual battle results. Land-based aviation had no effect against the Japanese carriers; they were all sunk by naval aircraft.[21] As Alan Zimm cautions: "One purpose of an operational wargame is to understand what could possibly go wrong and to gather insights on how a plan might progress in the face of enemy countermeasures. Umpires' decisions are revised to take into account modifications of the plan, lessons learned, to prevent the game from departing too far from what is considered the most probable course of events, or to allow different elements of the plan to be exercised."[22]

WORLD WAR II OUTCOME FOR JAPAN

The attack at Pearl Harbor, while devastating, did not locate any of the U.S. aircraft carriers in the Pacific Fleet, and after the U.S. victory at the Battle of Midway, the U.S. Pacific forces began to have success against the Japanese forces. The Japanese general staff decided to convene a wargame in the summer of 1942 to understand how the war against the United States would end. As the wargame was organized, the Japanese realized they needed to have players who understood the way Americans thought to play the U.S. roles. They knew that the Japanese culture differed enough from American culture that if they had no players who could reflect American cultural values and norms as they made decisions in the wargame, the wargame's results would have little value. In a twist of fate, an agreement between the United States and Japan that allowed for a prisoner exchange of sorts had been reached in the summer of 1942. When Japan launched its surprise attack on Pearl Harbor in 1941, the embassy staffs had remained in Washington, DC, and had been quickly rounded up and interned as Pearl Harbor smoldered. Japanese naval intelligence officers that had been assigned to the Japanese embassy in Washington were part of the interned group.

In August 1942 these naval intelligence officers were repatriated to Japan. The Japanese general staff had the officers met before their ship docked in Tokyo Bay and had them taken to naval headquarters. There, they were sequestered to keep their knowledge of the United States untainted. The wargame was then conducted, and the results demonstrated that the Japanese would not be able to match the U.S. military-industrial capacity once Washington was focused on the war effort.[23] Based on the wargame's results, the Japanese changed their strategy. Knowing that they would eventually be defeated, they decided to attempt to avoid having to unconditionally surrender to the United States by making each engagement of the war as bloody as possible, hoping to force the United States to negotiate terms of an armistice.[24]

DESERT CROSSING

In 1999 General Anthony Zinni, USMC, the commander of U.S. Central Command (CENTCOM), sponsored a wargame called Desert Crossing designed to focus on phase 4, the post-combat stabilization phase of CENTCOM's Iraq war plan. The key issues that were examined included security, reconstruction, humanitarian aid, economic development, and political stability. The results of Desert Crossing were eerily prescient in the areas of military action, political stability, leadership in Iraq, and an exit strategy.

In the realm of military action, the wargame found that it should be "swift, large-scale, and decisive," not only to overwhelm any remnants of Saddam Hussein's military but also to demonstrate a show of force to minimize violence and ensure security.[25] The actual execution of Operation Iraqi Freedom occurred with a much smaller ground force than was recommended by General Eric Shinseki, the Army chief of staff in 2002. Testifying before Congress, General Shinseki estimated a need for an invasion force more than twice the size of what was actually employed. Shinseki explained, "It takes a significant ground force presence to maintain a safe and secure environment to ensure that people are fed [and] that water is distributed, all the normal responsibilities that go along with administering a situation like this." With the looting of hospitals and the Iraq National Museum that began in April 2003, it became clear that the smaller U.S. invasion force was not capable of providing a safe and secure environment once Saddam's army was defeated, just as General Shinseki predicted.[26] In 2006 General John P. Abizaid, the departing commander of U.S. forces in the Middle East, told Congress that "General Shinseki was right that a greater international force contribution, U.S. force contribution and Iraqi force contribution should have been available immediately after major combat operations."[27]

Regarding political stability, the Desert Crossing finding was that it might not be enhanced by regime change and that Iraq's neighbors could in fact try to take advantage, particularly if there was internal fragmentation.[28] During Operation Iraqi Freedom, the post-invasion Iraqi government was formed primarily of Shiites who had sought refuge from Saddam in Iran. As a result, this enabled Iran to wage a proxy war against the United States in Iraq using their elite Al Quds forces.[29]

The wargame's finding regarding Iraqi leadership was that it would be crucial to identify potential Iraqi leaders well in advance of regime change, if possible.[30] In reality, the United States did identify an Iraqi exile, Dr. Ahmed Chalabi, to lead the post-invasion Iraq government, and he was flown to Iraq soon after the 2003 invasion as its potential leader. Unfortunately, allegations of corruption and a perception that he was part of the Shiite power base settling scores with former Sunni leaders soon eroded his influence.[31]

As for an exit strategy, the Desert Crossing finding was that the preferred end state for Iraq was a unified country with self-reliant political and economic systems, a stable security environment free from internal and external threats, respect for human rights and decent treatment of its own people, and recognition of its international borders and obligations.[32] The post–Iraqi Freedom reality was less optimistic. In 2011 Iraqi president Nuri Kamal al-Maliki, a Shiite, ordered the arrest of his Sunni vice-president Tariq al-Hashimi and charged him with running Sunni death squads, bringing the Iraqi government to the brink of collapse—one day after the last U.S. combat troops left Iraq.[33]

The wargame's results were classified at the time but have since been declassified and posted online. On the website, General Zinni, now retired, stated: "When it looked like we were going in, I called back down to CENTCOM and said, 'You need to dust off Desert Crossing.' They said, 'What's that? Never heard of it.'"[34] This story has an additional footnote. In 2017 we were conducting an NPS Mobile Education Team (MET) basic analytic wargaming course for CENTCOM and recounted the story of Desert Crossing and General Zinni's call to CENTCOM. One of the wargaming course attendees, a long-time CENTCOM planner, left the room and returned fifteen minutes later with a copy of the Desert Crossing final report. He explained that CENTCOM planners had made senior defense officials aware of the Desert Crossing results, but the National Command Authority gave the wargame's results little credence.[35]

This short history of wargaming is intended to provide the reader with a snapshot of the rich history and application of wargaming and its role in educating, planning, and executing military operations. Part II of the book is designed to put into practice the craft of wargaming for the reader to begin the journey of designing, developing, and executing their own wargames.

CHAPTER 5

Analytic Wargaming Fundamentals

■ ■ ■ ■

You have been tasked to conduct a wargame. You may have been in the room and the requestor looked you in the eye and told you to do a wargame, or your supervisor may have dropped by to tell you that one of his/her superiors needs a wargame done, and you are now tasked to lead the effort. In any event, you're now in charge of putting together a wargame in support of someone who we will call the wargame's sponsor. Wargaming sponsors come in all shapes and sizes, but two things are generally true about them: they are coming to you because they need help with a complex problem, and they really don't know the amount of organization or effort that it will take to design, develop, conduct, and analyze a quality wargame that helps answer their problem.

Peter Perla has stated that "wargaming is an act of communication."[1] In this case, the first communication comes from the sponsor to you, the leader of a team that will design, develop, conduct, and analyze the wargame. Chances are high that this first communication will not be detailed enough for you to understand exactly what the sponsor hopes to learn from this wargame. Further clarification and more details will almost always be required, but before you decide to take that on, you should first organize your wargaming team. The reason you want to form this team before you engage the wargaming sponsor is so you can do some preliminary research and determine some of the issues and challenges that you will need to clarify with your sponsor. And, as is often the case with interpersonal communications, three people listening to the same speaker will usually have their own different or unique take on the information that was communicated, so having the core team participate in the sponsor engagement is highly recommended.

THE CYCLE OF COMMUNICATIONS

We will cover the reengagement of the sponsor for the purpose of clarifying the wargaming tasking in the next chapter, but first we need to clarify this idea of wargaming as an act of communication. Wargames are based on a series of communications that are conducted between the wargame's sponsor, the wargaming team, and the wargame's players. The first act of wargaming communications comes when the sponsor requests that an organization conduct a wargame on the sponsor's behalf. The sponsor and the organization's wargaming team need to clearly negotiate the details of the wargame to ensure the sponsor's objective and issues are addressed to the best of the team's abilities and within any resource constraints.

The wargaming team is typically composed of a design group and an analysis group. The size and scope of the wargame will drive the size of these two groups. We do not advocate that individuals be in only one of the two groups but rather some personnel overlap should occur. For example, there should be an analyst in the design group who is involved in the wargame construction from the beginning of the process. The wargaming team then designs and develops a wargame that will enable the players to examine in detail the sponsor's objective and issues. Thus, the wargame itself is a vehicle designed by the wargaming team to communicate the sponsor's objective and issues in a way that enables players to make the decisions that your team has identified as necessary to answer the sponsor's objective and issues. As the wargame is conducted, the players make those decisions, which the wargaming team then records and collects information about—yet another type of communication. Finally, once the wargaming team has sifted through all the data collected, the team will close the communication loop by creating the final wargaming products to convey to the sponsor what the team has discovered about the sponsor's objective and issues.

THE FIVE PHASES OF WARGAME CONSTRUCTION

Analytic wargames are created, executed, and analyzed using a five-phase process. These five phases—initiate, design, develop, conduct, and analyze—are listed in chronological order. The execution of the design and develop phases should be thought of as a cyclical process where a wargame's playtest, one of the key tasks in the develop phase, will often inform an update of one or more elements of the wargame's measurement space or the design's foundation, the data collection and management plan, from the design phase. The tasks are not all inclusive, but they are the basic tasks that nearly all analytic wargames will require.

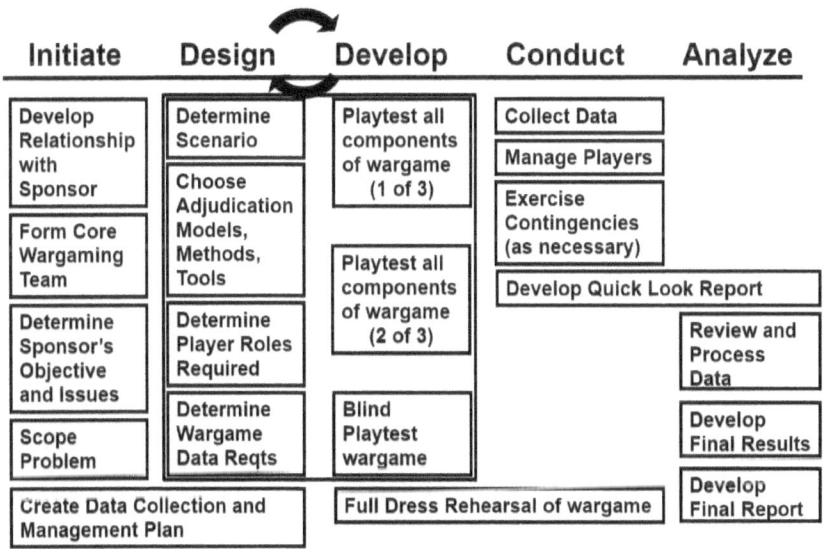

Five Phases of Wargame Construction

Initiate

The initiate phase is where the sponsor and the wargaming team reach an agreement on what the wargame will produce. The initiate phase transitions to the design phase once the first draft of the data collection and management plan (DCMP) is complete. (Some organizations may use other terms, such as data collection and analysis plan.) The DCMP is the foundation for the wargame's design. The primary focus of the DCMP is the translation of the sponsor's objective and issues into the information (data) that the wargame's players need to produce in order to provide the insights that the sponsor seeks. Often we talk about it being a decomposition of the sponsor's issues, but the process isn't always that straightforward. In practice, creating the initial DCMP can be the most challenging task faced by a wargaming team. We will discuss more of the details of the initiate phase in chapter 6.

Design

After the sponsor and wargaming team have agreed upon the wargame's objective and issues and the DCMP has been drafted, the next task is to create a wargame design that will allow the wargame to produce the information necessary to address the sponsor's objective and issues. The wargaming design team will then begin to identify the measurement space that the wargame will require for the wargame' players to produce this information. The three elements of the measurement space are the scenario(s), the methods, models, and tools needed for adjudication, and the data that will be required to begin the wargame (think of the data that would be found in the player's read-ahead packets, such as orders of battle, weapons system characteristics, etc., as well as any data the chosen MMTs require in order to be fully functioning on wargaming day). We will discuss more of the details of the design phase in chapter 7.

Develop

The initial wargame design will be brilliant—and it will not work, or at least not as designed. Wargame development is the process that informs the wargame design by having play-testers actually play the first design. Commercial wargame designers learned to get a crude design completed quickly and then to play-test it, and we strongly recommend the same practice for analytic wargames. To do development correctly, the play-testers need to attempt to "break" the wargame. Much like a dentist probing for cavities, the developers should thoroughly test each component of the wargame and the wargame in its entirety. It is important to understand that the design and develop phases are iterative phases. The play-testing of the initial design will reveal what is not working as designed, and why, informing how the design needs to be updated. It will also allow the play-testers of this initial design to begin to realize if additional details should be added to the wargame to enable it to address all the sponsor's issues. Spending too much time designing a detailed prototype of your wargame without play-testing often backfires, as there will be too much detail for the play-testers to understand the wargame's purpose, and they will be unable to discern why the wargame does not work as planned or what changes need to be made.

Most wargames will iterate several times between the two phases, updating the wargame's design (and potentially updating the DCMP) with each iteration. Through the iteration process of the design phase, you should also keep an eye on the ending analysis phase, and you should have identified the framework of the quick-look report.

Every method, model, and tool needs to be play-tested just like every other component of a wargame. What kind of input do the players need to provide to allow the MMT to be run? How long will it take to input players' decisions before the MMT can be run? How long will the run take? How long will it take before the output of the run can be processed and provided to the players? What is the white or control cell's contingency if the MMT will not operate?

It is important to play-test MMTs at the scale that they will operate in the wargame. If the wargame portrays a theater-level conflict such as NATO–Warsaw Pact but you test the MMT with a battalion-level engagement, you haven't gotten accurate answers to the questions above.

If computer simulations are to be used to adjudicate the wargame, consider if the simulations can be pre-run for a variety of potential scenarios; this way, the adjudication during the wargame can be done via a look-up table or by interpolation instead of relying on the simulation to operate on demand. If the simulation has a long run time and you need to run it as the wargame is being played, consider running it during breaks, over lunch, or after the conclusion of each day's wargaming activities.

You also need to ensure you've tested all MMTs in the actual wargaming venue with the venue's information technology (IT) personnel present. Even if you bring your own MMTs on the machines they run on at your home station, you need to consider any interface your machine must have in order to operate, especially if you rely on Internet access. Download speeds and local firewalls can have a tremendous effect on the operation of computer-based MMTs. You will also want IT personnel standing by during the actual wargaming play.

As the time to conduct the actual wargame draws near, a full rehearsal play-test needs to be scheduled and conducted. The purpose of this is to ensure the wargame will work the way it has been envisioned, so it is advisable that it be conducted at the actual wargaming venue. Think of this as a walk-through that should test every aspect of the wargame. At this point, the design should be fairly complete, although you may discover that it requires some final tweaks. All the other aspects of the wargame, such as the data collection process and the adjudication tools, need to be tested at the scale and intensity that the actual wargame will require. Key aspects to test include:

- Adjudication tools: Do they work, and do they work as planned?
- Data collectors: Are they trained, and do you have enough to ensure they don't get burned out collecting data for several hours?
- Facilitation: Has the facilitator checked out the venue to understand where the key players will sit and to see lines of sight between the facilitator and players and between individual players?
- White cell: Has the white cell staff been trained and exercised? Are they prepared to develop contingencies on the fly and search for data to answer player requests?
- Administration: Have you provided for in-processing of the players, cell phone collection, player break room(s), IT support, and food and coffee services?

Conduct

It is the first day of conducting your wargame. All the planning and preparation are about to pay off. However, wargames are probably more prone than any other activity to fail during execution. That's because wargames have these wildcards called players, and you simply have no way to know in which direction the wargame will go. Wargames need active management and direction. Seminar wargames rely on a skilled facilitator to lead the players through the wargame, eliciting the information that the analysts need to produce the final report. System wargames may have rule sets that allow the players to conduct the game without continual input from the wargaming team, yet a wargame director who ensures that the wargame adheres to the schedule and resolves any disputes or answers any requests for information from the players is still required.

If the wargaming team has done its due diligence and has designed, developed, and conducted a quality analytic wargame, the wargame will conclude with the quick-look report. As the last turn of the wargame is completing, the wargaming team is scrambling to produce the quick-look report. This report is designed to reveal to the players, at the wargame's conclusion but before the players depart, the top-level findings that the wargaming team has distilled from the wargame to date. The quick-look report, as well as key player post-game interviews, should appear on the wargame's schedule. The vetting of the quick-look report will provide the wargaming team with important feedback from the players. It also will provide a great framework from which to produce the detailed analysis report. The report's purpose is to confirm the emerging key insights garnered from the game before the players depart. First, the wargaming team needs to obtain player feedback while the game is still fresh in their minds. Second, the team needs to ensure that any corrections or adjustments that the players provide are appropriately adjudicated. To ensure that the quick-look report is valid, its revision needs a good facilitator and perhaps even an adjudicator. The framework of the quick-look report should be informed by the key issues the sponsor wants answered. For example, if the sponsor had three to five issues that the wargame was to address, the quick-look report should probably have three to five key insights. As a reminder, you should have the framework of the quick-look report determined before the start of the wargame.

The quick-look report provides a great starting point for the final analysis and the outline for the final analysis report, because both it and the DCMP were derived from the sponsor's objective and as such have been designed to specifically address those issues the sponsor has identified as critical. We will discuss the details of the conduct phase in chapter 9.

Analyze

The analysis of the completed wargame will depend greatly on the type of wargame that was conducted. Seminar wargames are likely to generate mostly quantitative data, whereas system wargames may have more qualitative than quantitative data; hybrid games will likely have a healthy mixture of each. The framework of the quick-look report provides the starting point. First, the information collected during the wargame needs to be thoroughly combed through to ensure that the key takeaways vetted in the quick-look report are underpinned by evidence. In most cases, they will be, and the analysis may reveal additional insights as well as the solid evidence to support the top-level claims from the report. On rare occasions, analysis may uncover evidence that contradicts a quick-look report finding. We will discuss more of the details of the analysis phase in chapter 10.

THE TROUBLED NATION OF ZEFRA

The craft of wargaming can only be learned through a combination of education and experience, with the emphasis on experience. Our best practice for wargaming education is to intersperse practical exercises between lectures or readings to provide students the opportunity to learn by doing. Wrestling with hands-on practical exercises puts wargaming students on the path to becoming apprentices and begins to bridge the gap between pure education and being assigned to a wargaming team without ever wrestling with any of the key tasks that a wargame requires. The intent of the wargame is to allow the reader to work through each phase of the wargaming process to actually construct an analytical wargame. A reader who actually takes the time to execute the practical exercises should have a basic wargame at the end of this process.

At this point we have provided the fundamental building blocks for a planner or analyst to construct a wargame to achieve a sponsor's objective. The next several chapters will provide more details and best practices to flesh out this set of building blocks. Some readers will be able to simply read through each of the proceeding chapters and be able to capture the basic essence of the analytical wargaming construction process. However, wargaming really is a craft, and most readers need more to support their learning process. Therefore, to help this process, we will ask the reader to design and develop a wargame over the next five chapters. You may be tempted to just read through the upcoming series of practical exercises, but to get the most out of this book, take the time to complete each exercise.

To set the stage for the upcoming exercises, we will now introduce you to the troubled nation of Zefra on the South Pacific island of Capricornia. (The full background information is included in appendix 2.) The island of Capricornia lies in the Coral Sea of the South Pacific. In topography and climate, it seems like an idyllic South Seas paradise, but dig deeper and you will discover its challenges. Two independent and completely different nations share this island: Daloon in the South, and Zefra in the North. Each nation occupies roughly half of Capricornia; they share a common border and dependence on the island's scarce fresh-water resources, which are located in the border region. Both are relatively impoverished nations with very little in terms of natural resources or major economic activity.

Daloon, a former Spanish colony, gained its independence in 1947 and initially enjoyed relative political stability, although it faced significant economic challenges. It has a relatively homogeneous and stable population. Defense treaties were maintained with Spain, and Daloon developed good relationships with other major powers. The major security challenge to Daloon comes from sharing the island with Zefra, a country whose history unfolded quite differently and one in which insurgency and internal strife were all too common.

Zefra was a French colony that was granted independence in 1951. It is a country dominated by a well-educated Bongo-minority population. The Bongo population arrived in Zefra before the French in the seventeenth century. They were primarily traders and initially established a good relationship with the Truscans, who were already established in Zefra. Under French colonial rule, the Bongos gained stature as functionaries of the colonial government and developed as an entrepreneurial middle class. The Bongo population has dominated the central government and led economic development since independence. This dominance in government, the civil service, and the judiciary further alienated the Truscan population and led to a series of local uprisings across the country. An attempt to crush this resistance in the late 1990s had the effect of unifying the rebels into an opposition movement called the People's Liberation Movement (PLM). Associated with the development of the PLM was a parallel armed component called the People's Liberation Armed Militia (PLAM).

Zefra erupted in a civil war between 2002 and 2009. In Truscan-dominated areas of Zefra, the PLM enjoyed considerable popular support.

With this, the PLAM was able to establish its control over significant areas of Zefra. However, the development of factions within the PLM limited its overall effectiveness. Internally, the PLAM was dominated by three major sub-groups, each forming around its own charismatic leader. Initially, these three sub-groups generally agreed on actions to be taken against the central government. But the leaders of the three factions espoused different visions for the ultimate aim—namely some form of autonomous Truscan homeland. The internal divisiveness over ultimate aims sometimes led to uncoordinated and ineffective operations against government forces.

Reports of atrocities in the Zefran civil war became particularly gruesome in early 2007. When cellphone videos of these began appearing regularly in the evening news, the U.S. government decided that it would need to make a generous and well-intentioned attempt to settle issues in the country. A small force of Marines landed in eastern Zefra to help sort out the belligerents. The U.S. initiative ended in failure, and soon after the Americans

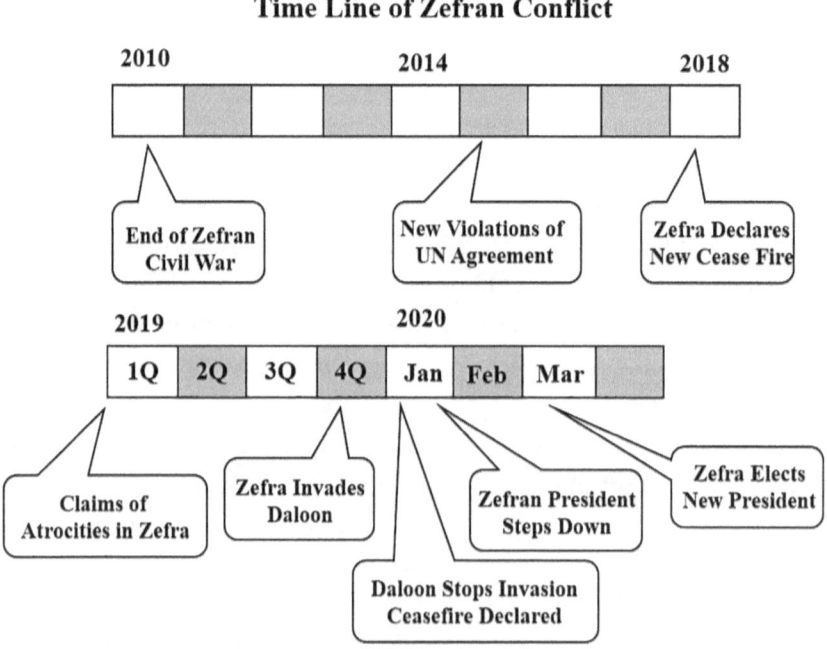

The Zefran Timeline to War

withdrew, there were atrocities where the native supporters of the Americans killed a number of their fellow countrymen, claiming they were being maligned for having collaborated with the Americans (who were seen in some quarters of Zefra as an occupying force). Animosity continued after the end of the civil war when U.S. promises to help the Zefran economy proved illusory—during this time, the United States had its own economic problems to deal with. Nevertheless, the ill feeling in Zefra toward the United States continues to complicate matters to this day.

Meanwhile, the civil war in Zefra caused a substantial flow of refugees across the border into Daloon. Within their numbers, the refugees harbored Truscan insurgents who had come from Zefra and found safe havens for future action on the Daloon side of the border. Daloon, at this point, had an immature security establishment with nascent armed forces and a very lightly armed border patrol. These resources were insufficient for Daloon to maintain effective control of its border with Zefra; nor were they able to stop insurgents, lodged within the safe havens of the refugee camps, from conducting operations from Daloon into Zefra.

In response to incursions by the insurgents, Zefra initiated a series of cross-border counterinsurgency penetrations into Daloon to deal with the insurgents' safe havens where the Daloon forces were seemingly impotent. Claiming the right of hot pursuit, the Zefran government of the day ignored diplomatic protests from Daloon and the international community, most notably from the European Union.

While ostensibly having the apprehension of the Zefran insurgents as their only objective, Zefran operations caused significant damage to local Daloon infrastructure and property. The level of violence and its apparently indiscriminate application generated a substantial migration of internally displaced persons away from the border area. Many ethnic Truscans, when apprehended by Zefran forces in or near the refugee camps proximate to the border, were treated brutally, and there were allegations of rape, torture, and amputations by Bongo militia men who seemed barely under control of any leaders, let alone of their national government.

Over time, migrations of ethnic Truscans were generally pushing deeper into Daloon. In some respects, this just spread the violence and bloodshed, as Bongo-led Zefran irregular forces probed deeper and deeper into Daloon in pursuit of Truscan refugees, although the target was claimed to be only the insurgents who were hiding among the apparently innocent refugees.

Meanwhile, within Zefra, factions of PLAM were inflicting tremendous violence on seemingly peaceable Bongo neighbors in the border regions and elsewhere. PLAM spokesmen claimed that these Bongos were not what they seemed and indeed alleged that many provided bases from which Bongo irregulars were crossing the border to attack the refugee camps in Daloon. By 2009 civilian casualties were rising quickly, with both Bongos and Truscans sharing responsibility for the butchery. At this point the United Nations (UN) High Commissioner for Refugees sought international condemnation for the atrocities on both sides, as well as commitments to separate the belligerents. Unfortunately in the early twenty-first century, Western nations had become embroiled in military operations in Afghanistan, Iraq, and Libya. In addition, they were still feeling the economic impact of the recession of 2008–9, so they were reluctant to commit precious resources to sort out yet another bloody mess.

In 2009 all parties to the violence in and near Zefra had exhausted themselves. Every party seemed to see some advantage in ending hostilities. Some of the parties saw it as a chance to reestablish norms of civil behavior and to seek a more peaceful environment for their children. But others saw it simply as a chance to rearm for the next time and to inculcate into a new generation fiery memories of the grievous harm that others had inflicted on their clans and tribes and a burning desire for revenge on the alleged perpetrators.

The civil war finally ended when the UN brokered a peace agreement that created an autonomous region under PLM/PLAM control within Zefra but adjacent to its border with Daloon. This agreement is credited with creating a period of relative calm that lasted for some years. In response, the government of Daloon sought to secure its borders. Several European nations provided some limited help to Daloon in the form of military training assistance teams and a small amount of surplus military equipment.

Within the international community were ongoing recriminations that too little had been done to help the people of Zefra. Thousands had died during the civil war, while the Western nations had seemingly been busy with their own problems. In the years after the Zefran civil war, evidence frequently emerged of mass graves on both sides of the border. These were found in proximity to the refugee camps in Daloon and initially were associated with the Zefran operations against the mainly Truscan insurgents within the camps. However, evidence also emerged that Truscans, probably associated with the insurgency, had committed heinous crimes in areas of Zefra that they controlled. Clearly, all sides in the matter had committed atrocities that showed this uncivilized and reprehensible behavior was widespread. The nations of the world pledged that the next time Zefra was in crisis, they would not stand idly by; they would do something.

This short background narrative of the troubled island of Capricornia is designed to set the stage for what will become "the Crisis in Zefra." This crisis will unfold over the next several chapters as you become more familiar with the details of the basic analytic wargaming fundamentals. The objective of this effort is to reinforce the educational element of the book in constructing an analytical wargame. It is not designed to replace the mentorship of a wargaming craftsman but hopefully will help crystallize the concepts for the reader.

PART II
FUNDAMENTALS

CHAPTER 6

Initiate

■ ■ ■ ■

You have been tagged to lead a wargaming effort. You have a rough idea of the sponsor's problem, but you have not yet engaged the sponsor to gain a clear understanding of the problem and the full scope of the effort. Your first task is to clearly define the problem so you understand the needs of the sponsor. This is not easy, and unfortunately too many analysts and planners are eager to show their gung-ho attitude by creating a wargame that attempts to answer a poorly defined problem. It is far more the norm that your sponsor will provide vague or conflicting guidance, objectives that need two or more wargames to answer, or a problem that is not appropriate for a wargame. The ability to quickly recognize these potential pitfalls comes with experience, which is why it is critical to practice the craft of wargaming. The eagerness to take a poorly defined problem and rush to answer it usually results in wasted resources, primarily your organization's and the sponsor's time, and ultimately a sponsor unhappy with wargaming products that do not provide the insights needed to address their actual problem. The initiate phase of the analytical wargaming process focuses on problem definition and developing answers to these critical questions. Each of the tasks in this phase is critical to ensure your analytical wargame will actually address the needs of the sponsor. This phase begins with the identification of a need or requirement to conduct a wargame and continues until the wargaming team has a clearly defined and, if necessary, scoped sponsor's problem that you adequately address in a wargame.

You, the wargaming lead, could engage the sponsor one on one, but it is important to recognize that very few individuals can design an entire wargame by themselves; even wargaming masters rely on others to review, critique, and flesh out their work. So unless you are a wargaming master, you will need to form a team to tackle this wargaming project, and you will find that having a diverse team with complementary skill sets and experiences will greatly increase your chances of creating and conducting a successful wargame. In a perfect world, the core wargaming team members will have experience with scenarios, doctrine, operations, and analysis. They should also have some wargaming education and some experience designing, conducting, and playing wargames. We recognize that many organizations do not have a cadre of wargamers who can be detailed full time to a particular effort, so your core team may have a mixture of full- and part-time members. The point is to identify early in the process those individuals whom you will need to advise, assist, support, and analyze the wargame and to have them involved from the beginning of the wargaming effort.

A wargaming best practice in preparation for the first sponsor engagement is to form your core wargaming team, because you will want the team with you each time you engage the sponsor. Once your core team is formed, you need to sit down and collectively plan the initial engagement with the sponsor.

SPONSOR ENGAGEMENT

We recommend that the wargaming team conduct a series of three sponsor engagements consisting of the initial engagement, the clarification engagement, and the scoping engagement. We have found that those wargaming teams who properly structure and execute these three engagements actually operate more effectively and efficiently during the design and develop phases of the wargaming process.

The immediate goal of the first engagement is problem definition. This is understanding the sponsor's objective and identifying the key issues for the wargame. Most sponsors do not think in these terms, so do not expect the sponsor to clearly articulate the singular objective of the wargame and then tick off a well-thought-out list of key issues. The majority of sponsors will come to you with a problem that even they themselves struggle to clearly articulate. In many cases, the sponsor's problem is complex and multifaceted, and the sponsor may be representing several stakeholders who have each provided several issues they believe your wargame should address. The problem may need not only wargaming but also other analytic techniques to answer. You and your core wargaming team must gain a clear understanding of the sponsor's problem. In many cases, the engagement process actually helps the sponsor gain a better understanding and clarification of the actual problem. This mutual benefit of problem clarification is one of the reasons why it is critical, if at all possible, that you engage directly with the sponsor instead of their staff. We have all played the game of "telephone" and understand the pitfalls of hearing information second- or third-hand.

The clarification engagement is designed for the wargaming team to clarify with the sponsor their understanding of the problem's definition as embodied by the wargame's objective and key issues. This will be more than a simple "read back" of the initial engagement, because the sponsor likely has not thought of the problem in terms of objective and issues. The intent of the scoping engagement is to let the sponsor know what the wargaming team can actually do in support of gaining insights into the sponsor's problem given finite resources.

While it may be possible to combine these three engagements into two or even one interaction, we do not recommend that an inexperienced wargaming team attempt to consolidate them. Many wargames fail because of poor communications between the sponsor and wargaming team, so think carefully before considering combining sponsor interactions. Even an experienced wargaming team should not reduce the number of engagements with a new sponsor, because these engagements also provide your wargaming team an opportunity to develop a relationship with the new sponsor. In some cases, especially with a large or complex study, more than three engagements are required to ensure your team has the proper focus for the wargame. The bottom line is that you, your team, and your sponsor need to all be in agreement about the objective. Later in this chapter, we will outline another wargaming best practice: a written sponsor agreement, which captures what the wargaming team and the sponsor have agreed to with respect to the wargame's objective, issues, constraints, limitations, and assumptions, as well as other critical details of the wargame.

Before the first sponsor engagement, the core wargaming team needs to conduct some preliminary research, which includes understanding a series of typical first questions. These include:

- Who is the sponsor, and why are they coming to you for this wargame?
- What are the primary responsibilities of the sponsor? What is the mission of the organization the sponsor works for?
- How does the sponsor intend to use the wargame's results, and who will be receiving the results?
- How much does the sponsor know about wargaming?
- Will the wargame be one part of a larger study, and if so, what is the objective for the larger study?
- What doctrine or future concepts apply to this wargame?
- Has the sponsor identified a preferred scenario or scenarios for the wargame?
- What is the operational timeframe for the wargame? Wargames exploring future concepts may be set ten to twenty years in the future, while planning wargames are typically for the immediate to near future. The timeframe may necessitate that the wargaming team make some assumptions to properly scope the wargame.
- When does the sponsor require the wargaming results? This will help you budget the time you will have to design and conduct the wargame.

It might be possible for the wargaming team to get many of these questions answered before the first engagement with the sponsor, or the questions may need to be answered during the initial engagement.

Based on the information gained from the above questions, the wargaming team should create a list of the key issues they believe the sponsor will want addressed in the wargame, along with any assumptions that must be made to appropriately frame it. In organizing for each engagement, there should be a single facilitator who will guide the engagement with the sponsor by asking a series of questions that the wargaming team has identified as crucial to the problem definition. The facilitator will ensure all the key questions are addressed during the engagement. All members of the wargaming team, with the exception of the facilitator, should expect to take notes during the sponsor engagements. However, there should be a single identified scribe responsible for maintaining a record of all questions and answers during the engagement process. The scribe is also responsible for consolidating the notes of all core wargaming members after each engagement to establish a clear record of the interaction. All members of the core wargaming team should attend each sponsor engagement, as the sponsor's answers may generate subsequent questions from a team member that will require further sponsor elaboration.

INITIAL ENGAGEMENT

The purpose of this initial engagement is to gain a better and hopefully complete understanding of the sponsor's problem and objective for the wargame. We distill this understanding into two main components: the sponsor's singular wargaming objective, and the key issues needed to address the sponsor's objective/problem. The problem the sponsor is wrestling to understand or gain insights into is typically the objective of the wargame. We tend to advocate that a wargame focus on a single objective; otherwise it may become too large and unwieldy and fail to adequately address all objectives. This may require you to conduct multiple wargames to fully address the sponsor's requirements.

When NPS brings a mobile education team to an organization to conduct a five-day basic analytic wargaming course, the student teams taking the course will execute a wargame by the end of the week that addresses a topic chosen and presented by a sponsor that their organization has identified. We do not coach the sponsor on what the students are specifically looking for; we simply tell the sponsor to communicate to the students what they need their help to address. In one such course, the wargaming topic was to examine the benefits and enhanced capabilities of incorporating the optionally manned fighting vehicle (OMFV) into the combined arms battalion (CAB). The sponsor told the student-formed core wargaming team that his problem "was to determine how to achieve combat vehicle overmatch in close combat against near-peer threats and deliver decisive lethality as part of a combined arms team in the future operating environment."[1] To add to the complexity of the problem, the OMFV's characteristics were not yet fully defined. There were several different technologies that could be integrated into it, so there was not one standard OMFV that the wargame was to assess. Unsurprisingly, there was considerable discussion between the sponsor and the team as the students sought a clearer understanding of the sponsor's needs. The wargame the students conducted at the end of the course came to be known as the "Next Generation of Combat Vehicles" wargame.

This initial engagement with the sponsor is focused on your team listening to the sponsor and asking questions as needed to clarify points or gain a better understanding of the sponsor's problem. This is not the time to attempt a scoping of the objective/problem to what the core wargaming team thinks it can accomplish, since the team does not yet have a clear understanding of the problem. There may be other critical information that surfaces in the initial engagement, to include sponsor-designated assumptions, scenarios, and potential players. Additionally, the sponsor may indicate that some issues are more important than others, which will be valuable information if the wargame needs to be scoped by the wargaming team. The sponsor will almost certainly have a deadline for the delivery of the final wargaming products, which will drive the wargame's schedule. However, the primary purpose for the initial engagement is simply gaining an understanding of the problem the sponsor wants your team to address in the wargame.

CLARIFICATION ENGAGEMENT

Once the initial engagement is complete, the core wargaming team needs to meet to process and distill the sponsor's requirements. Prior to the clarification engagement, the wargaming team needs to develop what it believes to be the sponsor's objective and issues for the wargame. The first task, during this step, is for the wargaming team to reach an agreement on the wargame's objective. It is not uncommon for a slight differing of opinions among the participants of the first engagement concerning the sponsor's actual problem and objective for the wargame. This difference in opinion is why it is critical for all members of the core wargaming team to attend the initial engagement with the sponsor. The process of developing a consensus among the core wargaming team and distilling the objective into a single sentence, if possible, helps to ensure that the core wargaming team captures the sponsor's true objective. Returning to our Next Generation of Combat Vehicles wargame, after the core wargaming team had a lively discussion with the sponsor, asking many questions, the core wargaming team convened its own meeting and attempted to distill a clear and concise problem statement from what they had heard from the sponsor. At the same time, they also sorted out potential issues from the initial sponsor's brief, identified terms used by the sponsor that required clarification, and listed assumptions that they had heard from the sponsor.

The core wargaming team concluded that the sponsor's objective for the wargame was to "assess how the integration of emerging technologies and characteristics into the design of an Optionally Manned Fighting Vehicle provides overmatch while shaping future urban Combined Arms Battalion operations."[2] Note that this objective provides more specificity than the original sponsor's problem statement from the initial engagement. This single sentence was distilled from the discussion with the sponsor to understand his actual problem. Also note that the term "decisive lethality," which had appeared in the sponsor's original problem statement, does not appear in this more succinct problem statement. The team concluded that lethality should be assessed in one or more of the key issues of the wargame.

After the identification of the objective for the wargame, the core wargaming team needs to develop a set of key issues that they must address to gain insights into the sponsor's problem. A key issue is a question that the wargaming team will need to answer during the course of the wargame to explore its objective. Typically, the wargaming team will work through a problem structuring exercise to begin to identify this set of issues. It is also possible that the sponsor may have identified some of these issues during the initial engagement. Once the wargaming team has established this set of potential issues, they need to review the list to sort out key issues from sub-issues. Sub-issues are issues that stem from another identified issue and that must be answered to address the higher issue. Once the wargaming team identifies the key issues, they should attempt to prioritize them. Some of the identified issues for the Next Generation of Combat Vehicles wargame included the following:

- What is the impact of OMFV on armored brigade combat team effectiveness on the future battlefield?
- How would an OMFV better enable a CAB to operate in an urban environment?
- Which enablers provide the most capability to the formation in an urban environment?[3]

The issues are written as questions, with the intent that by answering these questions the wargaming team can provide answers/insights to address the sponsor's objective. In this effort, the wargaming team actually identified ten key issues with six sub-issues. Some issues may be broad in scope and could require additional decomposition into a set of sub-issues or questions during the problem structuring process. For example, the third issue's requirement to address "enablers" in our Next Generation of Combat Vehicles wargame is too broad in scope. We need a clearer picture of the potential set of enablers to ensure we gain sufficient insights from our wargame to answer the issue. In this example, the wargaming team created the following sub-issues to specifically address potential firepower and sensor capabilities:

- Which OMFV cannon option enables the formation to provide the most lethality in an urban environment?
- Which OMFV sensor option enables the formation to provide the best situational awareness in an urban environment?

These two sub-issues bring a clearer focus to the wargaming team as they begin to design the wargame. However, these sub-issues are still too broad in scope, since they are not completely clear about the cannon or sensor options. We will address this point later in the chapter. The problem definition, issues, and sub-issues are identified during problem structuring and decomposition. This is a critical step in the process, and it is often rushed by planners and analysts.

Problem structuring exercises or methods are a set of techniques, usually used by a group in a collaborative manner, to help in structuring and decomposing a problem to provide insights into how to solve it. These qualitative operations research techniques date to the 1960s and were designed to help analysts decompose ill-structured or wicked problems.[4] There are many productive problem structuring techniques to include diagramming techniques (such as Rich Pictures, Influence Diagrams, and Causal Loop Diagrams) and facilitated brainstorming techniques that support creative and critical thinking.[5] Another effective problem structuring technique is the Army Design Methodology.

During this problem structuring process, the team will identify additional information that it will need to conduct the wargame, some of which the sponsor may have or can help obtain. Once that is identified, you will go back to the sponsor with a request for information (RFI). You will want to verify other information the sponsor provided in the initial engagement, such as assumptions that were heard. The wargaming team needs to develop an in-depth knowledge of the problem space to be able to adequately identify the list of necessary information. Several key questions guide this effort:

- Have there been previous wargames or other studies completed that have investigated some aspects of the problem?
- What doctrinal, organizational, or professional publications, instructions, white papers, or other documents apply to the problem?
- Who has the information (data) that will be required for the wargame, and how can it be obtained? Will you need the sponsor's help obtaining it?

At this time the team should carefully note any terms that the sponsor has used that will require further definition. Senior leaders in the U.S. DoD are well known for creating "buzz words"—colorful terms that work their way into conversations but that really have not been clearly defined. The term "irregular warfare" is a classic example—in the early 2000s as counterinsurgency campaigns were raging in both Iraq and Afghanistan, the U.S. Army Training and Doctrine Command Analysis Center (TRAC) analysts were asked to focus their analysis of that year's Unified Quest Title X wargame on irregular warfare. The analysts asked that the sponsor provide the definition of irregular warfare, but the sponsor did not have one.[6] In order to proceed, the TRAC analysts developed terms of reference (TOR), which included a proposed definition of irregular warfare along with several other terms being used by senior leaders, so that the sponsor and the analysts could agree on what each term meant for the purpose of the wargame. We return to the Next Generation of Combat Vehicles wargame and recall that the sponsor's original problem statement "was to determine how to achieve *combat vehicle overmatch* in close combat against *near-peer threats* and deliver *decisive lethality* as part of a combined arms team in the *future operating environment*." The italicized terms all require a specific definition that the analyst and the sponsor agree to, or, if no definition can be agreed upon, the terms simply need to be dropped from all conversation. With these examples, we conclude that it is a best practice for the sponsor and the wargaming team to agree on a TOR that includes all the important terms raised by the sponsor or that have emerged as the sponsor's problem has been distilled into the objective and key issues that are not doctrinally defined (for DoD, doctrinal definitions are found in Joint Publication 1-02, *Department of Defense Dictionary of Military and Associated Terms*). In conclusion, the sponsor should be able to provide or point the team toward some of the information that is needed, but do not expect your sponsor to be the sole source for information. Good wargaming teams develop a network of contacts and subject matter experts to leverage.

The clarification engagement is where the sponsor and the wargaming team agree on the wargame's objective and the key issues. The main focus of this engagement is to ensure the team heard the sponsor correctly and to gain the sponsor's agreement that the team has the correct objective and key issues for the wargame. During this interaction, the team should also present any assumptions for the wargame that they heard during the initial engagement, as well as any assumptions they believe are necessary for the success of the wargame.

The wargaming team will make more assumptions during the design and develop phases of the process, but this initial set of assumptions will help to establish the foundation for the wargame. It is at this time that an experienced wargaming team may begin to scope the wargame if necessary. Often the sponsor will ask the wargaming team to address more issues than can reasonably be accomplished in the time available for the wargame, but if the team is inexperienced or the sponsor is new to wargaming, we advise not to try and scope the effort at this point. It is better if the wargaming team does some additional homework to better understand the amount of effort necessary to address each of the sponsor's issues.

For an inexperienced wargaming team or a team working with a new sponsor, we suggest that the clarification engagement remain focused on agreement of the wargame's singular objective and on identification and prioritization of the issues. For this engagement, simply prioritize the issues, and tell the sponsor how the wargaming team has ordered the sponsor's priorities. If the sponsor agrees with this singular objective and issue prioritization, the wargaming team may explain that it may not be able to thoroughly address the lowest ranking priorities in the wargame, and the sponsor's input is being sought to ensure that everyone agrees on the prioritization of issues. Establishing the issue priority also alerts the sponsor of the potential requirement for a scoping engagement. After the clarification engagement has developed the clearly defined singular objective and issues, the wargaming team needs to decide if it can address all the sponsor's issues or if the problem needs to be scoped. If scoping is necessary, the wargaming team and sponsor must come to an agreement on the final scoped set of issues that the wargame will address.

SCOPING ENGAGEMENT

Scoping is simply taking the complete set of wargaming issues and reducing its number to a smaller set of issues that the wargaming team can address within the current resource constraints to accomplish the wargame's objective. The challenge is to retain the high-priority issues that will provide the sponsor meaningful analysis. It is critical that the sponsor and team agree to the scoping, which is the purpose of the scoping engagement of the sponsor. This scoping process needs to be captured and included in the final analysis product so that consumers will understand what the wargame did and did not cover in addressing the sponsor's question/problem.

Scoping requires the wargaming team to understand the complexity of each of the sponsor's issues, which will then provide a rough indicator of the amount of time the issue will take to design, develop, and address in the wargame. An inexperienced wargaming team or an experienced team working with a new sponsor should begin drafting the DCMP to better understand the complexity of the sponsor's wargame. An inexperienced wargaming team may want to create a preliminary design (covered in chapter 7) and then conduct a play-test of that design (covered in chapter 8) if they cannot determine if scoping is necessary at this point in the sponsor engagement process. If a design–play-test cycle is conducted, it should be done quickly, as the scoping engagement should take place shortly after the clarification sponsor engagement. The first step in preparation for the scoping engagement is to develop each issue's essential questions (EQs), which is also the first step needed to draft the DCMP. The EQs are those questions that need to be answered for the team to address all identified issues. Not all EQs will require a wargame to answer, but the team will find that many, if not most, of the EQs are questions that they need to answer through the wargame. The team will then focus the design of the wargame on being able to answer these EQs. We will fully discuss the DCMP and development of EQs at the end of this chapter.

Once the wargaming team has each of the sponsor's key issues distilled into the EQs and has roughed out the measurement space required to address each EQ to be answered in the wargame, the team will have a general idea of the wargame's initial design. This is the time to sketch out enough details of the design so the wargaming team can conduct the initial play-test of the wargame. This play-test will not only reveal design challenges but will also provide a rough understanding of the amount of resources (typically time) that will be required to address each of the sponsor's key issues. For a wargaming team, there are two key tasks that need to be considered with respect to time: the time it takes to develop the wargame, and the time it takes to conduct the wargame. The time that is available for the team to conduct the wargame can often be a limiting factor for the number of issues that can be addressed during the actual wargame, although there are other techniques that the team can leverage to address issues if the time to conduct the wargame is not sufficient. This time is often dictated by the due date of the results, the availability of key players, the availability of the necessary facilities to conduct the wargame, and other factors. Wargames are rarely more than a week long in DoD, with the primary constraint being the availability of the key players. Not many DoD organizations can afford to have key personnel gone for more than a week. At this point, it will be difficult for a team to know how long it would take to conduct a wargame that addresses all the sponsor's issues, so we recommend that the team focus on developing an assessment of how long it will take the team to develop a wargame to address all issues. Once the team is able to conduct that assessment, they are then ready for the scoping engagement with the sponsor.

When the wargaming team determines that they cannot address all of the sponsor's key issues in the allotted design and development time, the sponsor and wargaming team should have a frank discussion with the sponsor to reach agreement on the scoped issues. The wargame team should approach this sponsor interaction and engagement in a methodical way. The general idea is that there is a trade space between the time allotted for design and development and the number of issues that the wargaming team can adequately address. Many sponsors and wargamers believe that more time means the wargaming team can address more issues, so if the sponsor has some flexibility on when the wargame's results must be delivered, the delivery date can be linked to the number of issues that the team can design into the wargame. You should be cautious in making this direct relationship between more time and more issues. More time may mean you can conduct a longer game or additional wargames to address the set of defined issues. There is also the belief that simply adding more personnel to the wargaming team might allow more issues to be designed and developed without changing the results delivery timeline, but this is usually not the case, as there are few experienced wargamers who are not already fully engaged.

We have found that both the analyst's business model and the constraints, limitations, and assumptions code of best practice are useful frameworks for the scoping engagement. The analyst's business model is very simple. It has three criteria: good, fast, and cheap. The idea is that the sponsor for a wargame, or any other analytic project, can have the project completed satisfying two of the criteria at the expense of the third. If you can educate a sponsor who says, "I want an outstanding product, I want it now, and I do not want to provide the team any additional resources" that they cannot have all three, you can begin the scoping process. We recommend that the wargaming team use the TRAC Constraints, Limitations, and Assumptions (CLA) Code of Best Practice as a method to structure a scoping engagement with the sponsor:[7]

- A *constraint* is a restriction imposed by the study sponsor that limits the wargaming team's options in conducting the study. Time is the usual constraint; the results must be delivered by a certain date. There

may be others, such as a scenario that must be used or a particular individual specified to be used as a role player.
- A *limitation* is an inability of the study team to fully meet the study objectives or fully investigate the study issues. One such limitation may be the lack of subject matter expertise that is needed for the wargame, or the need to augment the team in order to design and conduct a wargame that will answer all the sponsor's issues.
- An *assumption* is a statement related to the study that is taken as true in the absence of facts, often to accommodate a limitation. Some assumptions may come from the sponsor, and some may be identified by the wargaming team as they design the wargame.

The sponsor needs to accept all key CLAs of the wargame. Wargaming teams often need to identify assumptions that help keep their players from taking the game off track, but the team needs to avoid making an errant assumption that precludes investigating some issue that is critical for the sponsor. However, the wargaming team should also use the CLAs to communicate to the sponsor the quality of the wargame that is to be delivered. The wargaming team may be limited in its capability to examine all the issues the sponsor has, so advising the sponsor that they may need more resources (time or personnel) should present a critical opportunity for the team to have a discussion about scoping the wargame so that quality results can be obtained for the sponsor.

The objective is to conclude the scoping engagement with an agreed set of key issues with the sponsor so the wargaming team can complete the initiate phase of the wargaming process.

SPONSOR AGREEMENT

One best practice that we learned from the U.S. Naval War College is the drafting of a sponsor's agreement between the sponsor and the team.[8] We first called it a "sponsor contract" and required the sponsor's signature, but some sponsors sensed a need to involve lawyers if they were going to sign a contract, so we now call it a sponsor agreement. Essentially, the sponsor and team have agreed upon the scope of the wargame and capture that agreement in a written document. We have no illusion that this will prevent "mission creep" or the addition of issues for the wargame to examine by a sponsor or a stakeholder at some later date, but it does provide a line in the sand for the wargaming team that says, "We had an agreement based on design and development time available, so if you (sponsor) need to add issues, we need to re-scope the wargame and drop issues that are currently to be included in the wargame." We recommend that this sponsor agreement include as a minimum:

- wargame objective
- wargame issues to be examined
- wargame details (type and format)
- who provides the wargame scenario (sponsor, wargaming team)
- who recruits/provides players (sponsor, wargaming team)
- timeline, to include:
  - date of sponsor/team initial progress reviews
  - date(s) that wargame will be played
  - date the final out-brief will be conducted with the sponsor
  - date the final report will be provided to sponsor
- Other enclosures include:
  - draft key CLAs
  - initial requests for information
  - draft TOR

DATA COLLECTION AND MANAGEMENT PLAN

The DCMP provides the foundation of the wargame's design. The plan's purpose is to lay out the roadmap that ensures all of the data required to initiate, conduct, and analyze the wargame is collected and processed effectively and efficiently. The creation of the DCMP begins once the wargaming team and the sponsor have agreed to the wargame's objective/problem and the key issues that the sponsor wants examined in the wargame.

Before the process of scoping the wargame is conducted with the sponsor, the wargaming team needs to assess how many of the sponsor's key issues they believe the wargame will be able to address in the time allotted. Not all key issues are created equal. There may be key issues that have few EQs, and thus many of those may be addressed in the wargame.

The wargame will likely be able to address fewer key issues that have many sub-issues and EQs. The wargaming team must also consider that there may be EQs or entire key issues that need to be addressed by means other than the wargame, and the wargaming team will need to determine if they can address those, and if so, how. Typically, these are questions or issues that could be addressed through outside research, doctrinal reviews, or quantitative models and simulations. For example, one of the issues in a force structure development problem could be to understand what threat size and composition the new force can defeat. The wargame would first help develop the concept of operation for this new force in a certain operational environment, and then the wargaming team could turn to an appropriate combat model or simulation to gather quantified data on its ability to defeat a threat. The understanding that to fully address the agreed upon issue requires support beyond the wargame is critical as part of the design and planning process to ensure there are adequate resources to address the issue.

Determining the Essential Questions

The first step in this assessment is to determine, for each of the sponsor's key issues, the set of corresponding EQs that comprise each issue. The goal is to develop a set of clear questions that are scoped to the smallest possible element. These EQs are a distillation or decomposition of the key issue, where a key issue may have one or many EQs. There may be several layers of decomposition—that is, a key issue may have several sub-issues, and those sub-issues may have sub-issues of their own, before discovering the EQs. For example, the third issue in our Next Generation of Combat Vehicles wargame example was decomposed into two sub-issues focused on cannon and sensor enablers. These two sub-issues are too broad, so we need to further decompose them to gain a little clarity. The sub-issue focused on the type of cannon equipped on the OMFV could be decomposed to address the two available options:

- How lethal is the formation with a 30 mm cannon–equipped OMFV in an urban environment?
- How lethal is the formation with a 50 mm cannon–equipped OMFV in an urban environment?

Once we get to the point where the question is clear and cannot be decomposed any further, we have reached the essential question we need to answer. It is important to note that some of the EQs required to answer an issue may not necessarily be questions that can be answered in a wargame. Essential questions may require that the wargaming team do research to answer, research that needs to be concluded before the wargame, perhaps to inform the wargame's design. EQs may point to additional initiate data that the team needs to collect. They may need the sponsor to provide an answer; thus, they become the topic of an RFI. For example, the EQs above will need a clear definition or assumption for several of the terms in the question, to include "lethal," "formation," and "urban environment," before we design the wargame. The remainder of the EQs, likely the majority of them, will be questions that the wargame will be constructed to address.

How will the wargaming team know they have created an EQ that needs to be addressed in the wargame? They will be able to look at the EQ and understand what player interactions are needed in the wargame to produce the information needed to address that particular EQ. They will know the specific *players* that must interact to obtain the EQ's response. They will know or be able to create the *scenario elements* so the question has the proper context that will be necessary to stimulate those players. They have determined that the wargaming team has *limitations* that will affect the quality of the information the wargame will produce. They will understand *assumptions* that must be made (if any) to further frame or clarify the necessary context of the scenario. They will understand the *MMTs* that will need to be created or obtained to adjudicate player interactions to address this EQ. And lastly, they will understand what *data* will be required so that the players have the information necessary to respond and the MMTs can properly adjudicate the player interactions. This *initiate data* is needed before the wargame begins, and it will consist of the data that the players will need to understand their roles and make decisions in the wargame. In addition, it is any data that any method, model, or tool will need to be ready to function when called upon at any time during the wargame's execution.

The answers to the wargame's EQs are called the *analysis data*, which can take on many forms but are generally qualitative in nature. In a seminar wargame, this data may simply be the recording of a player's decision, although the context of the decision—that is, *why* that player made the decision—is often needed to fully understand the decision that the player made. As you move along the spectrum of wargaming styles from seminar to system (rigid Kriegsspiel), this data may include more details and some quantitative data. For example, a system game focused on military operations would include threat situation, movement orders, operations, and potential adjudication results from either/both kinetic and nonkinetic operations.

Finally, there will be data required during the wargame that provides the players with feedback on the results of decisions that they made earlier in the wargame. This *feedback data* is important to keep the players informed and engaged and in many cases could/should represent the consequences of their decisions. A simple example is our system game focused on military operations. One piece of feedback data would include the results or consequences of their movement or operations. It is very likely that this feedback data will also make up some portion of the data that the analysts will need to do the post-game analysis and produce the results the sponsor is seeking, so the means to collect and/or record all feedback data that has been provided to the players needs to be devised.

The DCMP template is set up to organize the elements required to design an analytic wargame. Spreadsheets are a convenient management tool for a DCMP, where additional columns can be easily added to accommodate the wargaming team's design requirements.

The DCMP Core Elements

Note the core DCMP elements listed in figure 3. We will cover these elements in more detail as we continue to lay out the phases of wargame design. All EQs are designed with the expectation that there will be Player Information–Out, also known as analysis data. Most EQs will require entries for players, MMTs, and Player Information–In, or initiate data. Careful consideration should be made if Player Information–Feedback is not filled in, as this is a potential indicator that a player will be asked to make a decision whose impact will not be revealed to that player, which could negatively impact the player's willingness to continue to provide realistic and relevant responses. However, not all spaces of the DCMP's core elements may be filled in. There may already be sufficient detail in the scenario for a particular EQ, so that space will be left blank. Some EQs may not require additional assumptions.

The questions that the team derived from the Sponsor's Issues.	**Essential Questions (EQ)**
The players that need to interact in order to answer the associated EQ.	**Players** • TF CDR • POTUS • PLAN
Events or interactions that need to occur in the wargame so that the players can answer the associated EQ.	**Scenario Details** • Injects • Vignettes
The MMTs that are needed to adjudicate player interactions that are necessary to answer the associated EQ.	**Methods, Models, and Tools** • Combat Sim • Seminar
The limitations the study team has WRT answering the associated EQ.	**Limitations**
The assumptions that must be made to accommodate a limitation or to better define the measurement space for an associated EQ.	**Assumptions**
Information (data) required for the wargame that is requested from an external source.	**Requests for Info**
The information (data) that must be collected BEFORE the wargame begins.	**Player Info – In (Initiate Data)**
The information (data) that must be generated DURING the wargame to inform the players on the impact of their decisions.	**Player Info – Feedback (Feedback Data)**
The information (data) that we are seeking to answer this EQ! This information will be collected DURING the wargame.	**Player Info – Out (Analysis Data)**

The Core Elements of the DCMP

Once a solid draft of the EQs has been completed, the wargame design can begin. The data, scenarios and vignettes, MMTs, players, and assumptions (the five elements of the wargame's *measurement space*) are all informed by the EQs; they will be covered in depth in chapter 7.

The core wargaming team will probably need to be expanded after you have a complete understanding of the sponsor's wargaming problem. So who should be on the final wargaming team? How many members should it have? What are the roles of each of the team members? The size of the wargame (both number of players and the length of time that the wargame will be played) and the resources required for the wargame (personnel, funding, IT equipment, and time allowed to design the wargame) will help determine that. Even after you have a complete understanding of what the sponsor wants, you will still need to get a better idea of the wargame requirements through some research and preliminary design work before you can determine your final wargaming team composition. For larger teams (more than ten personnel), we recommend that the wargaming team consist of a design group and an analysis group, with the design group having at least one analyst and the analysis group having one non-analyst. This is to encourage cross-talk and coordination between the two groups as the wargame is designed and developed.

The initiate phase transitions to the design phase once the first draft of the DCMP is complete. Some organizations may use other terms (such as the Naval War College's Data Collection and Analysis Plan), but the purpose is similar. The DCMP is the foundation for the wargame design. The primary focus of the DCMP is the translation of the sponsor's objective and issues into the information (data) that the wargame will produce in order to provide the insights to the sponsor's key issues. Since the wargame is focused on players and the decisions they are making, most of this data will be qualitative in nature, but depending on the issue, there could be some quantitative data. We will discuss in chapter 10 techniques for analyzing this data. The critical point at the end of the initiate phase is the identification of this data and where you plan to collect it in the wargame. We often talk about the DCMP as being a decomposition of the sponsor's issues, but it is not always that straightforward. In practice, creating the initial DCMP can be the most challenging task faced by a wargaming team, but getting this correct will help reduce chaos and potential restarts later in the design process.

WARGAME PRACTICAL EXERCISES 1–4

The following set of practical exercises is designed to begin the wargame construction process. You will get more out of the book by actually taking the time to execute the exercises. The craft of wargaming is learned by doing versus by just reading or watching. The hope is that at the end of the nine practical exercises, you will have a basic analytical wargame. We will provide one set of potential solutions in appendix 3.

Practical Exercise 1: First Sponsor Interaction

Read the South Asia–Pacific Command (SAPCOM J-5) brief (in appendix 1); this will serve as your first interaction with the sponsor. You have just heard the sponsor (SAPCOM J-5) brief on the Zefra wargame. Prepare an initial progress review brief to apprise your supervisor of as much detail as you can about the wargame project you will design, develop, conduct, and analyze:

1. List the wargame's objective.
2. List the sponsor's key issues that you can identify in the brief. These should each be in the form of a question.
3. List any assumptions that the sponsor communicated or that you think will be required for this wargame.
4. List any RFIs that you will need the sponsor to provide.

Practical Exercise 2: Preparing for the Second Sponsor Interaction

You now have an objective and what you believe is the list of the sponsor's key issues. Take the list of key issues below and break them into groups by "must have," "good to have," and "nice to have." Then prioritize your list in the order that you believe are most important to address the wargame's objective. Do NOT use the language "Must have, good to have, nice to have" with the sponsor.

Current list of issues:

1. What assistance can SAPCOM provide to assist the Combined Joint Task Force Zefra (CTJF-Z) in stabilizing Zefra?
2. What capability gaps does the CJTF-Z have for its Zefra stabilization mission?

3. What force protection issues does the CJTF commander face?
4. What capacity gaps does the CJTF-Z have for its Zefra stabilization mission?
5. What kind of medical assistance can the UN task force (TF) provide to take better care of the refugees in the Daloon camps?
6. What kind of medical assistance can the SAPCOM TF provide to take better care of the refugees in the Daloon camps?
7. Sub-Issue: What unique medical capabilities does SAPCOM have to offer Doctors without Borders?
8. Sub-Issue: Should we pre-position USS *Comfort* for medical contingencies?
9. What activities are TOKEN involved in on the island of Capricornia?
10. What capabilities does CJTF-Z need to have to respond to the weaponization of nuclear material?
11. What kind of challenges does the Illustrious Fighters for Freedom (IFF) battalion pose to bringing stability to Zefra?
12. How effective will the UN TF be against the IFF if it decides to insert itself in the stabilization process?
13. How effective will the Marine expeditionary unit be against the IFF if it decides to insert itself in the stabilization process?
14. What unique capabilities does the PLAN TF have that might be leveraged in Zefra?
15. What kind of media issues should SAPCOM anticipate from the Zefra situation?

Practical Exercise 3: Essential Questions

Take issue 3 from your solution to practical exercise 2, "What force protection issues does the CJTF-Z commander face?" and break down this issue until you have questions that you believe can be answered in a wargame.

1. Create a list of essential questions necessary to gain insight into this issue.
2. Determine the format of the answers to these questions. The answers may be either qualitative, quantitative, or potentially both.
3. Identify the adjudication technique(s), covered in chapter 5, you believe will be used to support answering these questions. We will

provide more details after discussing methods, models, and tools in chapter 7.
4. Identify any questions for which you anticipate you will not find answers; it is critical that these be brought to the sponsor's attention if you cannot subsequently find some means to address them.

Practical Exercise 4: Constraints, Limitations, and Assumptions

After doing some initial research and obtaining responses to your RFIs from the sponsor, you are ready to draft your initial CLAs, knowing that these will be continually reviewed and updated as necessary throughout the wargame creation process.

- The RFI about the IFF's strength, composition, and disposition has been partially answered by SAPCOM J-2. They have located five platoon-sized infantry elements around the city of Kabra. They are 95 percent certain that the shelling of the refugee camp was conducted by IFF members and that it was done with at least two mortar sections. They estimate that the IFF battalion is between 50–75 percent strength of a fully-manned Zefran infantry battalion.

- You have a contact at the UN who has told you that both the UN Planning Toolkit and the UN Peacekeeping Operations Principles and Guidelines (2008) are being revised. CJTF–Zefra has the final drafts of the revisions, but your contact cannot get you copies until they have been published, which will be in about sixty days.

- You have a combat simulation that you can run to assess UN forces against the IFF. Unfortunately, in order to run this simulation, you need to get the Zefran terrain uploaded and the UN and IFF performance data generated and quality controlled. This will take at least ninety days. However, the Daloon Ministry of Defence has a ready-to-run combat simulation with Daloon armed forces and Zefran armed forces that was created to assess the Zefran incursion into Daloon that happened recently. They are willing to share that with you and provide any support needed to run the simulation and interpret the output.

At this time, develop your list of CLAs.

1. List any constraints imposed on you by the sponsor.
2. List any limitations that your wargaming team will have when attempting to respond to the sponsor's issues.
3. Create any assumptions to accommodate the limitations you listed, if possible. Keep in mind that not all limitations have assumptions, but many will have an associated limitation.
4. Now create a consolidated list of CLAs, ensuring ALL assumptions that you have identified are listed.

CHAPTER 7

Design

■ ■ ■ ■

According to Peter Perla, "Once the sponsor, designer, and analysts have agreed upon the definition of the problem, and decided how it may be usefully addressed through a wargame, the actual design work can begin."[1] The design phase of the wargaming process is where the wargame begins to take shape. During this phase, the wargaming team will establish the scenario for the wargame, identify the necessary methods, models, and tools to support player decisions, determine the roster of players, and capture the data needed for both the players and MMTs. Designing a wargame is a bit like designing a playground for children. The playground designer establishes the theme for the playground to attract and hold the interest of the children. With the theme in mind, the designer then chooses the playground equipment that best supports the theme and the enjoyment of the children. The playground designer needs to consider how many children to accommodate at any given time on the playground and the boundaries of the playground to contain them. In addition, understanding the age groups and skill sets of the children who will play on this particular playground is critical to the design process. Thus, just like a playground designer, a wargame designer must consider who the players will actually be, and, with the game's objective and issues in mind, choose the scenario and the methods, models, and tools, and obtain the necessary data. A wargame designer that accomplishes this should be able to successfully construct a useful wargame.

Wargaming design is conducted using an iterative process that involves wargaming development, which is discussed in detail in chapter 8. The idea is to get a draft design roughed out quickly and then actually conduct a play-test of the wargame to determine if the design works the way it was envisioned by the wargaming team. The play-test identifies those areas where the design does not work well, and then the wargaming team, armed with a detailed critique, updates the wargame's design. Once the design is updated, another play-test is conducted, and this iterative process repeats as necessary and as time allows.

"Experienced military officers, practiced operations research analysts, and accomplished computer programmers are not necessarily capable of designing useful wargames. Although some or all of the knowledge and skills of such people are important tools for a wargame designer to possess, the nature of game design requires a unique blending of talents."[2]

Peter Perla's words ring as true today as the day he wrote them. There are very few individuals who can sit down and design a useful wargame by themselves. Recognizing this as fact, we ensure, both in our resident wargaming course at NPS and in our mobile education wargaming course for defense organizations, that we create wargaming teams of four to six students to give the team a blending of the talents as expressed by Perla.

One of the most challenging aspects of creating a wargame is creating its design. It is infinitely more challenging if those trying to create the design do not fully understand the problem space into which the players need to be brought. Here again is where teams that rush off to design a wargame without a complete understanding of the problem find themselves in treacherous waters. The first vector of research should be to ensure that the team understands all the operational aspects of the wargame sponsor's problem. That includes doctrine, white papers that describe emerging concepts, concepts of employment for new weapons systems, and so on. More requests for information may well be in order as your team seeks to fully understand the problem space. Your team should aim to know more about the problem than the sponsor knows.

The second vector of research is to see if any other wargaming has been conducted to address the same or a similar problem space, taking

James Dunnigan's advice to "plagiarize."[3] This is where building your network of wargamers may help. Knowing what other wargaming teams have tried and how successful they were can be a tremendous help when building your own wargame's design. When borrowing from other wargames, be careful to understand what the purpose of the original wargame was. Your wargame is very unlikely to have the same purpose, so understanding how the other game differed from yours will help your team to understand how to parse the other aspects of it. Useful aspects to examine from other wargames include the scenario, orders of battle, MMTs, player roles, and assumptions. Remember, though, that your wargame has a very unique DCMP that you have created, so "cutting and pasting" from other wargames isn't the idea here; it is learning how another wargaming team approached a similar problem.

MEASUREMENT SPACE

We adapted the concept of measurement space from the combat simulators who use computer-based combat simulations to do quantitative studies for warfighters. Measurement space for a quantitative study is a function of the scenario, MMTs, and data. We will add two elements specifically for wargaming later in this discussion. The objectives of the study can only be met if the measurement space allows enough latitude to permit the systems under study to be assessed throughout a sufficient range of the systems' critical capabilities and attributes.

A simple example of an analysis of alternatives (AoA) conducted for the U.S. Army with the purpose of evaluating alternatives to replace the current main battle tank (MBT) will help illustrate the point of measurement space. Analyses of alternatives for the U.S. DoD are concerned with two things: cost and operational effectiveness. An assessment of operational effectiveness seeks to understand how effectively the force equipped with one of the alternative MBTs executes a given operation. Effectiveness is usually described using metrics such as lethality, survivability, and sustainability.

For this AoA, we need a force. For this main battle tank example, the force we will use is a combined arms battalion, which is a battalion-sized force that has main battle tank companies as part of its structure. We also need alternatives for the analysis effort. Each alternative will be a CAB equipped with a different type of main battle tank. For this example, we will have three different main battle tanks: the current MBT (this "alternative" is also called the base case), a product-improved (current) MBT, and a next-generation MBT.

The idea is to compare alternative CABs to see how each force's operational effectiveness changes with a different MBT integrated into its formation. The challenge is to pick the proper measurement space, consisting of three primary elements: scenario, MMTs, and data to support the AoA effort. All three of these elements need to combine to provide a sufficient measurement space that allows analysts to assess operational effectiveness differences between the three alternative forces.

Scenario

Tanks are meant to fight in open and rolling terrain, such as the northern German plain or wide-open deserts such as the Middle East. Tanks are primarily used to kill enemy tanks, hopefully before the enemy's tanks can shoot back. Open terrain also means that the other main nemesis of the tank, the anti-tank (AT) team, will have a hard time hiding, and thus the tank will not need an infantry escort to hunt out and eliminate the AT threat. Tanks are not as effective in restricted terrain, such as old-growth forests, triple-canopy jungles, steep mountainous terrain, or urban environments. They still can be used for some missions there, but they will not be able to showcase any advantage to the CAB such as increased main gun range, accuracy, killing power, or faster speed. When a tank is restricted to limited routes such as urban canyons, anti-tank mines and improvised explosive devices can cripple or destroy it, and the tank's advantages of speed and long-range killing of targets are negated. So for the purpose of this MBT AoA, the scenario should be in open or rolling terrain against a near-peer adversary that has tanks.

One complicating footnote in this process is that DoD would very likely want to also understand any critical operational effectiveness differences if the circumstance required the commander to employ the CAB in terrain that is not favorable for a tank, such as the streets of an urban environment or in a jungle. This could necessitate another scenario or two, or at least a few vignettes that will then allow the study to assess the CAB alternatives in a spectrum of combat situations.

MMTs

In this case, we will choose a closed-loop combat simulation that can run thirty or forty replications of the same battle so we can look at statistics for each variant. If the simulation isn't precise enough, we might not be able to discern differences in the alternative forces. For example, if the simulation were to determine if a tank is killed after it has been hit twice by a tank round, regardless of the type of round, and our next-generation MBT has an electromagnetic round that has three times the penetration of the current MBT round, we probably will not be able to see the effect of that new round, so we would pass on that simulation and choose one that would better account for the attributes of each of the alternative MBTs.

DoD would very likely want to also understand any critical operational effectiveness differences if the CAB has to be employed in different operational or strategic constructs, such as counterinsurgency operations. There are no useful computer simulations that can provide quantitative comparisons of a force's operational effectiveness in counterinsurgency operations, so in support of the main wargame, the wargaming team may utilize a seminar or matrix-style wargame to better understand differences between alternatives. This process would identify and produce qualitative insights into potential critical effectiveness issues and may establish additional hypotheses for future research.

Data

Data is very important but often overlooked. First, we need to understand the precision of the MMT that we chose, so we can find the performance data (data that specifies how well the MBT performs) that the MMT needs: probability of hits and kills for each MBT round versus enemy vehicles, penetration, speed, reliability, and so forth. For new technologies, performance data can be hard to come by, especially if we are considering technology that is still on the drawing board. If the technology exists, there may be test data available that can be used. Organizations that generate data for use in quantitative studies often have ways to approximate performance data for new or emerging technologies.

But there is other information that this study needs, and that is how each of the alternative force structures will fight. This may be a mixture of quantitative and qualitative data, as each of the three versions of the CAB (each equipped with a different alternative MBT) may fight differently (qualitative) and may have a different number of MBTs than an alternative (quantitative). These elements of data might be more difficult to obtain, or they might come after a series of studies. The qualitative information of how the CAB fights would likely come from wargames where experienced tank commanders, given a new tank variant, determine if their force should fight differently given the new capabilities. The Army might not decide to change the number of tanks in a tank unit until after the first quantitative study is complete and both the cost and operational effectiveness differences for all alternatives are known. The push to change (usually reduce) the number of new MBTs would then typically be influenced by current and projected budgets and would likely also involve a longer-term study that would account for any difference in reliability, operations, and maintenance costs.

Now that you have a better picture of what measurement space is, we will adapt the construct to wargaming. The measurement space of a wargame has five key elements: scenario, data, MMTs, players, and assumptions. In some sense, you can think of the measurement space as a playground with boundaries that you want the players to stay within, which encourages player interaction—ultimately producing the information that you need to address the sponsor's issues.

SCENARIO

The scenario is the most critical element of measurement space. The scenario sets the scene or narrative for players and establishes the world in which they will make decisions. It is the common framework for the sponsor, players, and analysts crafted by the wargaming team to support answering the sponsor's issues in the wargame. A scenario that is not compelling to the players almost always dooms the wargame to failure. Quite simply, if the players do not believe the scenario is plausible, they will not be able to play their roles with any enthusiasm or realism, drastically affecting the information that they provide. Polite players may do their best to push the "I believe" button, but the more outspoken players will push back and want to "fight the scenario." They will point out, with great authority and specificity, why the scenario would never happen. When players openly fight the scenario, it can infect the other players, and the wargaming team will be challenged to either adjust the scenario on the fly—which is nearly impossible and may mutilate the wargame's DCMP—or drag unbelieving players through a scenario they are convinced is pure fiction. Prior to constructing the scenario, the wargaming team must have a clearly defined problem for the wargame and the draft version of the DCMP. The DCMP will identify the potential decision points for players to address the essential questions listed in the DCMP.

Every scenario has a common set of components: background, player objectives, relationships, available resources, and information updates. The wargaming team fleshes out each of these components as necessary to establish an immersive environment for players to make decisions. The background establishes the general situation, which will include a specific geographic area and time period as part of the operational environment. Analytic wargames are always set in the future—the near future for most planning wargames, and ten or more years in the future for most other analytic wargames. A "road to war" is one method for capturing some of this information. It is a chronological storyline that traces how the source of conflict evolved from the current world situation. A compelling road to war can help the credibility of the scenario and perhaps deter those who want to fight the scenario. The background will also establish who the key actors are in the wargame and identify their general attitudes, intentions, and goals. These key actors will typically drive the player roles for inclusion in the wargame. Player objectives will establish what each player is attempting to achieve in the wargame and should provide a source of tension or conflict between some or all of the key players. Relationships will establish the organizational structure or command relationship of all players in the wargame. Available resources will establish what each player has at their disposal during the conduct of the wargame. One common resource item is the order of battle (OOB) for military units in a tactical or operational level wargame. The final component of the scenario is the update mechanisms in the wargame, which include how information is shared with the players and could include contingencies or injects to update the scenario.

DATA

An analytical wargame will have three different data categories: initiate, feedback, and analysis. The term "data" does not necessarily mean quantitative information; it can be qualitative as well. Data is the information needed to support the player before and during the game and the information from the players that supports the analysis effort. The key is to identify the actual data/information needed for the wargame and to ruthlessly cut any extraneous information. The general rule is to provide the players with the information that is reasonable to expect they would have in the same situation in real life. If the wargame uses computer-based models or other tools, they may require input data. Many computer-based combat simulations need to request input data for a date-specific scenario at least six months in advance, and once received, a data validation process is usually needed. Therefore, careful consideration should be given to obtaining data and the time it takes for the simulation to be prepared when deciding to incorporate a combat simulation into a wargame.

We review the three data categories we use. Both initiate and feedback data are needed for the design of the measurement space. The initiate data must be present before the actual wargame begins, and the feedback data is produced during the game by some adjudication process. However, the wargaming team needs to understand the nature of the feedback data in order to properly design the wargame's measurement space.

Initiate Data

The data needed before the wargame begins includes information that the players will need to understand their roles and make the decisions the wargame will require as it begins, as well as the data that any method, model, or tool will need to be ready to function any time during the wargame's execution. Each key player will usually require a read-ahead packet that will provide specific information about the scenario, their assigned role, responsibilities, and assets that they control. For a military commander, an OOB along with weapons system status and capabilities are usually provided.

Let's use as an example a simple Red versus Blue wargame assessing Blue's capability to defeat Red given a new suite of advanced sensors. Each side will need to know their OOB (information about their forces, to include strength, disposition, mission, etc.) as well as weapons system capabilities (range, speed, etc.). They will also need to know the scenario details—that is, the context of the battle (where, when, the road to war, etc.). Each side should also know some information about their adversary, so some thought needs to be put into deciding how much information should be revealed. In most cases, this information should match the information that would realistically be available in an actual combat situation given the collection assets that would be employed in the wargame.

Let's also assume we have an adjudication tool that will be able to determine the outcome of combat between the Blue and Red forces. The tool will likely need to be instantiated with each weapons system and sensor capability, location, and status. If a computer-based combat simulation is used as the wargame's adjudication tool, ensure that the time it will take for data to be produced and instantiated in the model is accommodated; many computer-based combat simulations require three to six months from the time data is requested until the time the simulation is ready to be used for the wargame.

Feedback Data

The data that is needed to keep the players engaged and to keep the wargame progressing is usually produced during the wargame. The challenge for the wargaming team is to develop the means to produce, process, and disseminate this data to the players. Some thought should be given to the difference between what each player should know and what ground truth is. Battle damage assessment, a report of the damage inflicted upon the opposition, is often inaccurate and delayed in actual combat operations. Should the wargame provide each player the ground truth—the actual status of each force—or restrict the information to only what the player's assets could be reasonably expected to deliver on that timeline? What mechanisms and personnel (data collectors, analysts, and controllers) will be needed to produce, collect, and disseminate the data? Is there a record of what data is provided to each player if this data will also be needed for the post-game analysis? If there is a significant time between the last round of player decisions and the feedback provided to the players that allows them to understand the impact of their decisions, the wargaming team needs to think about what the players will be doing when the feedback data is being produced. It is often the case that this feedback data is also analysis data—the data that the wargaming analysts will need after the wargame concludes to process and provide results to the sponsor.

The first round of Red versus Blue player decisions has concluded, and the wargaming white cell/controllers are determining the outcome of these decisions. Combat is being adjudicated by an adjudication tool. The players need to be informed how their decisions played out in combat. What losses did their side take? What losses did they inflict on the opponent? Did their forces accomplish their mission, and where are they now located? Because this wargame is assessing sensor capabilities, the wargaming team has ensured that the information being provided to each side is restricted to the information their sensors would actually produce. Because the information each player has available will be important to know when assessing the decisions made during the wargame, the wargaming team also needs a record of the information each side has been provided as well as what ground truth is at the conclusion of this first turn.

Analysis Data

This is the data that the wargaming team decided up front would be needed in order to produce the wargaming results that answer the sponsor's issues. This is the data that the wargame is designed to produce. This data may be collected or produced in many forms and by multiple sources. Data collectors using pen and paper may be transcribing player decisions, while automated tools may be used to collect other information from players and/or wargame observers. Because the conduct of a wargame can often take longer than anticipated, wargames may have to conclude before all the information that is needed is produced. A disciplined and well-organized wargaming team tracks the status of the required analysis data during the wargame and makes in-stride adjustments to ensure the most critical analysis data is collected before the wargame terminates and players need to depart. The wargaming team may also be scrambling to conduct post-game interviews with key players from each side.

Good wargaming teams realize that they will likely not have all the time needed to produce all of the required analysis data and have developed contingency plans that provide alternate means to collect missing data. Wargaming teams can make good use of surveys and interviews as contingency methods to collect missing data that the wargame had been expected to produce. Surveys and interviews can also be used as planned data collection methods. Surveys and interviews take time, which must be anticipated and planned for by the design team. Anticipate that the surveys players are asked to complete at their home station may not get completed in a timely fashion, or even at all, so it is not a good idea to depend on remote surveys as a primary data collection tool. You may have surveys that players complete after each day of wargaming, or even between turns (perhaps when awaiting feedback data), but a careful balance must be struck that extracts as much usable information from each of the wargaming participants as possible without exhausting or frustrating the participants with hours of mind-numbing requirements that distract their focus from their role in your wargame. Pre- and post-wargame surveys may be useful in assessing how the wargame may have changed participants' perspective on the use of a new technology or tactic, technique, or procedure.

The process is not over once the wargame has concluded after several turns. This is still a hectic period for the wargaming team. Each player may have planning sheets or forms designed for the wargame that need to be collected and delivered to the analysis group. If the players have feedback data, that should also be collected by the wargaming team and delivered to the analysis group. Data collectors complete their forms or spreadsheets. The quick-look report is produced, and participants are reconvened for the report's vetting to give the players a chance to correct the record if they were misunderstood, to clarify results, and perhaps to add a result that the wargaming team overlooked. Participants are informed of when to expect a coordinating draft of the wargame's final report. Key players are then taken for their post-game interviews. Other participants are completing post-game surveys. The wargaming team collects all the data produced and begins the task of detailed analysis.

METHODS, MODELS, AND TOOLS

The primary purpose of MMTs is to adjudicate player interactions. When you ask players to make a decision, you owe it to them to provide feedback on that decision; this is called feedback data or player data-feedback. Without any feedback, players quickly become disinterested in the wargame, and the quality of their subsequent decisions suffers. MMTs can range from a facilitator who is basically the judge and jury for a seminar wargame to a closed-loop combat simulation that provides quantitative data for a system wargame. In most cases, wargames don't need precise quantitative data. The adjudication mechanisms need to be realistic (believable) and timely. If you think you need the results from a combat simulation, you should consider running several alternate scenarios ahead of time so you have output that you can use to approximate most situations that the players will need adjudicated.

Common Wargame Adjudication MMTs

Most analytic wargames examining the complex operational environment of the future will require some level of MMTs, and in many cases these wargames will require multiple MMTs to fully address the set of sponsor issues. These MMTs will likely also require input from the wargame, such as a concept of operation, to support analysis. The complexity of modern combat, to include the whole of government contributions and the mixture of kinetic and nonkinetic lines of effort, will require well-thought-out wargames that require several different methods of adjudication. There is not a singular software-based "wargaming MMT" that we teach or recommend. The days of dusting off a computer-based combat simulation to conduct wargaming analysis of a kinetic NATO–Warsaw Pact fight for Western Europe are behind us. The MMTs you choose for your wargame will be dictated by your sponsor's issues and the answers required by the issues' essential questions. Once the first draft of your DCMP is complete, look down the MMT column to see the range of MMTs your wargame will require. Anticipate that your wargame will require multiple different adjudication MMTs. What follows are some of the more common adjudication MMTs.

Facilitator Adjudication

A facilitator listens to player positions, arguments, and actions and decides the outcome of those actions. Its strength is that it is simple; its weakness is that it depends on a knowledgeable and skilled facilitator.

Subject Matter Expert Panel Adjudication

Similar to facilitator adjudication, a panel of subject matter experts (SMEs) adjudicates outcomes of interactions of subjects of which they are experts. Your wargame may require more than one SME panel—for example, one for future technology and one to rule on cultural responses. An SME panel's strength is that it is very credible if you have the right expertise. Its weakness is that it may take a long time for a panel of SMEs to reach a consensus.

Consensual Adjudication

Consensual adjudication is a recent construct often found in matrix wargames.[4] The idea is that the players themselves propose an action and then present an argument for why their action should be successful. Opposing players then propose their counteraction and why that should render the initial proposed action ineffective. Based on the arguments, a simple adjudication method is devised (usually ascribing a percentage to success of the proposed action) and a die is rolled to determine the outcome. The strength of this method is that it is simple; the weakness is that it depends on the capability of the players to present cogent arguments. In many cases, a facilitator presides over this method to keep the adjudication credible and even-handed.

Simple Model Adjudication

Simple models often work well for adjudicating wargames. Because wargames are focused more on player decisions and interactions and less on quantitative outcomes, models need to be believable and realistic but not complex. Here are some simple adjudication techniques.

Simple Odds (Dice)

The simplicity of using dice to adjudicate a decision is alluring to many wargaming teams. The technique's strength is the simplicity and unambiguous results. The weakness is that many players believe the approach may be inappropriately random. Some senior leaders will reject a wargame that uses dice but will accept a wargame that uses an Excel spreadsheet "combat adjudication model" that replicates the roll of dice. Perception matters! Matrix gaming takes full advantage of a process called Simple Combat Resolution Using Dice.[5] This approach has gained a great deal of acceptance for adjudicating combat actions in a matrix game.

Combat Results Tables

These tables are often used in hobby wargaming. They usually rely on dice rolls, and they can be adapted to account for several different variables (see

Dunnigan's drive on Metz as an example[6]). This technique provides the appearance of being less random and more algorithmic. However, it can get complex quickly (column shifts for terrain, air power, day/night, and so forth).

Spreadsheets
Excel provides a valuable mechanism for constructing adjudication techniques. Typically, this technique provides the appearance of being more sophisticated (a spreadsheet can do dice rolls!). Its weakness is that if the wargaming team is not careful, spreadsheet models can get complex very quickly; the temptation is to add lots of "simple" functionality.

Combat Simulation Adjudication
The use of combat simulations for wargaming adjudication hit its peak in the late 1980s at the height of the Cold War. Most of the large wargames that focused on the NATO–Warsaw Pact battle for Europe had a combat simulation that was used for adjudication. At one point, federating (digitally linking) several combat models together to have an uber-combat simulation called a "federation" was seen as the height of adjudication sophistication, but results were mixed at best, as a failure in any one of the models that comprised the federation usually rendered the entire federation's output useless—and failures were frequent. Our assessment here is for using a *single* combat simulation. This approach is usually seen as credible by most players, especially if they have some prior experience with the simulation or believe that it provides a realistic adjudication of the type of decisions they are making. However, this prior knowledge may also be a weakness of this adjudication approach. The simulation may not be seen as credible, depending on players' knowledge of it, or it may be seen as a black box where no one understands how the simulation generates its results. Some players may be perceived as having an unfair advantage if they appear to be familiar with the particular simulation being used and can exploit its idiosyncrasies.

The wargaming team should assess the length of time that a cycle of adjudication using such a simulation will take during the wargame. This cycle starts when the players have made a decision in the wargame that requires simulation or model adjudication. The wargaming team first translates the players' decisions into input data that a computer technician can use to instantiate the simulation or model. The technician will run the simulation, perhaps dozens or hundreds of times, to produce the data for analysis. The wargaming team will need to analyze and then convert this data into useful feedback data so that the players understand the adjudication of their decisions. We had a personal illustrative experience in the early 2000s as Army analysts where the simulation vector-in-commander (VIC) was used as the adjudication model for a large wargame. Most everyone in the Army knew VIC was an analytic simulation frequently used by TRAC to conduct analysis for the Department of the Army, and it had credibility among most senior leaders. VIC took hours to run and required technical expertise as well as a team of analysts to extract the results, so the wargame had to be designed around the running of the simulation. The VIC cycle was about six to eight hours, so the decision was made to run VIC at night to adjudicate player decisions and provide the results to the players in the morning for the next wargame turn. After the wargame, the conclusion of the design team members was that VIC was not really necessary or essential for the conduct of the wargame. Instead, we could have used VIC to help produce a simple combat results table, potentially even one modified from a hobby game, which would have easily been used by the wargaming team to yield believable, useful results in much less time.

When the wargaming team decides to use a combat simulation, there may be a way to generate parametric look-up tables if the units that will be used in battle are reasonably standard. It would require several different sets of simulation runs to be made, but they could all be made prior to the wargame, and then the adjudication would be conducted by simply using the look-up tables (with possibly some interpolation) taking only a few minutes instead of several hours. If the wargaming team decides to have the simulation run during the wargame, the team must be ready for the possibility of a computer crash and design a contingency plan.

PLAYERS

The wargaming team must consider players when designing the measurement space of the wargame. The team needs to decide on both the player roles and the actual credentials and experience of the players in the wargame. Those credentials usually include a number of years of experience in certain positions or specific organizations (or both). In many cases, not all the players you want for your wargame will be available, or you will get a last-minute notification that one of your players cannot make it and you will need to find a substitute. In any event, you design your wargame based on players that will represent their roles credibly. Once the roster of the actual players who will attend is finalized, you need to assess the credentials of the players you have versus the credentials of the players you wanted. If there is a big difference, you may need to adjust some or all of the other elements of your measurement space. A simple example is a junior officer substituting for a senior officer in a command role. The junior officer will lack the senior's experience and knowledge, so a more detailed OOB that includes additional information on the force's weapons systems (data) may be necessary for the junior officer to adequately play the role.

ASSUMPTIONS

Assumptions can come from many sources. All scenarios set in the future will have some assumptions about the state of the world at that point in time. Your wargame sponsor may specify additional assumptions that narrow the scope of the wargame. You may also need to make assumptions both to limit the wargame's scope and to accommodate limitations of your wargaming team. In any event, these assumptions further restrict your measurement space. One example is the arms race between NATO and the Warsaw Pact. Most U.S. DoD analysis focused on acquisition examined only conventional combat in Western Europe, based on an assumption that no tactical nuclear weapons would be used. Most senior officials believed that once a tactical nuclear weapon was used, the war would escalate into a strategic nuclear exchange, and the outcome of the conventional combat would no longer be of interest. All key assumptions need to be vetted with your sponsor to ensure you have not "assumed away" a vital aspect of the sponsor's problem that needs to be examined in the wargame.

MEASUREMENT SPACE: IDEALIZED AND REALITY

When we talk about measurement space, we typically talk about two of the three primary components, the scenario and the MMT, as if there will be one of each for any particular wargame. In reality, this may not be true. In many cases, one scenario will suffice for a wargame, but there are other cases where senior leaders need to understand how well a new technology works in all environments and across the spectrum of conflicts, which may necessitate many scenarios or a primary scenario and several vignettes (or even multiple wargames). Vignettes should be used with caution, as their use will require that the players extract themselves from the scenario they are currently immersed in and then dive into another situation, and that leap can be difficult for some players to make. It is not unusual for wargames to need more than one MMT for adjudication purposes. Wargames that are hybrids may have elements of a seminar game that require a facilitator to adjudicate, and other elements where forces are committed to a combat engagement that requires some sort of mathematical model or combat simulation to adjudicate. One of the virtues of using the DCMP to design the foundation of a wargame (specifically its measurement space) is that after you have determined all the EQs that are needed to provide the necessary analysis data, you then specify what the measurement space needs to look like for each. This prevents the wargaming team from choosing a single scenario and a single adjudication technique, and then choosing what analysis data can be extracted from a measurement space artificially restricted by a premature choice of those measurement space elements. It is difficult for wargaming novices to imagine what the design of a wargame will look like until they have gained some practical experience in designing and participating in wargames. Most DoD personnel, uniformed or civilian, want a checklist or a template, but because a sponsor's objective and issues will vary greatly from wargame to wargame, each wargame's design will have unique aspects that are needed to produce the analytic data required by the wargame's DCMP. We noticed this checklist mentality when we first began teaching the Wargaming Applications course at NPS. We had the students play the hobby wargame *Midway*[7] about halfway through the resident course so they could see an example of a wargame. The objective of the student team's sponsored wargame was to conduct an AoA that compared three different ships, each conducting a variety of missions that supported a combined joint special operations task force in the Philippine Sea. The team's first design had a game board with a grid very similar to *Midway*. After the wargaming instructor observed their first play-test with the grid design, all concluded that it took far too long to move a ship from origin to destination and really did not support the wargame's objective very well. The students went back to the drawing board to redesign their wargame and found a way to leverage Google Earth maps for their computer-based game board. They also created spreadsheet tools to assess the real differences in the ships' performances: speed to complete the variety of missions presented, and fuel burn rates to determine the logistics burden that each ship incurred. This design worked much better, and the actual wargame exceeded all expectations. The lesson learned from this experience is that individuals tend to gravitate to what they know, and if the only wargame construct they know is a hex-based design, then that is what they will use for their wargame.

WARGAME PRACTICAL EXERCISE 5

This practical exercise builds on the work that was accomplished in the first four exercises. It will begin to flesh out the wargame and provide the necessary structure and foundation to actually begin testing the wargame.

This practical exercise will utilize the additional information in appendix 2. Use your results from the essential questions you identified in practical exercise 2 to answer issue 3: "What force protection issues does the CJTF-Z commander face?" The objective of this exercise is to begin fleshing out the measurement space of the wargame. This will include the scenario, methods, models, and tools, and data. Take the essential questions that you developed in practical exercise 3 and:

1. Confirm the format of the answer for each question (quantitative, qualitative, or both).
2. Determine the players who will need to participate in answering each question.
3. Determine the method, model, or tool that you will utilize to adjudicate the player's answers to these questions. In addition, for each question, specify the measurement criteria if they exist. This may be a range of values for a quantitative answer; for a qualitative response, it may be a narrative answer or a survey range of values.
4. Determine what data the players and the MMTs will need for each question in order to *start* the wargame. The data the players need will

likely go into their read-aheads. Depending on the MMT, the data may need to be requested *months* before your wargame is played.
5. Construct the basic scenario framework that will enable you to answer the identified questions.
6. Utilize the DCMP framework to organize your essential questions and what you will need to answer them. This guide will be used by the data collectors and wargame director to ensure the sponsor's issues are addressed and the proper information is collected from the players when your wargame is conducted.

CHAPTER 8

Development

■ ■ ■ ■

The process of development means playing the designed wargame and seeing which elements work the way they were designed and, even more importantly, determining which ones do not work as the wargaming team's design group intended. The development phase is not a stand-alone phase or simply the next step in the design process. Wargaming design and development are part of an iterative process. Frequently, the design group waits until the entire wargame is designed before transitioning to development. This is a recipe for disaster, because no matter how much time the design group spends on the wargame's design, it will not work exactly as intended. This shortcoming is typically discovered in the development phase.

In designing a wargame, the best practice is to lay out a rough design quickly that can be played by the design group and then iterate between play, redesign, play again, until a working wargame is developed. Development in the commercial or hobby wargaming industry works a bit differently. Commercial wargamers often have a development group that does not participate in the wargame's initial design, but that design is very sparse. Commercial wargame designers may sketch out the skeleton of the wargame on a single sheet of paper that is given to their stable of professional wargame developers to flesh out the details. These developers have several advantages over DoD wargamers in that many commercial wargame designs are similar, and the medium is almost always the same. For military-based wargames, this is typically a gridded or hex-based game board with counters to represent units, so it is not as if the developers started with a blank sheet of paper. The explosion of Eurogames, since the development of *Settlers of Catan* in 1995, is arguably the fastest growing sector of hobby games and is a great example of design construction.[1] Many of the games have economic themes and are usually designed to keep all players around until the end. The basic mechanics can be adapted easily to create a different scenario or to add a new wrinkle (such as new technology or a different warfighting concept), and the developers typically have years of experience working for the same designer, so a framework is all they need to begin. In any case, these wargame developers are responsible for turning the outline into a fully fleshed-out, and most importantly, playable wargame. The developers ensure the wargame is playable through play-testing, and they do it much the same way that DoD wargame design groups do: they get a workable design, play it, figure out what needs to be fixed, redesign it, and play it again. James Dunnigan, a prolific commercial wargamer, says: "Depending on the complexity of the game, you might have to play it anywhere from half a dozen times to dozens of times during the testing stage. This is only a fraction of the testing the game will get before it's finished. The bulk of the testing will take place during the blind testing phase."[2]

The goals of the development phase are to determine that the wargame does what the designer said it would and that it has the necessary structure to extract the information (data) the analysts need to provide insights into the sponsor's key issues. The iterative nature of the design and development phases will lead to completing several related but distinct critical tasks:

- scenario validation and enhancement
- data confirmation
- MMT testing
- verifying and updating player roles (confirming, adding, and deleting roles as necessary)
- rules and procedure updates
- DCMP refinement

These tasks are accomplished in the development phase through a series of iterative play-test events. The events include play-testing by the design group, blind play-testing, and a full dress rehearsal to include data collectors.

PLAY-TESTING

Play-testing ensures the wargame's mechanics work correctly and that the wargame is able to accomplish the stated objective. We recommend testing early and often in the design process. Unfortunately, many analytical wargames, especially planning wargames, lack a serious effort at play-testing. There are many reasons for this shortcoming, but the most cited reason is time. Too often, the design group attempts to develop the perfect wargame before testing it. However, without a thorough play-testing, there is no way to ensure the wargame will function as intended and provide the information (data) need for the analytical effort. The play-testing process is designed to stress the wargame components to find potential points of failure or design flaws, which also includes plans to collect the necessary data. The design group should approach the play-test as a challenge to see where they can break the wargame.

However, there is more to the play-testing process than simply looking for points of failure or design flaws. Play-testing provides an opportunity to discover potential friction points in the wargame's mechanics or areas that just do not function as anticipated by the design group. The design group should play the wargame as designed, reviewing rules and procedures as written in an attempt to ensure clarity and to streamline the process. The goal should be to help the players focus more on the wargame and less on understanding the administrative overhead of rules and procedures. Play-testing the wargame will not guarantee success, but the lack of proper play-testing will increase the likelihood the wargame will have challenges and potentially fail to achieve its objective or provide sufficient information for the analysis.

Once the design group, after multiple iterations of design and development, believes they have a workable wargame, they should schedule a blind play-test, which involves bringing in outside participants who have not been part of the wargame design or development process. This is a common practice in the commercial wargame industry where the designers bring a new set of eyes to the wargame structure: "Blind testing is nothing more than having the game played without the designer or developer in attendance. If this was a commercial[ly] produced wargame, you are, in effect, sending out the closest thing to a finished version of the game and the people who are playing it are approaching the game as if they had just bought it in the store."[3] For analysts and planners, this group of play-testers would be individuals who were not part of the design process, so they have little information about the operation or wargame. This untarnished view will typically reveal unexpected holes or issues with the construct of your wargame. We recognize that most planners and analysts, the target audience of this book, will likely not have the resources or time to conduct a full blind test, but it is critical that the wargaming team understand the advantages of this process and the potential disadvantage of having to skip it because of time.

The reason blind play-testing is vital to a wargame's success is because after several iterations of play-testing and updating rules and procedures, the design group knows how the wargame is supposed to work, and they overlook the inconsistencies or friction points of their wargame. At this point in the process, the design group is typically so familiar with their developed set of rules and procedures that they will automatically fill in any missing information or processes. The blind play-testers will not have the advantage of knowing the intentions of the design group and will be able to find issues missed by the design group. Unlike the commercial wargamers, we recommend that the design group observe the blind play-test and take copious notes. However, it is critical that the design group not interact with the blind play-testers unless the play-testers are so confused they cannot continue to play, which means there are some serious design flaws or very poorly written rules and procedures.

The last step in the play-test process is the conduct of a full dress rehearsal of the wargame. This can be combined with a standard play-test of the design concept, but it is not recommended. The focus of standard play-testing is the design and development of the wargame. The dress rehearsal provides an opportunity to test all of the elements of the wargame to include the flow of data both to and from the players. It is also critical at this point to include the rehearsal of the data collection by the analyst team and assigned rapporteurs. The responsibilities of all individuals who have roles during the wargame should be exercised, to include the functioning of the white and control cells. Elements that should be tested include the methods, models, and tools, the rules and procedures, the data collection process, and the analysis team that will be working during the wargame producing interim results to be leveraged for quick-look reports (large, multi-day wargames may require a facilitated quick-look report at the conclusion of each day's wargaming). The wargame design group should find players to play the wargame, much like the players for the blind play-test. These players should try and emulate the actual players as much as possible. For example, if you can borrow a flag officer's executive or aide to play the flag officer, they may provide additional insight into how the flag officer would react to wargame situations. We recommend at least an hour of actual, fully burdened wargame play to ensure that the volume of generated data and the pace of the wargame are sustainable by the assigned wargaming staff.

PLAY-TESTING THE DATA COLLECTION MANAGEMENT PLAN

An often overlooked area of play-testing is the functioning of the data collection process. To test the functioning, you should have first recruited and trained a set of data collectors or rapporteurs. These individuals are critical to the wargame process and are all too often an afterthought toward the end of the design and develop process. They should have full knowledge and understanding of the wargame's objective, issues, and players and of how the wargame is expected to unfold. In addition, these individuals should have a copy of the DCMP and understand their role in collecting the analysis data during the wargame. They should be brought in prior to the conclusion of the final play-test to ensure they have all this information. These individuals will be monitoring the players and the game play and utilizing the analysis data collection mechanism throughout the wargame. It is critical that they be part of the final play-test and rehearsal to ensure they have a clear picture of their role in the process. One great example of the impact of failing to play-test this component was an observed wargame where the group of data collectors was placed in a part of the room where they could not hear or monitor their assigned players. The wargame team would have discovered this difficulty with a simple play-test/rehearsal.

Prior to this play-test, the DCMP should have been screened and data collection forms developed specifically for the data collectors. While the DCMP spreadsheet is a great construct that can be used as the foundation of the wargame's design, its format is not useful to support data collection. The play-testing of the actual data collection process that documents the how and why of players' decisions is critical to ensure that all of the feedback and analysis data specified in the DCMP can be easily and efficiently collected and processed. Inexperienced wargaming teams often think that they can place much of the burden of data collection on the players. The thought is that the players can record their own decisions and provide the rationale for them using either a manual data collection form or on a digitized form using a laptop or computer terminal. On the first turn of the wargame, this process usually works well, with the players recording eloquent prose about their decisions and the rationales. By the third turn, the primary tasks that the players must accomplish have them so involved in the wargame that they only have enough time to scribble single words or unintelligible comments.

The data that needs to be collected from the players will often come in a steady stream throughout the wargaming process, and useful data will be produced not only during the wargame but at breaks as well. Without play-testing the actual data collection process, you will not discover the many groups of players that are discussing various aspects of the game, and the data collectors will miss many data-generating conversations. The best designed and executed wargame will not produce findings of value if the data collection team is not able to collect the necessary information for analysis. The bottom line is that the design group needs to play-test the data collection plan at the full dress rehearsal to ensure all the feedback and analysis data can be collected, which ensures success during the analysis phase.

Through the iterative design and develop process, the design group's wargame process and rules will have evolved toward what will be the final product. From experience, one common change from the design process is the wargaming team's recognition that the developed scenario will not adequately address all issues. This usually results in the development of a set of injects or vignettes to address these shortcomings. The iterative process also means that the wargaming team needs to constantly update the rules after each of these iterative steps. There should be one "keeper of the rules" who attends each play-test and dress rehearsal to capture the changes in the wargame.

There is an old military saying that the plan will not survive the first contact with the enemy. Wargames are very similar in nature. No matter how well the design group planned, designed, and developed (and redesigned and redeveloped), the wild card remains the players who are now immersed in the wargame with the freedom and latitude to make decisions. These decisions are designed to be affected by and to affect the wargame, and sometimes the direction they take the wargame will not have been anticipated by the design group. The most rigorous play-testing will not test every possible combination and permutation of potential outcomes. The design group needs to have a plan for when things go wrong or when they recognize that the wargame is not getting them all of the anticipated insights.

CONTINGENCIES

Very few wargames unfold exactly as planned, so a wargame's design needs to account for contingencies. The primary reason for exercising wargame contingencies is to obtain the analysis data or player data-out needed to complete the DCMP that did not materialize as anticipated. Because you cannot expect to know what analysis data will be missing, contingencies may have to be developed on the fly, during a break in the wargame, or overnight between days of a wargame. The requirement for the development of contingencies tends to increase for the less structured seminar and matrix wargames. Because the facilitator asks open-ended questions in these types of wargames, the players are provided more leeway in the direction they will go, which may not follow your DCMP.

Contingencies Executed during the Wargame: Injects, Branches, Sequels, and Vignettes

The wargame director will initiate one of these mechanisms as the wargame is being played. An inject is a situation or event that can be inserted into a wargame at the time and place of the wargame controller's choosing to obtain necessary analysis data. It provides a contingency plan that can ensure an essential question identified in the DCMP is examined during the course of a wargame. These injects are often crafted by the design group but can also be generated on the fly by an agile white cell in an emergency. Generally, they are used if the players have taken the wargame in a direction that will preclude collecting necessary data for a critical issue. For example, a player moves their force in an unexpected direction that allows it to miss an ambush that needs to occur to produce the required data of how well the force responds to an ambush. An inject would be a minefield discovered on the route the force is now traversing, causing it to backtrack and move into the ambush, generating the required interaction.

Injects can be used if wargame time is running out and there needs to be a refocus on a critical issue or to allow a shift in the wargame direction if more issues are added to the analysis plan. It is common to insert multiple injects during a seminar-style wargame, and an experienced wargame facilitator will have several prepared ahead of time. The process of presenting injects is typically seamless because of the general flow of a seminar wargame. The facilitator presents a situation to the players and follows up with one or more leading questions to prompt the players to begin a robust discussion. Injects provide an opportunity to update the situation based on the flow of the discussion and to implement an untaken branch during the wargame.

A branch is similar to an inject but is used to reexamine a player decision that has previously been made. Suppose a player decides not to use a new sensor suite to assess the threat level along a route that the player's force will take in the near future. The assessment that the player makes using the older standard sensor packages only reveals a small threat, and the force proceeds and encounters a much larger adversary force than was detected. The wargame director could "rewind the clock" and force the player to use the new sensor suite to see the difference in the assessment provided and have the player reassess the decision. A branch in the scenario (stepping back in time to revisit a decision point) provides an opportunity to gain further insight into the implications of critical decisions. The branch allows the players to explore additional options that would remain unexplored if the wargame proceeded linearly in time.

A sequel is a construct that allows the design group to examine what happens after a critical decision. Typically, a sequel allows a more in-depth look at a particular decision, assuming there is sufficient time in the wargame to do so. One use for sequels is to provide progressively harder missions/tasks to a successful commander in order to identify friction points or potential break points of the commander's forces. Opportunities to use sequels will likely present themselves as targets of opportunity in the wargame play that will augment the analysis effort, but care should be taken to not miss other critical analysis data that needs to be produced and collected.

A vignette is a small, simplified scenario. Vignettes are similar to injects, but they are used when an issue needs to be examined that the current scenario does not support. Adding a vignette to a wargame will increase playing time and may force other data to not be produced, so vignettes as contingencies should be used sparingly. When a vignette is introduced, the players will need to refocus their efforts, having been given a new set of circumstances in a new operational environment. For example, the primary scenario of a wargame may provide the opportunity to assess the performance of a sensor in all operational environments except for a dense urban environment that does not exist in the current scenario. A vignette set in such an environment can be used to assess the sensor in this last remaining environment. Care should be taken to use vignettes sparingly, as you do not want your players to have to shift back and forth between regions and environments. Using a vignette after you have addressed all the issues that the primary scenario supports will help to minimize the number of shifts that the players will endure. The process of introducing a new vignette into a wargame, especially a seminar-style wargame, is tricky. It typically changes the situation or scenario that the players have been operating under for some amount of time, and if they are truly immersed in game play, they may have some difficulty in changing gears to a new situation. It is best to try and introduce vignettes after some logical break in the wargame, such as lunch or the end of the day.

Contingencies Exercised outside of the Wargame: Surveys and Player Interviews

Surveys are a data gathering tool that can be used in addition to the play of the wargame. Pre- and post-wargame surveys can be used for a variety of purposes. You would use both types to assess the change in players' attitudes and perceptions about a new technology, concept, or doctrine. Surveys can also be used to obtain player data about sponsor issues that the wargame cannot address for some reason. The quality of this data usually will not be as good as that collected during the wargame with players interacting, but surveys provide a means to address more sponsor issues than the play of the wargame can produce in the allotted time. Good surveys, much like good wargames, require a rigorous design and develop process, so do not think of them as an easy method of obtaining data.

Player interviews should be scheduled at the end of every wargame to give the wargaming team a final opportunity to collect data found to be missing when the wargame ended. If the player interviews are not included on the original schedule, you will find key players dashing to the airport as soon as the wargame ends, so a best practice is to always schedule key player interviews for every wargame. Player interviews can be used to gain more insight into why decisions were made and can be used to explore alternate branches, albeit without any other player responses. The issues to be covered in the player interviews should be developed as data is determined to be missing throughout the play of the wargame.

The importance of the development phase cannot be overemphasized. It is critical to ensure that the wargame flows as anticipated by the design group and that the wargame provides the necessary information (data) to answer the wargame's objective.

RULES AND PROCEDURES

Rules and procedures are designed to keep the wargame on schedule and the players on task. A procedure lays out how the wargame will be executed, such as specifying that for each day of the wargame, two turns will be executed in the morning and one turn in the afternoon. It can specify the details of each turn, such as: "There are three phases in a turn: ISR, movement, and combat."

Rules specify what players can and cannot do. For a system wargame on a hex map, a rule may be that "each unit can only move the number of hexes indicated on the right-hand corner of the unit counter." Rules need to be written clearly and concisely—the rule just used as an example is not well written. Does the player have to move the unit the *exact* number of hexes specified on the counter, or is that the *maximum* number of hexes the unit can move? Rules need to have an explainable rationale. If a player encounters a rule that prohibits what is perceived to be a reasonable action, there needs to be an acceptable explanation or the player will begin to question the wargame's pedigree. Care should be taken not to create a volume of rules and procedures that will leave players uncertain of what actions they can and cannot take.

Design-Develop Iterations: Updating the Wargame's Design

We began the chapter introducing the iterative design-develop process where the goal was to quickly get a crude but playable design completed that could then be played (play-tested) and then updated (redesigned). It is important to note that redesigning your wargame will likely require you to reexamine each of the elements of measurement space (scenario, data, MMTs, players, and assumptions). Your DCMP also will need to be updated. Play-testing often reveals that analysis data that you identified in the DCMP will not be produced, and alternate means will need to be created. Play-testing also may reveal player roles that need to be added as well as roles that may be eliminated, consolidated, or turned over to the white cell. These changes are also noted in the DCMP. The rules and procedures should also be reviewed and updated for each and every play-test.

WARGAME PRACTICAL EXERCISES 6–7

The following set of practical exercises is designed to continue the work that was accomplished in the first five exercises. These practical exercises will begin to flesh out the wargame and provide the necessary structure and foundation to actually begin testing the wargame.

Practical Exercise 6: Play-test

You have cobbled together a crude design for your wargame and have play-tested it with your wargaming team. After the play-test, you revised, updated, and enhanced your measurement space and refined the MMTs that you chose to adjudicate your wargame. We recognize that it is possible, and frankly we hope, that the reader has a different wargame construct than the solution we provide; that is fine at this point. This practical exercise has two components—a directed set of conditions for our designed wargame and a play-testing of the reader's wargame. The solution presented in this book looked at designing this as a seminar- or matrix-style wargame. We recognized three potential adjudicating methods:

- seminar, free adjudication, with a need for a facilitator since there will be several seminar aspects of the wargame
- matrix, semi-rigid adjudication, with a need for a potential construct to handle UN and Internal Security Bureau or UN and PLAM engagements
- system, rigid adjudication, with a formal Daloon Ministry of Defence combat simulation to represent kinetic engagements between the UN and the IFF

For this exercise, you need to conduct a play-test of the wargame:

1. You need to conduct a second play-test, and you have recruited some blind play-testers, but you will only be able to play-test one of the three adjudication methods listed above. Which one do you play-test? For the two that you don't play-test, what could play-testing have done for those two methods?
2. Play-test through your designed wargame and identify what did and did not work as planned.

Practical Exercise 7: Final Rehearsal—Large Wargame

You are the wargame director of a large wargame. You were able to get a second blind play-test scheduled for half of a day to shake out all components of your wargame. You feel confident that the wargaming mechanics have been thoroughly tested and the support staff is ready for any contingencies the players might throw at them. Maybe you don't really need to do this final rehearsal. But something is nagging at you—what have you not tested?

1. List at least eight distinct wargame support functions that you should test during this final rehearsal.
2. Conduct a final rehearsal of your wargame to test those functions.

CHAPTER 9

Conduct

■ ■ ■ ■

In an analytical wargame, the design group has focused on designing and developing a wargame to produce the analysis data required to answer the sponsor's issues. The viability of the wargame cannot be known until it is time to execute and the actual players are introduced into the mix. Far too often, designers and analysts lose sight of the fact that the success of the wargame hinges on the ability of the players to make decisions in the wargaming environment they designed. The design group needs to ensure that the players themselves are ready for the roles they will assume in the wargame. The amount of preparation depends on several factors, including the complexity of the wargame and the experience of the player. Player preparation takes place before the wargame begins and has two primary components. First, the wargaming team needs to prepare and deliver a read-ahead packet to each of the players. The second, which may be foreign to many analysts, is the pre-wargame social.

PREPARATION FOR EXECUTION

The read-ahead packet should provide the players with enough information so that they understand both the scenario and the responsibilities of their role in the wargame. Practical experience indicates that the read-ahead packet should be sent to arrive about ten days prior to the wargame's start. If the briefing arrives more than two weeks early, it tends to be put on the back burner and never gets read. If it arrives any later, the player will not have time to read and digest the information or to call the wargaming team to clarify their role or request more information. The design group should plan on a follow-up phone call with the players to ensure that they have received the read-ahead packet and to demonstrate that the wargaming team values their participation and is striving to make sure that they have everything they need to be prepared for the wargame. This phone call will be a good time to check on whether the players might need any additional information or details to better perform their assigned roles. It is better to identify the need to generate additional information now rather than find out on game day that a player needs more information produced as turn one is unfolding. Read-ahead packets should be polished documents that not only provide players the information they will need for their roles, but also provide the administrative information they will need, to include the schedule, points of contact, travel and lodging information, directions to and from the facility, and access requirements for the facility as needed. For large, multi-day wargames, the read-ahead packet should be sent as a hard-copy booklet with a professional cover, and it needs to be proofread and edited. This document will give the players their first impression of the wargaming team, and if you want the players to take your wargame seriously and conduct themselves as professionals, you need to communicate your team's professionalism through this document.

The level of detail in the read-ahead packet depends on the player. Less experienced players may need more information to understand their roles and potential ranges of decisions. More experienced or senior players will typically require less information, but they may request additional data or details. If senior players ask for more details, even if they may appear to be unnecessary to the wargaming team, provide them. If the senior leader thinks the details are important, perhaps you should carefully look at the requested data to understand why the player thinks this data is needed. The design group needs to be careful to provide the players only the information they would reasonably expect to have for their role. Information about adversaries or other players should be restricted to what their sensors and other intelligence collection methods would have produced for them.

It is a good practice to schedule several social events over the course of a wargame. The length of the wargame will dictate the number and types of social events. The purpose of these social events is to provide players an opportunity to get to know each other and the key wargaming team members. There should at least be a pre-game mixer the evening before or the morning of wargame execution. The goal of this social is for the players and the principal wargaming team members to meet each other before the start of the wargame.

A mixer at the end of the first day of a multi-day wargame provides the wargaming team an opportunity to obtain feedback about the first day's events, allowing for minor course corrections to the following days' events as necessary. For multi-day wargames, providing a dinner to thank the players on the last or next to last evening of the wargame is a good gesture and can also provide an opportunity to solicit suggestions to improve or enhance the wargame if it is a recurring wargame that will be played again in the future.

EXECUTION

The design group should plan for a player in-brief the day of execution. This provides an opportunity for their players to get their heads into the wargame and gives those players who did not read their read-ahead packets a chance to get familiar with the wargame and ask questions to clarify their roles or request additional information. The wargaming team also will have an opportunity to update players if there are changes to the wargame's scenario or wargame play that they need to be aware of before execution.

The time that the wargaming team has with the players is limited and precious; however, the wargaming team should consider the first turn of the wargame to be a practice turn. The players need to be socialized to the way your wargame functions. They need to understand what information they will have to make their decisions, how their decisions are accounted for in the wargame, and what feedback to expect to apprise them of the impact of their decisions. The first turn of the wargame should give players an opportunity to clarify any aspect of the wargame they did not understand from the read-ahead packet or in-brief. The main objectives of the first turn are to ensure all players understand the boundaries within which they must operate, the rules and procedures of the wargame, key assumptions, wargame mechanics, and how their decisions may impact the wargame and other players. The first turn will also provide a warm-up for the data collectors and data collection process. The data collected during the first turn should be kept, but care needs to be taken during the analysis process. Depending on the wargaming style and complexity, players may spend more of the first turn just trying to wrap their heads around how to play versus being carefully focused on what they are doing during the wargame. Typically, you will see this more as an issue in system-style wargames, where players do not have a clear understanding of their own or the adversaries' potential full range of options, than in seminar wargames. The first turn will also allow both the white cell and control cell a chance to exercise their responsibilities. Expect the first turn to take longer than subsequent turns because of this socialization aspect. Depending on the complexity of the wargame, the design group needs to be cautious on using the analysis data collected from this initial turn, given that the players are learning how the wargame works and the adjudication process of their decisions, for independent conclusions.

As discussed in chapter 8, it is critical to be prepared for players taking the wargame in an unexpected or unintended direction. One additional concern, often seen in seminar-style wargames, is the occasion when a player cannot let go of an issue or topic that comes up in wargame play. One proven way to handle this situation is known as the "parking lot" technique. This method allows for tabling a topic of discussion while still acknowledging its importance. The intent is to keep the wargame progressing on schedule while acknowledging that there is an important unresolved topic to be addressed at a later time. Parking lot topics for revisiting are prominently displayed so all wargaming players can see the topics that have been recorded to date. These topics may be resolved as the wargame progresses, or they can be revisited if time is available in the wargame. If not resolved during the wargame, they may be addressed through post-game analysis. If they still cannot be resolved, they should be documented as an unresolved issue requiring further study in the wargame's final report.

Analytical wargaming is focused on the players' decisions in the wargame, and it is critical to capture these decisions and their rationale. The DCMP status needs to be continually monitored to ensure that the analysis data scheduled to be collected during a certain turn or day of the wargame has indeed been collected. If analysis data is missing, steps need to be taken to obtain that data if possible. If there is available time, injects or vignettes can be created and implemented during the wargame to obtain the missing data. If there is no time, the missing data may be obtained at the end of the quick-look report or through the key player interviews or post-wargame surveys scheduled at the conclusion of the wargame.

Wargame directors and facilitators need to be sensitive to last-turn "end effects," or players acting out of character because it is the last turn. There are a couple of proven techniques, which include ending early or not providing an end time or number of turns, that the wargaming director could use to avoid this last-move madness. Typically, planning on ending the wargame earlier than advertised is a simple and very effective method at the disposal of the wargame director. This allows the wargaming team to design into the process their own expectation that the game will end early, enabling them to ensure the wargame will still achieve its objective. Not letting the players know how much time or how many turns they have for the wargame will work, but some participants may be able to deduce what is going on based on the day's timeline. The day's activity timeline will usually provide for a conclusion time. This will occur because you will want to factor in and schedule a time to allow for player interviews and/or end of wargame surveys or questionnaires and the quick-look report. The player interviews and surveys are designed so the wargaming team can ask each player pointed questions, which in many cases are designed to get at some of the whys of players' decisions. The quick-look report is presented to the players after the wargame concludes but before the players depart. The report is similar in nature to a hotwash but is a more facilitated discussion with its primary purpose being to confirm top-level insights that the analysis team has identified and updated from emerging wargame results. It is important that the discussion focuses on correcting the record, not revising history by refighting the wargame or relitigating events that occurred during it. The analysis team must avoid reshaping results to conform to anyone's preconceived notion of what the results should reflect. The format for the report should reflect the structure of the DCMP, a key insight for each identified key issue from the sponsor. This approach ensures that the team has not missed key information (data) and serves as a great framework for the final report. It is likely that the quick-look report will point to data gaps that may be addressed with post-game player interviews. One key point to stress is that this is not an after action review. In an analytical wargame, the focus is not on what the players learned or experienced during the wargame. The design group should already have a good feel for what they learned from the wargame by the information collected during its course.

Player exit interviews provide the last best opportunity to fill any potential analysis data gaps identified by the analysis group during the wargame. These interviews should be scheduled as part of the wargame, and players should be aware of them and be prepared to participate. The purpose of these exit interviews is:

- to collect missing analysis data that the wargame did not produce
- to glean additional insights on the "why" behind critical decisions made during the wargame
- to provide the players an opportunity to comment on other aspects of the wargame

There are a great many moving parts to the wargame that are exercised on execution day. The play-testing that was conducted by the design group and the blind play-testers set the stage for success during execution. Designers and analysts need to remember that the focus of the wargame is on extracting the players' decisions and their rationale, the analysis data that the DCMP specifies. A good DCMP provides the necessary roadmap to ensure the data collectors are successful during execution of the wargame.

WARGAME PRACTICAL EXERCISE 8

This practical exercise, Conduct the Wargame, has two components, which include a directed set of conditions for our designed wargame and a requirement for your wargame. You are still the wargame director. The wargame is in its first of five days, and it already seems as if the wheels are coming off. Here are the many challenges that you are attempting to handle in the wargame:

- One of your data collectors called in sick and will be out for the entire wargame.
- Because of severe weather, the caterer has called to tell you that lunch will arrive thirty minutes late.
- The player representing the CJTF-Z commander has a crisis and must return to home station, departing this evening and not returning.
- The SAPCOM commander has a question about the legality of sharing U.S. secret info with NATO.
- The People's Liberation Army Navy task force commander wants to know if China has the capability to sink a U.S. amphibious assault ship from the Chinese mainland.
- Your primary facilitator has a bad cold and is starting to lose his voice.

These challenges are representative of many basic issues that have appeared in wargame after wargame. The list is not exhaustive, but it does provide a flavor of potential crisis events.

1. How would you address each of these issues to help keep the wargame on track?
2. Execute your wargame as designed and developed, and identify your own set of unanticipated crisis events.

CHAPTER 10

Analysis

■ ■ ■ ■

The purpose of conducting an analytic wargame is to produce knowledge and information that the wargaming team can process into *insights* and potentially additional *hypotheses* that address the sponsor's objective and issues. The DCMP is designed to identify the information that the wargame needs to produce, and the analytic wargame is constructed around the DCMP. In short, analysis is built into the wargame from the very beginning.

BEGINNING THE ANALYSIS

Wargaming analysis actually begins as the basic research about the problem is conducted and continues as the DCMP is being drafted, RFIs are being answered, and initiate data is collected. This important pre-wargame research shapes the wargame and may provide data that players will need to address wargaming issues, in some instances even yielding findings for some of the sponsor's issues. Once the wargame starts, data collectors record the information that the players generate. Careful tracking of the progress the data collectors are making in collecting DCMP analysis data allows the wargame's management team to redirect the wargame as necessary to ensure the required analysis data is produced and collected. In longer wargames, a quick-look report may be conducted at the end of each day. This requires that a team of analysts sift through the data collected that day to discover any preliminary top-level findings that will be vetted with the players during that afternoon's quick-look report session. The name "quick-look report" communicates to the sponsor, other stakeholders, observers, and the players that these preliminary findings will require further analysis before any of the report's findings can be confirmed.

At the end of any wargame, there should be two closing events. First, there should be key player interviews scheduled immediately after the wargame, to provide one last chance to verify earlier insights, clarify answers, or get analysis data that was not produced during the wargame. Second, there should be a final quick-look report. For a multi-day wargame, this will be a compilation of each day's quick-look report plus the preliminary findings from the last day. A useful format for the wargame's final quick-look report will have findings that correspond to each of the sponsor's key issues.

POST-WARGAME ANALYSIS

The final quick-look report's preliminary findings provide a framework for the post-wargame analysis. The DCMP provides an important road map for the conduct of the post-wargame analysis, and it is here where a well-researched and up-to-date DCMP will pay off.

The essential questions of the DCMP should now all have analysis data collected during the wargame and/or through other data collection methods. Each EQ belongs to an issue at some level, as the DCMP was designed by decomposing the sponsor's key issues into sub-issues, sub-sub-issues, and so forth, until the wargame's EQs were created by the design group. The analysis group will now need to work backward from the EQ responses to synthesize EQ and sub-issue findings, compiling them for all of the sponsor's key issues. Before we more fully describe the synthesis process, we need to talk about forming the post-wargame analysis group.

Once the final quick-look report is vetted with the players, the analysis group collects any remaining analysis data, including feedback data provided to the players. The team will then pore through the collected analysis data with the ultimate goal of either further underpinning the preliminary findings, or, in some cases, adjusting or even overturning those findings as contradictory evidence is found. Earlier, we discussed the best practices associated with forming the wargaming team. Forming the analysis group that will conduct the post-wargame analysis also has best practices. The composition of the analysis group will be dictated by the sponsor's key issues and the types of analysis data collected during the game. Every one of the sponsor's key issues should be examined to understand what qualifications the members of the analysis group should have to properly interpret and formulate analytic findings for each of the key issues. Some of the sponsor's issues may require that other personnel join the analysis group. Highly technical issues may require subject matter experts who know the technology being addressed so they can help the analysts interpret the veracity of the findings. Issues that focus on doctrine and tactics, techniques, and procedures may require military experts to augment the analysis group. Because a wargame's findings are largely qualitative, communications skills are very important. The skill of clearly and precisely communicating a finding in a sentence or paragraph is developed over many years and is not routinely found in less experienced personnel, regardless of their "analytic" education.

CHARACTERIZING WARGAME ANALYSIS FINDINGS

Care must be taken when compiling the wargame's findings. Because a wargame is a unique event, there are not multiple samples of a repeatable event that can be statistically characterized by averages, variances, or confidence intervals. In all likelihood, there will not be much quantitative analysis data; most will be qualitative data. Characterizing the findings associated with qualitative data can be challenging and may require discussion, calling in outside help, and even facilitation of the collected experts who are gathered to conduct the analysis. The rubric we adopt below to characterize findings is by no means universally accepted, but it should provide a useful structure that can be adapted as your organization sees fit.

OBSERVATIONS, INSIGHTS, AND RESULTS

Much of the data collected in a wargame can be characterized as an *observation*—for example, "The commander decided to commit forces to the attack." There may be a set of observations collected during the wargame to answer a single EQ, such as: "How well does the new sensor assist the commander in making force employment decisions?" The wargame may present the commander with many different situations to ascertain the conditions under which the sensor assists the commander in deciding to employ forces. These situations may cover a spectrum of terrain, weather, and operational contexts, with data collected for each instance. These observations then may be synthesized into an *insight* by the analysis group. Two insights from this particular EQ focused on the terrain as a variable might be: "The new sensor is useful in open, rolling and desert terrain" and "The new sensor is of limited value in jungle, complex, and urban terrain." In this example, each insight is a synthesis of observations that documented the commander's force employment decision for each of a variety of terrain conditions. If observations cannot be usefully synthesized into an insight, the original observations may be simply listed as observations for that EQ. A critical component of these observations, insights, and results is developing an understanding of the reasons behind players' decisions and actions. These reasons will help analysts gain insights into current hypotheses or identify potentially new hypotheses for additional research. The post-play interviews, questionnaires, and surveys will provide supporting analysis data to the analysis team to help their understanding of players' decisions.

In some cases, it may be appropriate to further synthesize issue insights into a *result*, which is a stronger statement than an insight. A result should have a fair amount of evidence that suggests the stronger characterization of the analysis data than an insight. A result from the above example could be: "Forces should never be employed in open, rolling, or desert terrain unless the new sensor has been used to obtain situational awareness for the commander." It is hard to imagine many results being generated solely from a single wargame, so characterizing findings as "results" should be done sparingly.

Analyzing a wargame's analysis data is really an act of synthesis, "the combination of ideas to form a theory or system."[1] The lowest level sub-issue will have one or more EQs associated with it. For each of the lowest level sub-issues (those from which EQs were directly generated), review all the data (observations) that correspond to the sub-issue's EQs and assess how well those observations address that sub-issue. This assessment should be tempered by the constraints, limitations, and assumptions that are associated with the EQs and/or the sub-issue. In particular, any limitation or assumption that affected the collection or the characterization of the EQs' observations needs to be accounted for in the analysis group's synthesis. This synthesis should develop one or more insights that correspond to that sub-issue if possible, or determine any observations that should be noted if observations cannot be synthesized or an insight is not warranted. This should be done for each of the lowest level sub-issues until all the EQ observations have been documented as observations or synthesized into insights for their generating issue or sub-issue.

Now the analysis group will work to synthesize the observations and insights of those EQ-generating issues into findings for higher-level issues. There may have been an issue that generated three sub-issues, each of which generated a number of EQs. Each of the three sub-issues now has had its EQ responses triaged, and those findings should now be synthesized into findings for the parent issue. This process will continue until the analysis group has worked through all the issues, synthesizing insights for the key issues the sponsor originally specified. At this point, the analysis group has findings for each key issue that have been produced by the synthesis of all of the information collected in the DCMP.

FINALIZING WARGAMING FINDINGS

Once all the key issues have findings, the analysis group will go back to the quick-look report and compare the findings produced through the analysis process with those findings that were communicated in the quick-look report. In most cases, the quick-look report's findings will have been corroborated, and the supporting evidence generated by the analysis can be added to the findings. In rare instances, quick-look report findings may not be supported by the analysis, and a hard look at the evidence the analysis group produced will be required as there is sure to be close scrutiny by the sponsor, stakeholders, and players who all left the wargame believing a finding that subsequent analysis has overturned. Typically, one overlooked aspect of wargames is that their completion is not the end of the research and analysis process. Wargaming, as an element of the cycle of research with analysis and exercises/experiments, should be designed to provide insights into future exercises/experiments or other analysis efforts. Good wargames tend to provide potential research hypotheses that field exercises, analytical simulation techniques, experiments, and other efforts to confirm/deny or update. This additional information should then be reincorporated into future wargames on the topic.

FUTURE WORK

It should be expected that wargaming results will reveal issues that require further investigation. The analysis group should be alert for sponsor issues that were not adequately addressed by the wargame. There will be new issues and identified hypotheses that were brought to light by the wargame that need further study and analysis. After all, this is one of the primary outcomes of an analytical wargame. The wargame should not be viewed by anyone as the end of the analytic process but should be seen as part of a larger analysis effort. This view does not mean just in terms of additional analytical wargames but also of exercises/experiments and other analysis techniques. Almost thirty years ago, Peter Perla clearly captured the thought that wargames, exercises, and analysis woven together in a "continuous cycle of research each contribute what they do best to the complex and evolving task of understanding reality."[2] Instead of using a wargame by itself, it should be incorporated with exercises/experiments and other analytical techniques to fully explore problems. This incorporation should include providing insight into how to focus the exercises/experiments as well as pulling data from these events. As an example, the wargame may help identify potential concepts of operations that the exercise or experiment could provide as an avenue to test these concepts. These exercises, if carefully analyzed, could provide ranges of potential mathematical values that could be modeled and offer additional topics for further wargaming. A historic example of this connection would be VADM Henry Mustin's exploration of using an aircraft carrier from the fjords of Norway in the 1980s. This effort started with analysis of the potential effects of providing close air support to NATO forces and was augmented with wargaming to develop an understanding of the range of operational and strategic implications. This cycle of research also included Admiral Mustin directing at-sea exercises to explore the actual ability to operate in the fjords.[3] The point here is that wargaming is not an isolated event, and if conducted properly, it will illuminate a path of additional study.

WARGAME PRACTICAL EXERCISES 9–10

The following set of practical exercises is designed to continue the work that was accomplished in the earlier exercises.

Practical Exercise 9: Quick-Look Report

You have the following DCMP extract (with the analysis data in italics) for three of the sponsor's key sub-issues (3.3, 3.4, and 3.5) to address issue 3 from practical exercise 2. Summarize the findings into one or two sentences for the quick-look report.

1. How does the UN commander intend to conduct patrolling in Zefra?

    a. What will be the size of the patrols?
    Patrols will be a fire team (four to five soldiers) led by a noncommissioned officer.

    b. How will the patrols be different between Bongo and Truscan territories?
    Patrols in Truscan territories will have an additional UN soldier to record any interactions between Zefran soldiers and Truscans.

    c. What conditions will the Zefran government put on UN patrols in Zefra?
    There will be two to three Zefran soldiers who accompany each UN patrol in Zefra, regardless of region (per agreement with Zefran president).

2. What immediate fire support is available if UN patrols take indirect fire?

    a. Under what conditions will Daloon allow a UN fire base that can fire missions into Zefra?
    The government of Daloon has allowed the UN forces to establish an artillery fire base on Zefran soil under the following conditions: Artillery can only be used in response to hostile action involving deadly force, and any civilian casualties will be cause for the government of Daloon to revoke this permission.

b. Under what conditions will Daloon allow UN close air support aircraft to sortie from Daloon airfields?
Same conditions as the artillery fire base above. Assets allowed include both fixed wing and rotary wing attack assets.

c. What are the other organic fire support options available to the UN commander, and how responsive are they?
Mortars. They require emplacement before firing and their range is limited, so a mortar team must be added to patrols if other fire support is unavailable. The UN commander will only employ mortars if UN troops patrol in areas that cannot be ranged by the artillery or in areas where there is a high probability of collateral damage.

3. What sized IFF element can the standard UN patrols defeat?

   a. How will the IFF choose to employ its forces?
   The IFF will normally operate in two- to three-soldier groups, but will send squad-sized elements (eight to ten soldiers) and mortar sections (three soldiers, one 120mm mortar) to conduct ambushes and raids.

   b. What is the UN commander's criteria for defeat?
   The UN commander further defines defeat as "rendering the opposing unit unable to complete its current mission due to casualties or fleeing the area."

Practical Exercise 10: Analysis

You have responses to the following three sponsor issues. Consolidate these responses into succinct answers to the sponsor's issues for the final report.

1. What size quick-reaction force (QRF) will the UN commander establish?

   a. How quickly will the QRF need to respond?
   Within fifteen minutes of a call for reinforcements.

   b. How will the QRF be transported?
   By helicopter. The Daloon government has allowed the QRF helicopter and soldiers to be based in Daloon.

ANALYSIS

    c. What sized IFF element can the QRF defeat?

    You now have results from the Daloon versus Zefran scenario in the Daloon MOD combat simulation. Analysis shows that a UN platoon can defeat an IFF squad 65 percent of the time. Assuming that the QRF will be able to augment surviving members of the UN patrol calling for assistance, parametric analysis shows that a UN platoon plus a UN fire team can defeat an IFF squad 85 percent of the time, and a UN platoon plus two UN soldiers can defeat an IFF squad 75 percent of the time. You will want to vet these results with the UN commander to see, given these results, what size QRF the UN commander wants, and how many helicopters will be needed to transport the QRF.

2. Under what conditions would Bongo forces attack UN forces?

    a. What is the objective of the attack?

    The objective of an attack would be to discredit the Truscans. Bongo forces will only attack UN forces if Truscans start getting traction with the UN and there are active initiatives to change the current government to allow the Truscans more say. They would attack disguised as Truscan militias from Truscan-dominated regions in Zefra.

    b. What is the expected size of a Bongo attack element?

    In order to emulate the Truscan militia, it would be no bigger than a fire team.

    c. What is the composition of the element?

    The fire team would only be armed with small arms, no machine guns or mortars.

3. Under what conditions would Truscan forces attack UN forces?

    a. What is the objective of the attack?

    Two distinctly different objectives: First, to send a wake-up call to the UN if they are too accepting of the ruling Bongo government and ignoring Truscan grievances. The Truscans might make this look like a Bongo ambush by only killing the UN soldiers on patrol. Second, to terrorize Zefran armed forces—this attack would seek to target the

Zefran soldiers when they accompany UN forces, but this would be a targeted attack intending to kill or maim Zefran soldiers without hurting UN soldiers or causing them to engage Truscan attackers.

b. What is the expected size of a Truscan attack element?
For the first instance, attack against the UN, it would be squad size or larger ambush with the intent of eradicating the entire patrol. For the second instance, only a few skilled militia who could slit throats and melt back into the jungle without drawing attention from the UN element, or maybe sniper teams.

c. What is the composition of the element?
For the first, any firepower the Truscans can muster, to include heavy weapons and mortars. Might try and steal them from Zefran armed forces or ISB so the attack looks like a Bongo attack. For the second, the Truscans will carry sharp knives, maybe even arrows tipped with poison, or use sniper rifles to strike from distances.

PART III
PLANNING AND MANAGEMENT

CHAPTER 11

Planning and Managing an Analytic Wargame

■ ■ ■ ■

The best-designed wargame will still fail if not properly planned and managed. Larger wargames have a planning and management staff that allows the wargaming team to focus on the creation of the wargame via the five phases, while smaller wargames may require the team to plan, create, manage, and analyze the wargame with minimal outside assistance.

SCHEDULING THE WARGAME

Several key factors will dictate the schedule for the actual playing of the wargame. First and foremost is the sponsor's timeline for results. The wargame planner needs to reverse-plan and determine how much time the analysis will take, which should include the updating and vetting of the preliminary analysis results with key stakeholders, finalizing the analysis results, and editing the wargame's final report. The length of time required for the analysis will depend on the length of the game and the amount of analysis data that is produced and processed, and this can only be known when the wargaming team has completed the wargame's design. The length of the wargame and the duration of the analysis then allow the scheduling of the wargame, which may depend on key player availability.

If key players are coming from outside of the organization conducting the wargame, scheduling will depend on their availability. If key players are flag officers or senior government officials, expect that their calendars need to be scheduled between six months and a year in advance, and that the scheduling of the wargame may depend on maximizing the number of key players that can be present during a certain time frame.

Having the proper facilities for the wargame is critical, yet many times this is not given careful consideration. Even facilities that were developed for wargaming were likely not developed with *your* particular wargame in mind, so make sure that you first identify the characteristics of the facilities your wargame requires before seeking out the venue. Closed wargames require more rooms and may demand a more robust IT infrastructure. Seminar wargames usually require a more open forum where the facilitator can easily see all the players and the players can be seated according to a specific plan. Hybrid games could require all of the above. The size of your wargame, to include number of players, number of support personnel, and the length of the game (hours, days, weeks), are all important factors that need to be considered and identified before choosing the facility. The time that you will have access to your players is very valuable and needs to be maximized, so plan on feeding your players in or near your wargaming facility so they do not have to search for meals. Catering lunch will be necessary for most wargames that are a day or longer.

Your players need to be immersed in your wargame, so it is a best practice to remove as many distractions as possible. Separate players from their cell phones, laptops, and other communications media during game play. However, have a communications room with easy network access that allows players to contact their organizations during scheduled breaks. Provide the players access to their cell phones at scheduled break times. Also give players an emergency contact phone number that will allow them to be pulled from the wargame in the event of an emergency.

DATA COLLECTION

The foundation of an analytic wargame is its data collection and management plan. The wargame is constructed for the sole purpose of obtaining the analytic data that will allow the post-wargame analysis to address the sponsor's key issues. Thus, the wargame's success depends on the data collection process and the data collectors.

The DCMP provides the roadmap for the data collection process. The wargame is constructed to enable the player interactions that will produce the analysis data identified in the DCMP to answer a particular issue. The DCMP should identify when (which includes the turn or day in a multiple day wargame) during the wargame that the design team expects the players to address the EQ to generate the analysis data. In a closed wargame operating in multiple spaces, it will be important to also indicate where that information is in the DCMP so it can be referenced quickly by the data collector or rapporteur. The importance of having well-trained and alert data collectors who are familiar with the entire DCMP cannot be overstated. Every item of analysis data specified in the DCMP can be produced during the wargame, but if that data is not collected, it is as if it never existed. You should spend time training and rehearsing your team of data collectors to ensure they are ready for the wargame. These data collectors should be intimately familiar with not only the wargame's objectives, issues, EQs, and players but also their role in the process. This will enable them to both capture their assigned analysis data and to recognize and capture potentially essential data coming from an unexpected source.

While the DCMP specifies the EQ that the analysis data should answer, it is important to understand the conditions that were present in the wargame when the players made those decisions and how those conditions influenced decisionmaking. In simpler terms, the data collected should include *what* the decision was, *why* the decision was made, and *when* the decision occurred. For example, in a study to assess the value of a new sensor package, the commander may have decided to commit a battalion to combat (the *what*) because he was very confident he knew the enemy's location (the *why*). The decision occurred in the morning of day two on the second turn (the *when*). Capturing the why is more challenging than the what, so the data collection methodology needs to be well thought out. Care needs to be taken not to burden the player with massive input requirements (for example, filling out a page-long form in detail about each decision), as this will compete with the wargame itself for the player's attention, potentially damaging the quality of play by having distracted or multi-tasking players.

This points to the need for a well-thought-out data collection plan that begins with the DCMP and then parses each EQ to ascertain the analysis data that needs to be collected for it. There may be several EQs with similar analysis data collection requirements, so we recommend designing a simple data collection form to ensure the data collectors capture all the elements needed by the analysis team for specific EQs. Some wargames may require several different data collection forms for different types of analysis data. Each form should have a space for the data collector to indicate additional data that key players need to provide during their interviews. At any rate, the idea is to provide clear and useful templates and guidance so the likelihood of the data collectors collecting the required analysis data is high.

Data collectors need to be present wherever and whenever the players interact to produce relevant information to the wargame's analysis. Closed games will require more data collectors, as there will be data collection events occurring in several rooms simultaneously. We have found, depending on the complexity of the wargame and data collection tasks, that data collectors are usually effective for about two hours at a time during the course of a day. Therefore, it is important that you understand how long you expect your data collectors to be working and, if necessary, establish a data collection rotation to ensure all information is accurately recorded. This can be done by having a second data collector for the more complicated set of tasks and simply rotate the collectors. You should try to schedule these rotations, with some period of overlap, to occur during a natural break in the process, such as between turns, to avoid missing any critical information. We will also reiterate that data collectors should be familiar with the entire DCMP and be trained as data collectors. Collecting data for the DCMP is a task that should be rehearsed (play-tested) and critiqued before the actual wargame, just as every other aspect of the wargame is play-tested.

In smaller wargames, the white cell and control cell are often combined. The white cell's main function is to keep the wargame progressing on schedule. The white cell needs to monitor the DCMP to ensure the interactions required for data collection are taking place as scheduled, and, if not, the white cell needs to ensure that contingency plans are created and activated to produce the required data. The white cell may also have to provide additional data to answer a player's request, create and apply an adjudication method for an unanticipated interaction, or rapidly develop an inject or a vignette to insert into the wargame to produce data collection interactions as necessary (as per the DCMP). Having at least one analyst in the white cell to maintain cognizance of white cell activity that affects the wargame is necessary, as these activities will help frame why players made the decisions they did, which in turn impacts data collected in the DCMP.

As the name implies, the control cell exerts the control necessary to keep the wargame on track and functioning. Control functions that need to be exercised include starting and ending wargaming events according to the published schedule, implementing shift changes for data collectors, analysts, IT crews, and any other support staff that work in shifts, responding to IT or other support system failures, ensuring catering functions such as food and/or beverages are executed on time, and escorting VIPs as the need arises. In short, they allow the wargaming team to focus on keeping the wargame, its players, and support staff on track and minimize any outside distractions that occur.

WARGAME PLAN

The wargame plan is a document that lays out every task that needs to be accomplished for the wargame's preparation, execution, analysis, and reporting. It lays out duties and responsibilities of wargaming support elements and personnel, including data collectors, white cell, control cell, analysis team (including augmentees), IT support, MMT support, and administrative support (VIP escorts, catering, parking, buses, and lodging). As a minimum, the plan will have a roster of every member of the wargaming team with their duties and a schedule that specifies who needs to be where and at what times. This will serve to deconflict any double taskings and identify scheduling conflicts. Training dates and times for data collectors, white cell personnel, and control cell personnel will be specified. The different means to collect and process data will be specified and may include identifying responsibilities for preparing and administering pre- and post-game surveys and observer questionnaires, preparing and facilitating quick-look reports, and conducting post-wargame after action reviews. The conduct of the analysis, to include members of the analysis team, may be augmented by subject matter experts for certain key issues that require specific knowledge and/or experience.

CHAPTER 12

Course of Action Wargaming

■ ■ ■ ■

During Operation Iraqi Freedom, V Corps commander Lieutenant General William S. Wallace observed, "This is not [exactly] the enemy we wargamed against."[1] This comment, often misquoted, provides a great introduction to both the capabilities and limitations of planning wargames. Wallace elaborated: "The enemy we're fighting is a bit different than the one we war-gamed against because of these paramilitary forces. We knew they were here, but we did not know how they would fight."[2] Asked whether the fighting increased the chances of a longer war than forecast by some military planners, General Wallace said, "It's beginning to look that way."

It is not news that the U.S. Defense Department planners overlooked the capability and capacity of the paramilitary forces that went on, after the fall of the Iraqi government, to mire the United States in a counterinsurgency struggle that took well over a decade to quell. The U.S. National Command Authority overlooked the insights from General Anthony Zinni's 1999 Desert Crossing wargame (described in chapter 4). Not knowing how the paramilitary forces in Iraq would fight was a failure of planners to understand the culture and the motivation of those who took up arms as

General Wallace's forces approached Baghdad, and it points to one of the worst practices we continue to see in planning wargames today: a failure to play a culturally correct, active adversary. This is not a new problem or a critique of planning or course of action (COA) wargames. Moltke encountered similar circumstances in the German wargames of the Schlieffen plan. His wargames adequately captured the logistics challenges that the German movement through Belgium presented at the time. As a result of the wargames' findings, the logistics capabilities were increased for the German units moving on the flank. However, these same wargames failed to identify the willingness of Belgian civilians to destroy the railroad ahead of the advancing German armies or to disrupt logistics behind the German lines.[3] Despite the demonstrated historic relevance of planning wargames, we have experienced some discussion in many venues that planning wargames are not really analytic wargames. Our goal with this chapter is to help demonstrate that planning, JP 5-0 (*Joint Planning*), or COA wargames are indeed analytic wargames and to provide analysts and planners with some insights into how to get the most of their planning wargames.

We contend that good planning wargames *are* analytic wargames. In these cases, we are defining planning wargames as those wargames designed to help organizations develop insights into their operations plans and contingency operations plans. Typically, planning staffs use these wargames as part of assessing all critical points in an operation during the COA analysis. U.S. doctrine does lay out a useful structure for conducting planning wargames, but there are gaps in how to actually conduct the wargame as well as a lack of organizational wargaming capability and capacity in planning headquarters throughout most of DoD to properly conduct the wargames. Planning wargames, when done correctly, provide commanders and their staffs with a powerful tool to assess operational COAs, providing key insights into the advantages, disadvantages, and risks of each friendly course of action when confronted with a thinking, adaptive adversary executing both its most likely and most dangerous courses of action. Most U.S. allies and partners and many potential adversaries leverage wargaming as a critical element of their planning processes.[4] These planning processes utilize wargaming to analyze staff-developed plans and courses of action, seeking to identify opportunities and vulnerabilities and assess risks, much like current U.S. DoD doctrine. For example, the British Ministry of Defence (MOD) recognizes that wargaming may need a large amount of time and resources but that "if prepared for fully, trained for regularly and resourced appropriately, however, wargaming should form an essential part of the Joint Task Force Commander's planning repertoire."[5] The British acknowledge the importance of training, resourcing, and practicing to ensure the wargames are successful. Yet despite this recognition, there are typically not enough resources to adequately wargame all planning. The combatant command planning requirement for noncombatant evacuation operations provides a great example of a wargaming workload for planners and analysts. Noncombatant evacuation operations are designed to support the State Department in evacuating noncombatants, nonessential personnel, and others who are at risk in a foreign nation. In one year, a combatant command (CCMD) had twenty-four noncombatant evacuation operations contingency plans under review. Following doctrinal requirements, this review would require, for a minimum analysis effort, between 72 and 144 COA wargames. The command's planners and analysts are required to conduct these wargames, since outsourcing them would be too cost prohibitive.

DOCTRINAL WARGAMING FRAMEWORK

Wargaming is a "conscious attempt to visualize the flow of the operation" based upon the capabilities of the adversary and an examination of critical events in a possible COA.[6] Wargaming is cited as a "critical portion of the planning process and should be allocated significant time."[7] That said, U.S. doctrine writers provided an escape for planners who always seem to be short on time as they rush to complete the planning process: "Based upon time available, the commander should wargame each COA alternative against the most probable and the most dangerous adversary COAs."[8] If we examine the U.S. doctrine through the lens of analytic wargames as this book describes, the framework for planners to construct useful wargames seems to be there.

Planning doctrine correctly identifies many of the critical elements for an effective wargame. These include:

- people making decisions
- a fair competitive environment
- adjudication

- consequences of actions
- iteration (i.e., new insights will be gained as games are iterative)[9]

Planning wargames have an *objective*: "COA wargaming allows the commander, staff, and subordinate commanders and their staffs to gain a common understanding of friendly and enemy COAs, and other actor actions that may (intentionally or otherwise) work in opposition to achieving the objectives or attaining desired end state conditions."[10]

Planning wargames have specified *issues*:

1. Determine how to maximize combat power against the enemy while protecting the friendly forces and minimizing collateral damage in combat or maximizing the effect of available resources toward achieving CCMD and national objectives in noncombat operations and campaigns.
2. Have as near an identical visualization of the operation as possible.
3. Anticipate events in the operational environment and potential reaction options.
4. Determine conditions and resources required for success while also identifying gaps and seams.
5. Determine when and where to apply the force's capabilities.
6. Plan for and coordinate authorities to integrate information-related capability early.
7. Focus intelligence collection requirements.
8. Determine the most flexible courses of action.
9. Identify potential decision points.
10. Determine task organization options.
11. Develop data for use in a synchronization matrix or related tool.
12. Identify potential plan branches and sequels.
13. Identify high-value targets.
14. Assess risk.
15. Determine COA advantages and disadvantages.
16. Recommend commander's critical information requirements.
17. Validate end states and objectives.
18. Identify contradictions between friendly COAs and expected enemy end states.[11]

Planning wargames have *rules and procedures*:

- "Each COA wargame has a number of turns, each consisting of three total moves: action, reaction, and counteraction. If necessary, each turn of the wargame may be extended beyond the three basic moves. The facilitator, based on Joint Force Commander guidance, decides how many total turns are made in the wargame."[12]
- "Each retained COA should, at a minimum, be wargamed against both the most likely and most dangerous enemy COAs."[13]

Planning doctrine even specifies the *analysis data* that the planning wargame should produce:

- wargamed COAs with graphic and narrative; branches and sequels identified
- information on commander's evaluation criteria
- initial task organization
- critical events and decision points
- newly identified resource shortfalls
- refined/new commander's critical information requirements and event template/matrix
- initial decision support template/decision support matrix
- refined synchronization matrix
- refined staff estimates
- assessment plan and criteria[14]

For all these positives, the general critique of the planning wargaming described in doctrine is that it still does not provide the detail necessary for planners to construct and execute useful planning wargames. We focus on the specified *methods* for planning wargames that the doctrine provides for depicting the range of actions that the competitors can take. There are four distinct methods: narrative, sketch-note technique, sophisticated, and full competitor representation.[15] The critical differences between these methods appear to be the amount of competitor involvement and the necessary time to execute the wargame. The narrative approach is a simple detailed narrative effort that captures the action, reaction, and counteraction of the players. In many cases, this wargame process becomes a scripted exercise designed to confirm the COA. The sketch-note method introduces operational sketches and details to provide a clearer picture. This method is the traditional route for many U.S. military organizations. The sophisticated level employs a more "extensive means" to capture the range of competitor actions and consequences. What is meant by more extensive means is unclear, but it can be implied that the wargame will involve more competitors in the analysis process. The final method is one where all "competitors in a conflict are represented and have equal decision space to enable a full exploration of the competition."[16] This most sophisticated level is the closest to the true analytical wargaming process that was described in part II of this book. This method of wargaming is actually necessary if the commander and staff really want to develop a complete understanding of the risks and weaknesses of a given plan as exposed by a thinking, adaptive adversary. For each of these methods, the wargame's white cell is supposed to provide the adjudication of the outcome, although the only adjudication guidance provided is a choice between "manual" and "computer-assisted."

There should be organizational concern that conducting a narrative or sketch-note COA wargame is simply a "walk-through" construct designed to confirm the current plan's COAs. The planning staff typically implements these types of wargames when they reach the wargaming step in the planning process and have little time, have invested little thought into how to design and conduct the wargame, and have little interest or command guidance to cause them to actually seek the strengths, weaknesses, and risks associated with any of the COAs. The result is typically a very pro forma wargaming process that does not allow for the discovery of potential risks and only serves to confirm the COA. These wargames do not have a true competitor with the availability of the full spectrum of potential decisions and thus would never have a chance of discovering the type of deficiency General Wallace referred to.

However, this lack of a full competitive wargame is not a new development. Early in World War II, from 1–5 May, Admiral Isoroku Yamamoto presided over a wargame aboard the battleship *Yamato* for a Japanese naval action that later became known as the Battle of Midway. Admiral Chuichi Nagumo served as the commander of the Midway strike force, and Yamamoto's chief of staff Admiral Matome Ugaki acted as the wargame's head umpire. There were few challenges to the plan's feasibility, but there were some command and control and situational awareness concerns in the wargame. Ultimately, the plan was approved, and many historians now contend that Yamamoto really just wanted a rubber stamp approval versus a true competitive wargame. Multiple historians have argued that Yamamoto constrained the U.S. player to scripted behaviors described as most advantageous to the Japanese.[17] The narrative is that the U.S. player was not allowed to execute a surprise flank attack on the Japanese carriers. This action prevented the Japanese staff from testing their plan to identify potential risks in the operation. The wargame should have allowed for plausible U.S. actions to allow the staff to understand the potential risks and to develop the appropriate contingency plans. This is one reason that doctrine suggests that the staff should wargame against both the most dangerous and the most likely enemy actions. Of course, if this is still a scripted enemy action without a true competitor, the staff will still not fully identify the plausible actions of the competitor. The Japanese actions at Midway and countless other examples should serve as a warning to future staffs of the potential pitfalls of improperly designed and executed wargames.

Unfortunately, the narrative and sketch-note methods of wargaming do not capture the fair competitive environment that is recognized as a critical element of the planning process and wargame. It is important to recognize that this competitive environment must include more than just the Red versus Blue kinetic military conflict. It should include the full spectrum of competitors across the political, military, economic, social, infrastructural, and information operational environments and the asymmetric realm.

FREE-THINKING ADVERSARY

Too often, military planning wargames plan against a static intelligence estimate focused on unit strengths and equipment but are short on innovation and dynamic thinking and lacking the culturally correct human dimension that represents the actual threat. Moltke understood the significance of having a free-thinking adversary in the wargame. When he took command of the Prussian army general staff from Count Alfred von Schlieffen, he expressed this concern directly to Kaiser Wilhelm II:

When I see how the strategic war games, which are presented year after year to your Majesty, regularly end with the capture of enemy armies of five to six hundred thousand, and in the course of a few days of operations, I cannot rid myself of the feeling that these in no way represent wartime relationships. I cannot direct such war games. Your Majesty himself knows that the armies directed by him regularly surround the opponent and thus apparently end the war with one blow. In my opinion these results can only be achieved when they are forced in such a manner that does not at all bespeak the basic rule, that war games should be a study of real war and that all delays and hindrances which appear in war needs to be taken account of. This kind of war game, in which your Majesty is aware, produced an opponent with more or less tied hands, must cause very false impression, which can be injurious if war comes.[18]

Today's world is much more complex than a simple Blue versus Red military kinetic construct and wargame of the threat. Most operations are potentially influenced by a range of operational conditions/conflicts. The planner needs to conduct an honest assessment to decide if the simple "action-reaction-counteraction" is a sufficiently robust construct to enable an adequate "Red teaming" review of the plans. Red teaming is a technique that provides a culturally appropriate Red cell with information above and beyond what that cell would typically know about the way the Blue force will fight. This methodology allows the adversary to find the flaws in the revealed concept or plan, in effect providing a worst-case look at the vulnerabilities of the Blue's COA.[19] Think of an adversary who was able to get a copy of the Blue plan ahead of time! Red teaming is a structured process executed by a team of trained and educated individuals that provides the organization the ability to critically identify technical issues and vulnerability in operations.[20] One purpose of the Red team is to help the organization overcome cognitive errors that sometimes come from group-think and confirmation bias, especially when Red is part of the planning process. Red teaming should not be confused with the functions of the intelligence organization (Red cell) that is supporting operational planning. The Red team is designed to tear apart the operational plan in hopes of discovering vulnerabilities, risks, and limitations. One great source for planners and analysts is the British MOD's *Red Teaming Guide*.[21]

Our experience with combatant commands has revealed a gap between the wargaming that U.S. doctrine specifies and the wargaming actually conducted at CCMDs. While we have provided educational courses to several CCMDs in an attempt to increase both the educational and experiential level of the wargamers, progress has been uneven. Most of our experience points to planning processes that almost never wargame more than one COA, and that rarely wargame that one COA against both the most likely and the most dangerous enemy COA. If CCMDs conduct any planning wargaming, it is typically one COA wargame, usually against a scripted, static "most likely" threat. Time is almost always cited as the reason for conducting the one pro forma wargame, although the planning process for future plans often takes more than twelve months. There are usually no dedicated wargame designers in CCMDs. Designing a wargame becomes more of a coalition of the willing, where operational planning teams are formed with a few staff sections providing one or two personnel to create plans and perhaps, if time permits, organize some sort of wargaming activity. If wargames are conducted, they often ignore any players other than military roles, so the whole of government and any nongovernmental actors are not included in the wargame's design or analysis.

For the few CCMD wargames that do attempt to play the adversary as a full competitor, having the J2 shop lead the Red team brings its own challenges. First, intelligence officers do wonderful jobs developing intelligence estimates, but few ever command military formations. If the Red commander is unimaginative and commands the Red force to mimic the intelligence estimate that the J2 provided the Blue commander to plan against, the outcome will reveal no surprises, the Blue force will easily prevail, and little will be learned about the weaknesses and risks associated with that COA. We recommend having someone with combat unit command experience command the Red force, with the J2 representative as the deputy. This would far better serve the intent to field a thinking, competitive adversary. This adversary should take more of a Red-teaming approach, which is where the adversary attempts to break the plan or COA to identify friction points or risk, giving the planners additional information to update their plans or concepts. We realize that time is always the critical shortcoming in many organizations, but the best practice is to wargame the plan or concept several times against an adversary. To make the wargame more useful and less predictable, you can vary the behavior of the adversary. The adversary can alternate between the most likely threat—in which case there are well-researched guidelines so the adversary conforms to its known doctrine, standard operating procedures, and tactics, techniques, and procedures—and the most dangerous one, where the threat is allowed to bring in new technologies and is not restricted to existing doctrine. In every case, the adversary should be a dynamic player, not a scripted opponent.

FACILITATING MORE WARGAMING

However, education and experience may also play a role in the dearth of wargaming at many planning headquarters. Most planners do not receive education in how to design and conduct a wargame as part of their professional military education, so often there is no knowledge base other than doctrinal publications. These planners tend to learn on the job and either rely on what they read in doctrine or follow the lead of what has been done in the past. Once planning headquarters stand up a robust wargaming capability and begin to conduct thorough COA wargaming as part of the planning process, we recommend that planning wargaming activity be expanded. Wargaming should be incorporated throughout the entire planning process. There should be a wargaming cell where analysts, advised by planners, develop the bones of the planning wargame using the DCMP construct built around the issues that the command needs to address.

Figure 4 applies one example of how to use wargaming principles throughout the planning process. This approach has been adopted by several U.S. organizations and has improved both the planning and wargaming processes. It identifies at least five opportunities in the planning process to incorporate wargaming principles versus using COA wargaming to just inform step four. The first two wargames are designed to support the initiation and development phase. These wargames could easily be executed as a seminar or matrix-type game with the goal of developing a strategic appreciation for the problem and helping identify potential COAs during the initiation and mission steps of the planning process. This early introduction of wargaming also gets the planners thinking about wargaming earlier

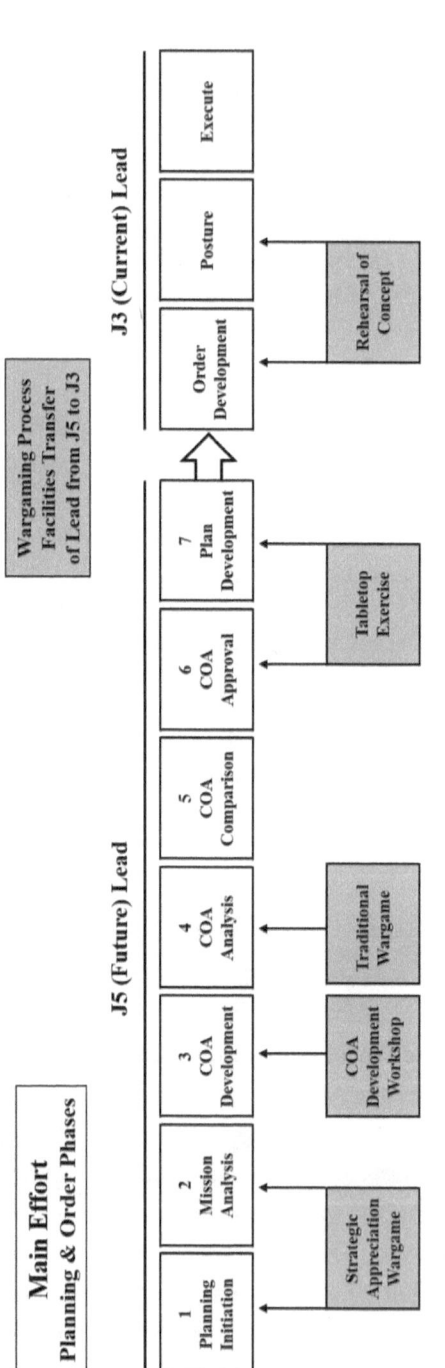

Applying the Wargaming Principles to the Orders and Planning Process

in the planning process. The traditional wargame support is designed to be a full competitor wargame. The final two wargames are designed as a tabletop exercise and rehearsal of concept drill to identify risks and necessary contingency plans. One key aspect of this effort is the establishment of the wargaming cell to support planners with this series of wargames. The objective of this cell is to support J5 and J3 planners in the development and execution of a series of wargames using the application of various wargaming tools and methods to illuminate elements of complex problems to improve planning and operations. This series of wargames maximizes the benefits of COA analysis wargaming by producing a better plan, providing the commander a better understanding of contingencies and risks, and placing the key scenario assumptions under more scrutiny. One important element is the acknowledgment that the wargaming center's mission is not to design and conduct the wargames but to provide guidance, organization, and structure that the planners can leverage as they create the wargame. This guidance includes educating the planners on best practices for designing and conducting wargames.

CHAPTER 13

Special Considerations for Less Structured Wargames

▪ ■ ■ ▪

There is a tendency, usually because of the complexity of the issues, for planners and analysts to use the less structured styles of wargaming, including seminar, matrix, and free Kriegsspiel, to support their efforts to gain insights into their issues or plans. Because of this tendency, we would like to address a few special considerations and some reminders of what is involved in these less structured wargames.

Seminar wargames are an important class of wargames that can be very useful for analysis. As a reminder, we are defining a seminar wargame as one in which a scenario, which may range from military to geopolitical or a combination of anything in between, is presented to a group or panel of selected subject matter experts who discuss and support developing insights into the issue(s) presented in the scenario. Seminar wargames are easily recognizable in that there is typically a single facilitator who encourages discussion and guides the topic of discussion, and there are role players who bring a particular expertise to the wargame who are usually seated in a semicircle, allowing the facilitator to easily make eye contact and observe the players as the wargame unfolds. Seminar wargames can be used for a variety of wargaming purposes and topics. Strategic wargames and political-military wargames are often either seminar wargames or wargames with a large seminar component. Operational-level wargames often have a seminar component as well, but the closer the operational focus gets to the tactical level of war, the more likely that the wargame will have less of a seminar component. However, most well-designed wargames defy neat categorizations, so wargame designers should not look to determine the construct simply by level of war (e.g., "It's a tactical game, therefore it should be a system wargame").

Seminar wargames have an important role as analytic wargames. Exploring and defining new doctrine, operational concepts, and tactics, techniques, and procedures can all be done well using a seminar wargaming environment where the wargame seeks to leverage the players' expertise in these areas. Seminar wargames can also be used as educational wargames for the players to gain a better understanding of a complex analytical problem. In this role, they can be used to better educate planners and/or analysts to understand and refine cogent issues for further study or future wargaming.

Seminar wargames are usually thought of as open wargames, where all the players sit in the same room and have access to the same information, but they can be designed with a closed component. One such construct is called "closed planning, open execution." Imagine a seminar wargame with two teams of coalition partners, where each player uniquely controls his or her forces or assets. The NATO International Security Assistance Force (ISAF) construct in Afghanistan lends itself to this. A seminar wargame on Afghanistan may allow a team of NATO ISAF members to go into a room to plan out their next move against the "adversary," which may also be a team that includes the Afghan Taliban, the Pakistan Taliban, the Haqqanni network, poppy farmers, and warlords, who are allowed to go into another closed room and conduct their own planning. Then each group concludes their planning meeting, and all members reconvene around a table and, in an open seminar format, respond to the facilitator when called upon to make a decision or take an action.

BOGGSAT VERSUS SEMINAR WARGAMES

We have introduced you to the term BOGGSAT—bunch of guys and gals sitting around a table—and you recognize it for what it is and know it is not really a wargame. However, to the casual observer, a seminar wargame and a BOGGSAT may appear very similar, in the sense that both typically represent a group of subject matter experts discussing an issue. What separates the two?

First, from experience, a BOGGSAT has little in terms of a structure developed to capture insights into essential questions and issues. The seminar wargame, like any good analytic wargame, is designed around the DCMP. A keen observer of a seminar wargame will note that the facilitator's questions have purpose and focus, and a set of data collectors is recording players' decisions as they are made in the wargame. In many cases, the BOGGSAT's facilitator is the individual who is actually conducting the research, and they tend to focus on their own checklist and to be the one recording the responses of the individual providing information. Many BOGGSATs do not have the underlying analytical development of a DCMP to ensure that the planner or analyst is getting all the information they need to address issues. In many instances, the analysis typically takes on the format of an after action review—what did we learn from the discussion? A seminar wargame will have the data collection records, and the results will need to be synthesized by the analysis team.

A wargaming team should not consider choosing a seminar wargame because it looks easier to create than any other form of wargaming. In actuality, seminar wargames are the most difficult from which to get good analysis results, and because of that, they require careful planning, a robust DCMP, well-trained data collectors who are familiar with the entire DCMP, and a skilled facilitator. The bottom line is the format of the wargame needs to be chosen because it is best suited to answering the sponsor's issues, and many of the best wargames are not a single format but rather hybrids of two or more formats.

FACILITATION OF SEMINAR AND LESS STRUCTURED WARGAMES

Facilitating a seminar wargame is challenging, and not everyone is a good facilitator. Facilitators must have certain skills to be effective. First, they have to be able to draw out comments from players who are reticent—not all players are eager to jump in and voice their views. The polar opposite, those players that cannot wait to share their ideas and be heard, often need to be managed so they do not dominate the game or take it on a tangential path. Facilitators need to be unbiased and also be perceived as unbiased by the players. A facilitator may need to curtail a player's input but must do so in a way that is not perceived as advocating against that particular player's position; it must be seen as an action taken solely to keep the wargame progressing. A useful way to keep seminar games on track is the parking lot technique. The "parking lot" can be a white board or a pad of butcher paper on an easel that all the players and observers can see. When an issue cannot be expeditiously resolved, it is recognized as needing further scrutiny at another time. The recognition is formalized by annotating the issue on the parking lot. After each turn, the facilitator and analysts record these issues and decide the best way to proceed with them. If no further investigation can be done during the wargame or in post-game analysis, it should be mentioned in the final report as an issue requiring further inquiry.

The facilitator also needs to be careful to be perceived as unbiased in managing the wargame's path. The facilitator's duty is to investigate all of the issues that the DCMP has laid out, so the game is steered to examine each of those issues to the fullest extent allowed in the allotted time. However, the facilitator cannot be seen as steering the game to any preordained results. Players who believe the facilitator has a certain outcome for the game in mind may not be invested in the process, and their contributions to the wargame will have little or no value.

Facilitators of wargames with flag officers need to be particularly adept at managing these senior players. The Army's Unified Quest had several skilled facilitators who were retired military officers that had been peers with most of the senior flag officers that were players. These prior relationships allowed the facilitator to understand how to relate to each of the senior players, and because the facilitator was known to the players, there was a better appreciation of what the facilitator had to accomplish. There are professional facilitators for hire, but care must be taken here. One of the combatant commands we visited relayed a story of a professional facilitator hired to facilitate a wargame where the players were senior flag officers (three and four star). For whatever reason, the flag officers did not respond well to this facilitator, and the wargame was of limited value.

ADJUDICATION TECHNIQUES FOR LESS STRUCTURED WARGAMES

Most true seminar wargames, where the facilitator is guiding the discussion, do not have need for a formal adjudication technique but, as already noted, the only absolute in wargaming is that there are no absolutes. Therefore, the range of MMTs that you may use in a seminar or other less structured wargame is unlimited, but you must use caution introducing these MMTs; they have a tendency to add complexity and potentially interrupt player immersion in the wargame. The essential questions in the DCMP will dictate the number and types of necessary MMTs in the wargame. It will be reasonable to expect that with a larger number or greater complexity of these MMTS, a system wargame would be better to use than a seminar wargame. If adjudication is required in these less structured wargames, these adjudication techniques can range from the facilitator acting as the adjudicator, to reliance on the group, to a computer-based combat simulation.

Facilitator-Focused Adjudication

The judgment of the facilitator is used to provide the players feedback on the outcome of their decisions. This is essentially a free Kriegsspiel-style wargame. This requires that the facilitator be knowledgeable about conditions required for specific outcomes and choose ones that are logical for the situation—ones that are not perceived as biased toward a particular player or advocating for a certain outcome. It is important in this situation that the group/players recognize the facilitator as an expert in the field, or you run the risk of them challenging or debating the facilitator adjudication.

Consensus-Focused Adjudication

A facilitator may have the participants attempt to reach some agreement on an appropriate result from an interaction. This is essentially a matrix-style wargame. This consensus can incorporate an element of randomness: the participants will propose that certain outcomes have associated probabilities or likelihoods of success, and a random number generator (maybe represented by the roll of dice) will dictate which outcome is chosen. The random number method will use the probabilities previously agreed to, so that, for example, the outcome the participants feel is most likely will be the one that the random number generator is most likely to select. One additional method could include players making arguments for or against the likelihood of success and then having an open discussion prior to a vote. These consensus-focused techniques may be useful to identify likely decision points in the scenario being explored so a future game might create a more detailed or robust adjudication for similar interactions. Unlike true seminar wargames, which do not require an extensive discussion about how you plan to handle adjudication, planners and analysts will need to plan for informing the players of the process and should consider that they may not be able to complete as many turns because of the time needed to conduct the consensus adjudication process.

Facilitator with Advice Adjudication
Rather than relying on the facilitator's judgment to determine all results, the facilitator may seek advice on select interactions from an expert observer who has been invited to participate in the wargame. This is essentially a free Kriegsspiel with a white cell of subject matter experts to handle adjudicating actions and decisions. This approach may be particularly appropriate in areas such as a future technology or emerging doctrine where facilitators will not have the necessary knowledge to render an accurate adjudication. The players will be given the feedback following consultation between the facilitator and the appropriate subject matter expert. Keep in mind that this approach will take longer to execute than the facilitator-focused adjudication, since you will have to defer to the white cell for a decision. Planners and analysts need to develop a mechanism for how information is provided to the expert observers and how decisions are adjudicated within these groups, and the results are transmitted to the players. This flow of information is critical to the wargame process, and if you are not careful and this flow of information takes too long, you run the risk of breaking the immersion of the players in the wargame.

Expert Panel Adjudication
A panel of subject matter experts may be employed when a wargame is dominated by issues that require expert rulings on the feasibility of player actions. This, like the previous scenario, is essentially a free Kriegsspiel with a white cell of subject matter experts to handle adjudicating actions and

decisions. The main difference tends to be the number of required experts and the breadth of areas they must cover in the wargame. Often such topics are not so simple that a single expert can give a conclusive response. A panel, particularly one comprising disparate perspectives, may be particularly enlightening. Such a panel could assess the impact of military actions on the social, cultural, economic, or behavioral fabric of a local population. If the wargame is focused on future technologies, the panel would rule on the feasibility of certain technology capabilities. A downside is that there may be no one obvious resolution to player interactions. From our experience, one common issue with this approach is that the white cell of experts becomes too large and thus takes too long to make a decision or a consensus cannot be reached. In many of these cases, the issue is a weak mechanism for the group to actually adjudicate the players' actions or decisions. Unfortunately, there is also a tendency for these larger groups to not be consistent in their decisions over longer wargames consisting of multiple turns or decisions. You also need to be cautious that the white cell is not making decisions each turn without keeping an eye on how their previous decisions might influence the current decision. One last critical point is that the planner or analyst needs to make sure they are collecting more than just the decision from the white cell. They must have a process in place to capture the discussion and the whys behind the decisions.

Mathematical and Computer Model Adjudication

Seminar wargames may sometimes require the adjudication of physical interactions, such as the outcome of two forces doing battle. Look-up tables, combat results tables, and computer-based combat simulations are prominent adjudication examples. The technique the wargaming team decides to use should be determined by the precision of the analysis data needed and the time available for the MMT to cycle through the input and output—in most seminar games, the primary analysis data sought will be player decisions, not quantitative data, so incorporating a computer-based combat simulation should be done with careful consideration to the value-added it provides (contrasted with simpler techniques such as combat results tables or look-up tables) versus the overhead that is needed to prepare (six months to incorporate data and instantiate a scenario) and run (cycle time from start of input to providing output).

SEMINAR AND LESS STRUCTURED WARGAME ANALYSIS

As with all analytic wargames, analysts, planners, and game designers derive the essential questions they need to answer from the sponsor's issues. The analytical focus with which the DCMP is developed will determine the quality of the feedback and analytic data collected and therefore the veracity of the analytic results. Since game outcomes rely on player decisions, which often include an element of surprise, the development of the DCMP by the wargaming team needs to be extensive, flexible, and extendable, and needs to anticipate carefully to avoid surprises. A wargame in which the collection of valuable evidence was overlooked will have very little value.

Seminar wargames focus on qualitative data, which often has two components: the "what" and the "why." A player's decision to take some action (the what) is easily recorded: for example, "'Doctors without Borders' would only accept medical supplies from the United States and would not accept military doctors working at their facilities." The rationale behind the decision (the why) may not be communicated, so the analysts need to devise methods to collect the rationale. This can be done by player interviews, data sheets that players fill out, or the pursuit of a specific component by the facilitator for specific decisions: "What is your rationale?" Although we think of a seminar portion of a wargame with all the players in a room as open, players' motivations are known only to themselves and those they choose to inform (as in a closed planning session), so a player may not want to reveal the rationale to the entire gathering for obvious reasons. Player contributions to data collection may be subject to natural human foibles: players will have an incomplete picture and may supplement it with assumptions (right or wrong), or players may try to defend a contentious decision rather than unemotionally state only the facts. Because memories may fade with the passage of time, it is important to gather rationales as soon as possible after decisions have been made. Key player interviews can be scheduled each day or even after turns if the schedule permits. Having players fill out rationales on data forms either manually or using computer software may be an option if it does not take an inordinate amount of time or distract the player from the wargame itself.

CHAPTER 14

Educational and Experiential Wargames

■ ■ ■ ■

Educational and experiential wargames—with their focus on producing better educated, better trained, or more experienced players—have important roles in the defense community. While this book concentrates on planners and analysts producing analytic wargames, many of the best practices contained within apply equally well to educational and experiential wargames. The five phases we presented for the construct of analytic wargames (initiate, design, develop, conduct, and analyze) apply to the development of both educational and experiential wargames. However, wargame developers too often overlook or give insufficient attention to the analyze phase. These wargames should include some form of pre-wargame assessment (analysis) to better understand the current education/experience level of their players and a post-wargame assessment/analysis to determine if the wargame imparted the desired education/experience to the players.

Next we examine each of the transitional tasks that are defined in the five phases chart. The data collection and management plan may seem to not be needed for experiential or educational wargames. But remembering how the DCMP is used to build the foundation for an analytic wargame should give us pause. Could a construct such as the DCMP be used to build the foundations of experiential and educational games? Absolutely. The process of deconstructing the defined problem into its constituent components, and then understanding what elements of measurement space will be required to address each component, provides the road map to follow for the design of any type of wargame. While we call these components essential questions for an analytic wargame, they are defined differently for experiential and educational wargames. The transitional "full dress rehearsal" task needs to be conducted to ensure that the wargame has set the conditions to impart the requisite experience or education. Finally, the quick-look report of an analytic wargame will not be required for an experiential or educational wargame; however, there should be some consideration, before the wargame is declared a success, to assess what knowledge or experience the wargame has transferred to the players. As with an analytic wargame, we recommend a mechanism more rigorous than a simple after action review. We discuss defining the components of the DCMP and assessing the effectiveness of experiential and educational wargames in greater detail in the following paragraphs.

EXPERIENTIAL WARGAMES

An experiential wargame provides its players with experience that should be relevant to the players' current or projected duty positions. The structure that the DCMP provides for an analytic wargame can easily be leveraged for an experiential wargame. An experiential wargame should build the game's foundation around the experience that the wargame is designed to impart to its players. A training wargame is an example of an experiential wargame, and the idea is to have the wargame's players experience their duties in a simulated environment.

Training Wargames: Background

As computer simulations came into being, both the analytic and the training communities embraced computer-based wargaming tools. In the U.S. Army, the human-in-the-loop (HITL) computer simulation JANUS was used by both the analytic and training communities through the early 2000s.

For many years, a different version of JANUS was maintained for each community. The biggest differences in the simulations were in the details of the technologies represented and the data. The analytic community typically conducts futures studies that seek to understand what concepts and technologies the future force should embrace. Incorporating these new technologies requires frequent updating of the simulation code as well as a degree of precision for every system represented to discern subtle differences in operational and system effectiveness of both current and future weapons systems. This precision, in turn, requires classified performance data. In contrast, the training community does not need the same degree of precision and often prefers to use unclassified data, which is less restrictive on both facilities and users. The analytic community used JANUS, with active friendly and adversary players, to help produce and refine concepts of operations and courses of action that could then be instantiated in closed-loop combat simulations for quantitative analysis purposes. Today the simulation OneSAF provides an HITL wargaming capability for the analytic community.[1] The training version of JANUS was used to train commanders from platoon through brigade level in applying tactical doctrine and combat techniques.[2] JANUS was replaced by the Joint Conflict and Tactical Simulation system, which is still widely used by the training community along with some analytic users.[3] All of these HITL simulations require humans making decisions, but are they wargames? Wargaming purists would judge by whether there is a live, thinking adversary responding to the decisions and actions of the humans playing the "good guys."

As the commercial gaming industry began to develop and publish military-focused games, the military community investigated using or adapting commercial-off-the-shelf (COTS) products for military use. In 1995 the U.S. Marine Corps adapted the commercial first-person shooter (FPS) game Doom to train tasks such as mutual fire team support, protection of the automatic rifleman, proper sequencing of an attack, ammunition discipline. and succession of command.[4] In 2000 the U.S. Army adapted the game Delta Force 2 to create a tactical training simulation that familiarized soldiers with the capabilities of the new Land Warrior system for dismounted infantry.[5] The U.S. Military Academy at West Point's Department of Military Instruction also used this simulation to teach military science.[6] As with all simulations, there are abstractions of the real world that need to be acknowledged, and the tasks that the software will be designed to train personnel on need to be carefully chosen and rigorously described so that both the simulation developer and the user are clear on the specifications that the adapted simulation needs to adhere to when delivered. As with the HITL simulations, the question of whether COTS FPS games are wargames is germane. Most FPS games are designed to be played by individuals, and there is usually the choice to "play against the computer," meaning there is an automated adversary, usually referred to as "AI" (artificial intelligence). As the topic of AI is a prominent one, with computers now being able to win at the ancient game of *Go*,[7] we will not treat AI in any great detail. However, in looking at COTS FPS games, we suggest that you look to determine if the game allows multi-sided play with actual players on opposing sides.

Wargaming can be a good choice for training collective tasks for higher commands and staffs, particularly for command and control. The U.S. Army Mission Command Training Program uses a spectrum of tools, including elements of wargaming, to "conduct or support combined arms training for Brigades, Divisions, Corps, Army Service Combatant Commands, Joint Force Land Component Commands, and Joint Task Forces in order to create training experiences that enable the Army's senior commanders to develop current, relevant, campaign-quality, joint and expeditionary mission command instincts and skills."[8] Key elements of the Mission Command Training Program include a "free-thinking" opposing force (OPFOR) and advanced technology to gather data.[9]

Foundation for a Training Wargame

The methodology to design a training wargame is very similar to the principles we have outlined for analytic wargame design. Problem definition is identifying the tasks that the wargame will be designed to train. These tasks will typically be collective training tasks. By U.S. Army definition, a collective training task is a "clearly defined, discrete, and measurable activity or action that requires organized team or unit performance and leads to accomplishment of the task to a defined standard."[10] These tasks often come from or are derived from task lists, such as the Universal Joint Task List maintained by the U.S. Joint Chiefs of Staff.[11] Services often have their own lists, such as the Army Universal Task List.[12] TRADOC Pamphlet

350-70-1, "Training Development in Support of the Operational Training Domain," provides an excellent guide to the development of training tasks. Each task needs to specify the conditions—for example, identifying the situation and describing the operational environment in which the team or unit should be able to perform the task to standard—with the standard criteria for determining the minimum acceptable level of task performance under operating conditions.[13] Analytic wargaming practitioners will recognize that the operational environment described simply presents the details that the wargame's scenario needs to represent. To allow the wargame to assess if the standards have been achieved, the other two principal components of measurement space—data and methods, models, and tools—need to be designed to allow for this assessment. The DCMP we use for analytic wargames, with minor modifications, allows for the creation of a solid, rigorous foundation for a training wargame using the task, condition, standard construct discussed. We recommend the use of the DCMP specified in annex C, appendix 3, of ABCA Publication 354, *Operational Assessment of ABCA Exercises and Experiments*.[14]

To truly test the training wargame's efficacy, you can plan to conduct both pre- and post-wargame surveys with the players to see if any training proficiency can be attributed to the wargame. As with any training simulation, care needs to be taken to design a wargame that rewards sound decisions and penalizes poor ones. Wargames that have excessive randomness or that are not careful with abstractions of lesser but still important details can inadvertently provide "negative training" by rewarding poor decisions and/or penalizing good decisions. This can be particularly challenging when designing training wargames with new or future technologies or concepts, as innovative decisions or creative uses of new technologies may be hard to accurately represent or assess. This points to the need for extensive play-testing of training wargames to ensure constructs that might impart negative training are identified and eliminated.

EDUCATIONAL WARGAMING

Traditional wargaming at U.S. DoD educational institutions has waned or morphed as computer simulations, often mistakenly thought to have replaced wargaming, were inserted into the curriculum. Wargaming events such as the capstone wargame that all students played at the Naval War College in the years leading up to World War II are making a comeback in the curricula at many DoD professional military education institutions as they revisit the role of wargaming in military education.

Educational wargames also have roles outside of educational institutions. Wargames exploring new operating environments and new threat technologies, force structures, and doctrine can be used to help commands and staffs begin their intellectual engagement on new missions that should continue as that command begins to create concepts of operations, courses of action, and plans to prepare.

Foundation for an Educational Wargame

Since an educational wargame is meant to impart learning to a player rather than producing data for analysis, the analytic wargame DCMP, at first glance, does not seem relevant. However, the structure that the DCMP provides for an analytic wargame can easily be leveraged for an educational wargame. Instead of building a DCMP around a sponsor's key issues, an educational wargame should build the game's foundation around the learning objectives that the wargame needs to impart to its players. Instead of producing analysis data, each learning objective should specify the knowledge that it is meant to convey to the players.

PLAY-TESTING EDUCATIONAL AND EXPERIENTIAL WARGAMES

Properly planned and designed educational and experiential wargames should impart new knowledge or provide valuable experiences to the players. Pre- and post-wargame surveys are frequently used to assess their success in doing so. Both the wargame and the surveys need to be tested before the wargame is conducted, and the best practice of conducting a blind play-test can pay big dividends in this regard. Be sure that the players you choose for this blind play-test are a good representation of the players the wargame is actually targeting. Test the pre- and post-wargame surveys on these players. After action reviews can also be used as a secondary collection tool, but we do not recommend them as either the sole or even the primary method of collecting assessment feedback.

In some cases, wargames can serve more than one purpose. Educational and experiential wargames can provide analytic insights as the players begin to realize unique aspects of the scenario's region and/or adversary capabilities that point to new concepts and/or technologies that could be incorporated into the existing force structure to make it more competitive or render the adversary less capable. Identifying these potential new concepts or technologies is an analytic insight that could also suggest an issue to be examined in a future analytic wargame. However, capturing these analytic insights will require some data collection process above and beyond the constructs designed to assess training or knowledge transfer. After action reviews with players may provide such a method. In the series of planning wargames suggested below, it is easy to see how an educational wargame that focuses on mission analysis can also produce analytic insights about force composition that could inform the composition of the forces being examined in the COA analysis.

SERIES OF WARGAMES FOR THE DOD PLANNING PROCESS

The DoD planning process presents opportunities for planners to leverage analytic, educational, and experiential wargames.[15] The traditional use of analytic wargames to conduct step four of figure 4, COA analysis, can be prefaced by an educational wargame for steps one and two to initiate and conduct mission analysis for the planning process. Having the commander and primary staff play in an educational wargame to learn about a new operational area or adversary will help the planning team visualize and internalize the commander's intent since their sponsor for their COA wargame, the commander, will better understand the challenges that need to be addressed in the plan, resulting in more distinct and relevant mission guidance. Once the COA wargaming and analysis are complete and a COA is chosen, an experiential wargame can be conducted with the commander and staff to flesh out the details of how the commander wants to execute the chosen COA, which would then be incorporated into the actual operations order.

TRAINING EXERCISES: WARGAMES OR NOT?

Any discussion of military wargaming inevitably brings up exercises, which are often referred to (albeit incorrectly) as wargames. Peter Perla's definition of wargaming in *The Art of Wargaming* included the phrase "whose operation does not involve the activities of actual military forces."[16] We interpret the dropping of that caveat in Perla's later wargaming definitions as a tacit acknowledgment that in *some* events where actual military forces are used, that event may also be considered a wargame. We also want to acknowledge that one of the many virtues of wargaming is an ability to gain key insights on the execution of pending or potential military operations *without* the huge resource investment of deploying and maneuvering large numbers of personnel and equipment. The U.S. Army has a list of exercise types that commanders may utilize for various training purposes, and some can be considered wargames, and some are not. These training exercises are developed using a Mission Essential Task List (METL) that forms the basis of the exercise design.[17] Regardless of whether the exercise is considered a wargame, the procedure of using the DCMP to track tasks, conditions, and standards for a training wargame can also be used to ensure any training exercise has a solid foundation and can be adequately evaluated. The Army regulation governing exercises directs senior commanders to:

1. Evaluate exercise performance to (a) measure the attainment of exercise objectives, (b) detect deficiencies and voids in procedures and doctrine, (c) determine requirements for developing concepts of operation, (d) assess capability to perform wartime missions.
2. Record the results of evaluation.
3. Track issues recorded in after action reports and meet requirements for post-exercise joint reporting.
4. Correct deficiencies within command or agency capabilities.
5. Apply lessons learned to future training.[18]

For item 1(a), "Evaluate exercise performance to measure the attainment of exercise objectives," we recognize that the DCMP can be used to list and roster the exercise objectives as well as specify measurement criterion. Similarly, item 2, "record the results of evaluation," speaks to the need to create a method of collecting data—again, the DCMP. Columns can easily be added to the DCMP to address items 3 (tracking issues) and 4 (annotating the status of deficiency correction). Finally, item 5, "apply lessons learned to future training," brings to mind the design-develop phases of analytic wargaming in that lessons learned from the execution of an exercise, much like lessons learned from a wargaming play-test, should be used in the design of the next iteration of the training exercise.

We next review some common exercise types to assess if they could be considered wargames. In the command post exercise (CPX), the forces are simulated, involving the commander and the staff, and communications within and between headquarters.[19] A CPX is an example of an exercise that does not deploy large numbers of troops but instead exercises commanders' and staffs' ability to command and control simulated formations in a realistic environment. But is a CPX a wargame? By the wargaming definition we use, there needs to be an active, thinking adversary for a CPX to be classified as a wargame. Many CPXs have a scripted set of events, often derived from a METL, that drives the exercise instead of human players representing a thinking, adaptive adversary; such CPXs are not wargames. The goal or objective of most CPXs is to provide a venue for a unit's commander and staff to train and increase their planning, coordination, and synchronization proficiency for conducting operations. It is possible to garner insight into how commanders will fight or employ new equipment or doctrine, but this is typically not the focus of a CPX.

Another training event is the rehearsal of concept drill. Rehearsals are used to give commanders and staffs a better understanding of key elements of an existing plan, including the concept of operations, control measures, decision points, and command and support relationships.[20] For most rehearsals, the adversary is not explicitly represented, as the plan was developed and previously wargamed against a specific threat COA; thus, rehearsals without an active adversary are not considered to be wargames. It is possible to gain insights into the COA from a rehearsal of concept drill if the players are provided more freedom in discussions during the process.

In a map exercise, a facilitator gives a series of military situations to the players, who solve them on a map. If the series of military situations is scripted, such as one derived from a METL, then it likely is not a wargame. If an active adversary or OPFOR commander is reacting to each situation that a friendly commander is solving, then it could be considered a wargame. A map exercise could easily become a wargame if the students developed a solution that is then fought out on the map using a free Kriegsspiel-type wargame with an active adversary.

A field training exercise (FTX) simulates combat conditions in the field and emphasizes command and control at all levels in battle functions using actual and simulated forces.[21] The U.S. Army directs that its FTXs employ a realistic OPFOR using the doctrine, tactics, matériel, and weapons systems of potential adversaries.[22] If this is done, the FTX would be considered a wargame for those participants who were making decisions and reacting to actions taken by a thinking adversary.

The best litmus test to assess if a given training exercise is a wargame might be found in a quote from the U.S. Navy's wargaming pioneer, Capt. William McCarty Little: "Now the great secret of its power lies in the existence of the enemy, a live vigorous enemy in the next room waiting feverishly to take advantage of any of our mistakes, ever ready to puncture any visionary scheme, to haul us down to earth."[23] The existence of such an enemy indicates the exercise is indeed a wargame.

CHAPTER 15

Best and Worst Practices

■ ■ ■ ■

This chapter will examine some of the more common worst practices of analytic wargaming through the lens of the five phases of wargame design (initiate, design, develop, conduct, and analyze) that we have seen from our more than seventy years of combined wargaming experience. Wargames can fail for myriad reasons, and we do not claim to cover them all. Wargame failures occur because of actions taken or not taken during each of the five phases, and some of the most common and egregious failures will be examined, along with the best practices that, if followed, would likely prevent such failures.

INITIATE PHASE

The initiate phase is where the sponsor and the wargaming team should reach an agreement on the objective and key issues that the wargame will address. The three worst practices we discuss are creating a wargaming team without analysts, failure to finalize and agree on the problem definition with the sponsor, and failure to scope the wargame.

Forming the Core Wargaming Team without Analysts

An analytic wargame needs analysts on the wargaming team. For a large wargame, we recommend that the team have both a design and an analysis group. Analysts are excluded from the wargaming design process for many reasons. Often, analytic organizations are not collocated with the organization that has been tapped to produce the wargame. A prime example is the Army's annual Title X wargame Unified Quest. The tasking to produce the wargame belongs to the U.S. Army Training and Doctrine Command (TRADOC) Army Capabilities and Integration Center based at Fort Eustis, Virginia. The TRADOC analysts are based at Fort Leavenworth, Kansas. Like DoD, many of our allies concentrate their analysts in analysis-focused organizations and have few or no analysts collocated with military units that often require analysis support. Thus, warfighter-centric events that need analysis support require prior coordination and may require resourcing to support travel for planning, workshops, and the execution of the event.

"Out of sight, out of mind" might be the phrase that describes this phenomenon, but sometimes it isn't a simple oversight. Analysts naturally want to bring more analytical structure to wargames, and that usually adds time to the wargaming design process. From our experience, organizations that do not make the up-front commitment to developing this analytical structure tend to create wargames that do not adequately address the sponsor's objective and issues. So not inviting the analysts can be seen by warfighters or other non-analysts as a way to avoid what they believe is unnecessary complexity. Sometimes, the analysts are invited at the eleventh hour to analyze a wargame that has not been designed to produce the data necessary for the analysis. There can be a tainted "reward" for such a maneuver: the event's findings will have the analyst's fingerprints on them, allowing the perpetrators to add unwarranted credibility (the analyst organization's "seal of approval") to results from a shoddily designed wargame. This happened at one of the Unified Quest wargames prior to 2006 that was focused on the ongoing counterinsurgency fight in Iraq, and the primary task was to analyze how well the force could conduct irregular warfare. The analysts asked for the current definition of irregular warfare; they were told that it was still being worked out but that they should analyze it anyway!

Analysts who are too comfortable at their home station bear some of the blame for wargames that lack the appropriate analysis support. For the wargame analyst who isn't physically located with the rest of the wargaming team, frequent travel, video teleconferences, and phone conversations may be required to ensure the wargame is designed with the necessary rigor. In these cases, the analyst needs to be persistent in order to remain involved in the design process for a remote wargaming event.

Best Practice: Wargaming Team
Analysts need to be included on the wargaming team. For large wargaming teams, it may be useful to have both a design and an analysis group, but it is not as if all the tasks the wargaming team needs to accomplish can be neatly binned. These groups need to interact frequently and coordinate most if not all of their efforts. For large wargaming teams, we recommend that an analyst serve in the design group to help ensure the wargame can produce the information the DCMP requires. This has two immediate benefits: first, the analyst will understand the impact the wargame's design will have on producing required feedback and analysis data as per the DCMP (which the designers may be ignoring), and second, the analyst gets some professional development on how the design team goes about creating a wargame. We also recommend a non-analyst serve in the analysis group to ensure that the sponsor's issues are well understood and properly represented in the analyst-developed DCMP and to obtain professional development by seeing how analysts translate the sponsor's issues into the foundation of the wargame.

Failure to Agree on the Problem Definition with the Sponsor

Agreeing on the wargame's objective and issues is simply problem definition, and on the surface it sounds so simple that students often ask, "Is problem definition really a challenge?" As Peter Perla points out, "Often the sponsor's goals will be unclear."[1] Sponsors who are extremely busy may provide only top-level guidance and might not be available for any subsequent attempt to clarify or scope the problem definition, so wargaming teams are often left to work through staff members who may or may not have a good idea of the sponsor's actual intentions. Wargaming teams sometimes attempt to run with a poorly defined problem for a variety of reasons: assuming the sponsor knows what they are asking for, reluctance to confront a sponsor when their objective and issues are unclear, or a willingness to accept a poorly defined problem so the wargaming team has leeway to steer the wargame in a direction that minimizes their effort. Sometimes sponsors may ask for something that a wargame simply cannot deliver because they are not aware of the capabilities and limitations of wargaming, or they confuse wargaming with quantitative studies best completed using closed-form models and simulations.

For organizations that don't want to or have not learned how to do analytic wargaming, the substitute that those tasked with doing a wargame sometimes employ is a BOGGSAT (bunch of guys and gals sitting around a table). The recipe for this check-the-block "wargame" goes something like this: The sponsor asks for a wargame on a particular topic but without much specificity. Instead of engaging the sponsor to make sure key issues are illuminated, recorded, and addressed, the wargaming team runs with the sponsor's vague problem statement because they know almost any answer they come up with will fit the problem statement. The team then dusts off an applicable scenario, convenes the preselected player team in a convenient conference room, appoints a "facilitator," and kicks off the BOGGSAT. Once the facilitator runs out of questions, the laptop comes out, and each player is asked, "What did you learn about [the vague problem statement]?" If the assembled players are fairly clever and know the sponsor's predispositions and pet peeves, they can come up with "findings" that they know will resonate with the sponsor. The players' comments are then assembled into a final report and fed back to the sponsor—block checked, mission completed.

BOGGSATs occur for a variety of reasons, and it isn't always the wargaming team trying to shirk its duties. If a command does not understand how analytic wargames are created and conducted, then sponsors will not provide adequate guidance or the proper resources (usually time and personnel) needed for sponsor–wargaming team interactions and game design and development. Unreasonable timelines for conducting wargames set conditions that preselect the BOGGSAT as the only wargaming "technique" that will allow the topic to be "addressed" within the meager time allotted. If the wargaming team has never been educated on how to conduct an analytic game, a BOGGSAT may be the only wargaming technique that they have experienced, and it becomes the template that provides the roadmap that is followed ("this is the way we've always done it"). For organizations where BOGGSATs are the norm, a wargaming team doing its due diligence will need to first educate the sponsor organization so it understands the advantages in problem structuring/definition and analytical insights into their problem that can be gained by conducting a proper analytic wargame. The analytical process of designing these wargames tends to offer the organization a clearer understanding of the actual problem and issues it is facing and better insights into how to proceed in resolving these issues or a clear roadmap for additional analytical efforts to address them. In most cases, it comes down to sponsor–wargaming team communication, and there is no substitute for the wargaming team building a solid relationship with the wargaming sponsor and agreeing to the problem definition.

Best Practice: Sponsor Contract
We adopted the concept of the sponsor contract from the U.S. Naval War College. When the wargaming team and the sponsor have completed the sponsor engagement process and agree on the objective and the key issues to address, they sign a formal agreement that specifies what the wargame will address, which often includes the key constraints, limitations, and assumptions of the effort. While no document can ever prevent mission creep, this contract lets the sponsor know that what both parties have agreed on can be accomplished in the time provided. Should the sponsor (or anyone else) wish to insert additional issues or add constraints, the sponsor contract provides the starting point to re-open the scoping process to either obtain more resources or drop some of the issues agreed to in the original contract.

Failure to Scope the Wargame

If a wargame has not been properly defined, it cannot be scoped, so the scoping problem is compounded when the wargaming team fails to first define what the wargaming problem is. In this case, the wargaming team will be in trouble because the problem is so vague that they will not know what resources will be needed to complete the task, making scoping impossible.

However, properly defined wargames are sometimes not scoped when they need to be. This can happen for several reasons. It can occur when a sponsor is unrelenting and wants every issue addressed in full without providing the additional resources the wargaming team needs. When this happens, the team has some limited options that need to be exercised with caution. A known sponsor priority for the issues can help the team decide how to scope the wargame's design. The wargame can be refocused to address the top-priority issues with the most detail and then address the lower priority issues with a less rigorous treatment. It is important to address every key issue to some degree, but the prioritization allows the team to apportion resources appropriately. Research may reveal that some of the sponsor's key issues have already been addressed in other wargames or studies, so recording (and properly attributing) these results in the wargame's final report may be a suitable alternative to addressing the issues in the wargame. Lower priority issues can also be addressed outside of the actual playing time for the wargame, using survey instruments or during the key player interviews. Other less preferable options include a balanced treatment of all issues but addressing few or none with the appropriate rigor, or dropping, against the sponsor's wishes, issues believed to be the lowest priority. Neither of these last options are particularly good ones.

Failure to scope also happens when the wargaming team is reluctant to tell the sponsor the wargame needs to be scoped. This is simply a failure of the wargame's leadership. The wargaming team has to be frank with the sponsor in order to meet the sponsor's needs, and bad news gets worse with age. The biggest problem with this is that the wargaming team rather than the sponsor will now have to decide the prioritization and level of treatment that each of the sponsor's key issues will receive. Why attempt to divine the sponsor's intent when a thirty-minute conversation will eliminate all doubt?

Best Practice: Scoping
Scoping techniques are described in detail in chapter 6; however, prior sponsor education may help to mitigate challenges with scoping. Tell the sponsor that three sponsor engagements, including a scoping engagement, are needed in order for the wargaming team to be successful. This plants the idea in the sponsor's mind that scoping will be necessary. And if the problem is such that no scoping is required, no harm has been done. If the team approaches the sponsor with a schedule of wargaming events that includes three sponsor engagements, subsequent in-progress reviews, a schedule of

play-tests, the final rehearsal, and the days of actual wargaming play, the sponsor should get the impression that the wargaming team is organized and professional, and the sponsor will be more willing to accept the team's recommendations on scoping and any other matters that need sponsor approval.

DESIGN PHASE

The design phase is where the wargaming team uses the initial draft of the DCMP as the foundation on which to construct the wargame's measurement space. The primary worst practices are symmetric or simplistic adversary representation, designing a wargame without a DCMP, failing to plan for contingencies, improper balancing of realism and playability, and constricted measurement space.

Symmetric or Simplistic Adversary Representation

This is one of the most frequent and egregious worst practices we see in DoD, especially in planning wargames. If you do not represent the adversary accurately, your wargame's results are essentially useless, and you have wasted your and the players' time. However, we often see combatant commands using a scripted threat or having an intelligence officer standing by to guess how the adversary might react to a certain event. Or they may just recruit an experienced U.S. military officer to step in and "play Red." After all, war is war, isn't it? Fortunately, some of our CCMDs are realizing that they cannot conduct any useful planning unless they invest time, effort, and resources into learning how their potential adversaries think and act. The DoD's regional CCMDs that face our two near-peer threats understand this. Indo-Pacific Command stood up a Chinese strategic focus group in 2012 to better understand that nation's perspective and perceptions with respect to the United States.[2] European Command stood up a Russia strategic initiative in 2016 to better predict Russian behavior and avoid surprises such as the Russian annexing of Crimea.[3]

Best Practice: Representing Adversaries
When you begin to design your wargame, you should learn as much as you need to about the adversaries so that you can accurately depict their

actions in your wargame. If you need to represent China or Russia, go to the above-mentioned CCMDs and seek to leverage their expertise. Player recruitment should also actively seek out the proper expertise to play in the wargame, as well as subject matter experts as they are needed. Our planners need to ensure our war plans have been tested against a dynamic, thinking, culturally accurate adversary so that our armed forces are prepared for what they could face when those plans have to be executed. Contrary to the guidance in JP 5-0 about COA wargaming, planners should consider having an experienced post-command officer command the adversary instead of a member of the intelligence staff section. Instead, have an intelligence officer act as the commander's deputy so the commander's basic warfighting skills can be combined with the intelligence officer's unique knowledge of the adversary.

Designing a Wargame without a DCMP

By now you realize that the DCMP is the foundation of an analytic wargame, so we hope it seems infeasible to design a wargame without one. Sadly, it is done all the time. We've already talked about the BOGGSAT that often occurs when the perpetrators either don't have the time to do a useful wargame, or they already know what the boss wants to hear and can steer the assembled players toward what they believe is the sponsor's preferred solution.

Analytic wargames can also be produced without DCMPs when the wargaming team does not know better. Required wargaming education in our military education programs is sparse, and most of the courses that can be taken don't teach wargaming design. Without any wargaming education on the five phases of analytic wargaming, teams use either constructs they have seen in the past or ones they find in doctrinal pamphlets or hobby games, or they otherwise improvise.

Best Practice: DCMP—Foundation of a Wargame's Design

The DCMP forms the bones upon which a wargame's design is fleshed out. A well-crafted DCMP provides the wargame designers a roadmap from the sponsor's key issues to the wargaming events and interactions that the designers need to create. The DCMP also provides an in-game progress reporting system that allows data collectors to understand what analysis data has been collected and DCMP gaps that indicate required analysis data that has not yet been collected. Forming the draft DCMP beginning with essential questions is described in chapter 6, and the design process is discussed in chapter 7. The DCMP is a living document that will likely require updating with every play-test and redesign.

Failing to Plan for Contingencies

Wargaming teams that are overly arrogant or ignorant may go into the wargame believing that it will go off exactly as planned, but this rarely happens. Typically, the wargame will be taken off track at some point and will grind to a halt. Players, data collectors, facilitators, and the white cell will all be wondering what to do next. The unprepared wargaming team will then have to scramble to steer the wargame back where it needs to go.

Best Practice: Plan for Contingencies

While not every wayward path can be anticipated, thorough play-testing, especially blind play-testing, can help identify critical junctures at which players could take the wargame in unexpected directions. Multiple blind play-tests provide a great opportunity to learn about your wargame and refine its rules and procedures. Recruiting experienced wargamers as players for a blind play-test can pay huge dividends. Experienced wargamers should be encouraged to try to break your game so you can learn and repair any obvious paths to game derailment that they find. Knowledge about key players often helps, as other wargaming teams may have some recent experience with one or more of your players. The staff of senior players may be able to make you aware of hot-button topics or pet peeves that will trigger the player.

Play-test your white cell's capability to respond to contingencies. The white cell needs to be able to create assumptions to thwart unproductive paths and injects to steer the wargame back on track.

Reality versus Playability

While all wargames need to be realistic enough to be believable, a balance between realism and playability must be struck when designing a wargame. Designers need to be cognizant of the scale or level of the military operation—strategic, operational, or tactical—and the roles of the players in their wargame and attempt to only focus on the necessary level of data and information. For example, if the players are representing the staff of a joint task force, there is no need for them to be diving into data at the unit level. These are the types of information and activities you should capture in combat results tables or other MMTs. More detail and complexity are often needed to make wargames more realistic; however, the more complex the wargame becomes, the larger the rule set gets.

Large rule sets can lead to players struggling with the decisions they have to make, becoming hesitant to make any decision because they do not fully understand how your wargame is designed to work or what their options are. Large rule sets will mean that each turn of your wargame will take a fair amount of time, and adjudication will often be more complex. Your wargame will need to cover many key issues, so it will be necessary for the lead to balance the appetite of the team to add more realism when the marginal return for that realism may be small. Unnecessary realism occurs when wargame designers either decide to explicitly represent phenomena in great detail that could be represented much more simply while producing similar effects, or choose to represent phenomena that add little to no value to achieving the ultimate objective of the wargame. Often the design team thinks this unnecessary realism is required, only to discover through play-testing that the realism either could be represented much more simply or has no significant effect on the wargame's outcomes. In many of these cases, the phenomena can be simplified by developing an implicit representation. A simple example is representing close air support (CAS) in support of ground operations where the wargame's focus is on the capability of the ground combat forces. You can explicitly represent CAS aircraft, friendly and enemy air defenses and fighter cover, and have a portion of a wargaming turn devoted to determining which CAS aircraft are interdicted before they make it to their target; then, of the surviving aircraft, which ones are affected by enemy air defenses; and then, after assessing the impact of air defenses, determining which aircraft would successfully engage the target and what the effects of CAS munition were that struck a particular enemy unit. An alternative is to implicitly model the effects of CAS by assuming that for every X CAS sorties, Y percent will survive enemy aircraft and air defenses and Z percent will successfully engage their targets, resulting in W percent of enemy ground combat power lost. So the player chooses the number of CAS sorties and enemy targets, consults a look-up table, and then determines the ground combat power decrement.

Best Practice: Reality versus Playability
Frequent play-testing is the key to discovering the appropriate balance between realism and playability. Wargames that are never play-tested almost always get bogged down in unnecessary detail, making them take too long to play and missing opportunities to cover more issues or to cover issues in greater depth. Several play-tests may be necessary to get the proper balance. A blind play-test using experienced wargamers and concluding with a specific after action review (AAR) that solicits their comments on playability and realism will produce useful insights on the wargame's design for the wargaming team.

Constricted Measurement Space

We recall that measurement space has three principal components: scenario, data, and MMTs. The wargaming team needs to create a measurement space that allows the players to explore all of the sponsor's key issues. Most wargames focused on the future are looking to assess new technologies, concepts, or capabilities. The measurement space is too constricted when the players are not able to make decisions that will allow the wargaming team to adequately assess those technologies, concepts, or capabilities important to your sponsor within your wargame. Examples include a scenario that does not have the terrain that stresses a particular capability, a lack of data to represent the qualities of a new technology, or an MMT that does not have the precision to discern any differences in alternate representations of technologies or weapons systems. Scenario deficiencies often occur because a wargaming team is forced to use a particular scenario that may not be well suited to the wargaming problem the sponsor has communicated. In DoD, there are specific classified planning scenarios that must be used for analysis, and often sponsors specify their use in wargames or other analytic studies to comply with DoD requirements.

Another reason for a constricted measurement space rests with the wargaming team's choice of MMTs. Organizations that routinely do wargaming may have a suite of MMTs that have been used for past wargames, and the temptation exists to continue to use the same MMTs because they worked well for the last wargame. Of course, this ignores the principle to design the wargame to the current sponsor's objective and issues, which may be totally different than the objective and issues for the last sponsored wargame that the organization did. The Army's Unified Quest wargame, conducted by TRADOC, had looked at kinetic, NATO–Warsaw Pact conflicts for many years, incorporating a suite of combat simulations to adjudicate combat outcomes. A member of the Unified Quest team during that time came back to TRADOC as a senior leader about a decade later and wanted the team to go find all those combat simulations he used to use so they could do Unified Quest the way he remembered. The problem was that the wargame was now looking at counterinsurgencies in Iraq and Afghanistan, and those simulations were of little or no value in representing the current challenges that it needed to address.

The challenge with data is ongoing; representing newly fielded or future weapons systems requires some projection and guesswork, and sometimes the data is not precise enough to be used to compare and contrast new, future, and existing technologies.

Best Practice: Expanding Measurement Space

In DoD, excursions to DoD-approved scenarios are usually allowed, so the wargaming team may need to be creative and expand a scenario to allow all the key issues to be thoroughly examined. This can be done within the context of the mandated scenario by designing vignettes that specify different forces, or another scenario may be used. In any case, these adaptations need to be vetted with and approved by the sponsor.

The wargaming team should carefully examine the issues that need to be examined and the attributes of the systems and technologies that need to be portrayed in the wargame before looking for an existing MMT that "could" model the required attributes. Adapting an existing MMT can take significant resources and will require new data to be developed. Developing your own MMT also will be challenging, will require resources, and will need some independent validation (as will any new behavior instantiated in an existing MMT). The key is for the team to first understand what needs to be represented before reaching for an off-the-shelf software solution that may take months and significant resources to adapt to the requirements.

Data is often the long pole in the tent for new technologies and weapons system prototypes. The creation of useful and verifiable data is always a challenge. If the sponsor wants future technologies or weapons systems that do not yet have a prototype, there will be no test data available, so the team will have to do some research and likely will need the sponsor's help in developing projections for the required data. Even if test data is available for a newly fielded system, care needs to be taken to ascertain that the data is an accurate representation of the system's capabilities. Acquisition program managers will be quick to forward favorable test data, while pessimistic test data may be held back for further study and scrutiny.

DEVELOP PHASE

Wargame development is the process that informs the wargame design by play-testing the latest design. To do development correctly, the developers need to attempt to "break" the wargame. The developers should thoroughly test each component of the wargame and the wargame in its entirety. The four primary worst practices in the development phase are failure to conduct any development, failure to conduct a blind play-test, failure to test MMTs, and failure to conduct a full rehearsal.

Failure to Conduct Any Development

Time is always a critical factor when creating a wargame. Because designing a wargame is challenging, wargaming teams tend to spend too much time attempting to create a detailed design before ever attempting to play-test it. The naive wargaming team may actually believe that their design will be perfect and work exactly as planned, skipping the development phase entirely. Or time may simply slip away while the team is still busily designing the wargame as the event approaches. This usually ensures failure, because if the wargaming team has spent a lot of time designing without play-testing, the design is likely to be complex. The more complexity a wargame's design has, the more play-testing it requires. No matter what the reason, skipping any development is a huge mistake. Your team's initial wargame design will have flaws, some of them showstoppers. You have to play the wargame to find its flaws.

Best Practice: Play-test Early and Often
We recommend that the team adopt a "one-third/two-thirds" rule and get the first design drafted to a playable form using only one-third of the allocated design-develop time. Keep it simple; it is much easier to create a playable wargame by starting with a simple design and adding detail than starting with a complex design that will require the elimination of extraneous or game-crippling details. We also recommend that the play-testers work quickly and return the play-test results to the design team quickly, with a goal of conducting at least three play-tests before the final rehearsal.

Failure to Conduct a Blind Play-test

So much is learned through a blind play-test that it is hard to imagine not conducting one, but wargaming teams routinely miss this opportunity. Play-testers who have helped design the game have a difficult time finding the wargame's flaws because they are too familiar with it. Remember that wargaming is an act of communication; the sole purpose of the wargame's rules and procedures is to communicate the wargame design to the players, and the effectiveness of the wargaming team's communication can only be assessed by outside players. In many cases, especially with wargames that have a fairly extensive or complex rule set, the designers know what the rules *should* say but do not, because no one has taken the time to update the rules and test them after a design-develop cycle. These flaws will be obvious to blind play-testers who will quickly come across situations not covered by the rules and procedures, or they will find contradictions in the rules. Keep in mind that most players, with the exception of power players who really get into wargaming, rarely read through all of the rules in the read-ahead material.

Frequent design flaws discovered by blind play-testers include gaps, inconsistencies, and imprecision in written rules and procedures; no written sequence of play for wargames that have several actions for each turn; situations requiring contingencies such as injects or vignettes; and gaps in the wargames design that will allow the players to take the wargame off track. The blind play-test gets a fresh set of eyes on the wargame design to test its robustness to players' unexpected actions and also provides a wonderful opportunity to see how well the team has communicated the rules and procedures that govern the wargame.

Best Practice: Blind Play-test
The best blind play-testers are those who will emulate the actual players or will at least have a similar background. Play-testers who are wargamers are also useful, as they may provide best practices on wargame mechanics that they have learned through experience. One or more members of the design team should be observing (but not directing) the blind play-test and recording where the design (to include rules and procedures) needs to be updated.

Failure to Test MMTs

MMTs can require a fair amount of overhead and can fail for so many reasons that the wargaming team should first consider if their use is worth the trouble. Naive wargaming teams often think that using a computer-based MMT is like using a coffeemaker. Just unplug it, tote it to the wargaming venue, and plug it back in. It should work just fine! MMTs may require network accessibility with precise connection requirements, and many computer-based simulations use classified data, so there may be several issues to be considered. One issue that is sometimes overlooked by planners and analysts is that the security conditions in their organizations may prevent or interfere with the use of computerized MMTs or that the computerized system may not work or unexpectedly crash.

Best Practice: Testing MMTs
The MMTs need to be tested at the actual wargaming venue, especially if they depend on network connectivity. Bringing all the hardware and software provides a better chance of success than having your software run on others' machines and network. Even if your MMT is something simple like an Excel spreadsheet, you still need to test it on the computers you will actually use for the wargame to ensure they have the same version of the software that you developed the MMT in, and that the machines have the appropriate permissions to allow your software to run. Do this several weeks before your wargame, especially if this is a critical component of the wargame. You do not want to discover the MMT will not function the night before your wargame starts!

You must ensure you have the proper expertise to run and troubleshoot the MMT. If the MMT takes a significant amount of time to produce results, you will need to build your wargame's schedule around the MMT's input-output capabilities. The time required to receive input and produce results needs to be discovered through a fully burdened play-testing.

You may be able to avoid bringing complex or resource-intensive MMTs to the wargaming venue at all. If the MMT's purpose is to provide adjudication, it may be run ahead of time to output a range of possible results so that hard-copy look-up tables can be used during the wargame instead of running the MMT as players wait for results.

You should always have a manual backup procedure ready in the event that your computer-based MMTs do not work correctly or the security situation prevents or interferes with their use.

Failure to Conduct a Full Rehearsal

As the time to conduct the actual wargame draws near, a full rehearsal needs to be scheduled and conducted. Full rehearsals are skipped for a variety of reasons: the venue is not available, the team runs out of time, key personnel are not available, and so forth.

Best Practices: Full Rehearsal

The purpose of this final play-test is to ensure the wargame will work the way it has been envisioned, so it is advisable that it be conducted at the actual wargaming venue. Full rehearsals should test every aspect of the wargame, including all MMTs and administrative and support functions, to the fullest extent possible.

All the aspects of the wargame, such as the data collection process and the adjudication tools, need to be tested at the scale and intensity that the actual wargame will require. We had a student wargaming team that was headed to San Diego to conduct the wargame at the sponsor's location, and only three of the four team members were able to travel. The team did a play-test at NPS that was only about half the scale of the actual wargame, yet the three students were in constant motion, running paper data slips and inputting moves into their spreadsheet adjudication tool. It was obvious to the instructors that they would need more personnel than the three students to keep the wargame flowing smoothly. A fully burdened play-test would have exposed this problem, and fortunately the instructors' experience substituted in this case. The three students, now armed with the knowledge that they needed to recruit and train additional data runners, were able to do just that from the staff in San Diego, and their wargame was a success.

The key aspects of a wargame that need to be tested include:

- Adjudication tools: Do they work, and do they work as planned?
- Data collectors: Are they trained, and do you have enough to ensure they don't get burned out collecting data for several hours? Have the data collection forms been tested to see if they are organized and have enough space to record decisions and their rationale, and have a place for any additional data collector observations? An AAR with the data collectors after a fully burdened play-test will usually reveal some good ideas for streamlining the data collection process and updating the data collection forms.
- Facilitation: Has the facilitator checked out the venue to understand where the key players will sit and whether there are lines of sight between the facilitator and players and between individual players?
- White cell: Has the white cell staff been trained and exercised? Are they prepared to develop contingencies on the fly and search for data to answer player requests?
- Administration: Have provisions been made for the in-processing of the players, cell phone collection, player break room, IT support, and food and coffee services?

CONDUCT PHASE

A good wargame design certainly helps keep the players on task, but worst practices still need to be anticipated. The three worst practices that occur during the wargame are failure to anticipate that some or all of the players will not be prepared to engage at the start of your wargame, failure of the wargame director to manage the wargame, and failure to properly end the wargame.

Unprepared Players

The wargaming team should plan for players who have not prepared to play the wargame. Unprepared players will be hesitant to make decisions, will take longer to make decisions, and will become frustrated if they believe that they would have made better decisions if they understood the wargame better. If read-ahead packets have not been sent out or were sent out but not read (which often happens with senior officials who handle real-world crises frequently), you will be dealing with unprepared players. If the rules and procedures for your wargame are fairly complicated, they will be hard for the players to grasp without seeing how the wargame actually works, and the players will arrive with questions. Wargaming teams should plan for unprepared players because it is almost guaranteed that each wargame will have several players who will require help getting up to speed.

Best Practice: Building Player Preparation into the Wargame
A good read-ahead packet can go a long way toward mitigating the problem of the unprepared player if the packet is well organized and produced. If you have a fairly complex rule set, you may include a sample turn or a short tutorial in the read-ahead that show how the rules and procedures are implemented within a turn of the wargame. By the way, it is a good idea to play-test your read-ahead packet by providing it to the players you recruit to conduct your blind play-test. If they have read and understood your read-ahead packet but still have many questions about the conduct of the wargame, your read-ahead may require some work. An AAR after your blind play-test should solicit player comments about your read-ahead.

Every wargame should start with an in-brief that reminds the players about the details of the scenario to include the road to war, the current state of the world, and the objective of the wargame. These in-briefs provide the unprepared player with an opportunity to get the top-level details that were contained in the read-ahead and gives those who have read it an opportunity to clarify any details that were missing or confusing.

The first turn of the actual wargame may need to be a practice turn, especially for complex or unique wargame designs. The idea of the practice turn is to get the players familiar with the way the wargame design uses the decisions that the players have been asked to make. At the end of the practice turn, every player should be confident about how their decisions will be used, what the boundaries of their decision spaces are, and what kind of feedback the wargame will provide that informs them of the effect that their decision had on the wargame.

Complex wargames may require that player guides be assigned to the players. These should include written player guides, how game turns occur, and the summary of critical rules and tables. You should not expect players in more complex wargames to have a complete understanding and remember these rules without some aid. These player guides help the player understand what decisions need to be made, what latitude the game rules provide for player actions, and what options a player has for a given situation. Player guides should have strict instructions about what they can and cannot provide. They do not exist to help the player "win" or provide an unfair advantage; they are there to ensure the player knows his or her options and understands what actions can be taken during a move. These player guides can be temporary—that is, only for the practice turn or for the first few turns—or they may be permanently assigned if the rules and procedures are so complex that the players will need help throughout the wargame. A data collector can also act as a player guide, but a workload assessment needs to be made to ensure both tasks can be completed without compromising the analytic data collection. If at all possible, you should protect your data collectors so they can focus solely on collecting the information you will need to answer the essential questions and issues. Understand the risks associated with their ability to collect data if you add any other duties to their primary role.

Failure to Manage the Wargame
Often, little consideration is given to the management of the wargame. For a small wargame or wargaming team, most of the team's time is focused on getting a playable wargame that will produce results, and the conduct of the actual wargame is only thought about as the day approaches. Often, it is assumed that the facilitator of the wargame also manages the wargame, and unless the wargame is small (fewer than ten players), the management aspect of the wargame will add an unwelcome and distracting burden to the facilitator. Large wargames need a dedicated director to ensure the players and the primary wargaming staff are focused on the wargame. We will loosely define the primary wargaming staff as those personnel who directly or indirectly interact with the players as the game is being executed, such as facilitators, the white cell, and data collectors.

Best Practice: Directing the Wargame
Wargames need a director who ensures that the wargame adheres to the schedule, produces the necessary analysis data, and functions smoothly with no undue distractions or interruptions. The bottom line for all types of analytic wargames is that the wargame needs to produce the feedback and analysis data specified in the DCMP, and anything that may detract from that needs to be minimized or eliminated by the wargame's director. The status of the DCMP needs to be closely monitored, and the wargame director may need to improvise if unexpected holes in the analysis data need to be filled. For large wargames, the director is a full-time job, so no other major role, such as facilitator, should be assigned. The director is in charge of everything that has an active part in the wargame's execution that the principal wargaming staff is not doing. This includes managing the data collectors, the control cell, the white cell, facilitators, analysts, and SME panels. VIPs need to be properly briefed and escorted, and other accommodations may need to be made depending on rank and seniority. Access to the wargaming venue may need to be controlled. Catering must happen on time. The duties of the wargaming director are not technical in nature, so the wargaming director does not need to be a member of the wargaming team. The director needs to understand how the wargame is constructed, how the wargame functions when it is being conducted, and most importantly, what the wargame needs to produce in terms of the analysis data. A simplistic definition of the director's duties is to keep the wargame progressing so that the players produce, and data collectors collect, all the feedback and analysis data required to address all of the sponsor's issues.

Ending the Wargame

Ending the wargame without revealing the emerging insights via the quick-look report is a worst practice that can often torpedo any of the wargame's analytic findings. If a finding is based on erroneous data (the data collector misunderstood the player, or subsequent discussions during the wargame reversed a finding), then the final analysis will be built upon a poor foundation, and the credibility of the entire wargame's analysis will be open to question.

Another worst practice is not providing an experienced facilitator to facilitate the quick-look report. While the intent of the quick-look report is to verify the analytic insights the analysis team has produced to date, some players may try to seize this as an opportunity to refight the wargame or perceive it as a platform to advocate for a position or opinion that they want to be heard. Having a strong facilitator to obtain the appropriate player feedback and reach consensus on disputed issues is crucial.

A related worst practice is relying on an AAR for the production and collection of analysis data. AARs are usually open-ended and typically ask the players to tell you what they learned. The analytic wargame is not designed to educate the players; it is designed to produce analytic data for subsequent analysis. While an AAR may be a good tool to gain insight into making the analytic wargame better (typically administrative or support issues), it should not be used to produce or update analytic data.

Best Practice: Ending the Wargame
Direct the analysts as they produce the preliminary findings that will be presented and reviewed during the quick-look report. When the analysts present the preliminary findings to the players, it is important for a skilled facilitator to be present to adjudicate the finalized preliminary findings that both the analysts and the players agree to. The facilitator ensures that the adjudication is resolving any disputes about the findings that relate to misunderstandings or improperly collected data and is not refighting the wargame. It is not unusual for players to attempt to spin reasons that they made certain decisions during the game or to try and have rulings or game adjudications overturned. If your players are senior officials, a strong facilitator will be needed to keep a lid on this kind of activity. This is not the purpose of the quick-look report.

Immediately after the quick-look report should be the player interviews. It is a best practice to have included the scheduled key player interviews well before the wargame started so there is no misunderstanding that these interviews are required. They should always be scheduled after the final turn but before the wargame is formally ended. The purpose for key player interviews is twofold. First, they provide the analyst one final opportunity to collect analysis data that was not produced during the wargame. Second, they allow the data collectors to better understand reasons behind the key decisions that were made during the wargame. In multiday wargames, it is a best practice to either schedule key player interviews at the end of each day or to have a daily quick-look report. Asking key players to provide their rationale for decisions that were made over a day ago is usually asking too much of them. It is often overlooked by planners and analysts, but a great best practice is to have players complete the interviews, surveys, and questionnaires prior to conducting the quick-look report, AAR, or hotwash. This will enable you to gather their independent views untainted by the group discussion.

Last-move madness is a real effect for many wargames with a defined number of turns or a time limit. Many players become so immersed or engrossed in the wargame that they really want to "win." The tendency on the last turn is for these individuals to go for broke and attempt anything, no matter how wild, unlikely, or uncharacteristic, on this final turn to win the wargame. A best practice for this is to end the wargame earlier than the players expected. This can be achieved by not letting the players know how many turns there are in the wargame or by ending it one turn earlier than announced by the wargaming team. The first approach of having an expressed open-ended number of turns is less disruptive to the players' planning process and is typically easy for the players to accept. Ending the wargame one turn earlier than announced may receive some complaints in the quick-look report that the players were in the process of setting up a devastating attack that would occur on the last turn. From an analytical point of view, this is likely more acceptable than the potential of a wild action on the final turn.

ANALYSIS PHASE

It is virtually impossible to capture everything that can or might go wrong during a wargame. However, there are a couple of worst practices to watch out for in the analysis phase. The three worst practices that occur are failure to crosswalk findings to the sponsor's issues, failure to recruit SMEs to augment the analysis team, and failure to vet the final draft with stakeholders.

The analysis of a wargame will be affected adversely by any of the worst practices that occurred during the previous four phases, so it is important when the wargaming team is making choices that might save time (for example, skipping a play-test or not training data collectors) to consider how the analysis may be affected. For this discussion, we assume that none of the earlier worst practices occurred.

Failure to Correlate Findings to Sponsor's Issues

A worst practice that often occurs in wargames is producing an analysis report that fails to adequately address some of the sponsor's key issues. This usually happens when dominant personalities in the wargame bring out additional issues they think are of primary importance or place too much importance on one or two key issues, and the analysis team unwittingly begins to refocus the analysis. While the quick-look report provides the players a voice in the wargame's analysis, the players should not be allowed to hijack the process or the findings.

Best Practice: Addressing All the Sponsor's Issues
A properly completed DCMP ensures that the wargaming team can address all the sponsor's issues, since all the feedback and analysis data collected during the wargame can be traced back through sub-issues to the relevant key issues of the sponsor. This ensures that you have sufficient analysis data to synthesize into findings for each of the sponsor's key issues. One way to assist the quick-look report facilitator is to ensure the focus is on confirming analysis data that underpins the preliminary findings, not on readjudicating the wargame's outcomes. Structuring the quick-look report to include preliminary findings for each of the sponsor's key issues is a good first step to structuring the analysis of all the collected data. This starts the in-depth analysis on solid ground and sets the analysis team up for success with solid direction as they begin to dig through the collected data and start to synthesize results.

Failure to Recruit SMEs to Augment Analysis Team

Another worst practice is a failure to provide access to subject matter experts whose unique knowledge and experience are needed to verify or underpin some of the analysis findings.

Best Practice: Including the Appropriate SMEs in the Analysis Team
While analysts are skilled at decomposing issues, the ability to synthesize analysis data from essential questions to form higher-level insights often requires subject matter expertise that relates to the key issue the questions belonged to. Producing the analysis for a wargame examining future technologies will require that the analysis team have access to technology subject

matter experts. Cultural SMEs may be required for wargames focused on analyzing how a country's diverse population responds when interacting with foreign forces. A best practice is to anticipate these analytic requirements, and have the SMEs recruited, scheduled, and integrated into the analysis team for the post-wargame analysis.

Failure to Vet Final Draft with Stakeholders

The last worst practice that we discuss is failure to vet the final wargame report with the appropriate personnel. Analysts often think writing the final report is their job, and they provide the final word on the wargame's findings. However, the wargame is a collaborative effort, and the wargaming team should ensure that the report appropriately and accurately reflects all contributions.

Best Practice: Vetting the Final Report

The wargame's players and the stakeholders, including the sponsor, all provided some level of expertise and knowledge to the final product, and, much like with the quick-look report, these participants need to have a final say in the findings. Players and stakeholders need to be restricted to substantiation of the findings, not refighting the wargame, so the report needs to be firmly managed and deadlines set for responses and rebuttals. First, the final report should be vetted with the key players who produced the raw analysis data to ensure that the findings are consistent and accurate. Key stakeholders may also need to vet the report. Who has a final say in the report will be a function of the wargaming team's organization and the sponsor of the wargame, but just as with the quick-look report, the vetting of the final report will need firm leadership to ensure its findings are not hijacked by those pursuing other agendas.

APPENDIX 1

Practical Exercise Zefra Brief

■ ■ ■ ■

This appendix provides your tasking from the South Asia–Pacific Command (SAPCOM) J5. We have intentionally only included the tasking in this appendix but recognize that the reader may have forgotten the introduction to this crisis from chapter 5. We recommend that you first review the Zefra scenario in appendix 2 to get a full picture of what is currently happing in Capricornia.

Good morning. I am Colonel William "Bull" Schitter, the deputy J5 of the South Asia–Pacific Command. In less than thirty days, the United Nations [UN] Combined Joint Task Force [CJTF]–Zefra, led by Brigadier Joseph Brock, will land on Capricornia and start the mission to stabilize Zefra. Stabilizing Zefra is a goal that is shared by the UN and the United States. As you know, there are no U.S. forces in CJTF–Zefra, which is unfortunate because SAPCOM and the United States have a vested interest in a stable Zefra, and we stand ready to help stabilize Zefra if and when any of our assets are needed.

To that end, SAPCOM is deploying an Amphibious Ready Group–Marine Expeditionary Unit to stand ready off the coast of Capricornia. Its mission is to assist in restoring stability to Zefra. If CJTF–Zefra can restore stability in short order without any outside assistance, SAPCOM will stand by. If CJTF–Zefra needs assistance, we will provide any assistance required. However, we do not want to escalate any tension between the United States and China. Therefore, any U.S. assistance provided cannot be perceived as explicitly violating the terms of the UN resolution. That said, we will not remove any options from the table because if the UN mission should falter, then SAPCOM needs to be prepared to take any measures necessary to safeguard the peoples of the island of Capricornia.

SAPCOM needs you to conduct a wargame to examine what measures SAPCOM needs to be prepared to take. First, what assistance is CJTF–Zefra likely to need that SAPCOM can provide? I want you to look at nonintrusive assistance—that is, assistance that does not require U.S. boots on the ground. But I also want you to examine options that could require deploying U.S. forces on the island. Clearly these options will be sensitive, so this study needs to remain classified SECRET//NOFORN and Close Hold. Although we would like some basing options on the island, we know that Daloon is very hesitant to host any foreign military, so don't plan on SAPCOM forces having basing options in Daloon.

We will need an assessment of the CJTF-Z combat capability so we can better understand what capability and capacity gaps CJTF-Z will have against the most likely and the most dangerous activities that the situation in Zefra could present. Knowing these gaps will allow us to better understand what SAPCOM can do to enhance their chances of success and lessen their risk.

In particular, force protection will be critical for the task force commander, so looking at the force protection challenges that the TF commander will face is something that will be critical to know. We cannot ignore "whole of government" for this operation. There are medical and security requirements that are factors in stabilizing Zefra. Doctors without Borders [Médecins Sans Frontières (MSF)] operates both in Zefra and Daloon, and they appear to be understaffed and overwhelmed. What kind of assistance can either the UN TF or the SAPCOM TF provide to take better care of the refugees in the Daloon camps? Does SAPCOM have any unique medical capabilities that should be offered to MSF? We have a Navy hospital ship, USS *Comfort*, in Sydney harbor. Should we pre-position that for contingencies?

There is a private security company called TOKEN operating on Capricornia. It provides security services for the nuclear plants in Zefra, for MSF, and for the Chinese firm working the natural gas fields off the coast of Daloon. TOKEN's headquarters is in Macau, so they themselves are a Chinese organization. However, many of the actual TOKEN employees on the ground are ex-Special Operations Forces, mostly from Western nations. Knowing what TOKEN is up to and having TOKEN contacts on the ground on Capricornia, preferably in Zefra, would be useful. They have to make a profit, so there may be some way we can work with TOKEN on issues of mutual interest.

Intel reports that there may be nuclear waste that is missing from Zefran reactors. What are the most likely and most dangerous uses of this material by the Zefran Internal Security Bureau? What are the most likely and most dangerous uses of this material by the Truscan Peoples' Liberation Armed Militia?

There are unconfirmed reports of a rogue battalion that calls itself the Illustrious Fighters for Freedom [IFF]. It was formed by a former Zefran armed forces officer. We do not yet have a good intelligence estimate on this IFF battalion's strength or disposition; the SAPCOM J2 is working on this now. Refugee camps in Daloon were shelled with 120mm mortars last week, suspected to be from this battalion, so it is a safe bet this battalion sympathizes with the Bongos' cause. What kind of challenges does this force pose to bringing stability to Zefra? Can the UN TF handle it if it decides to insert itself in the stabilization process? What about our Marine expeditionary unit?

The People's Liberation Army Navy has a task force headed to Capricornia as well. What unique capabilities does this TF have that might be leveraged in Zefra?

We need to be careful about perception of U.S. involvement. Both the *New York Times* and *Al Jazeera* have offices on the island, and both have been actively reporting on the ongoing crisis. SAPCOM needs to be prepared for press involvement.

I need results in fourteen days. I cannot entertain questions at the present time. My action officer, Major John Payne, will provide you any assistance you need. Thank you, and good luck!

APPENDIX 2

Zefra Scenario

■ ■ ■ ■

The Zefra scenario is designed to provide you with enough background information to understand the situation in Zefra and to help construct your own wargame as part of the practical exercises in part II of the book. In addition, there is enough scenario background information to construct a more developed wargame for educating future planners and analysts. There is too much information here to provide a player—it will overwhelm the players.

The island of Capricornia lies in the Coral Sea of the South Pacific. In topography and climate, it seems like an idyllic South Seas paradise, but dig deeper and you will discover its challenges. Two independent and completely different nations share this island: Daloon in the south, and Zefra in the north. Each nation occupies roughly half of Capricornia; they share a common border and dependence on the island's scarce fresh-water resources, which are located in the border region. Both are relatively impoverished nations with very little in terms of natural resources or major economic activity.

Daloon, a former Spanish colony, gained its independence in 1947 and initially enjoyed relative political stability, although it faced significant economic challenges. It has a relatively homogeneous and stable population.

Defense treaties were maintained with Spain, and Daloon developed good relationships with other major powers. The major security challenge to Daloon comes from sharing the island with Zefra, a country whose history unfolded quite differently and one in which insurgency and internal strife were all too common.

Zefra was a French colony that was granted independence in 1951. It is a country dominated by a well-educated, Bongo-minority population. The Bongo population arrived in Zefra before the French in the seventeenth century. They were primarily traders and initially established a good relationship with the Truscans, who were already established in Zefra. Under French colonial rule, the Bongos gained stature as functionaries of the colonial government and developed as an entrepreneurial middle class. The Bongo population has dominated the central government and led economic development since independence. This dominance in government, the civil service, and the judiciary further alienated the Truscan population and led to a series of local uprisings across the country. An attempt to crush this resistance in the late 1990s had the effect of unifying the rebels into an opposition movement called the People's Liberation Movement (PLM). Associated with the development of the PLM was a parallel armed component called the People's Liberation Armed Militia (PLAM).

Zefra erupted in a civil war between 2002 and 2009. In Truscan-dominated areas of Zefra, the PLM enjoyed considerable popular support. With this, the PLAM was able to establish its control over significant areas of Zefra. However, the development of factions within the PLM limited its overall effectiveness. Internally, the PLAM was dominated by three major sub-groups, each forming around its own charismatic leader. Initially, these three sub-groups generally agreed on actions to be taken against the central governments. But the leaders of the three factions espoused different visions for the ultimate aim—namely some form of autonomous Truscan homeland. The internal divisiveness over ultimate aims sometimes led to uncoordinated and ineffective operations against government forces.

Reports of atrocities in the Zefran civil war became particularly gruesome in early 2007. When cellphone videos of these began appearing regularly in the evening news, the U.S. government decided that it would need to make a generous and well-intentioned attempt to settle issues in the country. A small force of Marines landed in eastern Zefra to help sort out the belligerents. The U.S. initiative ended in failure, and soon after the Americans withdrew, there were atrocities where the native supporters of the Americans killed a number of their fellow countrymen, claiming they were being maligned for having collaborated with the Americans (who were seen in some quarters of Zefra as an occupying force). Animosity continued after the end of the civil war when U.S. promises to help the Zefran economy proved illusory—during this time, the United States had its own economic problems to deal with. Nevertheless, the ill feeling in Zefra toward the United States continues to complicate matters to this day.

Meanwhile, the civil war in Zefra caused a substantial flow of refugees across the border into Daloon. Within their numbers, the refugees harbored Truscan insurgents who had come from Zefra and found safe havens for future action on the Daloon side of the border. Daloon, at this point, had a very immature security establishment with nascent armed forces and a very lightly armed border patrol. These resources were insufficient for Daloon to maintain effective control of its border with Zefra; nor were they able to stop insurgents, lodged within the safe havens of the refugee camps, from conducting operations from Daloon into Zefra.

In response to incursions by the insurgents, Zefra initiated a series of cross-border counterinsurgency penetrations into Daloon to deal with the insurgents' safe havens where the Daloon forces were seemingly impotent. Claiming the right of hot pursuit, the Zefran government of the day ignored diplomatic protests from Daloon and the international community, most notably from the European Union.

While ostensibly having the apprehension of the Zefran insurgents as their only objective, Zefran operations caused significant damage to local Daloon infrastructure and property. The levels of violence and its apparently indiscriminate application generated a substantial migration of internally displaced persons away from the border area. Many ethnic Truscans, when apprehended by Zefran forces in or near the refugee camps proximate to the border, were treated brutally, and there were allegations of rape, torture, and amputations by Bongo militia men who seemed barely under control of any leaders, let alone of their national government.

Over time, migrations of ethnic Truscans were generally pushing deeper into Daloon. In some respects, this just spread the violence and bloodshed, as Bongo-led Zefran irregular forces probed deeper and deeper into Daloon in pursuit of Truscan refugees, although the target was claimed to be only the insurgents who were hiding among the apparently innocent refugees.

Meanwhile, within Zefra, factions of PLAM were inflicting tremendous violence on seemingly peaceable Bongo neighbors in the border regions and elsewhere. PLAM spokesmen claimed that these Bongos were not what they seemed, and indeed alleged that many provided bases from which Bongo irregulars were crossing the border to attack the refugee camps in Daloon. By 2009 civilian casualties were rising quickly, with both Bongos and Truscans sharing responsibility for the butchery. At this point the United Nations (UN) High Commissioner for Refugees sought international condemnation for the atrocities on both sides, as well as commitments to separate the belligerents. Unfortunately in the early twenty-first century, Western nations had become embroiled in military operations in Afghanistan, Iraq, and Libya. In addition, they were still feeling the economic impact of the recession of 2008-9, so they were reluctant to commit precious resources to sort out yet another bloody mess.

In 2009 all parties to the violence in and near Zefra had exhausted themselves. Every party seemed to see some advantage in ending hostilities. Some of the parties saw it as a chance to reestablish norms of civil behavior and to seek a more peaceful environment for their children. But others saw it simply as a chance to rearm for the next time and to inculcate into a new generation fiery memories of the grievous harm that others had inflicted on their clans and tribes and a burning desire for revenge on the alleged perpetrators.

The civil war finally ended when the UN brokered a peace agreement that created an autonomous region under PLM/PLAM control within Zefra but adjacent to its border with Daloon. This agreement is credited with creating a period of relative calm that lasted for some years. In response, the government of Daloon sought to secure its borders. Several European nations provided some limited help to Daloon in the form of military training assistance teams and a small amount of surplus military equipment.

Within the international community were ongoing recriminations that too little had been done to help the people of Zefra. Thousands had died during the civil war, while the Western nations had seemingly been busy with their own problems. In the years after the Zefran civil war, evidence frequently emerged of mass graves on both sides of the border. These were found in proximity to the refugee camps in Daloon and initially were associated with the Zefran operations against the mainly Truscan insurgents within the camps. However, evidence also emerged that Truscans, probably associated with the insurgency, had committed heinous crimes in areas of Zefra that they controlled. Clearly, all sides in the matter had committed atrocities that showed this uncivilized and reprehensible behavior was widespread. The nations of the world pledged that the next time Zefra was in crisis, they would not stand idly by; they would do something.

BACKGROUND: SITUATION

Two independent nations share the island of Capricornia: Daloon in the south and Zefra in the north. The two are of about the same size and share a border that runs roughly east to west through the middle of Capricornia.

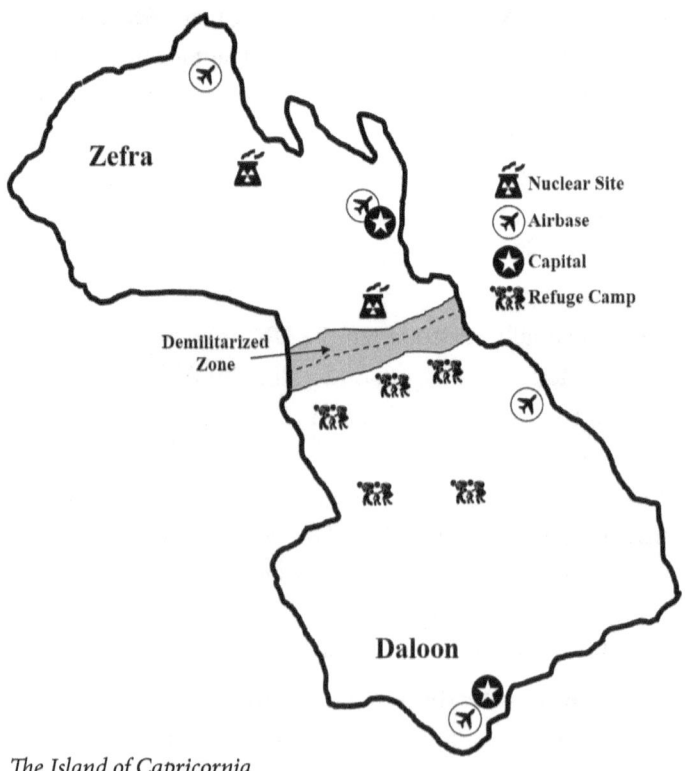

The Island of Capricornia

Violations of the UN Peace Agreement

The period of peace following the Zefran civil war was brief. By 2015 a more extremist central government was in control in Zefra and was prepared to violate the peace agreement by disbanding the autonomous region (established under UN auspices) and replacing it with three provinces. Almost immediately, the PLAM and other opposition groups began a protracted insurgency campaign against the Zefran central government. However, their overall effectiveness was hampered by infighting between the three dominant factions within the PLAM.

The Zefran government reacted with aggressive counterinsurgency action, but it failed to achieve a decisive victory. Meanwhile, the fighting had a tremendous humanitarian impact on the population in Zefra. Large segments of the Zefran population, mostly Truscan, fled to Daloon and to the major urban areas in Zefra to escape the violence throughout the countryside.

During this conflict, Daloon was much more capable of securing its border. However, insurgents of Zefran origin operating from Daloon territory conducted raids and operations in Zefra.

Daloon's forces decisively defeated an attempted cross-border pursuit of Truscan insurgents by Zefran forces into Daloon in the spring of 2016. In the aftermath of this attempted incursion by Zefran forces into Daloon, the Daloon government declared an area up to 10 kilometers on the Zefran side of their common border to be an exclusion zone for Zefran armed forces.

Daloon regularly monitors the exclusion zone and has enforced it on several occasions over the past few years. The so-called exclusion zone encompasses some of the major fresh-water sources that supply both sides of the island. Daloon control over this essential resource is a potential point of major friction between the two countries, particularly in periods of drought.

International pressure on the Zefran government did not have an appreciable effect on the humanitarian conditions; however, it did change the government's approach to prosecuting the conflict. In 2018, bowing to international pressure and facing the economic consequences of continuing to prosecute military operations, the Zefra government declared a cease-fire. In reality, however, it continued to conduct its campaign, but by other means.

The Zefran government had been encouraging the formation of Bongo militia forces under the umbrella of the Zefra Association (ZA) in areas where opposition to the PLAM was strongest. The government began arming the ZA before the cease-fire and used them to conduct proxy operations against the PLAM. The ZA was soon playing a major role in the fighting and was partly responsible for the ravages that the civilian population was forced to endure.

The arming of the ZA inflamed existing inter-communal conflicts and resulted in the deliberate killing of tens of thousands of noncombatants and a vast displacement of civilians. It also provoked a reaction from the PLAM against the ZA areas of support. Thousands of villagers were forced from their homes as a consequence of the fighting and the depredations of both the ZA and the PLAM. The fighting has continued to generate a flow of refugees from Zefra into Daloon, stressing the latter's capability to support this displaced population. Daloon remains concerned that Zefra's internal strife might spill over into Daloon with the refugee flow.

Zefra Invades Daloon

In December 2019 the government of Zefra mounted a significant attack into Daloon. The international community saw this as a crass move by the Zefran president to unite his people, both Bongos and Truscans, in a universal cause against an alleged external threat: Daloon. The lack of evidence that Daloon was an aggressor seemed irrelevant to the Zefran government. The much more sophisticated armed forces of Daloon brought the invasion to a halt, but at a considerable price in casualties, which the small army of Daloon could ill afford. The Daloon ground forces were unable to expel the Zefran forces entirely or to reestablish the international border. Small pockets of Zefran forces remained inside Daloon territory, up to 10 kilometers south of the border.

Daloon appealed once more to the international community to assist it against the incursion and to deal with the internal Zefran issues that had led to the attempted invasion. In January 2020 the president of Zefra, having failed in his objective of seizing the resources of its southern neighbor and of unifying his nation to fight for a common purpose, stepped down and called for new presidential elections.

The new president of Zefra (elected in April 2020) has been far subtler than his predecessors in his policies. Currently he seems to welcome a foreign military presence in his country as a means of quelling the insurrection. His cooperation does come at a price. He demands that foreign military action should be seen as closely coordinated with the Zefran armed forces. This means, for example, that patrols must be conducted with equal-sized forces from the foreign powers and from Zefra.

International Conference for Zefra

An International Conference for Zefra (ICFZ) was convened in Rome in March 2020 under European leadership to address the continuing humanitarian crisis in Zefra. The United Nations provided legal authority with a Security Council resolution invoking Chapter VII of the UN Charter (Action with Respect to Threats to the Peace, Breaches of the Peace, and Acts of Aggression). A majority of Security Council permanent members supported the resolution, with China abstaining. China apparently had a side deal with the United States that it would abstain as long as any coalition force did not include the United States. The ICFZ sought to work with the government and people of Zefra and with the United Nations in a sustained effort to initiate civil discourse between the belligerents, to provide humanitarian assistance, to promote the rebuilding of democratic institutions, to assist in social and economic development, and to combat poverty.

The conference agreed that the first step was to deploy a multinational force to establish a safe and secure environment. From this baseline, the components of the United Nations and other institutions would assist Zefrans to move toward a more attractive future. The conference participants pledged to assist in the development of a democratic political process, to support humanitarian and economic assistance, to promote the protection of human rights, and to initiate practices for a recommitment to the rule of law.

The conference established an overarching objective to end the humanitarian crisis in Zefra, with a view to creating the conditions under which the Zefran people could govern themselves in a free, safe, secure, and inclusive society that values the primacy of human rights and the equality of all individuals under the law. The conference established further sub-objectives:

- The separation of all belligerents and neutralization of forces that are creating instability, perpetrating acts of inhumanity, and generating the humanitarian catastrophe. The multinational force must establish at least local cessation of hostilities and security as a prerequisite for other relief and development operations to take place.

- Integrated and complementary solutions to the humanitarian crisis, combining immediate humanitarian intervention with a large-scale mid- to long-term rehabilitation strategy. Agencies involved will include the UN High Commissioner for Refugees, the World Food Program and partners, the World Health Organization and partners, the UN Children's Fund (UNICEF), the UN Development Fund for Women (UNIFEM), the UN Development Programme (UNDP), and the Food and Agriculture Organization (FAO).
- The restoration of the rule of law in Zefra through the rehabilitation and restructuring of the police, judiciary, and corrections system, including individual accountability and command responsibility. It is necessary to refurbish, strengthen, and restore legitimate national police and judicial services including internal and external oversight mechanisms. Law reform, judicial reform, and accountability for past crimes will need independent agency input in coordination with the UNDP.
- The international community will insist on equitable political involvement for all segments of the population regardless of region, or ethnicity, will work toward constitutional change and creation of a nationally representative parliament, will assist in reform of the appointment of ranking civil servants, and will assist with conduct of elections together with the UNDP.
- The restoration of the country's productive capacity and livelihoods is essential to the long-term prospect for peace and to elevate the human condition in Zefra. Once a secure environment and the rule of law have been established, this will be led by the UNDP, FAO, World Bank, and other international financial institutions and development agencies—supported by international donor assistance. This will first require the government to interdict illicit drug activities and to gain full and effective control over its territory.
- The disarmament, demobilization, and reintegration of ex-combatants, including women, children, and youth. The force will be assisted by civilian police and UNDP disarmament, demobilization, and reintegration programs for disarmament, security, and stabilization.
- The future requirements for Zefra armed forces will be the decision of an elected government. Swift revitalization of the national police

will reduce the need for an army as a security force. The multinational force will protect arms recovered from combatants pending the need to turn them over to legitimate security forces.
- A reformed education system will be a prelude to long-term stability, economic development, and cultural change. First priority will be given to access to primary education followed by economically relevant secondary education. Agencies will include UNICEF, UNDP, and UNIFEM.

Status Report April 2020

The new president of Zefra claims a strong mandate to govern—87 percent of the vote in last month's election. But the election went largely unsupervised by the international community (the government of Zefra claimed it could not ensure the personal safety of the international observers, so there were none). Consequently, there are suspicions of massive fraud, but little proof. However, the president claims to be the "father of the people of Zefra," with his election as the evidence.

He appears prepared to use every available means to embarrass the U.S. government, its forces in the area, and any other organization affiliated with the United States. The president feels a righteous indignation that foreigners have come to Zefra to solve problems that should have been left to the people of Zefra, under their chosen leader. The president will cooperate with CJTF-Z in many respects. The president and his backers see the international funding coming into Zefra with CJTF-Z as a source of cash to their allied tribes and clans. However, the president feels that CJTF-Z is a temporary phenomenon and that Zefrans will have to find a suitable long-term resolution of their own.

The government of Daloon has suffered for years from the instability in Zefra and frequent threats from its government. Its recent prosperity has given Daloon resources to build a small but highly capable military force. In this, it has benefited from a commercial alliance with the TOKEN Counter-Threat Corporation. TOKEN employees are embedded in most military units of Daloon. TOKEN employees are also present in Zefra where the company has contracts to provide bodyguards and site security for many of the international agencies, nongovernmental organizations (NGOs), and humanitarian efforts.

China is a key player in the region, albeit one staying aloof from the coalition operation in Zefra. China has industrial and commercial links with both Zefra (coal mining and nuclear plants) and Daloon (off-shore natural gas). The PLA Air Force (PLAAF) has a small ongoing presence at two airbases in Zefra and occasional larger deployments into training areas in Zefra. The PLA Navy (PLAN) has a task force in the general area that has been making local port visits. China has strong objections to a U.S. combat role in or near Zefra and thought it had a bilateral agreement with Washington that U.S. combat forces would not be involved—however, the United States has pointed out that this applied only to ground forces within the coalition contingent, and was not intended to apply to any U.S.-only activity. China is now suspicious that the United States will use any coalition failure as an excuse to deploy unilaterally.

BACKGROUND: ATTITUDES AND GOALS— THE FACTIONS WITHIN ZEFRA

The Government of Zefra

Since nationwide elections two months ago (following a failed attempt in late 2019 to invade Daloon), there is a new administration in Zefra, under a new president. The new president (inaugurated in April 2020) was formerly a rear admiral and chairman of the military council (the highest rank in the Zefran armed forces). He resigned his commission when there was an apparent overwhelming demand from his countrymen that he should enter politics and lead his nation out of its abysmal situation.

The armed forces of Zefra treat the new president as their commander-in-chief, and with his military credentials, he is highly respected throughout the military services and very active in this role.

Despite his claims to be running a new cleaner administration, many of the same old figures have resurfaced in positions of considerable authority. In response to criticism in this respect, the president claims that he has only a small pool of qualified experts to draw from, and the nation needs leaders who have leadership experience and can get the job done. The fact is that many in leadership positions are members of the president's family, and many of these had leadership positions in the days of the civil war and the violence and atrocities that followed—if they were not complicit in these incidents, there is little evidence they tried to improve the situation.

The president has also promoted into positions of power a cadre of military friends who had been close to him throughout his career in the armed forces. Already, this new president seems to have put a finger on every possible lever of power in Zefra. While he claims his new administration will follow democratic norms, there seem to be few opportunities for dissenting voices to be heard. That said, there is no convincing evidence yet that the new president's administration has a hand in any of the recent violence.

Zefran Armed Forces: The Zefran Army

The Zefran army was designed largely as a home-defense force. It also provides sinecures for many leaders in the Bongo community and is rife with cronyism and black marketeering. The bulk of the army is organized as one division of six brigades and some divisional troops.

A separate brigade, the Zefran Republican Guard, stands apart from the division and has favored status within the army. The level of training throughout the army is low, with the exception of the guard brigade. The Zefran Republican Guard is mechanized and capable of field operations, unlike the remainder of the army.

Army units are generally equipped with late-twentieth-century equipment acquired secondhand from France, Britain, and Russia. The Republican Guard has acquired some modern sensor capabilities—night-vision devices, small unmanned air vehicles, and ground surveillance radars.

Information that is widely available indicates that a rogue commander from the Zefran Republican Guard with his unit is in the vicinity of Kabra. This commander has positioned the battalion (known as the Illustrious Fighters for Freedom or IFF) astride Route A4, also known as the Capricorn Highway. Most of the troops are in the hills north and south of the highway and west of Kabra. In reference to CJTF-Z, the IFF commander has been quoted as saying: "We will turn back these foreign dogs, or leave their bones drying in the hot, hot sun."

Ministry of the Interior Forces: Border Guards

The Zefra-Daloon land border has traditionally been patrolled on the northern side by the Zefran Border Guards, a force of about 2,600 personnel. They operate from a series of guard towers and camps along the border. The border guards will patrol the border area with forces up to platoon strength. They are armed with small caliber infantry weapons, with some limited indirect fire from mortars up to 120mm caliber.

From the time of the civil war, this force had a reputation for brutality against Zefran citizens who might be suspected of trying to flee south as refugees (of course, most of these were Truscans). Several atrocities during the civil war were attributed to Border Guard patrols that came across groups who were in hiding near the border waiting for a time when they might cross safely into Daloon. Several mass graves of up to a hundred corpses have been found within five kilometers of the border where the dead appear to have signature wounds and mutilations long associated with Border Guard methods.

Internal Security Bureau

The Internal Security Bureau (ISB) is 100 percent Bongo and fiercely loyal to the government. It is the government's principal instrument to quell dissent and is believed to be behind several of the recent atrocities that have been committed against the Truscan population.

The ISB has been rumored to attack innocent fellow Bongos and give the incident the trappings of an attack by Truscan insurgents. The motives are twofold: first, to whip up popular feelings of disgust and suspicion among Bongos for their Truscan neighbors; second, to give legitimacy throughout the international community when the Zefran government imposes harsh anti-terrorism measures against Truscans in Zefra.

Irregular Forces

A number of irregular forces operate within the territory of Zefra. The Zefra Association (ZA) started as a government-sponsored Bongo nationalist militia. It has been associated with atrocities committed on Truscans, and the Zefran government claims it has no control over the ZA in such matters. However, some evidence has been emerging that there are still links to the Zefran government and that those activities for which the government needs "plausible deniability" get assigned to the ZA.

There is recent evidence that the alleged head of the ZA and the head of ISB are actually half-brothers and that both are cousins of the new president of Zefra. The president has been quick to point out that allegations of a family relationship between him and the head of the ZA are absolutely unfounded, that he actually has no power at all over the ZA, and that he has been using whatever influence he may have to clean up the ZA and direct it away from the evil ways of the past.

There were audits in December 2019 of spent-fuel waste from Zefra's two nuclear sites that suggested a considerable amount of high-level waste (highly toxic radioactive material) was unaccounted for, as much as 140 kilograms (kg). There were rumors at the time that rogue elements of the ZA had penetrated the nuclear sites and extracted nuclear waste stored in sealed and shielded containers while the ISB security forces for the reactors looked the other way. The waste amounted to 28 containers, each holding 5 kg of waste in 50 kg of shielding. The International Atomic Energy Agency (IAEA) expressed considerable concern at the time. However, some months later, the reaction from government officials in China and Zefra was that Chinese engineers had made a mistake at the time of the audits and that, in fact, they could now account for all of the high-level waste. The IAEA was never given any detailed account of the alleged disappearance and the subsequent investigation. However, stories have surfaced of highly radioactive material that could be available to terrorist groups for a price, and the contacts that have offered to arrange a potential sale are all from Bongo tribes in Zefra.

The Internal Solidarity Movement (ISM) claims to be a Bongo right-wing separatist movement, but it has developed into a drug-based criminal cartel. While it did indeed start life as a political movement, its perpetual need for financing of its activities led it into an early alliance with existing criminal cartels in Zefra. Initially, the ISM leadership felt they would be able to dominate the criminal element due to the "purity" of their own ideals. But over time the attraction of easy money from drug smuggling came to dominate ISM decisions. The ISM has been implicated in a number of mass killings, but it remains unclear if these are politically motivated or are more like gang violence intended to support their criminal activities.

The People's Liberation Movement (PLM) is a political movement for a Truscan opposition group seeking autonomy within Zefra. The Peoples' Liberation Armed Militia (PLAM) is the armed component and the dominant opposition group in Zefra. Much of the leadership of the PLM retains considerable respect in Zefra and internationally for their intent to better the life of average Truscans. The PLAM, on the other hand, has frequently been linked to brutal attacks on Bongos throughout Zefra.

During the Zefran civil war, the PLM constituted a "government in waiting" hoping to replace the Bongo autocracy, and the PLAM leaders apparently took their orders from the political leadership of the PLM. But since the civil war ended, the PLAM has become more independent of the PLM. It became a home for Truscans who wanted to take the fight to their Bongo neighbors by any means available. In the last few years, with a number of bloody stains on its reputation, the PLAM has frequently been described as a rogue element.

The People for a Greater Zefra (PGZ) is a moderate, multi-ethnic party seeking an inclusive, democratic Zefra. The People's Force (PF) is the armed wing of the PGZ. The PF is the most sophisticated armed group that exclusively targets government assets.

The Insurgency

Within Zefra, an insurgency has been brewing since the days of the Zefran civil war. During the civil war, various factions fought the central government in the role of an opposition party, a viable replacement for the Bongo-led autocracy. By the conclusion of the civil war, with the autocracy left largely intact, the government's opponents became an insurgency, the aim of which was to show that the Bongo-led autocracy could not govern Zefra except in a few selected areas, and then only with the most savage of methods. Indeed, a goal of the insurgency was to show that when the autocracy did govern, it was with a heavy hand, well supported by brutal security forces.

The Chinese-Zefran Connection

In 2015 China began to increase its investment in Zefra. While Zefra remained a relatively poor nation, its abundance of coal reserves near its southeastern coast attracted Chinese industries looking for raw materials.

As industrial relations between Zefra and China warmed, an informal military friendship developed in parallel. The Bongo leadership in Zefra was particularly attracted to Beijing's overtures as they came without the criticism of Zefran leaders commonly received from the United States, Europe, and Australia. Talks with Western nations always included comments from those nations critical of the heavy authoritarian hand used by the Bongos against the Truscan majority in Zefra—in particular, the U.S. leadership sought more democratic rights for the people of Zefra. No such criticism came up during talks Zefran politicians had with leaders in Beijing, however; indeed, Beijing appeared to appreciate that Bongo leadership in Zefra seemed more focused on stability than on democratic rights. Also, the government of Zefran began to see a potential alliance with China as insurance against any future repeat of the U.S. Marine landing in 2007, memories of which remain an impediment to better relations with the West.

Port visits to Zefra by PLA Navy ships began in 2015 and have grown in importance to both nations. PLA transport aircraft also became such frequent visitors to Zefran airbases that a small but permanent Chinese presence was established in 2018 at two of the military airfields. These are PLAAF personnel who load and unload the visiting transport aircraft and provide support services including refueling and minor maintenance; they have no combat training. In the past, these transports carried replacement crew members for visiting PLAN ships, military exports from China to support Zefra's military forces, and items required by Chinese troops who deploy to Zefra to use local training areas. There are now typically two or three air transport flights a week between Zefra and PLAAF bases in the Guangzhou Military Region of China. Elements of PLA's 15th Airborne Corps have deployed to Zefra in company strength for out-of-area training about four times a year for one or two weeks at a time (none of these forces are in Zefra at the current time).

Nuclear Plants and Ballistic Missiles
The Chinese State Nuclear Power Technology Corporation has had a cordial and productive arrangement with Zefra for nearly a decade. The main product of this arrangement has been the recent commissioning of two power generation sites in Zefra, each with two CAP1400 reactor units. For some time, this was a trilateral arrangement that also involved two American players: Westinghouse and Oregon State University (OSU). Westinghouse provided design expertise, and OSU provided support for testing and safety of the facilities.

Daloon's Security Forces
With its newfound resources, the Daloon government soon launched a program to develop a modern armed force that would be more effective in the protection of its border region. Although it was offered large quantities of

relatively unsophisticated equipment, the Daloon government deliberately spurned these quick-fix deals from the arms industry. Instead, it opted to develop its armed forces with limited quantities of state-of-the-art equipment, particularly in the areas of intelligence, surveillance, target acquisition, and reconnaissance (ISTAR), electronic warfare, communications, and non–line-of-sight precision strike.

The army's first integrated unit reached initial operational capability (IOC) in 2013 and full operational capability in 2014. The second integrated unit reached IOC in 2014. By 2016 there were three integrated units operating under a central command structure. A small fleet of fast patrol boats was acquired for protecting Daloon territorial waters. These craft employ stealth technology, over-the-horizon radar, and long-range missiles.

Daloon's small air force has manned and unmanned components. The manned element is composed of a regiment of armed, rotary-wing utility aircraft. There are sufficient aircraft to move one integrated unit in two lifts. The air force's unmanned aircraft are used primarily for ISTAR tasks in support of both the army and the navy. There are a limited number of strike platforms that are capable of supporting both the army and the navy with a variety of precision lethal and non-lethal payloads.

The Daloon armed forces include a small special forces unit with integral air and naval resources. This elite force numbers no more than five hundred troopers, apart from aircraft and boat crews and support personnel. The level of training is superb, the leadership and morale are excellent, and their equipment is sophisticated and well maintained. These special forces personnel are highly respected by the people of Daloon for their high professional standards and commitment to the nation.

That Daloon was able to develop a sophisticated, modern force in a relatively short period can be attributed to their acquisition and training concepts. Acquisition contracts required the suppliers to provide initial and continued operator training for Daloon military personnel, and an obligation to provide comprehensive maintenance was integrated into the purchase agreements.

Collective training and staff training were also contracted services, most of which has been provided by the TOKEN Counter-Threat Corporation, an international company based in Macau, with branch offices in Switzerland and Hawaii. TOKEN employees provided operational mentoring teams down to sub-unit level until the integrated units became fully operational. TOKEN continues to provide staff training and supports collective training throughout the armed forces.

There have been rumors that TOKEN staff have participated in military operations with the Daloon armed forces (going beyond simply training the personnel). In particular, the TOKEN staff working with the elite special forces seem to have been caught up in the enthusiasm often seen in such forces. In early 2020, the chief executive officer of TOKEN acknowledged that such problems have come to light, but he says new control measures by the company have taken the issue in hand. However, it appears that some TOKEN employees in Daloon and Zefra have not yet read the company memo on that.

TOKEN Counter-Threat Corporation

TOKEN is a private military corporation with a murky history, although the current management pledges that their scandalous past is now behind them. TOKEN started by providing "security training" for its clients. In the early years TOKEN was based in southern Europe and recruited its employees largely from *La Légion étrangère* (the French Foreign Legion). Business was good, and as TOKEN grew, it recruited from other nations, particularly from ex-military personnel with a special forces background. Many of TOKEN's current clients are in southern Asia and the South Pacific region.

In view of its new focus in the South Pacific, the company headquarters was moved to Macau, and there are rumors that TOKEN may be providing the Chinese Red Army with information on Western military tactics. This may be the reason that Macau authorities seem to have looked the other way when TOKEN employees have ended up in strange circumstances.

One of TOKEN's most lucrative contracts presently is with the government of Daloon. TOKEN employees, many of whom are former U.S. service personnel or intelligence operatives, are now embedded in most units of Daloon's armed forces, ostensibly as trainers. However, TOKEN employees are rumored to have taken on operational roles from time to time, especially those working with the elite special forces of Daloon.

In addition to its training role with the Daloon military services, TOKEN employees have been contracted with many NGOs to provide security in high-threat environments. TOKEN has the contract to provide bodyguards for the Chinese workers in Daloon and perimeter security for the enclaves where they live.

Many TOKEN employees are also known to be inside Zefra employed as bodyguards for western charities and for other NGOs. The Zefran security services are highly suspicious of the TOKEN employees in their country—they reason that information collected by TOKEN personnel in Zefra could easily be passed to the Daloon military through the TOKEN company links.

Since the alleged incident in late 2019 of 140 kg of missing high-level waste from the CAP1400 reactor sites in Zefra, TOKEN personnel have taken over security duties at the two locations. Its contract specifies that TOKEN will provide only facility security and will have no role in operations, maintenance, nuclear safety, or auditing of waste products. Previously (and when the alleged incident took place), a special unit of Zefra's ISB was assigned responsibility for site security. (There have been suggestions that ISB may have colluded in the issue of the apparently missing waste products. Even if there was no such collusion, the ISB procedures were apparently so lax that just about anyone could have had access to the waste storage areas.) Soon after the Chinese on-site engineers claimed that significant waste products had gone missing, Beijing officials encouraged the Zefran leaders to replace ISB personnel at the sites with TOKEN personnel. The TOKEN head of security at the sites is a Chinese national sent from the TOKEN head office in Macau following the hand-off from the ISB to TOKEN in early 2020. At the time, Zefran authorities objected that authority for site security should remain theirs, but, as a bargaining point, China pointed out that ongoing operation of the sites still depended upon Chinese good will and the support provided by the Chinese engineers. ISB personnel reluctantly left the site in early 2020 during the hand-off to TOKEN.

Combined Joint Task Force Zefra

Under a UN mandate (and Security Council Resolution 9000), a coalition force has deployed to the South Pacific to assist in resolving the many issues between Zefra and Daloon and within Zefra itself. While not part of this force, the United States has offered support in more strategic areas.

The Australian commander of CJTF-Z and his New Zealander deputy are confident that this force can make a real difference and provide succor to the people of Zefra. However, they are aware that this could be a time-consuming process, and have chafed under U.S. pressure to show results, and soon!

The U.S. President

As election season approaches in the United States, the president and the political advisors are planning their re-election campaign. The major foreign policy story is the troubles in Zefra. The president's political advisors are saying that the best solution would be if the problem could just go away quickly. There are substantial voting factions in California and Florida (key battleground states) who immigrated from Zefra and Daloon over the decades; they would look very favorably on a president who solved some of the serious problems in their homelands, but time is short for this.

The president wants the coalition force to be successful but is impatient to see results—and there have been none so far. Through the Chairman of the Joint Chiefs of Staff, the president recently tasked the commander and staff of South Asia and Pacific Command (SAPCOM) to develop plans for a U.S. amphibious landing in Zefra to provide support to the coalition. This could be a "game changer" in Zefra (and potentially with American voters come election time). But if this landing were to be costly in U.S. casualties or were to get the United States bogged down in some long-term commitment in Zefra, it could play very badly in the upcoming election.

South Asia and Pacific Command

In 2016 the massive expanse of U.S. Pacific Command (PACOM) was split roughly along the equator and the southern border of China. PACOM has kept its name and, with a reduced geographical area, it now concentrates on China, North Korea, and eastern Russia—substantial challenges, without question.

One of President Barack Obama's goals from early 2012 was that DoD "will of necessity rebalance toward the Asia-Pacific region." Splitting PACOM into two geographic combatant commands was an obvious way to allocate more defense resources to this region. While the physical resources have not doubled, creating two geographic combatant commands has expanded the staff resources that can tackle more problems developing in the Asia-Pacific region. With SAPCOM headquarters established in Guam, its approaches can be seen as more sensitive to local issues of South Asia and the South Pacific. SAPCOM still has a huge area of responsibility in its own right. And nations in the area create substantial problems: India and Pakistan, Burma and its neighbors, and, of course, Zefra and Daloon. While

China is not within the SAPCOM boundaries, it has been a major player in South Pacific issues for well over a decade, often leaving U.S. foreign policy in tatters. Fortunately, the United States has valuable allies in the region, particularly Australia and New Zealand.

However, with the recent difficulties on the island of Capricornia, the SAPCOM commander has come under considerable pressure from Washington. First, the commander and staff have looked in public like they were surprised by recent events. Widely read U.S. papers have been asking: "Why did SAPCOM not see this coming? Why are they not *doing* something? How long will it take to sort out what should be a minor problem in a tiny nation?" Some bolder papers have been asking questions: "Should the SAPCOM commander be replaced with someone more assertive, and more sensitive to South Pacific issues? Can't the Pentagon find someone more willing to take a leadership role in this critical part of the globe?"

Second, some political advisors to the president have pointed out that relieving the current SAPCOM commander could play out nicely in the Washington press: the president would look decisive but not have to commit U.S. troops to the operation. So far, the president has rejected this advice and announced his complete confidence in the U.S. military leadership, both in the Pentagon and at SAPCOM. But the president and his political advisors are certainly growing impatient to see some results in Zefra.

DESIRED END STATES

ICFZ operations will have met their objectives once a sufficiently secure environment has been established in which:

1. Relief and development agencies can work safely in cooperation with a legitimate democratic government.
2. Refugees, internally displaced persons, and former combatants are being repatriated without fear of reprisals.
3. International standards of human rights are honored by the government.
4. The humanitarian crisis has been resolved due to the coordinated efforts of the government, UN agencies, and NGOs to provide aid, and control of security can be handed over from the multinational force

to legally reconstituted government security forces or a follow-on UN security force.

Coalition Forces

Australia has agreed to accept responsibility as the lead nation of the coalition forces (Combined Joint Task Force Zefra). New Zealand agreed to provide the deputy commander of the military force and significant resources for the components of CJTF-Z. Australia, Canada, New Zealand, Britain, Germany, Norway, and the Netherlands have agreed to provide military forces and civilian police forces. Small elements, generally civilian police and medical and logistics components (with no combat capability), have been offered by Singapore, the Philippines, and India. France and Spain have agreed to provide other elements of national power, but because of previous involvements in the area, neither will contribute ground forces. Both of these countries and Russia, which has also agreed to be a member of ICFZ, will limit provision of support to the strategic level. The United States will not provide combat forces to the coalition but has offered selected resources for surveillance, intelligence, and reconnaissance (filtered as required for coalition consumption). The United States has also offered to back-stop coalition forces should they run into significant problems. However, China has objected that such an offer violates the conditions of the China-U.S. agreement at the Security Council that led to China abstaining rather than vetoing the UN initiative.

Daloon has indicated it may provide limited support if requested. However, Daloon is very sensitive over its colonial past, and the presence of foreign troops in the country is highly distasteful to most citizens. The Daloon government has thus restricted the number of foreign personnel allowed inside Daloon and has also restricted foreign personnel to remain on their assigned bases except for transiting to Zefra to accomplish their military mission.

The coalition, represented by a deployed military force (CJTF-Z), is largely under first-world leadership. The United States gave this initiative its blessing, although with some doubts about its credibility in terms of military effectiveness. China acquiesced as long as U.S. combat forces are not involved. The military leadership in CJTF-Z believes it has a handle on the situation and is skeptical that any U.S. military action would be to the long-term benefit of CJTF-Z, believing that "those Americans just do not understand the nuances of this very complicated situation."

The New Zefran President

The new Zefran president claims he has the support of his people and that he wishes to bring peace to the nation, soon to be followed by prosperity for all. He has announced that there is a spirit of cooperation with the international forces that are arriving in the region to help. Of course, he emphasizes, this assistance should be consistent with the traditions of Zefra, where the president is the "father of the people." He has also demanded that the foreigners do only what needs to be done to deal with the insurrection, and then leave immediately; anything less would be an affront to the national sovereignty of Zefra.

The president has offered that foreign military forces can patrol in Zefra in strengths up to platoon level as long as they are accompanied by Zefran forces of the same size. He claims this is to ensure that locals are not spooked by having foreign troops operate in their proximity, with the Zefran troops readily available to translate, to negotiate, and to smooth over issues that may seem culturally alien to the foreign troops.

Daloon

The government and people of Daloon are growing frustrated with their northern neighbor. The refugee camps are overflowing. Criminal elements from Zefra are affecting the peaceful way of life. The economy is in a nose dive. Unwelcome foreign military forces (from the coalition) are using the nation as a base for operations in Zefra. Something must be done soon.

The Media

The U.S. media are generally supportive of Western intervention in Zefra. However, many questions have been raised over whether the White House policies are influenced more by the upcoming U.S. elections than by an honest desire to improve the situation for average Zefran. Many journalists are also pressing the U.S. leadership over the effectiveness (or lack thereof) of the coalition forces: should the United States step in when the coalition seems to be getting bogged down? This issue re-emerges every time the coalition appears to be at an impasse, or where it seeks compromises instead of confrontation, or when the coalition leadership makes a move that goes down poorly with the American public.

The media from many coalition members support Western intervention. Press in Australia and New Zealand have been strong supporters of the coalition and see the South Pacific leadership as a means of re-asserting Australia and New Zealand as senior players in regional politics. *Al Jazeera* in particular has been critical of the "White Man"–led intervention. *Al Jazeera* points out that there is a high percentage of Muslims in Zefra, and they would be more comfortable with outside intervention if it were under the umbrella of, say, the Arab League. The Muslims of Zefra may well see the intervention as yet another Christian crusade meant to subjugate Muslims. Even an intervention led by the Association of Southeast Asian Nations could remove the stigma of the intervention appearing to be the neocolonial powers of the white race dealing with unruly natives. *Al Jazeera* has also pointed out that the issue of governing Zefra may be more related to superpower politics, with Zefra a pawn in the regional interplay between the United States and China.

PLAYER OBJECTIVES

President of the United States: Summary

The crisis in Zefra caught the White House off guard. The president is running for re-election this year (2020), so the staff has been focused mostly on a campaign for a second term. Now the situation in Zefra has developed, and the president's leadership in the international arena is being questioned. It would be nice if the problem of Zefra would just go away!

The United States agreed to see a UN-supported coalition joint task force deploy to Zefra and Daloon to deal with things. To get agreement at the UN Security Council, the United States arranged a side agreement with China that no U.S. forces would be part of the coalition mission. The Russian economy is in tatters, so Russia abstained as this was framed as Vladimir Putin taking a role as "peacemaker." With the China-U.S. side agreement, China was prepared to abstain as well, allowing the UN force to deploy.

The U.S. leadership has discussed various roles for the nation. In particular, the president is frequently advised on the local situation and on U.S. options by the geographic combatant commander of SAPCOM.

Many immigrants from Zefra now live as U.S. citizens in Florida and Pennsylvania, and the president's political advisors see these as key battleground states in the coming election. These Zefran-Americans may hold a balance for what is shaping up as a very close election race. The political advisors to the president are well aware of the fine balance between showing early success in Zefra and ensuring that the lives of U.S. service personnel are not risked needlessly.

The objectives are to:

- Keep a lid on the problems of Zefra.
- Deal firmly with any challenges to freedom of navigation and to U.S. support to allies and friends, especially challenges from China.
- Demonstrate leadership in foreign policy.

The criteria for decisionmaking are to:

- Do what is best for America and for the American people.
- Provide assistance to allies, to friendly nations, and to others (in that order). Ensure re-election come November 2020.

President of China and General Secretary of the Communist Party of China: Summary

China is very concerned about the unrest in Zefra and its potential to spread to Daloon. China has commercial interests in both countries. The nuclear power plants in Zefra were constructed by Chinese engineers, and a cadre has remained to keep the plants operating. Chinese forces have occasionally trained in Zefra, thanks to an ongoing cordial relationship with Zefran leaders and with the military forces of Zefra. This has been limited to small units (company level) to ensure no one sees it as aggressive.

For convenience, small groups of personnel of the PLA Air Force are stationed at airbases in Zefra to handle Chinese transport aircraft. This amounts to about fifty personnel commanded by an air force major at each of two airbases. They have small arms for self-protection. This is not a combat force.

For many years China has been investing in the recently discovered natural gas fields off the east coast of Daloon. While Chinese relations with

Daloon are not as cordial as they are with Zefra, the people of Daloon have benefited greatly from the Chinese investment. The support to the natural gas industry has resulted in a considerable boost to the employment of Daloon citizens.

When the problems in Zefra were taken to the UN, China initially saw a UN-supported coalition force as a low-cost option to protect Chinese workers in Zefra and potentially in Daloon as well. The main concern was that the coalition force would be led by the United States, with a considerable number of U.S. troops arriving in Zefra. When the U.S. administration offered a side deal that U.S. forces would not be part of the coalition in return for China not vetoing the initiative at the UN, this seemed like an excellent bargain to deal with Zefra without U.S. interference. If any U.S. actions seem to violate this agreement, the Chinese reaction will be: "Typical of the Americans interfering where they have no business!"

China's objectives are to:

- Ensure the safety of Chinese nationals in Zefra and Daloon.
- Prevent the situation from leading to an increase in U.S. influence in the Asia-Pacific region.
- Demonstrate leadership in foreign policy.

China's criteria for decisionmaking is to go to *any extent* to ensure U.S. influence in the region does not increase. Under appropriate conditions, this might include military actions, as long as China appears to be the "good guy."

Prime Minister of Australia: Summary

The Commonwealth of Australia currently has a shaky minority government from an election held two months ago. Before that election, the current prime minister led an administration that had a strong majority in Parliament and, at that time, it agreed to participate in the UN-sponsored coalition force to deal with issues in Zefra and to contribute considerable resources to that force.

If things go sour during the Zefra commitment, it might lead to the current administration losing the confidence of Parliament, forcing yet another election. Given the mood of the nation, a prime minister in such circumstances is likely to be soundly defeated should that election become necessary. Unfortunately for the prime minister, there are many ways the commitment to the Zefra operation could be seen as a failure. Even if there is success in a purely military sense, negative media coverage could contribute to the government's downfall. This could be in the form of stories about refugees suffering, superpower confrontation at Australia's front door, mass atrocities against local populations, or outbreaks of disease so close to Australia.

Australia's objectives are to:

- Retain the support of parliament (and the electorate).
- Fulfill the agreed mandate to the UN and to the international community.

Australia's criteria for decisionmaking are to:

- Ensure the safety of Australian civilians.
- Avoid unnecessary hazards to Australian military personnel.
- Assist and support fellow members of the coalition first, then Allies (like the United States). Avoid antagonizing China (Australia's largest trading partner).

President of Zefra: Summary

The situation is fluid. Just a couple of months ago, you were elected president of Zefra. In the meantime, a UN-backed coalition is moving into the area to deal with instability in Zefra. You want to demonstrate to the world that you can administer Zefran affairs without outside interference. However, you are prepared to be fairly ruthless in this approach, which has served Zefra well in the past (at least the Bongo population of Zefra). You are fortunate to have a very good relationship with the current regime in Beijing. Zefra has been, directly or indirectly, the beneficiary of Chinese technology. If you can get the various ZA factions to conform to your leadership, it provides a means to improve the situation for Bongos and hobble any political or military gains the Truscans might hope for. The magic of your relationship with the ZA is "plausible deniability"—you can claim these are rogue elements that have no connection to your administration (as long as everyone keeps their mouths shut).

Your objectives are to:

- Ensure that U.S. troops do not intervene.
- Get the UN-sponsored coalition force out of Zefra and out of the South Pacific as soon as possible. Have Zefra return to the situation before the foreign interventions (Bongos in charge).
- Ensure that fellow Bongos, and especially old-time cronies, benefit financially wherever possible, and ensure that those *devious Truscans* gain nothing.
- Ensure "plausible deniability" for any covert action that might otherwise be attributable to the Zefran government.
- Appear in public to welcome foreign aid, especially funds. Offer to provide assistance to the UN-backed coalition (but keep them tied up so they do not cause trouble).

Your criteria for decisionmaking are to:

- Choose what is best for the Bongos of Zefra.
- Choose measures that will place the Truscans of Zefra in a bad light.
- Choose options where negative media coverage will be avoided for the president and administration of Zefra.

President of Daloon: Summary

The situation is fluid. Just a couple of months ago, a new president of Zefra was elected. That looked like it might settle things down. However, stability issues in Zefra persist.

Unrest in the refugee camps in Daloon continues. Zefran elements are sneaking across the border into Daloon to attack refugees; the Zefran government argues that the refugee camps are providing shelter to insurgents who cross into Zefra to attack innocent Bongos (a likely story!).

As for the UN/coalition force moving into the area, it would be wise to give this force some support. However, the people of Daloon have always been suspicious of any foreign troops operating in Daloon.

You are concerned about the very good relationship between Zefra and China. Chinese companies have been operating in Daloon, mainly to invest in the natural gas fields. But politically, you have always been hesitant to develop a closer relationship with Beijing. You are very concerned about rumors about rogue elements in Zefra acquiring nuclear waste and missile parts. With the current levels of unrest, this could be a recipe for a dirty bomb, and someone might want to toss it across the border into Daloon.

The TOKEN Corporation has provided considerable support in the rebuilding of the Daloon military forces, although the cost has been considerable. But lately TOKEN has been picking up contracts all over the South Pacific region, including several in Zefra. Given the reputation that TOKEN has for trying to make a buck, you wonder if some of your secrets are being passed through TOKEN to elements in Zefra or even to TOKEN's apparent friends in Beijing, who could be passing them on to Zefra.

Your objectives are to:

- Keep Daloon and its people safe.
- Keep non-Daloon forces from rampaging in Daloon; this applies to Zefran elements crossing the border, but also to foreign troops of the UN-backed coalition.
- Encourage NGOs to provide aid to the refugees in the camps; otherwise the Daloon government would have to fill the bill.

Your criteria for decisionmaking are:

- Choose measures that keep Daloon out of its neighbor's troubles.
- Choose alternatives that keep costs to the Daloon government (and taxpayers) down; get foreigners to cover costs wherever possible—the coalition, the U.S. government, the Chinese, the NGOs—anyone other than the people of Daloon.

Commander, South Asia and Pacific Command: Summary
The crisis in Zefra caught you and your staff a bit off guard. There was an election in Zefra a few months back, and the feeling was that things would settle a bit. But now things are getting hotter. Due to international pressure from news stories of the problems in Zefra, the UN has backed a coalition force to reestablish some form of normality. The United States agreed to see the UN/coalition task force deploy to Zefra and Daloon to deal with things. To get agreement at the UN Security Council, the United States

arranged a side agreement with China that none of its forces would be part of the coalition mission. The Russian economy is in tatters, so Russia offered to abstain as long as this was framed as Vladimir Putin taking a role as "peacemaker." With the China-U.S. side agreement, China was prepared to abstain as well, allowing the UN force to deploy.

For this area, you are the main military advisor to the National Command Authority. You have a command created from the southern part of what was PACOM, which retains responsibility for mainland China, Taiwan, and everything north of the equator. You have military resources in the area, but you must assign their missions with care. It is clear that Zefra and the Coral Sea are potential flashpoints. Your moves will be watched with considerable attention in Washington and in Beijing.

The U.S. leadership has discussed various roles for the nation. The political advisors to the president are well aware of the fine balance between showing early success in Zefra and ensuring that lives of U.S. service personnel are not risked needlessly. The presidential election in November this year (2020) gives whatever move you make strong political overtones in a domestic sense. White House advisors will be screaming for your head if any such moves will damage the president's chances of re-election.

Your objectives are to:

- Accomplish missions as assigned by the National Command Authority to provide the commander in chief with the best available military advice.
- Deal firmly with any challenges to freedom of navigation and to U.S. support to allies and friends, especially challenges from China.

Your criteria for decisionmaking are to:

- Ensure, where possible, the safety and well-being of U.S. service personnel and citizens. Do what is in the best interest of U.S. foreign policy.
- Provide assistance to allies, to friendly nations, and to others (in that order).

Commander, CJTF–Zefra

The Combined Joint Task Force Zefra has a UN mandate and a British commander. The troop-contributing nations include Britain, Canada,

Australia, and the Netherlands. While most of the military activity is expected to be land-based, CJTF-Z has naval and air resources. The military leadership in CJTF-Z believes it has a handle on the situation and is skeptical that any U.S. military action would be to the long-term benefit of CJTF-Z.

The objectives are:

- Success in the assigned missions, especially the separation of all belligerents and neutralization of forces that are creating instability, perpetrating acts of inhumanity, and generating the humanitarian catastrophe. The multinational force must establish at least local cessation of hostilities and security as a prerequisite for other relief and development operations to take place.
- Safety of the displaced persons and refugees (mainly Truscan), cooperation with other agencies to maintain safety of own troops and of civilians return to peace and stability in Zefra, and cooperation as appropriate with any humanitarian operations in the area.

The criteria for decisionmaking are:

- Support any activity that is consistent with the mission.
- As long as the main mission is not impacted, support local civilian initiatives as appropriate.

Commander, PLA Naval Task Force "South Pacific" (Chinese)

The Chinese navy has a task force in the South Pacific conducting a series of friendly port visits. This is part of improving friendly relations with governments of the islands of the South Pacific. But recently China became very concerned about the unrest in Zefra and its potential to spread to Daloon. China has commercial interests in both counties. In Zefra, the nuclear power plants were constructed by Chinese engineers, and a cadre has remained to keep the plants operating.

From time to time Chinese forces have trained in Zefra, thanks to an ongoing cordial relationship with Zefran leaders and with the military forces of Zefra. This has been limited to small units (infantry company level) to ensure no one sees it as too aggressive.

For convenience, small groups of personnel of the PLA Air Force are stationed at airbases in Zefra to assist Chinese transport aircraft passing through. This amounts to about fifty personnel under an air force major at each of two bases. They have small arms for self-protection. They have some equipment for loading and unloading transport aircraft.

For many years, China has been investing in the recently discovered natural gas fields off the coast of Daloon. While Chinese relations with Daloon are not as cordial as they are with Zefra, the people of Daloon have benefited greatly from the Chinese investment. The support to the natural gas industry has resulted in a considerable boost to the employment of Daloon citizens.

When the problems in Zefra were taken to the UN, China initially saw a UN-supported coalition force as a low-cost option to protect Chinese workers in Zefra and Daloon. Once the U.S. administration agreed to a side deal that its forces would not be part of the coalition, China refrained from vetoing the initiative at the Security Council; this seemed like an excellent bargain to deal with Zefra without U.S. interference. But if the United States should interfere, many in Beijing will say: "Typical of the Americans. . . . they just cannot resist interfering where they have no business!"

The objectives are to:

- Follow orders from Beijing (and do not deviate!).
- Keep Beijing advised of the local conditions as they develop, particularly in terms, first, of U.S. Navy and Air Force activity, and second, of the moves by the UN-backed coalition forces.

The criteria for decisionmaking are to:

- Comply with orders from the Central Committee in Beijing. Ensure that U.S. forces do not get the upper hand.
- Monitor the UN-sponsored coalition force to ensure it operates independently of any U.S. forces and with no influence from U.S. SAPCOM.

Head of the Zefra Association (Bongo)

The situation is fluid. A few months ago, Zefra elected a new president. In the meantime, a UN-backed coalition is moving into the area to deal with instability in Zefra. The new Zefran president needs the help of the ZA (Zefra Association), whether he realizes it or not.

As one of the most respected and feared leaders of the Bongo community, you feel it is your duty to the Bongo tribes to defend them in *any way you can*. The insurrection by Truscans against the lawfully elected administration must be suppressed. Women have been raped, stores looted, and innocent civilians injured or killed by rebelling Truscans. *This must stop!*

Zefra is fortunate to have a very good relationship with the current regime in Beijing. Zefra has been, directly or indirectly, the beneficiary of Chinese technology. The ZA may be able to exploit some of this technology: putting some of the nuclear waste together with a tactical ballistic missile makes a very potent dirty bomb—even if the ZA does not actually have a dirty bomb, making its existence *plausible* will make you a feared and respected leader! So the ZA may wish to fabricate evidence to support rumors of such a bomb.

Another rumor you might want to support is that Truscans have a dirty bomb and are prepared to use it. This rumor would be particularly plausible if components could be found on Truscans, or if a small dirty bomb were set off in a Bongo community; surely any attack on Bongos will be attributed to Truscans, and probably to the People's Liberation Armed Militia.

Your objectives are to:

- Ensure that Bongos come out on top, all the time, everywhere! And ensure that Truscans (the ones who survive) are kept in their place.
- Have Zefra return to the situation before the foreign interventions (with Bongos very much in charge).
- Ensure that fellow Bongos, and especially old-time cronies, benefit financially wherever possible, and ensure that those *devious Truscans* gain nothing.
- Support "plausible deniability" for the president of Zefra in any covert action the ZA needs to take.

Your criteria for decisionmaking are to:

- Choose what is best for the Bongos of Zefra.
- Choose measures that will place the Truscans of Zefra in a bad light.

- Find means to discredit Truscan leaders. Use whatever evidence that can be found or manufactured to put these criminals away for good.
- When there are opportunities, embarrass the UN-led coalition forces and encourage them to leave Zefra and allow the elected leaders to govern.

Military Leader of the People's Liberation Armed Militia (PLAM) (Truscan)

The situation is fluid. Just a couple of months ago, Zefra elected a new president. But this was an illegitimate election process. Truscan observers claimed that there was electoral fraud on a massive scale. How can anyone believe that a nation that is 75 percent Truscan would freely elect a Bongo as president?

The last hope of the Truscan people is the UN-backed coalition moving into the area to deal with instability in Zefra. One way or another, this coalition force must take action against the Bongo oppressors. We will fabricate incidents to encourage this, if we must. Such incidents may even draw other international players into our conflict—particularly the United States. We are fighting for democracy in Zefra, and who better to have on our side than the leader of the free world.

In Zefra, human rights violations abound. Our women have been raped, Truscan businesses have been looted, and innocent Truscan civilians have been injured or killed by rampaging Bongos. *This must stop!*

Typical of Bongo duplicity, they have exploited their relationship with Beijing. The Bongo-controlled administration of Zefra has been, directly or indirectly, the beneficiary of Chinese technology. We believe there are rogue factions among the Bongos that may be able to exploit this by putting some of the nuclear waste together with a tactical ballistic missile to make a very potent dirty bomb. Members of the Zefra Association seem to be behind this.

The objectives are to:

- Seek freedom for all members of our Truscan tribes. We demand democracy in Zefra!
- Push to have new and fair elections where the majority (the Truscans) can have the democratic government they deserve.
- Put Bongos (those who survive, anyway) in their place.
- Rid Zefra of the ongoing cronyism of the Bongos—it has been a scourge on our country for decades.

The criteria for decisionmaking are to:

- Choose what is best for the Truscans of Zefra.
- Create incidents where the media show the innocence of Truscans and the duplicity of the Bongos.
- Find means to discredit Bongo leaders. Use whatever evidence that can be found or manufactured to put these criminals away for good.
- When there are opportunities, take measures to motivate the UN-led coalition forces to move against the Bongo oppressors.

NGO (Médecins Sans Frontières): Summary

A large number of NGOs are operating in Zefra and Daloon. One of the best known is MSF. Many NGOs have a presence in Zefra, Daloon, or both. The mission of most of these is to relieve the suffering of civilians (refugees and internally displaced persons). The NGOs run hospitals and other medical facilities—a specialty of MSF. Some NGOs also have sites where civilians can be provided safety, food, water, and clothing. Médecins Sans Frontières generally keeps an arms-length relationship with governments and military forces. The rationale is that MSF must be widely viewed as aloof from all sides of a conflict. If any side perceives MSF personnel to be favoring some other side, then they can become vulnerable. MSF believes their staff will be safer if they show no bias toward any of the sides in the conflict.

To provide security for its medical facilities and its personnel, MSF has a contract with the TOKEN Corporation. The intent is to have security for MSF operations but without relying on military forces. While the cost of this contract is steep, it is a price to be paid to maintain the independence of MSF.

The objectives are to:

- Deliver emergency aid to people affected by armed conflict, epidemics, health care exclusion, and natural or man-made disasters.
- Prioritize the safety and health of the displaced persons and refugees (most are Truscan). MSF will cooperate with other NGOs to provide for innocent civilians.
- Maintain neutrality and impartiality in the name of its medical ethics and the right to humanitarian assistance and claim full and unhindered freedom in the exercise of its functions.

- Respect their professional code of ethics and maintain complete independence from all political, economic, or religious powers.
- Exploit opportunities with the media to publicize the good works of MSF and thereby to encourage public donations for the cause.

The criteria for decisionmaking are to:

- Support any activity that will relieve human suffering, as long as the ethics and reputation of MSF are not in jeopardy.
- Improve the locals' situation (as long as the main objectives are not impacted).

The TOKEN Corporation, District Operations Manager in Zefra/Daloon: Summary

The TOKEN Counter-Threat Corporation is a private military company with headquarters in Macau. TOKEN has a substantial presence in Zefra and Daloon from which it makes a considerable profit for the shareholders. When our customers need people who can deal with any threat, they turn to TOKEN. So, when there is some new threat, there could be a new contract for the TOKEN Corporation!

TOKEN employs retired personnel from various elite organizations: the British SAS, the French Foreign Legion, U.S. Special Forces and other special operations units, Australian commandos, the German Grenzschutzgruppe 9 and Bundeswehr Fallschirmjäger (paratroopers), the Israeli Mossad, Hong Kong's Special Duties Unit, the Dutch Korps Commandotroepen, and others.

The objectives are to:

- Turn a profit for the shareholders.
- Keep employees safe. According to our advertising brochure, TOKEN's employees are our most valuable resource and their safety will be put first—usually (as long as the first objective is not compromised).
- Always conduct a cost-benefit analysis when we might have to put our employees at risk. In many areas where we operate, life comes cheap—and that might have to apply to our own people from time to time.

The criteria for decisionmaking is that decisions should be made on the basis of the well-being of the corporation. In annual reviews, managers will be judged on the contributions they have made to the bottom line. Bonuses will be distributed on the basis of the profitability of new initiatives.

Reporter for the *New York Times*: Summary

The crisis in Zefra caught the White House off guard. This year (2020) is an election year in the United States, and the president is running for re-election, so the staff has been focused mostly on a campaign for a second term.

For Zefra and the South Pacific at large, the White House has never clearly stated a proper role for the United States. Should it stand off? Should the Truscans, who seek democracy, get U.S. support? What about the UN-backed coalition force? It seems to be getting nowhere fast! Is China getting the upper hand in the South Pacific? Has the White House bungled things again? Is a U.S.-China rivalry likely to lead to superpower conflict?

The objectives are to:

- Get a scoop, *any scoop*, ahead of the other journalists.
- Investigate U.S. initiatives: What is the White House really trying to achieve? Is the administration really trying to solve problems in Zefra, or is it just trying to suppress problems until the president has been re-elected?
- Confirm that the only reason the White House is interested in Zefra is to promote the president's credentials in the elections in November 2020.
- If appropriate, reveal to the American people the inadequacy of the reaction of the U.S. government.
- Confirm or deny rumors that Chinese technology may be used in Zefra to build a dirty bomb. Find out if Bongos, Truscans, or someone else is behind this.

The criteria for decisionmaking:

- Check apparent facts with a second source.
- Run a story if the facts seem to support it (say, 90 percent reliable). If a story embarrasses the U.S. administration, they probably deserve it. If

it motivates the U.S. government to support democracy (as they claim to), that would be even better.

Reporter for Al Jazeera: Summary

The crisis in Zefra caught the White House off guard. This year (2020) is an election year in the United States, and the president is running for re-election, so the staff has been mostly focused on the campaign for a second term.

For Zefra and the South Pacific at large, the White House has never clearly stated a proper role for the United States. Should it stand off? Should the Truscans, who seek democracy, get U.S. support? What about the UN-backed coalition force? It seems to be getting nowhere fast! Is China getting the upper hand in the South Pacific? Has the White House bungled things again? Is a U.S.-China rivalry likely to lead to superpower conflict, and possibly a nuclear exchange?

Al Jazeera in particular has been critical of the Western-led intervention. Al Jazeera points out that there is a high percentage of Muslims in Zefra, and if the outside intervention included personnel from Muslim states in the region (e.g., Indonesia), the Muslims of Zefra may well see the intervention as yet another Christian crusade meant to subjugate Muslims. Al Jazeera has also pointed out that the issue of governing Zefra may be more related to superpower politics, with Zefra a pawn in the regional interplay between the United States and China.

The objectives are to:

- Get a scoop, *any scoop*, ahead of the other journalists.
- Investigate U.S. initiatives: What is the White House really trying to achieve? Is the administration really trying to solve problems in Zefra, or is it just trying to suppress problems until the president has been re-elected?
- Confirm that the only reason the White House is interested in Zefra is to promote the president's credentials in the elections in November 2020.
- If appropriate, reveal to the American people the inadequacy of the reaction of the U.S. government.
- Confirm or deny rumors that Chinese technology may be used in Zefra to build a dirty bomb. Find out if Bongos, Truscans, or someone else is behind this.

The criteria for decisionmaking are to:

- Check apparent facts with a second source.
- Run a story if the facts seem to support it (say, 90 percent reliable). If a story embarrasses the U.S. administration, they probably deserve it. If it motivates the U.S. government to support democracy (as they claim to), that would be even better.

APPENDIX 3

Practical Exercise Solutions

This appendix will provide a solution to the practical exercises in this book. It is recommended that the reader not look ahead but rather attempt each practical exercise in sequence.

CHAPTER 6 PRACTICAL EXERCISE 1 SOLUTION

- List wargame's objective: Determine the contributions SAPCOM can make to stabilizing Zefra.
- List all the key issues that the sponsor wants answered. These should be in question form:

1. How can SAPCOM assist the CJTF-Z in stabilizing Zefra?
2. What capability gaps does the CJTF-Z have for its Zefra stabilization mission?
3. What capacity gaps does the CJTF-Z have for its Zefra stabilization mission?
4. What force protection issues does the CJTF commander face?
5. What kind of medical assistance can be provided from the UN TF to take better care of the refugees in the Daloon camps?

6. What kind of medical assistance can be provided from the SAPCOM TF to take better care of the refugees in the Daloon camps? Two sub-issues: What unique medical capabilities does SAPCOM have to offer MSF? Should we pre-position USS *Comfort* for medical contingencies?
7. What activities are TOKEN involved in on the island of Capricornia?
8. What capabilities does CJTF–Zefra need to have to respond to the weaponization of nuclear material?
9. What kind of challenges does the IFF battalion pose to bringing stability to Zefra?
10. How effective will the UN TF be against the IFF if it decides to insert itself in the stabilization process?
11. How effective will the Marine expeditionary unit (MEU) be against the IFF if it decides to insert itself in the stabilization process?
12. What unique capabilities does the PLAN TF have that might be leveraged in Zefra?
13. What kind of media issues should SAPCOM anticipate from the Zefra situation?

- List any assumptions that the sponsor communicated or that you think will be required for this wargame.

    1. The United States will not be allowed any basing in Daloon.
    2. The IFF (rogue) battalion affiliates with the Zefran Bongos.

- List any requests for information that you will need the sponsor to provide.

    1. Order of battle for Amphibious Ready Group–MEU
    2. OOB for PLAN TF
    3. Known TOKEN employees on the island and in the island's supervisory chain
    4. Specific medical capabilities present in SAPCOM, CJTF-Z, PLAN TF
    5. OOB for CJTF-Z
    6. J2 intelligence estimate on IFF battalion

CHAPTER 6 PRACTICAL EXERCISE 2: PREPARING FOR THE SECOND SPONSOR INTERACTION SOLUTION

Must Have
1. What capability gaps does the CJTF-Z have for its Zefra stabilization mission?
2. What capacity gaps does the CJTF-Z have for its Zefra stabilization mission?
3. What force protection issues does the CJTF-Z commander face?
4. How can SAPCOM assist the CJTF-Z in stabilizing Zefra?
5. What capabilities does CJTF-Zefra need to have to respond to the weaponization of nuclear material?
6. What kind of challenges does the IFF battalion pose to bringing stability to Zefra?
7. How effective will the UN TF be against the IFF if it decides to insert itself in the stabilization process?

Good to Have
1. How effective will the MEU be against the IFF if it decides to insert itself in the stabilization process?
2. What unique capabilities does the PLAN TF have that might be leveraged in Zefra?
3. What kind of medical assistance can the UN TF provide to take better care of the refugees in the Daloon camps?
4. What kind of medical assistance can the SAPCOM TF provide to take better care of the refugees in the Daloon camps? Sub-issues: What unique medical capabilities does SAPCOM have to offer MSF? Should we pre-position USS *Comfort* for medical contingencies?

Nice to Have
1. What activities is TOKEN involved in on the island of Capricornia?
2. What kind of media issues should SAPCOM anticipate from the Zefra situation?

PRACTICAL EXERCISE 3 SOLUTION

The following provides our view of the nine sub-issues and twenty-three essential questions we felt were necessary to provide sufficient information for answering issue 3 from practical exercise 2, "What force protection issues does the CJTF-Z commander face?"

1. How will the UN commander protect UN camps in Daloon?
    a. Will UN provide its own guards?
    b. Will Daloon provide guards for UN camps?

2. What kind of medical treatment facilities will be used/set up to treat UN troops?
    a. Will the UN deploy its medical detachment on the ground in Daloon?
    b. Will Daloon have any conditions on its employment?

3. How does the UN commander intend to conduct patrolling in Zefra?
    a. What will be the size of the patrols?
    b. How will the patrols be different between Bongo and Truscan territories?
    c. What conditions will the Zefran government put on UN patrols in Zefra?

4. What immediate fire support is available if UN patrols take indirect fire?
    a. Under what conditions will Daloon allow a UN fire base that can fire missions into Zefra?
    b. Under what conditions will Daloon allow UN close air support aircraft to sortie from Daloon airfields?
    c. What are the other organic fire support options available to the UN commander, and how responsive are they?

5. What size IFF element can the standard UN patrols defeat?
    a. In what way will the IFF choose to employ its forces?
    b. What are the UN commander's criteria for defeat?

6. What size quick-reaction force (QRF) will the UN commander establish?
    a. How quickly will the QRF need to respond?
    b. How will the QRF be transported?
    c. What size IFF element can the QRF defeat?

7. Under what conditions would Bongo forces attack UN forces?
    a. What is the objective of the attack?
    b. What is the expected size of a Bongo attack element?
    c. What is the composition of the element?

8. Under what conditions would Truscan forces attack UN forces?
    a. What is the objective of the attack?
    b. What is the expected size of a Truscan attack element?
    c. What is the composition of the element?

9. What chemical, biological, radiological, and nuclear (CBRN) capabilities and capacities does the UN TF have?
    a. How does the UN TF handle decontamination from a dirty bomb attack?
    b. How does the UN TF handle the use of a biological weapon?

PRACTICAL EXERCISE 4 CLA SOLUTION

Constraints: Response due in fourteen days

Limitations:

- Do not have the strength, composition, or disposition of the IFF
- Do not have the latest UN peacekeeping operations doctrine
- Cannot get Zefran terrain or IFF and UN TF performance data into the combat model in time to represent IFF-UN TF kinetic engagements

Assumptions

- The IFF mirrors a Zefran infantry battalion at 75 percent strength.
- The 2008 UN doctrine will be adequate to represent the CJTF-Z operations.
- The Daloon versus Zefran scenario in the Daloon MOD combat simulation will adequately represent a UN-IFF engagement.

CHAPTER 7 PRACTICAL EXERCISE 5: DESIGNING THE MEASUREMENT SPACE SOLUTION

The following provides our view of the measurement space to address the nine sub-issues and twenty-three essential questions we felt were necessary to provide sufficient information for answering issue 3 from practical exercise 2.

1. How will the UN commander protect UN camps in Daloon?
    a. Will the UN provide its own guards?
    b. Will Daloon provide guards for UN camps?

    - Scenario: UN troops about to land in Daloon
    - MMT: Facilitated discussion (seminar)
    - Data: UN OOB, capacity and location of UN camps and facilities in Daloon
    - Players: UN commander and Daloon president

2. What kind of medical treatment facilities will be used/set up to treat UN troops?
    a. Will the UN deploy its medical detachment on the ground in Daloon?
    b. Will Daloon have any conditions on its employment?

    - Scenario: UN troops about to land in Daloon
    - MMT: Facilitated discussion (seminar)
    - Data: UN medical capabilities and capacities
    - Players: UN commander and Daloon president

3. How does the UN commander intend to conduct patrolling in Zefra?
    a. What will be the size of the patrols?
    b. How will the patrols be different between Bongo and Truscan territories?
    c. What conditions will the Zefran government put on UN patrols in Zefra?

- Scenario: UN commander planning patrolling in Zefra
- MMT: Matrix
- Data: Map of Zefra with Truscan and Bongo areas, cities, populations, UN OOB
- Players: UN commander and Zefran president, possibly Truscan militia leader

4. What immediate fire support is available if UN patrols take indirect fire?
    a. Under what conditions will Daloon allow a UN fire base that can fire missions into Zefra?
    b. Under what conditions will Daloon allow UN close air support aircraft to sortie from Daloon airfields?
    c. What are the other organic fire support options available to the UN commander, and how responsive are they?

- Scenario: UN planning patrolling in Zefra
- MMT: Matrix
- Data: Map, UN OOB including ranges and capabilities of all indirect fire assets, capacity of Daloon airfields
- Players: UN commander and Daloon president

5. What size IFF element can the standard UN patrols defeat?
    a. In what way will the IFF choose to employ its forces?
    b. What is the UN commander's criteria for defeat?

- Scenario: IFF planning attacks against the UN
- MMT: Facilitated discussion (seminar), some sort of matrix, combat results table, or combat modeling and simulation to adjudicate UN-IFF kinetic engagements
- Data: Map, UN and IFF OOB, performance data for all UN and IFF weapons systems
- Players: UN commander and IFF commander

6. What size QRF will the UN commander establish?
   a. How quickly will the QRF need to respond?
   b. How will the QRF be transported?
   c. What size IFF element can the QRF defeat?

   - Scenario: UN patrols come under attack and need reinforcement
   - MMT: Facilitated discussion (seminar), some sort of combat results table or combat modeling and simulation to adjudicate kinetic engagements
   - Data: UN, Zefran Internal Security Bureau (ISB), Truscan PLAM, IFF OOB, performance data for all weapons systems
   - Players: UN commander, Zefran ISB, Truscan PLAM, IFF

7. Under what conditions would Bongo forces attack UN forces?
   a. What is the objective of the attack?
   b. What is the expected size of a Bongo attack element?
   c. What is the composition of the element?

   - Scenario: UN patrolling in Zefra
   - MMT: Facilitated discussion (seminar)
   - Data: UN, Zefran ISB OOB
   - Players: UN commander, Zefran ISB

8. Under what conditions would Truscan forces attack UN forces?
   a. What is the objective of the attack?
   b. What is the expected size of a Truscan attack element?
   c. What is the composition of the element?

   - Scenario: UN patrolling in Zefra
   - MMT: Facilitated discussion (seminar)
   - Data: UN, Truscan PLAM OOB
   - Players: UN commander, Truscan PLAM

9. What CBRN capabilities and capacities does the UN TF have?
    a. How does the UN TF handle decontamination from a dirty bomb attack?
    b. How does the UN TF handle the use of a biological weapon?

    - Scenario: Dirty bomb hits Daloon, biological weapon reported by MSF
    - MMT: Facilitated discussion (seminar)
    - Data: UN OOB, nuclear and biological effects estimates
    - Players: UN commander, MSF, Daloon president

CHAPTER 8 PRACTICAL EXERCISE 6: PLAY-TEST SOLUTION

Matrix Adjudication

The first priority would be to test the matrix wargame component, because that is the most free-flowing of the three. Players decide which actions to take, and that could happen at any time, so seeing a new group of players decide which actions need to be adjudicated will help the game director to be better prepared for what may happen. In theory, matrix games are adjudicated by the players, but a best practice for using matrix adjudication for an analytic wargame will usually require facilitation or at least hands-on management by a wargaming team member.

You should try to recruit players who closely match the actual players you will have play the wargame. Since matrix games depend on the creativity of the players to propose actions, opportunities to adjudicate proposed actions can happen at any point through the wargame.

Seminar Adjudication

If you had a rookie facilitator, choosing between the matrix adjudication and rehearsing your facilitator are both strong candidates for the play-test. If you decided to rehearse a new facilitator, you might actually prep the play-test team to throw some curveballs at the facilitator to prepare for the wargame.

Daloon MOD Simulation

The combat simulation really will not benefit much from blind play-testers; however, the simulation should be tested. If you are going to run this simulation during the actual wargame, you do need to play-test the simulation at the wargame venue to ensure it will work and to get an estimate of the cycle time to take input and provide output. You can test the later part any time, and you really don't need players to do the testing this requires. Better yet, generating a range of runs that could be used to create look-up tables with varied force strengths for the opposing sides to be used by the white cell in the actual wargame would be ideal and would alleviate the cycle time concern and the potential of the simulation crashing during the actual wargame.

PRACTICAL EXERCISE 7: FINAL REHEARSAL, LARGE WARGAME SOLUTION

Plan on conducting your final rehearsal at your wargaming venue. Prior planning should ensure that you schedule the venue two or three working days before the actual wargame kicks off so you have time to set up, do the rehearsal, and respond to items that need attention.

1. Test the data collectors; make sure the forms they use work as intended and the time it takes to get data from the players is what you anticipated. Practice an entire turn with the data collectors collecting, see what they turn in, and ensure you are getting the analysis data you need. Conduct an AAR with the data collectors to see if the process can be improved.
2. Test the white cell; see how they respond to player requests for additional information. Have them create an inject and a vignette to respond to missing analysis data.
3. Test the control cell; see how they intend to track the staffing of the data collectors, white cell, VIP escorts, and analysis cell.
4. Have the analysis cell use the collected analysis data to generate a daily quick-look report after the half day and have it briefed and facilitated with the players.
5. Conduct an AAR with the analysis cell and the data collectors to see if the data collection process is adequate or needs to be improved.

6. Test the adjudication mechanisms that provide feedback data to the players. Once the players receive that feedback data, is there a record of it? It is likely analysis data as well, so it needs to be collected or recorded somewhere and provided to the analysis cell along with the other collected data.
7. Test the facilitator at the venue to ensure there are good acoustics and lines of sight between the facilitator and all the players.
8. Test any pre- or post-wargame surveys on the play-testers (should be done with plenty of time to revise, not day before).
9. Confirm catering.
10. Do an AAR for all wargame support functions play-tested to address any issues.

CHAPTER 9 PRACTICAL EXERCISE 8: GAME DIRECTOR MANAGING CRISES

You are still the game director. The game is in its first of five days, and the wheels already seem to be coming off. Here are the challenges that you are handling and the solutions and best practices (in italics).

1. One of your data collectors called in sick and will be out for the entire wargame. *You can move a data collector up in the rotation, while recruiting another data collector. You will want to train this new person by having them shadow an existing data collector or providing other training. Grabbing an analyst will usually work in a pinch as they are familiar with the DCMP, but then you need to consider how that affects the analysis that needs to be done later.*

    Best practice: *Have a few additional data collectors trained and ready to go.*

2. Because of severe weather, the caterer has called to tell you that lunch will arrive thirty minutes late. *Is there any flex in the schedule? If so, you may not need to change anything. Can the end of the day be extended instead of moving an event? If so, you simply have a longer lunch hour. If not, you may need to move an afternoon event to start when lunch would have started.*

Best practice: Build thirty to sixty minutes into the schedule. No one objects to finishing early. Extending hours will always be challenging.

3. The player representing the CJTF-Z commander must return to home station; the player will depart this evening and will not return. *This is a tough one. For Zefra, this player is critical. Is there someone from your organization with some UN experience who could step up and participate? You would need to locate that person and get them up to speed tonight, and it would be even better if they could shadow the player before they leave.*

    Best practice: Consider having additional players, such as deputy commanders, for key roles. In some cases, having a command team with a commander and several staff officers is useful and could actually allow more experience to be leveraged in decisions, while also providing a potential replacement should this happen. The downside is decisions by consensus may take longer.

4. The SAPCOM commander has a question about the legality of sharing U.S. secret info with NATO. *This is a question for your white cell to handle. Do you need the actual answer, and if so, how long will it take? Will this hold up the wargame, or can you park the issue and move on? If the wargame depends on having an answer now, then your white cell (or you) needs to make an assumption to keep the game moving. It is important this assumption is recorded and then later researched.*

    Best practice: You cannot anticipate all the players' questions, but for Zefra, this one could have been anticipated. The white cell needs to observe play-tests and actively seek potential questions so they have responses whenever possible.

5. Your primary facilitator has a bad cold and is starting to lose his voice. *Good luck. If you can facilitate, maybe you dive on this grenade if you have a deputy game director who can take over, or perhaps your deputy can facilitate.*

    Best practice: Have contingency wargaming staff members. You should have some of your wargamers trained as facilitators. It is a good idea

CHAPTER 10 PRACTICAL EXERCISE 9: QUICK-LOOK REPORT

The following provides our view of an initial quick-look report to address the three sub-issues (3.3, 3.4, and 3.5) for issue 3 from practical exercise 2.

3.3. How does the UN commander intend to conduct patrolling in Zefra?

Patrols will be a fire team (four or five soldiers) led by an NCO accompanied by two or three Zefran army soldiers, regardless of region. In Truscan-dominated territories, an additional UN soldier will record any interaction between Truscan residents and the Zefran soldiers.

3.4. What immediate fire support is available if UN patrols take indirect fire?

Artillery, fixed and rotary wing aviation, and mortars. Artillery and aviation assets are based out of Daloon and can only respond to deadly force attacks. Basing in Daloon can be revoked if the agreement is violated or civilian casualties result from the employment of Daloon-based assets.

3.5. What size IFF element can the standard UN patrols defeat?

Available data is inconclusive; the answers to the essential questions did not answer the issue. A key player interview with the UN commander to get an assessment would be useful to get insights. If the Daloon versus Zefran scenario in the Daloon MOD combat simulation had been pre-run and the facilitator had a set of look-up tables, you could use these to provide an estimate. You can have the analysts run the model (probably will need Daloon model expertise to assist) to examine several different size force-on-force engagements so you can create some statistics. You should get the feasible sizes of the force engagements through key player interviews with the UN commander and the IFF commander, and you should ask the IFF commander under what conditions he would flee an engagement with UN troops.

PRACTICAL EXERCISE 10: ANALYSIS

The following provides our view of an initial quick-look report to address the three sub-issues (3.6, 3.7, and 3.8) for issue 3 from practical exercise 2. In this case, the data from the game is a series of if/then statements and conditions. These provide a single set of insights and are not all inclusive.

3.6. What size QRF will the UN commander establish?

The UN commander will have a platoon-sized QRF that is transported by helicopter and able to respond in fifteen minutes. It will be based at an airfield in Daloon.

3.7. Under what conditions would Bongo forces attack UN forces?

If Truscans start getting traction with the UN and there are active initiatives to change the current government to allow the Truscans more say, Bongo forces will consider conducting fire team–sized attacks. The purpose of the attack would be to discredit the Truscans. Expect the attackers to be disguised as Truscan militias armed only with small arms, and the attacks would be conducted from Truscan-dominated regions in Zefra.

3.8. Under what conditions would Truscan forces attack UN forces?

Two distinctly different objectives. The first is to send a wake-up call to the UN if they are too accepting of the ruling Bongo government and are ignoring Truscan grievances. The Truscans would attack with a squad-sized or larger ambush, and the intent would be to eradicate the entire patrol. In order to make it look like a Bongo ambush, they may only kill UN soldiers and allow the Bongos to survive, and they may steal and employ Bongo weapons such as machine guns and mortars. The second objective is to terrorize Zefran armed forces. This attack would seek to target the Zefran soldiers when they accompany UN forces, but this would be a targeted attack intending to kill or maim Zefran soldiers without hurting UN soldiers or causing them to engage Truscan attackers. These attacks would be commando-style using only a few skilled militia members to slit throats or use poisoned arrows, or it may be conducted by sniper teams. They would seek to avoid targeting UN soldiers and provoking any UN patrol responses.

APPENDIX 4

Wargaming Gateway Exam

This exam is designed to evaluate the novice's understanding of the basic elements of wargaming as captured in the five phases of wargaming (initiate, design, develop, conduct, and analysis) presented in the book. It provides a good assessment of the reader's understanding and a potential tool for use in an organization's wargaming education program.

PART 1: WARGAMING FUNDAMENTALS

1. True or False: The role of wargames is to help investigate human decisionmaking, not to assist in calculating the outcome of combat engagements.

2. True or False: Wargames are designed to be run hundreds of times with the main purpose of producing massive amounts of quantitative output data for further analysis.

3. True or False: Wargames can be used to produce concepts of operations or courses of action that can then be integrated into closed-loop combat simulations.

WARGAMING GATEWAY EXAM

4. The most essential element of a wargame that drives its entire structure is:
   a. scenario
   b. objectives (objective and issues)
   c. rules
   d. players

5. The one element that you probably will NOT find in a pure seminar game is:
   a. scenario
   b. objectives
   c. rules
   d. players

6. The modifications to Perla's objectives include:
   a. "models" is replaced by "methods, models, and tools"
   b. "objectives" is replaced by "objective and issues"
   c. both a and b
   d. none of the above

PART 2: WARGAMING FUNDAMENTALS—SEVEN ELEMENTS

7. Select three of Perla's seven elements that you think are the most important and briefly describe why that element is important.

8. The purpose of a wargame is to create an environment in which ____ produce the information and output required to answer the sponsor's ____.
   a. computers, questions
   b. players, objective and issues
   c. essential questions, information
   d. mathematical models, measures of effectiveness

9. A wargame's data collection and management plan derives ____ from issues or sub-issues, and then specifies ____ for data collectors to collect.

a. computers, questions
b. players, objective and issues
c. essential questions, information
d. mathematical models, measures of effectiveness

10. If a wargame needs to assess combat outcomes, designers may incorporate ____ to produce output used to calculate ____.
    a. computers, questions
    b. players, objective and issues
    c. essential questions, information
    d. mathematical models, measures of effectiveness

11. The "fog of war" is better represented in a(n) _____ wargame. Command, control, communications, computers, intelligence, surveillance, and reconnaissance issues are better examined in a(n) _____ wargame.

12. A game in which players have access to information on all other players' forces and capabilities is a(n) _____ wargame.

13. According to Perla's seven elements, the key difference between hobby and professional war games is the element of _____.

PART 3: DESIGN AND DEVELOPMENT OF WARGAMES

14. True or False: All game rules are finalized and ready to be played without further change by the time the wargame is ready for the first play-test.

15. True or False: Game rules will probably need to be amended each time the wargame is play-tested.

16. True or False: You should expect to update rules at every play-test and even at the final rehearsal.

17. True or False: A game is best crafted when design and analysis groups work independently of each other.

18. True or False: It is a good idea to put an analyst in the design group.

19. True or False: The design and analysis groups should work together closely to ensure the sponsor's objective and issues are met.

20. The components of the "project team" always include:
    a. the sponsor and the design group
    b. the analysis group, the data collection team, and the sponsor
    c. the design group and the analysis group
    d. the subject matter experts, the military players, and the civilian analysts

21. Which of the following is NOT true concerning the rules of a war game?
    a. Rules must be constantly updated.
    b. The "keeper of the rules" must attend or collect feedback from all play-tests and preplay because there will be changes.
    c. Rules are established once at the beginning of the design process and then strictly adhered to throughout design, development, and conduct of the game.

22. Which of the following is one of the design and development corollaries?
    a. get a crude design quickly completed and develop (play) it
    b. play-test often: do not spend a large block of time designing without any play-testing
    c. heed Dunnigan: "keep it simple" and "plagiarize"
    d. all of the above

23. True or False: Goals of wargame development ensure that any player can win the game.

24. True or False: The player's objectives are the same as the game's objective.

25. True or False: You may not want to reveal the purpose of the game to the players.

26. Measurement space is a function of the _____ , _____ , and _____ created for the project.

27. _____ is taking the designed game and playing it in order to find out where the design breaks down.

28. Risk is predominantly an open game, with the exception of the cards each player holds. How would you redesign Risk so that another feature of the game was closed?

PART 4: CONDUCTING WARGAMES

29. True or False: If you provide a detailed read-ahead packet for every player, there is no need to schedule a briefing.

30. True or False: You should follow up the sending of a read-ahead packet by contacting all key players to ensure they have received the packet and have no questions.

31. True or False: A professional looking, well-formatted, and well-edited read-ahead packet will affect the amount of time and the degree of seriousness players will invest in their wargaming participation.

32. Name one facility-related and one analysis-related challenge that setting up a closed wargame presents.

33. Name one activity or role that members of the analysis team could have during the execution of the wargame.

34. Taking care of the players is often overlooked, especially when the players are coming from other geographic locations. Name two considerations that a study director needs to address in order to free the players from distractions.

35. The initial game play of a wargame may intentionally be designed for a purpose other than to produce data for the DCMP. If the game play

is not intended to help answer the sponsor's questions, what purpose could this game play serve?

36. Should you provide your players with a behind-the-scenes look at the methods, models, and tools that you will use to adjudicate the game? Justify your answer.

PART 5: ANALYSIS OF WARGAMES

37. True or False: Wargaming analysis planning should not begin until the game has been developed to a satisfactory level.

38. True or False: Wargame analysis should rely solely on after action reviews conducted with the players after the wargame has concluded.

39. Which of the following is NOT TRUE regarding the analysis plan?
    a. There is no "silver bullet" for the plan.
    b. The analysis plan is drafted after the game design is finalized in order to understand what information is possible to collect.
    c. The game must be designed so the analysis group can collect information relevant to the sponsor's objectives.

40. Who is primarily responsible for the derivation of the essential questions?
    a. scenario writers
    b. analysts
    c. sponsor
    d. players

41. The wargame's objective and issues come from:
    a. scenario writers
    b. analysts
    c. sponsor
    d. players

42. The information collected in the DCMP will come from the:
    a. scenario writers
    b. analysts
    c. sponsor
    d. players

PART 6: ANALYSIS METHODS

43. Analysts are busy before, during, and after the actual wargaming event. After the wargame is over, but before the players have left, the analysts need to produce this product: _____

44. Why is the product you named above produced before the players leave?

PART 7: SPONSORS

45. True or False: The wargaming team–sponsor interaction is an iterative process that requires regular communication to ensure objectives are met and the game remains focused.

46. True or False: The wargaming team should design the game from the sponsor's initial interaction; excessive interaction with the sponsor will only make the game harder to design.

47. True or False: Sponsors always know exactly what they want and what your team is capable of producing, so never negotiate with a sponsor.

48. You agree to do a wargame for a sponsor who wants a quality wargame but does not have any additional resources for the wargame. Using the analyst's business model, what do you caution the sponsor about with respect to the wargame you will design? It will not be _____ .

49. You agree to do a wargame for a sponsor who wants a quality wargame and wants it very quickly. Using the analyst's business model,

what do you caution the sponsor about with respect to the wargame you will design? It will not be _____.

50. You agree to do a wargame for a sponsor who wants a wargame produced very quickly and does not have any additional resources for the wargame. Using the analyst's business model, what do you caution the sponsor about with respect to the wargame you will design? It will not be _____.

51. The sponsor should be made aware of the _____ set of CLAs developed by the study team.
    a. key
    b. full

PART 8: CONSTRAINTS, LIMITATIONS, AND ASSUMPTIONS

52. True or False: Limitations are imposed by the sponsor.

53. True or False: Assumptions can come from both the sponsor and the study team.

54. True or False: You may use the analyst's business model to cause a sponsor to reconsider a constraint, such as time.

55. Explain why CLAs are important to a decisionmaker who is being briefed on the results of a study.

56. One of the three constraints, limitations, and assumptions criteria is "accepted." Explain the importance of this criteria.

57. True or False: A constraint is the inability of a study team to fully meet the study objectives or fully investigate the study issues.

58. The two sets of CLAs are _____ and _____.

59. A(n) _____ is a statement related to the study that is taken as true, often to accommodate a limitation.

60. Assumptions should be replaced by _____ once they are known.

PART 9: SEMINAR WARGAMES

61. True or False: An important attribute of seminar wargame facilitators is that they are unbiased, and perceived as unbiased.

62. True or False: An important attribute of seminar wargame facilitators is that they are welcoming of different points of view, ensuring full coverage of issues.

63. True or False: An important attribute of seminar wargame facilitators is that they exclude those reluctant or reticent participants, since the loudest voices usually have the most valuable opinions.

64. In order to visit an alternative future, a seminar wargaming facilitator may "rewind the clock." This is more commonly referred to as a _____.

65. A good seminar wargaming facilitator will have several (perhaps notional or mental) index cards that contain _____ used to introduce new information or a new situation into the game. These can also be used to add complexity to a problem as it unfolds.

66. Is it a good idea to have the study director also be the facilitator of a large seminar wargame? Justify your answer.

67. For what purpose would a facilitator use the "parking lot" technique?

68. Describe why you would use "closed planning and open execution" for a seminar wargame.

69. Describe how a wargame and a closed-loop combat model can be both leveraged in a study to obtain useful analysis results.

70. Briefly describe the difference between free and rigid Kriegsspiel.

APPENDIX 5

Case Studies in Wargaming Design

■ ■ ■ ■

In the resident Wargaming Applications course taught at the Naval Postgraduate School, teams of four to five students initiate, design, develop, conduct, and analyze a wargame for a real-world defense sponsor. Between 2009 and 2018, student teams designed, developed, conducted, and analyzed more than fifty wargames for more than thirty sponsors, and no two wargames were the same. For the first five years of the course, the only requirement to document the results of the wargame was a final out-brief that was provided to the sponsor, usually through a video teleconference, about a week after the conclusion of the wargame. This gave the students about a week to analyze all the data and synthesize that information into key findings that informed the sponsor's objective and issues. In 2015 we decided to formalize the analysis reporting and required an unclassified executive summary for the purpose of documenting all wargames' design and results. We also required that the wargame design team provide a final out-brief and a final report to the wargame's sponsor. One element of the craft of wargaming is being exposed to a variety of wargame designs and mechanics. There is no substitute for actual experience, but in this appendix we present a collection of actual wargame case studies that demonstrate various constructs that proved useful in addressing the sponsor's issues to give you a sense of the potential range and scope of wargames. Each case study will contain a brief introduction to the problem, the final sponsor/design team–agreed objective, the scenario, key players, game format and type, the MMTs that were used to adjudicate the wargame, and some critical lessons learned during the wargame design process. In some cases, the descriptions are terse, but we believe they will provide enough of a flavor of the wargame for the reader.

CASE STUDY 1: SOUTH CHINA SEA CONFRONTATION 2030 (Sponsor: Distributed Lethality Task Force)

Introduction: For many years, the U.S. Department of Defense's planning doctrine included a six-phase construct for the escalation of military operations: 0 (shape), 1 (deter), 2 (seize initiative), 3 (dominate), 4 (stabilize), and 5 (enable civil authority). When the U.S. armed forces applied this concept, they would first seek to shape the battlespace (phase 0) with the goal of conducting operations (phase 1) that would deter an enemy from escalating a situation into a kinetic engagement (keep from transitioning from phase 1 to phase 2). If deterrence failed, then the kinetic engagement would occur, which would then force a decision to either escalate or try and find a way to transition back to phase 1.

NPS student wargaming teams were challenged to create a wargame that would allow the assessment of the Navy's distributed lethality (DL) concept. Distributed lethality is an operational employment concept that combines increased surface warfare striking power with increased targeting capabilities in a geographically dispersed force. Using technologically advanced offensive and defensive weaponry and increased networking capabilities, DL harnesses the complete joint sea, air, and land force to provide increased combat power and force projection globally. The wrinkle in this wargame was the sponsor wanted to assess the DL's capability to deter an adversary, not fight it. The challenge, of course, is that the effectiveness of military deterrence is directly tied to how effective the force is in combat, and this depends in a large measure, especially in the Navy, on the first mover or strike advantage or the perceived advantage. Designing a wargame to assess if a force has successfully deterred an adversary presented multiple challenges to the wargame team, to include simply defining what "deterrence" meant. Students worked long and hard to create a wargame design that would allow them to assess deterrence.

Objective: Analyze the effectiveness of the distributed lethality concept at deterring a near-peer adversary in a highly contested environment.

Scenario: It is the year 2030. China has continued to build up its armed forces and continues to flex its muscle in the South China Sea, taking actions that antagonize and threaten its neighbors. In particular, the U.S. Navy's mission is to exert sea control and deter this adversary from further escalatory actions and to force China to back down from some of the actions that it is currently taking. Two separate vignettes in the South China Sea explored the effectiveness of distributed lethality compared to a carrier strike group. It should be noted that the number of vessels involved is definitely a dependent variable in understanding the deterrence value of DL, and it was held constant as the teams explored other potentially confounding factors. Each vignette added complexity by increasing the area of responsibility, incorporating noncombatants, lengthening the time of operations, and modifying objectives to add realistic complex problems to the wargame.

Key Players: Command and staff teams that represented the armed forces of China and the United States.

Game Format and Type: The game format was closed planning with open execution and was a hybrid combination of system and seminar. There were four phases for this particular wargame: planning, white cell adjudication, seminar adjudication, and final survey.

Planning: Upon initial receipt of the scenario brief, players were allotted one hour to complete an operational plan. This was a closed planning session, where each team prepared its plan in secret. Required products at the completion of the planning phase included a scorecard and a graphical overlay of the team's course of action. Each side had the identical hexed map of the South China Sea. Each team would plot its actions on a clear acetate overlay synchronized with the hexed map. The scorecard provided initial objectives, individual unit movements, a perceived threat index, as well as the top enemy actions that would increase the perceived threat. On one side of the acetate, the team would summarize its scorecard, but the U.S. team wrote its rationale to the right of its clear acetate overlay, and the Chinese team did so to the left. This set the stage for adjudication.

White Cell Adjudication: The white cell collected both overlays and synchronized them to their (identical) map of the region. By doing this, they could then see both U.S. and Chinese actions and positions and see where forces crossed paths. They then used a panel of subject matter experts to decide the objectives that had and had not been met for each side. Players were not present for this adjudication.

Seminar Adjudication: The student team had determined that deterrence could only be assessed through the examination of each sides' perceptions of the other side's actions. The overlays were brought from the white cell into an open seminar room where both overlays were posted over the same map again. Because each side wrote rationales on opposite sides of the map, the facilitator could easily read both sides' rationales and objectives. From the composite picture on the actual map, the facilitator could see where ships and planes from each side would have interacted with the opposing side's ships and planes. The subject matter expert panel's adjudication of objectives met and not met was annotated on the overlays. The facilitator then engaged both commanders to determine what perceptions each side had of the other side's actions, and what actions, if any, each side would have taken given their perception. Each individual team member had the opportunity to discuss the advantages and disadvantages of their plan and how DL helped or hindered their planning process.

Final Survey: Upon completion of the seminar, the analysis team used a survey to answer any remaining questions. The survey was the final portion of the data collection and completed the wargame data collection requirements.

Key findings included the following:

- Distributed lethality expanded strategic response and messaging options for the United States that differed from the messaging option of a carrier strike group. China saw the employment of a carrier strike group as an escalatory measure; conversely, the employment of an adaptive force package, in most cases, allowed presence of offensive weapons without escalation.
- The perceptions of U.S. rules of engagement and a lack of non-lethal and escalatory weaponry constrained distributed lethality's capability to influence and deter in phase 0 and phase 1. The U.S. Navy

must place a greater emphasis on the strategic messaging campaign for distributed lethality. Since this is a new operational employment technique, many nations are uninformed on the complete capabilities and increased offensive power that distributed lethality provides the surface fleet.
- Logistical changes are needed to adequately support distributed lethality. The logistical requirements under DL are the same or greater than those required to support a carrier strike group.
- Modifications to the command and control structure are needed to keep the flexibility created under distributed lethality. Command ship determination(s) should be based not on seniority but on asset location and capabilities of individual ships.
- There is a need to clarify the tactical procedures under distributed lethality. Although a dispersed force allows for greater geographic coverage, it also limits maneuver for each individual ship due to intelligence, surveillance, and reconnaissance (ISR) coverage responsibilities.
- U.S. political and naval leaders must propose a national level policy for retaliatory actions from a loss of a small craft used in the distributed lethality adaptive force packages. It was uncertain what the correct level of political or military response should be for enemy offensive actions against a small craft.
- Allied partners believe a carrier strike group provides a higher level of deterrence compared to a distributed lethality adaptive force package. The international players believe a carrier strike group shows the United States is willing to fully support their efforts; conversely, the employment of an adaptive force package is seen as a consolatory action.

Innovations and Lessons Learned: The overall design of the wargame to assess deterrence was a classic analog workaround for a closed system. The idea of having each team create overlays in exclusion, matching them up to do an initial assessment of potential interactions, and then convening a seminar discussion to learn both sides' perceptions of the other's actions was a clever method to capture some of the fog of war without having to digitize the wargame.

We caution our students about how much detail of the wargame they should provide the sponsor during in-progress reviews. In particular, the

DCMP is something we usually tell the team not to share with the sponsor, as this is a bit like seeing sausage being made. Most sponsors will not know what they are looking at, but if the DCMP is provided to them for comment, they may feel compelled to pick it apart to show that they are invested in the process. In this case, the sponsor actually adopted the team's DCMP as their task force's analytic agenda. This reinforced to us the old axiom that there are no absolutes in wargaming.

CASE STUDY 2: EMPLOYMENT OF NON-LETHAL CAPABILITIES FOR VISIT, BOARD, SEARCH, AND SEIZURE OPERATIONS (Sponsor: Royal Canadian Navy Maritime Command Pacific Operational Research Team)

Introduction: The selected problem was maritime interdiction operations, in particular visit, board, search, and seizure (VBSS) operations. This topic provides input for the work of NATO Systems Analysis Study 094 (Non-Lethal Weapons Concept Development), which cooperates with the NATO Defence Against Terrorism Non-Lethal Capabilities program on organizing a NATO Non-Lethal Technology Exercise focused on evaluation of the employment of non-lethal capabilities (NLC) during VBSS operations.

Objectives: The objectives of the wargame were twofold: To assess costs and benefits of NLC employment during VBSS, and to assess costs and benefits of NLC employment for force protection. Secondary objectives included development of a wargaming capability that could be used to train planning procedures and to assess potential benefits of new capabilities.

Scenario: Military ship (MS) *A* (a frigate with an onboard boarding team) is patrolling international waters off the coast of country *X* as a part of an international counterpiracy/counternarcotics task force. Intelligence indicates a suspicious cargo vessel (container ship that is longer than 50 meters with an assumed fifteen to twenty persons onboard, including crew and possibly several undeclared passengers) within the MS *A* area of responsibility. The MS *A* captain receives an order from the coalition higher headquarters to board and search the vessel; if there is a positive find of a contraband, they are to seize the ship and escort it to a port in country *X*.

MS *A* approaches the suspected vessel; the vessel is initially compliant, stops when ordered to do so, and allows the boarding team to approach and board. Once the boarding team gets onboard, the situation rapidly deteriorates, and force (up to and including lethal) must be employed by the boarding team. After the Blue team gains control of the target vessel, they search it and find significant illicit cargo. At that point they seize the vessel and escort it to a port in country X.

Key Players: The wargame design student team acted as the White team; the boarding party was played by variety of U.S. and non-U.S. (e.g., Pakistan navy) military subject matter experts from Navy, Army, and U.S. Marine Corps background.

Game Format and Type: This game was an open hybrid wargame that utilized a tabletop phase that was followed by a seminar discussion. The tabletop wargame included a schematic drawing of the target ship and capability cards for each lethal/non-lethal system employed by the boarding party. Two lethal/non-lethal options were gamed. The non-lethal weapon (NLW)–equipped boarding party was designated as a hybrid option since they retained their lethal capability, albeit somewhat reduced due to mandatory trade-offs; the baseline option was designated lethal. In addition, there would be predetermined probabilistic combat result tables for the likelihood of injuries and incapacitations. The analysis team would act as the boarded vessel's crew (White/Red team) and would provide courses of action for the crew. The boarding party component of the scenario was then analyzed using a seminar wargame approach. The reasoning behind separating the VBSS and force protection components of the scenario was that they happened at different scales (spatial and temporal), and therefore keeping them together would make the game unnecessarily complicated.

Adjudication MMTs: The analysis team recorded feedback from players during and after the game. The data collection sheet included the weapon chosen, action taken by the boarding team, and resulting outcome adjudicated by the white cell by using an adjudication (spreadsheet) model. At the end of each turn, players were asked to record their personal remarks on the effectiveness of the weapon chosen and how different choices may have resulted in a different outcome for the given scenario. At the end of the turn-by-turn game, the player workbook containing all player-input values was saved for analysis. Players were asked to fill out survey questionnaires for feedback on metrics such as severity, likelihood of certain occurrences, risk, cost, and trade-offs associated with non-lethal weapons. Upon conclusion of the VBSS game, proceedings of directed discussion on escort phase were conducted, followed by the survey to answer questions associated with the protection of the mother ship during escort phase.

Key Findings: The following recommendations are made based on the results of this wargame:

- The game developed may be used as a training aid to train boarding teams on situation handling and understanding repercussions associated with their actions.
- Use of NLWs by the boarding party can be effective in de-escalating certain situations.
- Rules of engagement for handling and use of NLWs need to be developed very carefully. Sailors may be naturally hesitant to use NLWs in an escalating situation.
- The game may be played with more players and diversity of results can be collected for further insights into the problem. Examples of insights that emerged but were not part of the initial objectives or issues included:
    - *Mother ship protection during escort phase*. The directed discussion on protection of the mother ship during the escort phase comprised of two types of results: individual answers to questions regarding procedures and potential weapons usage and answers to survey questions by the participants.
    - *Small boats* are a great threat in the maritime environment because of their low cost, ease of deployment, and success record. The aim is to stop this threat before it reaches the mother ship. Following are the results of discussions with players.

1. What could be initial actions by the escort?

- Track small boats entering a predetermined assessment zone with available sensors: navigation radar/surface radar.
- Ready to deploy organic helicopter and rigid-hulled inflatable boat (RHIB). One or two RHIBs can easily intercept the threat and warn it while covering the mother ship.

- An initial classification of boat by using visual sighting capabilities
- Initial warnings by using Marine VHF 16
- Evaluate its intent (friendly or hostile) toward mother ship, monitor its course and speed changes by using both radars and visual sighting.
- The mother ship can change its course to see whether the small boat is following it.

2. How do actions change after visual confirmation of identity of the boat?

- After visual confirmation, if small boat is unclassified, the mother ship uses all its means to attract the boat's attention. There are many non-lethal capabilities as well as lethal capabilities to warn and deter this boat. These weapons can be installed on the mother ships and organic units.
- In order to intercept a fast attack boat, a faster platform needs to be employed. These are helicopters, RHIBs, or unmanned systems.
- Helicopters are extremely useful against small boats. Their speed and maneuverability capability are a great advantage. Helicopters are the only choice to defend the mother ship without putting it at risk. Helicopters also can be equipped with non-lethal weapon capabilities. The main disadvantage is the helicopters may not be available all the time when needed, so non-lethal capabilities should be explored.
- RHIBs are highly maneuverable platforms with their shallow drafts. They can easily intercept the threat with their high-speed capability. These boats might be armed with lethal or non-lethal weapons to neutralize small boat threats.
- Unmanned aerial vehicles are useful to conduct a sufficient ISR and can be used for early detection and visualization of small boats.
- The Protector unmanned surface vehicle plays a prominent role in minimizing safety risk to the sailors and armed forces by allowing them to avoid direct contact with the potentially mission-critical operations.
- A long-range acoustical device is a military-grade weapon system that sends out mid- to high-frequency sound waves designed to disorient and possibly incapacitate personnel. It can be used for prevention of unlawful acts and dangerous approach of a target to a guarded entity. It can transmit signals within a range of up to 5,000 meters. The

effectiveness of long-range acoustical devices may depend on the range, the numbers, and their locations on the mother ship.
- The area denial system is a type of non-lethal weapon that directs electromagnetic energy. It is used to stop and deter adversary boats from a relatively long range. It can save countless lives by providing a way to stop individuals without causing injury before a deadly confrontation develops. It is designed for area denial, perimeter security, and crowd control.
- The laser weapon system is also a directed-energy weapon. This weapon could take a target out of action easily. It has proven its effectiveness in small boat engagements. Fast engagement of this weapon is a great advantage against small boat threats.
- Small boats have great difficulty keeping a steady course in massive waves. Creating artificial waves in the way of approaching fast boats would derail them and therefore save the mother ship from considerable damage.
- Other non-lethal capabilities are non-lethal slippery foam, dazzle guns, optical devices, and flares.
- Helicopters and RHIBs are considered the most effective way to intercept the threat. Based on the discussions, the weapons are ordered according to their importance level.
    a. Helicopter
    b. RHIB
    c. Long-range acoustical devices
    d. Laser weapon system
    e. Close-in weapon system
    f. Unmanned aerial vehicles
    g. Area denial system
    h. Optical devices
    i. Flares

3. What if terrorists use a tourist boat for deception?

Terrorist organizations may build some deception tactics toward the mother ship. Terrorist organizations could have the purchasing power to buy an expensive tourist boat to deceive military warships.

This should be considered as a great deception tactic, and every fast-moving boat should be considered a threat to the mother ship.

4. What is the possibility of selecting homeports with little or no likelihood of such an incident occurring?

It is not always possible to select a homeport. We expect that small boats can pose a serious threat to the mother ship in shallow waters. Selecting a route to homeport out of shallow waters would reduce the risk. Also, geographic location makes all the difference, and therefore predetermining which ports to take the ship can be challenging.

5. When should the escort make the switch from non-lethal to lethal, if at all?

While non-lethal weapons provide an option to reduce risk against the threat, lethal force may be required to protect the mother ship. The time is a big factor on deciding to apply non-lethal or lethal force. Fast boats should be tracked in longer distances. When they are monitored entering predetermined assessment zones, non-lethal capabilities should be used according to escalation of the conflict. If the commander has no option to stop the threat, he can switch to lethal capabilities such as the main gun, close-in weapon system, special force engagement, or helicopter capabilities. There is no formula to determine which activity or set of activities to employ. It is just a decision process.

6. How effective will non-lethal weapons be in this scenario?

Addressing non-lethal weapons in this scenario may not be enough. The threat is a fast boat, and the incident happens in a short time. To intercept an asymmetric threat such as a fast boat requires highly maneuverable platforms such as helicopters and RHIBs.

Innovations and Lessons Learned: This team was led by a Pakistan navy officer who had experience. The team decided that instead of playing the wargame once, they would play the game many times with new players each time. Each playing of the game would first bring the player through the exercise with the VBSS team armed with lethal weapons, the standard equipping scheme for most navies. Then the same player would be asked to re-equip the team with a mixture of lethal and non-lethal capabilities, and then the player would replay the scenario to see how the choices of non-lethal weapons impacted the result. This was the first NPS analytic wargame designed and executed as a repeatable wargame and demonstrates that with careful consideration during the design process, it is possible to use the same wargame to collect multiple sets of data. There are definite advantages in collecting additional analysis data from repeated execution of the wargame.

CASE STUDY 3: FLEET DESIGN AND EXPEDITIONARY ADVANCED BASING OPERATIONS IN THE BALTIC SEA (Sponsor: Fleet Design, Concepts, and Experimentation Division at U.S. Fleet Forces Command)

Introduction: This wargame assessed how players employed different modular designs and expeditionary capabilities during a Baltic Sea wargame. Players effectively planned and executed distributed maritime operations (DMOs) to gain and maintain sea control in a cluttered, constrained, and contested battlespace.

Objective: The sponsor tasked the wargame team to explore the following areas:

1. Assess specified command and control structures and the ability to support distributed maneuver in a contested environment.
2. Assess each specified modular designs' support to mission execution. Evaluation areas include integration, distribution, and maneuver in accordance with the current Fleet Design Campaign Plan.
3. Identify which current and/or near-future technologies best support mission execution in a contested maritime environment (technologies must meet a time horizon of 2023).

Scenario: In 2024, Russia pursues regional expansion, believing that the United States is overcommitted to a geopolitical struggle in the South China

Sea. Seeking to capitalize on a reduced NATO presence, Russia begins fomenting unrest in Sweden with the intent of isolating Gotland Island from the mainland. Using information operations and cyber technologies, the Russians begin to organize far right groups disenfranchised by current immigration policies. Additionally, the Russians are using naval forces (both military and commercial vessels) to probe the sea and littoral areas around Gotland Island. Russia seeks to seize Gotland Island to achieve greater situational awareness of the maritime approaches to key Russian ports and further project control over shipping and natural resources within the Baltic Sea.

Key Players: Russia and the United States

Wargame Format and Type: The wargame effort utilized a turn-based, closed, mixed system, and seminar game. The game was conducted over two days. The first day featured player instruction on distributed maritime operations and dynamic modularity from the sea (DMS) concepts and a tutorial game session. At the end of the first day, players were directed to plan how they would design and employ their choice of forces the next day. The second day involved six hours of game play and two hours of open seminar discussion. The geographic extent of the game board included the Skagerrak in the east; St. Petersburg in the west; southern Finland in the north; and the northern coast of Germany in the south. Forty-five nautical mile–wide hexagons provided the movement spaces.

The game team closed the Red team off from the Blue team, and within the Blue team, naval/air forces and ground forces were separated from each other at times to test DMS command and control concepts. This construct limited each team's awareness to the fleet tactical grid established during game play. The game explored optimal fleet design by assigning each team a budget and list of possible modular fleet design (Blue) and anti-access/area denial (Red) capabilities. The budget served as a limiting mechanism and allowed the game team to identify those technologies that players believed best applied to the mission. Players included a mix of U.S. Navy surface warfare officers, U.S. Marine Corps combat arms officers, and U.S. Marine Corps logistics officers. Before play, players received instruction on DMS and DMO concepts, the objectives for the game, and focus areas associated with the sponsor's game objectives. Of note, all DMO information was obtained from the U.S. Fleet Forces website, the last wargaming team to focus on this area, and conversation with stakeholders at the Naval Postgraduate School. No briefing materials were provided by U.S. Fleet Forces. The Marine Corps Warfighting Lab provided two briefs on expeditionary advanced basing dated August 2017 and 30 April 2018.

Players were tasked with choosing the units they wanted to employ and placing them on the board as allowed. The teams moved their units three at a time, considering implications for sensor and weapons targeting coverage, force protection through mutual support, fuel consumption and resupply, and the information effects of force dispositions with regard to deterring the adversary. Data collected from the game included fleet design choices, unit moves, and adjudication outcomes, and player perceptions of opportunities and limitations afforded by their fleet capabilities and adversary actions. Data was collected both passively during game play as well as actively during open seminar discussion.

Adjudication MMTs: A newly developed set of MMTs provided adjudication of sensor and weapons engagement outcomes based on platform capabilities. Game injects included degraded satellite communications and intelligence reports that forced player consideration of the game's objectives. At the end of play, an open seminar session allowed players to discuss the impacts of their fleet design and the implications for current DMO/DMS concepts.

Key Findings:

- When fighting in a cluttered and contested environment, expeditionary capabilities must be integrated into modular design. An integrated fleet tactical grid, reinforced by the physical presence of naval forces ashore, restricts enemy options and forces the enemy to invest more time and resources to overt military activities. Ultimately, this reaction helps drive the U.S. diplomatic narrative and places pressure on enemy decisionmakers.
- Commanding and controlling a distributed force is a challenge. The disaggregation of friendly forces makes "mission type" orders essential to operating in degraded situations. Additionally, distributing forces places greater demands on individual battle staffs. It is likely that battle staffs will have to increase in size and undergo advanced training such as the Rapid Response Planning Process to accommodate an increase

in mission tempo and become more comfortable incorporating supplementary capabilities (e.g., fighting autonomous vehicles).
- Distributed, land-based detachments and capabilities reduce the exposure of high-value surface combatants, simplify logistic requirements, and allow U.S. forces to better establish a well-integrated fleet tactical grid. Diplomatic efforts will be critical to emplacing the right capabilities in the right places.
- Autonomous platforms and expeditionary capabilities increase the agility and robustness of surface modular designs, allowing premier strike platforms greater stand-off from enemy threats. In a cluttered environment like the Baltic Sea, this stand-off provides a surface action group more maneuver space and places pressure on an enemy to locate high-value assets.

Innovations and Lessons Learned: The unique aspect of this game was that the sponsoring organization, U.S. Fleet Forces command, agreed to have a student team composed of U.S. Marines design a wargame to assess how well the future thinking of the Navy (DMO) meshed with the future concepts that the Marines were developing (Expeditionary Advanced Basing Operations [EABO]). This provides a good demonstration of understanding the experience level of your players and what they can bring to the analysis effort. One of the key tenets of EABO was emphasizing the Marines' role in assisting the Navy with sea control. This particular geographic area also posed a unique challenge. There were some schools of thought that postulated the EABO concept was only useful in the Pacific with less restrictive sea lanes; this scenario in the Baltic presented many unique situations that are not found, or are less challenging, in most South China Sea scenarios.

CASE STUDY 4: DISTRIBUTED LETHALITY—
EASTERN MEDITERRANEAN
(Sponsor: U.S. Navy N96)

Introduction: Distributed lethality is an operational employment concept that combines increased surface warfare striking power with increased targeting capabilities in a geographically dispersed force. Using technologically advanced offensive and defensive weaponry and increased networking capabilities distributed lethality harnesses the complete joint sea, air, and land force to provide increased combat power and force projection globally. (Note: The distributed lethality concept began as a U.S. Navy surface force construct that was transformed into DMO.)

Objective: Conduct an analysis of distributed lethality's capabilities and limitations during phase 0 (shaping operations) and phase 1 (deterrence operations). N96 requested that the wargame include allied nation integration with distributed surface forces in a joint and combined maritime conflict and to explore how unmanned systems impact the Red team decision calculus.

Scenario: The scenario, situated in the Eastern Mediterranean (EMED), was played twice with different force compositions. The basis of the scenario was that Blue launched Tomahawk land attack missiles (TLAMs) into country Orange. Country Red, ally of Orange, threatened to start shooting down TLAMs and made aggressive threats. The first run of the wargame explored the effectiveness of combining a distributed lethality adaptive force package (AFP) with a small contingent of a NATO TF compared to a full contingent of a NATO TF. The second run of the game combined a separate AFP with a smaller contingent of a NATO TF. Each scenario made use of a different unmanned system: the TERN medium-altitude long-endurance unmanned aerial system and medium displacement unmanned surface vessels (MDUSVs).

Key Players: United States, Russia, NATO

Game Format and Type: Closed planning, open execution; mixed system and seminar. Upon initial receipt of the scenario brief, players were allotted forty-five minutes to complete an operational plan. Required products at the completion of the planning phase included a scorecard and a graphical overlay of the team's course of action. The scorecard provided initial objectives, individual unit movements, a perceived threat index, as well as the top enemy actions that would increase the perceived threat. The graphical overlay produced by each team depicted their unit's movements. Players utilized simple map graphics to show areas of movement, feints, blocking positions, and recon/attack positions. Additionally, players were asked to provide a proposed ISR structure, rules of engagement, command and control construct, communications architecture, and a brief logistical overview. The map graphics were vital to adjudicate the success of the sub-objectives and helped spur discussions regarding points of contention (i.e., enemy blocking position along an axis of advance). This analysis did not include a cost comparison of the options.

White Cell Adjudication: During the initial white cell adjudication portion of the wargame, subject matter experts discussed both plans via the graphical overlays and determined which objectives the game did not address.

Seminar Adjudication: The seminar wargame represents the most significant event for data collection. Each team member had the opportunity to discuss the advantages and disadvantages of their plan and how distributed lethality helped or hindered their planning process.

Final Survey: Upon completion of the seminar, the analysis team used a survey to answer any remaining questions from the DCMP not answered during the seminar. The survey was the final portion of the data collection and completed the wargame data collection requirements.

Key Findings:

- Distributed lethality increased Red's perceived threat level. The combined task force (CTF) without the AFP integration did not provide the same amount of deterrence and decreased Red's perceived threat level. The threat of dispersion by Blue forces caused Red to anticipate a larger threat area. In response, Red overextended their forces to find Blue assets. Red players accepted gaps in coverage to find Blue assets.
- The employment of the distributed lethality concept by Blue altered Red's decisionmaking process by forcing Red to exchange persistence for coverage. Distributed lethality forced Red to prioritize the surface picture at the expense of ASW. The search for guided missile destroyer TLAM shooters took priority and left Red susceptible to NATO surface ships if scenario escalated to phase 2 or 3. All Red maritime patrol and reconnaissance aircraft and tactical air assets were forced into ISR roles searching for surface vessels, leaving gaps in ASW and AAW.
- The distributed lethality concept allowed for creative employment of forces. Blue NATO forces in the CTF can better take advantage of geography in EMED and position forces for escalation to phase 2 or 3

by staying in territorial waters of NATO allies for extended periods of time and by conducting constant transits to and from home ports. Blue players took advantage of expectation from Red that Blue would align forces around high-value units. When LHA was present in scenario, Red devoted over 50 percent of assets into finding LHA; Blue dispersed forces by allowing non-AFP surface assets from the CTF to provide support to the LHA.

- Challenges to traditional command and control architecture under DL. The command ship determination in the scenarios was based on location and capability of platform. Individual ships need detailed command authorities for escalation. The distributed forces caused increased risk for loss communications; flexibility of DL concept is lost if individual commanders are constrained by restrictive rules of engagement.
- Distributed lethality created greater logistics challenges in phase 0 and 1 for Red forces in the EMED. The AFPs integrated with CTF can leverage allied ports for resupply in the EMED. There are significantly fewer options for Red force resupply in the EMED. Blue forces can employ DL to stress Red logistic channels by forcing Red to push out further, leading to less time on station for air and surface assets. However, a prolonged distributed lethality operation could face increased logistical requirements where Red will shift focus from disrupting blue offensive capabilities to disrupting Blue logistic chains with conventional and non-conventional means.
- The use of unmanned systems in distributed lethality provided Blue with options not feasible with manned systems. Red forces were more inclined to engage unmanned systems during phases 0 and 1. Blue recommended saving TERN for use in phase 2 and using manned systems for surveillance during phases 0 and 1 to force Red decisions. Blue forces can use MDUSVs in pickets with less fear of loss. It is advantageous for Blue to saturate the battlespace with MDUSVs to create noise. Blue also showed the utility of using MDUSVs as a tattle-tale and/or shadow of Red assets. The national policy for loss of large unmanned systems was brought up as a point of contention from both sides. There was uncertainty about what the response is for the loss of large unmanned systems.

- Allies believed AFP is a good concept that allows for easier integration. A continued messaging campaign to showcase the abilities of the distributed lethality concept is necessary to facilitate the understanding of the usefulness of distributed lethality. Allied forces saw distributed lethality as a combat multiplier.

In summary, this wargame demonstrated the predicament that distributed lethality places on opposition forces. The perceived threat area caused by the threat of distributed lethality caused an overextension of forces and numerous gaps in coverage in both scenarios with an AFP integrated with the CTF. The use of unmanned systems with distributed lethality can provide creative employment options for future AFP TF commanders. In the EMED, allied and partner nation support is key to the sustainment of a prolonged distributed lethality operation. Allied and partner nations integrated with distributed lethality also provide a difficult decision for opposition forces in the EMED due to the availability of territorial water and home ports to set forces up for escalation to phase 2 and 3.

Innovations and Lessons Learned: A key lesson learned here is to have regional subject matter experts on the wargame design team to ensure the unique dynamics that occur between regional and global powers in a specific geographic area are accurately modeled. This wargaming team had Turkish navy and air force students who helped the other team members understand the dynamics between the United States, NATO, Russia, and Syria that impacted the wargame's modeling effort.

CASE STUDY 5: CARRIER PRESENCE WARGAME (Sponsor: U.S. Navy N98)

Introduction: The Design for Maritime Superiority describes the mission of the U.S. Navy as:

> The United States Navy will be ready to conduct prompt and sustained combat incident to operations at sea. Our Navy will protect America from attack and preserve America's strategic influence in key regions of the world. U.S. naval forces and operations—from the sea floor to space, from deep water to the

littorals, and in the information domain—will deter aggression and enable peaceful resolution of crises on terms acceptable to the United States and our allies and partners.

If deterrence fails, the Navy will conduct decisive combat operations to defeat any enemy.

In a region of increased international tension, the U.S. Navy must decide whether or not to send a CSG [carrier strike group] into the region to maintain stability. The goal of this wargame is to attempt to quantify the deterrence value of the CSG. The proposed effort will seek to represent the value of CSG presence through a risk framework complementary to current Navy combat modeling.

Objective: Provide analysis to inform the design of an algorithm that quantifies the deterrence value of a CSG. The wargame output will be used to validate and improve the game theoretic conceptual model and provide input to the model's parameters. Issues that were examined include:

- The interaction between the global power and the regional power in phase 1 and any interactions that contribute to the regional situation transitioning out of phase 1. The sponsor specifically requested to account for the transition to phase 2 with a recognized reward structure similar to that in phase 1; however, due to the time and scope limitations of the wargame, this transition was not accounted for in the wargame.
- The contribution of the smaller regional nations to the interaction between the global and regional powers, and its effect on the regional environment.
- Validation of viable courses of action for each nation player within the diplomatic, information, military, economic construct.

Scenario: The wargaming team considered a scenario where several nations within the South China Sea have territorial disputes that cause tensions to rise.

Key Players: The game consisted of two main "players" (the United States and China) and a regional nation "green cell" panel that represented other countries of interest in the region. The regional nations considered were Vietnam, Taiwan, the Philippines, Singapore, Indonesia, and Malaysia.

Game Format and Type: The wargame was designed as a hybrid game, having aspects of open, closed, and seminar-style wargames. The United States and China "players" (each played by a three-person team) were in two closed, separate rooms, while the regional nation panel was in an open room to which all players had access. The regional nation panel, led by a facilitator, made decisions for each regional nation as a group.

Adjudication MMTs: The DCMP allowed for the collection of both qualitative and quantitative data. Data collected during the wargame included:

- Diplomatic and military moves: actions, requests, and the associated costs of the two main players, as well as responses from the targeted regional nation
- Measure of regional influence: a subjective measure of the disposition of each regional nation towards the actions and requests of the United States and China
- Regional nation requests: requests and statements made to the United States and China
- Post-game survey: player thoughts concerning the most and least influential actions taken by each nation during the course of the game

Data Analysis: The majority of data collected was qualitative. The quantitative data (the measure of regional influence and costs) were analyzed using simple graphing techniques to identify trends and points of interest in the game.

Key Findings:

- The wargame remained in phase 1 throughout ten full rounds of game play. No actions were taken by any player that caused the game to escalate to phase 2 or de-escalate to phase 0.
- Presence of the CSG in the phase 1 environment had minimal effect on player decisions.

- Only minor advantages were realized by the presence of the CSG in the South China Sea during the phase 1 scenario. Often those advantages did not justify the risk to the CSG as tensions increased during the game. Although the U.S. team was "forced" to make a military move with the CSG at least every four turns, its use was limited to port calls and freedom of navigation–style sailing in and around the South China Sea. The U.S. team used its CSG to conduct a bilateral military exercise with the Vietnamese, which was viewed favorably. During the post-game debrief, the Chinese team remarked that the presence of the carrier had no impact on their decisionmaking process. It offered little deterrence to Chinese objectives of expanding territorial claims and incrementally improving its regional position. The regional nation panel viewed the presence and participation of smaller U.S. naval vessels as more productive and beneficial.
- The regional nation players viewed economic incentives from the United States and China as strong influential measures. Military exercises were also viewed favorably. Actions taken by the United States and China that escalated tension in the region were viewed negatively, while any action taken by the main players to de-escalate tensions elicited a positive response.
- The Chinese viewed any U.S. military presence in the region as escalatory and took action to counter U.S. efforts. For example, when the U.S. team based P-8s in Vietnam, the Chinese team countered by conducting a "trade war" against Vietnam. Ultimately, the Vietnamese succumbed and asked for the withdrawal of U.S. aircraft.
- Vietnam was seen as the most influential regional player, while Taiwan was seen as the least influential. There are two possible reasons for this observation. First, the fictitious scenario we wrote started the game with China and Vietnam having economic disputes and a tense relationship. We feel this may have artificially forced the focus of a majority of the game on resolving the tension between those two countries. Unfortunately, since only ten rounds were played, the length of the wargame did not allow for additional scenarios to develop. Secondly, the regional panel had no representative from Taiwan, and as a result, little attention was devoted to Taiwan's part in the wargame.

- The lack of subject matter experts on the regional nation panel proved to be a limiting factor in the wargame. Due to this fact, the regional panel was conducted as a seminar-style wargame, and decisions were made collectively by the players on the panel.
- The United States achieved on average 3.2 "influence points" per cost unit spent, as compared to China, which averaged 2.8. These ratios captured the cost of influence, which was our main quantitative metric collected. On every round, we used a paper worksheet to capture each player's diplomatic and military move. The worksheet data was then entered into the DCMP Excel spreadsheet. The spreadsheet allowed us to record and manipulate the cost and regional influence data easily, resulting in a relatively quick and straightforward analysis that helped identify which game events were impactful.
- The United States and China experienced diminishing returns as the game progressed. In other words, the longer the game was played, each nation had to spend more to increase its regional influence.
- The United States saw no effect on regional influence when a second CSG was introduced into the region.

Summary: Our analysis and observations from the wargame show that the presence of a CSG had little impact in a phase 1 scenario, most notably due to issues outlined in the bias section. While the presence of the CSG did little to deter Chinese actions in a phase 1 environment, the wargame participants believed it would prove effective in preventing actions that would lead to transition into phase 2. The economic instrument of power proved to be the most influential method to increase regional influence in the scope of our wargame. Economic incentives were consistently viewed as favorable, while military interaction between the United States and China was viewed unfavorably. Our wargame results reinforce the need to examine the phase 2 environment and how the presence of the CSG influences individual country actions. Future work would benefit by addressing the issues highlighted within the bias section of the report.

Innovations and Lessons Learned: This case study provides a cautionary tale about the inherent biases that were introduced into the study based on the nature of how the wargame was designed, developed, and implemented.

- A well-defined scenario was essential to placing the game players in the appropriate mindset for the wargame. However, as some of the game results show, the scenario was a factor in driving player actions. For example, Vietnam was the initial focal point for the U.S. and Chinese players, simply because the written scenario began in that particular state. Given longer game play or scenario injects, the design team may have seen an adjustment to the game's focus. The scenario also highlighted border tensions between Malaysia and Indonesia. In response, the U.S. team used one of its diplomatic moves to hold talks to resolve the issue. This was noted in the post wargame survey as one of the least influential U.S. diplomatic moves.
- Regional influence, as defined by the wargaming team, gave an initial advantage to the United States.
- Since one objective of both the United States and China was to increase its influence within the South China Sea, this placed the Chinese team in a position requiring it to take swift action to gain the favor of its neighbors. The lack of subject matter experts on the regional nation panel proved to be a limiting factor in the wargame. The design team was unable to secure representatives from Vietnam, Taiwan, Singapore, and Malaysia. Due to this fact, the regional panel was conducted as a seminar-style wargame and collectively made decisions for each nation on the panel. A few players on the regional panel were military members from Indonesia and the Philippines. While they provided excellent insight from a military point of view for their particular country, they acknowledged a lack of complete familiarity with the political and diplomatic perspectives.
- Allowing a single diplomatic and single military decision per round was also a limiting factor, affecting the players' ability to take all necessary actions. It is conceivable that multiple diplomatic or military moves would be desired in a single turn. However, to aid in analysis and to examine cause and effect, the wargame team placed this limitation into the game rules.
- Regional nation military forces were not considered as usable in the wargame. The addition of these forces could have changed the course of decisions for the main players. In the scope and size of this wargame, their addition was deemed to add too much complication to the game play.

- Although the game objective for the main players was to minimize cost, the resources available to spend were considered unlimited. This is unrealistic but was implemented so as not to restrict the player's actions. It is also recognized that the cost for the Chinese to operate in their "backyard" would be much less than for U.S. forces operating at a greater distance. This fact was not accounted for. Also, the cost for a particular action was a subjective assessment determined by the wargame team, or by the game adjudicator during play.
- The wargame did not capture the impact of a transition to the phase 2 environment. Although the wargame allowed for transition to phase 2, no player action resulted in a shift out of the phase 1 environment. Due to the fact that force-on-force adjudication between the main players was not accounted for in the wargame, no sufficient mechanism existed to allow conflict or measure the resultant probability.

CASE STUDY 6: LITMUS WARGAMING IN THE SOUTH CHINA SEA
(Sponsor: U.S. Navy)

Introduction: The LITMUS (Littoral Combat Ship Integrated Toolkit for Mission Engineering Using Simulation) wargame initiative resulted from a desire by the U.S. Navy to explore the use of the existing LITMUS agent-based combat simulation to provide Red team and Blue team players with a virtual wartime environment similar to commercial video game software. The LITMUS wargame provides players the opportunity to control air and surface naval assets in simulated engagements. Through this construct, LITMUS executes a tactical scenario and provides simulated real-world information back to the user. The objective of the wargame was to assess the capability of the LITMUS to provide players a realistic simulated naval experience.

Objective: In order to assess the utility of LITMUS for analytical wargaming, six tactical questions related to a simulated tactical scenario in the South China Sea were examined:

- What is the best employment of the *Zumwalt* destroyer (DDG-1000)?
- When and what do Blue and Red (U.S. and Chinese forces) launch to gain ISR and targeting?

- What are typical flight profiles for airborne assets in this scenario?
- At what times do combatants change emissions control (EMCON) status or modify formations?
- How are MDUSVs employed?
- If Blue has a choice, do they attack the Red surface action group (SAG) or the logistics group?

Scenario: South China Sea in 2030. Natuna Besar, Indonesia, has been occupied and surrounded by Chinese forces. U.S. and allied forces plan to both attrite the enemy Chinese naval forces and deny resupply to the island to force a withdrawal by the occupying forces without the need to conduct an amphibious assault of Natuna Besar. This last option would involve numerous casualties and therefore is a last resort.

Key Players: Teams representing China and the United States at an operational level

Game Format and Type: The DCMP focused data collection on four phases of the wargame. The initial brief and questions phase queried all participants if they had any questions about what was asked of them after review of the player read-ahead packet and in-brief. The familiarization phase captured players' initial impressions of the game and user interface. Data collectors focused their efforts on recording the players' questions and the requested user controls not yet present in the wargame environment.

The wargame phase consisted of players executing the wargame as Red and Blue players with the South China Sea scenario objectives. This phase allowed data collectors to capture in-game player recommendations and answers to the proposed tactical questions during the real-time conduct of the wargame. Finally, the post-wargame phase offered players the opportunity to summarize their impressions of the wargame, provide surface warfare officer insight into the tactical questions, and recommend prioritization efforts for the software developers.

Key Findings:

- How is the *Zumwalt* (DDG-1000) deployed? The Blue force utilized the DDG-1000 together with other units in the SAG. However, the Blue side normally deployed the DDG-1000 to the front of the ship formation to utilize its improved stealth characteristic. However, this was limited by LITMUS's capability to deploy the ships in a formation. Ideally, Blue wanted to deploy the DDG-1000 at the front of the SAG formation. During the seminar discussion, the participants reinforced how the DDG-1000 should be employed at the front of a formation (approximately 15 miles in front of a formation) where it may utilize its stealth as an advantage, since this is one of the primary advantages it brings to the fight.

- When and what do Blue and Red (U.S. and Chinese forces) launch to gain ISR and targeting? The participants utilized their air assets primarily for ISR. Since both Blue and Red had fixed wing assets, these were primarily utilized at the beginning to find the enemy assets. For the Blue, both F-35s from the LHA-6 and the MH-60s from the DDGs were used to provide increased levels of ISR while the ships stayed in EMCON A. Blue used the fixed wing to project ISR further than the helicopters could go. In addition, the DDG-1000 utilized their advanced sensors and their helicopter to provide ISR after air platforms were launched. Finally, the MDUSV was utilized, but its capability to provide ISR was somewhat limited due to the sensor configuration inside of the scenario in LITMUS. Red utilized their J-20s to make large, box-shaped patrol routes where the Red player thought the Blue forces were operating. In addition, Red used smaller patrol routes with his helicopters to conduct ISR. Due to the inability of players to target aircraft with LITMUS, targeting was only conducted with surface combatants and not with aircraft; this feature is being worked on by the developers. Participants reinforced the F-35's importance in gathering ISR during the post-wargame discussion because it may distribute real-time updates to all ships in the operation.
- What are typical flight profiles for airborne assets in this scenario? Due to LITMUS's inability to analyze the flight profiles, this answer is rather limited. The players were unable to control the altitude or flight profile of the airborne assets inside of the user interface. Some of the aircraft were flying at appropriate altitudes, while others were flying at surface level. Red utilized a box-shaped patrol route for their J-20s to identify the ship locations. However, further development of LITMUS's user interface needs to be conducted to fully analyze this question.

- At what times do combatants change EMCON status or modify formations? The participants changed EMCON status for two major reasons in this scenario. First, aircraft often turned on emission for short intervals to identify targets in their area of operations and gain situational awareness for all friendly units. Ships also emitted in short intervals to gain situation awareness. Blue emitted primarily with their DDG-1000 due to its increased stealth.
- How are MDUSVs employed? MDUSVs were used to provide both deception and radiate to identify enemy assets. During the wargame, players would move the MDUSVs away from their SAG in an off-axis manner and radiate along a given azimuth. This provides deception so the enemy thinks there are more ships present in an area than in reality. In real life, using link 16, an MDUSV may provide information about the area of operations to ships that are not emitting.
- If Blue has a choice, do they attack Red SAG or the logistics group? In this scenario, the Blue force always attacked the Red SAG first before the logistics group. This was partially due to the attack guidance built into the user interface of LITMUS, as participants could not select the targets they would engage (it was automatically selected by the system). In addition, the Red logistics group was much farther away than the Red SAG; for both iterations of the wargame, the Blue forces attacked the Red SAG first.

Innovations and Lessons Learned: This was a unique wargame in that we wanted to examine if we could take a closed-loop analytic wargame designed to examine tactical and operational interactions between subsurface, surface, and aviation assets in a maritime environment and convert it into a wargaming adjudication tool. Ultimately, LITMUS was not appropriate for addressing the analytic questions of this effort, but it did identify issues for LITMUS to correct for future research. The cautionary tale from this effort is to be careful bringing in pre-designed and pre-developed software tools to provide administrative and adjudication support for the wargame. Under the best of conditions, these automated platforms will require time to adjust to the specific objectives and scenario of tour wargame.

CASE STUDY 7: HIGH NORTH
(Sponsor: SOCOM J-3I)

Introduction: Human activities have increased in the Arctic due to the melting of sea ice, and as such, there is a heightened interest in the region. Record low extents of Arctic sea ice over the past decade have focused scientific and policy attention on links to global climate change and projected ice-free seasons in the Arctic within decades. The five Arctic coastal states—the United States, Canada, Russia, Norway, and Denmark (of which Greenland is a territory)—are in the process of preparing Arctic territorial claims for submission to the Commission on the Limits of the Continental Shelf. Changes to the Arctic brought about by warming temperatures will likely allow more exploration for oil, gas, and minerals. Large commercial fisheries exist in the Arctic. Although there is significant international cooperation on Arctic issues, the Arctic is increasingly being viewed by concerned countries as a potential emerging security issue. This security issue stems from the geographic importance and potential capability of military use within the High North such as permanent basing options, power projection, large force exercises, and the extension of global reach.

Objective: The purpose of the High North seminar wargame was to analyze likely Russian courses of action and the use of hybrid warfare at the diplomatic/strategic level necessary for Russia to establish dominance of the Arctic. The wargame illuminated potential Russian actions that could be used without crossing the NATO Article 5 thresholds. Additionally, potential NATO responses and exploitable weaknesses within the NATO coalition, combined with current capability gaps, were identified that could become a hindrance to the development of a comprehensive and effective response to Russian courses of action.

Scenario: A scenario was established based on current Arctic realities in 2015 and advanced in five-year increments through 2025 based on projected build-up. Five scenario "injects" were used by moderators to facilitate discussion of actions and counteractions of the wargame players.

Key Players: Role players representing the key states with Arctic interests

Game Format and Type: The wargame was conducted as a seminar wargame.

Adjudication MMTs: The analysis team recorded all feedback and interaction from players during and after the wargame. The data collection and management plan included all the sub-issues and key information requirements to answer the sponsor's objective. Data collectors conducted private interviews with players as required in order to understand the reasoning behind their actions when not explicitly stated. Upon conclusion of the wargame, a quick-look report was issued and a back brief was conducted by the analysis team with the players to confirm their actions and lines of thought. Following the quick-look report, the High North Wargaming Team conducted a deeper and more detailed analysis of all data collected during the game.

Russian Actions and Observations

- Russia will use benevolent Arctic proposals and initiatives to distract attention away from tactical and operational measures designed to strengthen their position in the Arctic.
    - During game play Russia proposed an agreement to make the Arctic a "Nuclear Free Zone" knowing that the U.S. submarines are far superior to Russian submarines. The purpose of this proposal was to distract Russia's adversaries and provide space for other efforts. An unexpected result was a display of Russian leadership on Arctic conflicts, marked by environmental concerns and de-escalation. Decelerations such as this have the potential of gaining the support of nongovernmental organizations and the populations of concerned states.
    - Russia also proposed to take lead on further developing search and rescue (SAR) infrastructure. This would require cooperation amongst coastal states and the development of SAR-specific boundaries based on capabilities instead of sovereign claims. Russia saw this as an opportunity to justify expanding its operations and way to reinforce its current claims. Russia strengthened this proposal by co-opting China.
    - The USSOCOM J3I can play a role in averting such a situation by participating in SAR planning, assessments, and exercises in the Arctic. This will deny Russia the opportunity to exploit a gap under the guise of protecting human life.

- Russia will attempt to exploit any opportunity available to exert its influence in the Arctic.
  - The ethnic Russian population of Svalbard quickly became a focus of all players. Coastal states proposed that a team of international observers should be placed on the island to prevent any flareups. Russia demanded to be a part of the observation team. Russia believed that the ability to position an official on the island would help facilitate future subversive actions.

- Russia will rely heavily on information operations.
  - Throughout the wargame, Russia used every opportunity to push IO themes stressing U.S. and coastal state impotence and lack of leadership. Russia was also able to divert U.S. and partner force assets from the Arctic area.
  - In response to an injected Islamic terrorist attack against ethnic Russians in the Baltics, Russia announced concern for all ethnic Russians. This was sufficient to cause NATO states to focus on resolving the Baltic situation and preventing a replay of Ukraine. Russia players confirmed that their intentions were to exploit the inject to draw attention away from the Arctic.
  - In response to an inject regarding a Chinese oil tanker sinking and causing a massive oil spill, Russia accused the United States of ultimately targeting the ship and being a cause of the sinking. China demands that institutions be developed to handle such incidents. This led to an agreement between Russia and China to begin building SAR infrastructure, citing the lack of U.S. and partner nation involvement and the need to execute the measure despite any other assistance.

NATO Actions and Observations

- Canadian claim to the Northwest Passage is a national sensitivity, and a dispute with other NATO partners (the United States in this game) can be leveraged by Russia in the attempt to drive a wedge between Canada and other NATO partners.

- Canada reaffirmed its claim to the Northwest Passage. This immediately caused friction between coastal NATO partners. Russia attempted to exploit this by acknowledging Canada's claim as valid.
- NATO Arctic states will not immediately look to NATO to resolve their Arctic disputes, but would rather handle most of them bilaterally with Russia or other states in order to expeditiously resolve conflicts.
- During the Russian nuclear submarine in Canadian waters inject, a distress call was initiated after losing power and was caused by unexplained detonations. The United States and Canada quickly sought to de-escalate the situation and prevent the incident from being labeled as an Article V violation. Russia attributed the incident to faulty navigation.
- NATO/Arctic states may rely on a belief that Russian and Chinese development in the Arctic is economically unsustainable.
- Throughout the game Russia continued to expand its bases and operations. Canada and the United States eventually stated that they will allow Russia to "bankrupt itself on the Arctic."
- If this theory is valid, there may be an opportunity to accelerate Russia's expenditures in the Arctic. By conducting surveys and exercises with Special Operations Forces personnel in the region, false signals can be sent to Russia, stimulating Russia to exert more control and exhaust itself economically.

General Actions and Observations

- All Arctic players agreed that there should be an international information sharing database to track and regulate the details and locations of ships transiting the Arctic.
- By fostering a relationship with the Article Council, USSOCOM can be better prepared to counter Russia's actions in the Arctic.
- China is likely to have a significant influence in the Arctic. Although the wargame did not indicate Chinese military interest in the Arctic, they signaled commercial interests such as using the Northern Sea Route and investing in commerce and ports. These activities may have a side effect on environmental issues that may be able to fix resources in the Arctic region.

Conclusion: The eleven-week study, development, and execution of the High North wargame yielded significant data points that have long-term predictive value. Efforts should be made to ensure deficiencies such as SAR are clearly delineated in order to deny Russia the opportunity to exploit them in the future. An inherent overreliance on Article V triggers in the Arctic can potentially weaken NATO's credibility in other theaters. Additionally, coastal NATO states will decidedly choose to use the Arctic Council as a forum to handle Arctic concerns while USSOCOM must remain and invest in becoming a viable member in the discussions led by the Arctic Council in order to counter future Russian efforts.

Innovations and Lessons Learned: This case study highlights the capability of a wargame to provide insights and hypotheses for additional follow-on study. In this case, two of the wargaming team students went on to do a thesis on this topic.[1] They incorporated the use of an adjudication tool called Senturion, a simulation capability that analyzes the political dynamics within local, domestic, and international contexts and predicts how the policy positions of competing interests will evolve over time.[2]

CASE STUDY 8: TRIDENT DELPHI
(Sponsor: U.S. Navy Special Warfare Command [NSW])

Introduction: In effort to move from NSW's counterterrorism and counterinsurgency operational objectives of the past seventeen years, this wargame looked at near-peer conflict in 2030.

Objective: The purpose of this wargame was to explore and identify potential NSW supporting effects for theater commanders in potential 2030 maritime conflicts with near-peer adversaries and to demonstrate to NSW the ability of analytical wargaming to develop insights into NSW issues. Issues to be studied include:

- How can NSW set the conditions for the theater to support joint force commander (JFC) actions in the event of hostilities?
- How can NSW provide deterrent options to prevent conflict escalation?
- How might potential adversaries respond to NSW operational concepts under consideration?

- How can NSW create effects in phase 2 operating without air or maritime superiority?

Sub-issues to be studied include:

- How can NSW support increased domain awareness for the JFC?
- How can NSW employ unique mobility capabilities in support of JFC operations (surface/subsurface)?
- How can NSW employ select advanced capabilities in support of JFC operations?
- How can NSW employ operational deception in support of JFC operations?

Scenario: The first day focused on the European Command area of operations, and the second day focused on the Pacific Command area of operations.

Key Players: Players of the wargame included senior and junior members of the U.S. Navy Surface Warfare community, mid-grade/junior/chief petty officers of the Naval Special Warfare community, mid-grade Army Special Forces officers, mid-grade Air Force Special Operations pilots, junior intelligence officers, and regional experts from the National Security Affairs department at NPS.

Game Format and Type: The wargame was conducted as an open seminar–style wargame. After introductory briefings on NSW history, capabilities, future technology, and game format, players were separated into four teams—two representing U.S. theater planners, a Red cell, and a "wildcard" team tasked with unconventional concept development. The teams were briefed on scenario context and operational vignettes and were tasked to create Naval Special Warfare concepts of operation for consideration generating desired effects. The concepts were then briefed to the group and evaluated via facilitated discussion for feasibility, effects, and risk.

Adjudication MMTs: Adjudication was controlled by the facilitator who facilitated a discussion to achieve a consensus on actions/decisions based on player arguments focused on feasibility, effects, and risks.

Key Findings: Consistent with the purpose of this wargame, the primary results revealed a number of operational concepts for NSW to generate effects in future conflicts. These concepts revealed the following high-level takeaways:

- Consideration for employment in phases 1 and 2 of a future conflict can inform better decisions in phase 0. During game play, players often referred back to capabilities developed in earlier phases to create desired effects in phases 1 and 2.
- NSW requirements and opportunities were similar in the two scenarios studied in European Command and Pacific Command. Many of the primary considerations, including escalation management, information operations, and maritime domain awareness, were similar. These were very distinct from recent operational employment focused on land-based counterterrorism and counterinsurgency.
- The wargaming method itself proved valuable in preparing the force for these near-peer conflicts in several ways:
  - For planning, by generating employment concepts for effects as intended
  - For strategy and resourcing, by highlighting differences between past operational approaches and requirements, and future ones
  - For training and education, by informing members of NSW, the fleet, and other communities on capabilities, limitations, and opportunities for utilizing NSW

Innovations and Lessons Learned: The unique aspect of this wargame was that its purpose was multifaceted, with a dual purpose of "explore and demonstrate." The genesis of this was the time frame, 2016–17. The United States was in the latter stages of the Afghanistan and Iraq wars and was refocusing on China with the "pivot to the Pacific." Special operations organizations were realizing that their parent services had been without their services for so long, they had forgotten what capabilities that special operations units could bring to a more conventional battle against a near-peer competitor. This wargame's analytic purpose was to analyze emerging and proposed technologies to assist NSW in understanding how the technologies could best be leveraged in a conflict. The educational portion of the wargame was to demonstrate to the Navy the capabilities that NSW had that could be leveraged if paired with conventional naval operations against a near-peer adversary.

APPENDIX 6

The Crisis in Zefra: A Matrix Game

■ ■ ■ ■ ■

The Crisis in Zefra is an example of using a matrix wargame to gain analytical insight into a sponsor's problem and issue. We designed this wargame to address issue 3 ("What force protection issues does the combined joint task force [CJTF] commander face?") from practical exercise 2, and it is intended for you to pull from the book and conduct on your own.

AIM

The aim of this wargame is to introduce players to the concept of matrix games in an analytical setting. This wargame's objective is to provide insights into the challenges and requirements for the CJTF-Z to stabilize Zefra. This wargame was designed to address the specific issue: What force protection issues does the CJTF commander face? The compact nature of this example, with a small number of players and limited scenario, is one way to demonstrate a matrix game, how it supports analytical analysis, and many of the elements presented in the book. As analysts, we are trying to capture insight into the myriad of possible security issues the CJTF commander may face attempting to stabilize the island. The analytical wargaming style we are using is a matrix game with a consensus-focused adjudication for most actions, but since we do expect some amount of tactical engagement, we will have methods, models, and tools to cover kinetic results.

HOW TO PLAY

Player actions in the Crisis in Zefra, like most matrix games, are resolved by the facilitator using a structured sequence of arguments from the players. Each player, in turn, will take an action in the form of an "argument." A successful argument (action) will advance the narrative of the game and the player's position in achieving their objective. The Crisis in Zefra will use the "Pros and Cons" system. This method contains three basic elements for each presented argument:

- The active player states argument (action) as: Something That Happens.
- The active player states: The Number of Reasons Why It Might Happen (Pros).
- The other players then state: A Number of Reasons Why It Might NOT Happen (Cons).

The facilitator adjudicates on the success or failure of the argument. A simple example may help clarify this approach. The president of Zefra might argue:

"I intend to demonstrate my resolve for stability in the capital by breaking up the Truscan protestors who have occupied the manufacturing zone with my police supported by the secret police, making the protestors disperse. I can achieve this action because:

- I have an experienced core of police officers who are not afraid of unarmed protestors.
- The police are equipped with light armored vehicles so they can concentrate themselves near the protestors quickly.
- The secret police have the ability to use excessive force and the protestors fear them.

- The manufacturing zone is isolated from the main population, so there is less room for the protestors to hide and more room for them to disperse."

This action has four arguments in support of it (4x Pros). The group of players agree that all four arguments are reasonable, so the facilitator will accept each of them. The facilitator will now seek counterarguments from the other players:

- The manufacturing zone is likely to have big industrial complexes with walls and security fences, unsuitable for the light armored vehicles, where the protestors will be hard to reach.
- The manufacturing zone is full of material that the protestors could use to fight off the police, like pieces of pipe and lumps of concrete.

This represents two counterarguments (2x Cons). However, the group does not believe that the first counterargument really makes sense and argues that the protestors are more likely to be protesting outside the factory. If they were occupying a derelict site instead, who would care? The facilitator should have a discussion of why they do not believe this is a valid counterargument to provide the players the opportunity to make the case for why it is valid. To continue this example, we will assume that the discussion was not successful and there is only one accepted counterargument so the facilitator will only accept the second counterargument (1x Con).

The success of the action/argument is then adjudicated by taking 2x D6 with a base chance of 7 or more to succeed. Please note that by needing a 7 or more, the game will have a "narrative bias" because 7+ represents a 58 percent chance of success if all things are equal. In this example, with a total of 3x Pros and 1x Con, the player will add 2 to the dice score for determining success. Using only 2x D6 is to encourage players to come up with a few good reasons rather than a laundry list of lots of trivial ones.

The advantage of this system is that you formalize the Pros and Cons of an argument, and the role of the facilitator becomes that of ensuring that the Pros and Cons carry equal weight—perhaps making compelling reasons worth two Pros and two or three weaker reasons against only worth one Con. You need to ensure you don't end up with an extensive list of trivial reasons or a player restating a reason already accepted in a slightly different way in a desperate attempt to gain points.

One very useful benefit of the Pros and Cons system is that it provides reasons for failure should the dice roll not succeed. You can also more easily run the game with very knowledgeable players.

NOTES ABOUT ARGUMENTS

One point to remember is that any reasonable argument is allowed in a matrix game if it is relevant to the scenario. It is common for players new to matrix games to argue that another player is influenced by something or them agreeing to a course of action. The player is present and can simply be asked—so that a little time between turns to allow the players to negotiate with each other (in secret if necessary) makes for a better game. Arguments are for actions during a turn. If players want to negotiate with each other, they can do so in between turns.

Sometimes players get carried away with their arguments and try to do several actions at the same time, which is not allowed. A player only gets one action a turn because part of the narrative and insight comes from players deciding the priority of actions. The action could be large, but it must be a single action, so mobilizing the militia and providing the police with heavy weapons would be two separate actions—which do you want to do first?

If a player's argument fails to succeed, the player will get a "Second Chance" chit. This is retained, and the player can use it at a later stage in the game to re-roll the dice. This technique tends to balance the game for beginners and prevent an unlucky player from getting placed at a big disadvantage early in the game and being demoralized.

TURN LENGTH

A game turn in Crisis in Zefra is approximately one week. This should be considered a variable length of time ranging from a few days to a couple of weeks. Therefore, player action/arguments need to be something that could reasonably occur during this time period. As an example, conducting a mortar attack on a refugee camp by clandestine forces is clearly

SECOND CHANCE	**SECOND CHANCE**
CJTF-Z	**ZEFRA**
This permits you to re-roll the random number generator when deciding on the outcome of a Matrix Argument	This permits you to re-roll the random number generator when deciding on the outcome of a Matrix Argument
SECOND CHANCE	**SECOND CHANCE**
DALOON	**PLAM**
This permits you to re-roll the random number generator when deciding on the outcome of a Matrix Argument	This permits you to re-roll the random number generator when deciding on the outcome of a Matrix Argument
SECOND CHANCE	**SECOND CHANCE**
IFF	**ZA**
This permits you to re-roll the random number generator when deciding on the outcome of a Matrix Argument	This permits you to re-roll the random number generator when deciding on the outcome of a Matrix Argument

Crisis in Zefra Cards

possible in a game turn, but arguing about the requirement to conduct reconnaissance, equipping, organizing, and moving to the refugee camp may require a preparatory argument to increase the likelihood of success.

At the end of the turn, the facilitator should review all of the arguments, both successful and unsuccessful, that occurred during the turn. The facilitator should also review any previous successful arguments (situations) that are still in effect if these arguments have not been countered during the turn. The facilitator will then generate a new set of established facts based on the set of successful and failed player arguments for the next turn. In establishing this baseline of new facts, the facilitator should consider reasonable unintended consequences that are expected to occur beyond the immediate results of the player's argument.

INTER-TURN NEGOTIATIONS

The players may want to engage in discussions/negotiations with each other before the beginning of the turn to strike a deal. As an example, one player arguing during the turn that they will "influence the president of Zefra" will not work since the president is a player who will simply counterargue the point. These discussions can be open or private from other players. The inter-turn negotiations provide the opportunity to potentially influence the other player. As a reminder, this is an analytical wargame, so it is essential to capture these discussions and offline deals and negotiations.

ELECTIONS

It is very likely that during the course of the game, there will be one or more arguments calling for elections. Zefra has just conducted an election, and another one would not be unexpected. However, in Crisis in Zefra, there needs to be a minimum of at least one turn before the call for elections and the execution of elections. In addition, this call for elections should not occur prior to other actions/arguments that would/could influence the popularity of the president. If an election does occur, the following process is suggested to determine the outcome: Each player will receive one vote. In addition, you will add to the player votes the "popular standing" in which the player character and their supporters are held among the general populace. This can be captured by recording each time the players argue for an action that increases their support or popularity. You should record the advantage each player has gained by marking their playing piece with plusses and minuses (so the other players are aware of their general standing as well). This means that during the game, some players' popularity will go down as well as up, and there may well be a good deal of off-table negotiations taking place before the actual votes are cast.

SECRET ARGUMENTS

Secret arguments are possible in the game if a player wants to take an action that they want to keep hidden from the other players. It could be that you have taken some action that you believe will impact another player if they take a particular action. In this case, the player will simply write down their argument on a piece of paper and present it to the facilitator, announcing to the other players that you are making a secret argument. The facilitator will treat this as any other argument and make a determination of success or failure but not inform the other players about the action.

However, the facilitator should not allow too many secret arguments in the game. These arguments have a tendency to destroy the developing narrative of the wargame. They also eliminate the opportunity for counter-arguments, which is one of the advantages of matrix games.

MEASURE OF SUCCESS

The facilitator should be careful declaring success or failure as a simple "Yes" or "No" proposition. Many player arguments are probably best judged on a sliding scale of success or failure in terms of numbers or the quality of the outcome. The roll of the dice can help in determining the full impact of success or failure. For example, if a 7 or greater is required for success and the player rolls a double 6 (12), this can indicate an especially notable success. So, if in the previous argument, the People's Liberation Armed Militia (PLAM) succeeded in stealing nuclear waste and rolled a double 6, they might gain some advantage in helping to weaponize it or having enough material for several weapons. If they rolled a 7, then they might only have acquired a bare minimum of nuclear material. Conversely, if they rolled a double 1, it could represent a disastrous failure where closed-circuit TV footage is leaked to the media of the PLAM attempting to break into the nuclear facility.

KILLING ARGUMENTS

It is completely possible during the course of this wargame that one of the players argues for something that will kill off another player. Matrix games are designed to allow players to argue for anything that is reasonable, so this action has some potential, and the facilitator should assess it like any other argument. As an example, assassination attempts are common occurrences, but depending on the arguments, they may not be very likely to succeed. If a player is killed off in the wargame, it does not prevent the player from continuing to make arguments; nor is another character appointed to step into the vacant leadership position.

BIG PROJECTS

There is the possibility during Crisis in Zefra that some actions and events may represent a large investment in time and resources and may require multiple arguments in order to achieve ultimate success. In general, a big project should take no more than three successful arguments; otherwise the game will start to focus on a single event. As a reminder, once a successful argument has started an ongoing action, it will continue until another argument stops it. In Crisis in Zefra, one player may want to develop a missile-delivered weapon of mass destruction. This would require the player to acquire the weaponized material, the delivery mechanism, and the skill to develop the weapon in order to succeed.

METHOD, MODELS, AND TOOLS

Capricornia Stability Index

The Capricornia stability index is designed to create a little tension in the wargame and to keep the players focused on their objectives. The index is a sliding scale from -6 (open civil war in Zefra) to 6 (country stabilized) and is intended as an indicator of the general feeling among the players of whether the situation is getting better or worse on the island. The index starts at 1 and is adjusted up or down after all players have completed their actions during the turn. After all play is complete, the facilitator and players will discuss how the collective actions of all players have either improved or worsened the situation and shift the index appropriately.

Zefran Presidential Influence Index

The Zefran and Daloon presidential influence indices are designed to measure the influence, political capability, and popularity of each country's president. The index, a scale from -1 (ousted or dead) to 10 (president for life), is used to judge how well each respective player is doing in the game. Each player will start at 5 on their respective influence index. Once per turn, the Zefran or Daloon president may use presidential influence to focus and energize their administration to take a second action during their turn. This will cost them some of their influence, and the player will immediately reduce their influence by 1. After all play is complete, the facilitator and players will discuss how the situation in each country and the specific actions of the country may have improved or worsened their influence and shift the index appropriately.

Insurgency Consequences

The Zefra president has an active insurgency in his country that he must stop. Once per turn, if the leader of the PLAM is still alive and active (with active defined as at least two ongoing events—protest, riot, or direct action), the PLAM player will roll a six-sided die at the end of their turn, consult the insurgency results table and take the appropriate action. The ongoing and active insurgency hurts the Zefran president's influence, and there is a good chance that unless the president stops the insurgency, he will lose influence in the country. For example, assume that the PLAM still has an active protest going on at the university and a riot in the business district.

Insurgency Results Table Zefra Presidential Influence Track						
Roll	1	2	3	4	5	6
Effect	0	0	0	-1	-1	-2

Kinetic Operations

Crisis in Zefra utilizes the simple combat resolution using dice (SCRUD) method to resolve all kinetic operations. The general rule is that each player will receive one six-sided die for each combat type unit involved in the operation. Each player will roll their appropriate number of dice, and each die will be modified based on the quality of the unit (see SCRUD Modifier Table). The dice are compared to each other with the higher dice roll winning. For example, the CJTF commander intends to attack an Illustrious Fighters for Freedom (IFF) outpost containing two IFF units with three infantry companies—supported with ISR to destroy the IFF units. The group agrees, because of the ISR support, that CJTF commander is likely to successfully engage the IFF before they melt into the countryside. The CJTF commander, with three units, rolls three dice for a result of 5, 3, and 2. However, because these are superior troops according to the SCRUD modifier table, the results are modified up to 7, 5, and 4, respectively. The IFF player rolls two dice for the two units in the engagement, with the result of 4 and 3. IFF forces are rated above average so the IFF dice rolls are modified up to a 5 and 4 respectively. The two players then rank order their dice from highest to lowest and compare the results to determine the victor (highest die win). In this case, the CJTF will destroy both IFF forces since the CJTF modified rolls of 7 and 5 will defeat the IFF modified rolls of 5 and 4.

SCRUD Modifier Table		
Quality	**SCRUD Modifier**	**Units**
Superior	+2	UN Forces
Above Average	+1	IFF, Daloon Forces
Average	0	Zefra Regular Forces, Militia
Below Average	-1	Protestors, Rioters

THE CRISIS IN ZEFRA MATRIX WARGAME

There is continuing trouble on the small South Pacific island of Capricornia. A decade later, Zefra is still feeling the impact of its civil war. The country is still in tatters. The ruling Bongos are still suppressing the Tuscans, insurgent and splinter Zefran military groups are still active in the country and thousands of Truscan refugees still flow into the neighboring country of Daloon. A strong Truscan insurgency continues to brew within the country. During the civil war, various factions fought the central government in the role of an opposition party, a viable replacement for the Bongo-led autocracy. By the conclusion of the civil war, with the autocracy left largely intact, the government's opponents became an

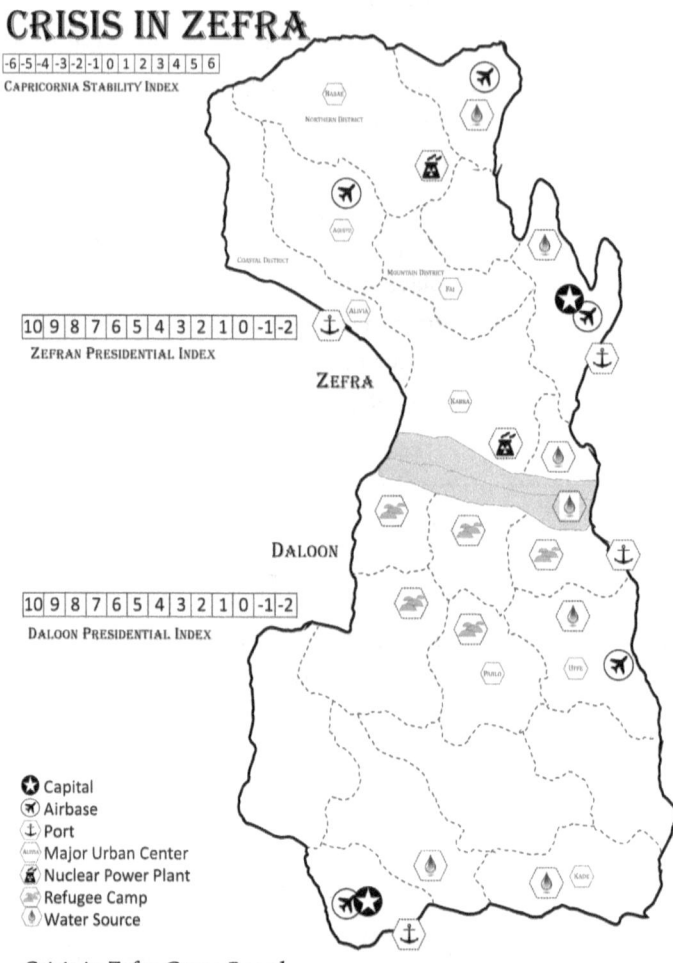

Crisis in Zefra Game Board

insurgency, the aim of which was to show that the Bongo-led autocracy could not govern Zefra except in a few selected areas, and then only with the most savage of methods. Indeed, a goal of the insurgency was to show that when the autocracy did govern, it was with a heavy hand, well supported by brutal security forces.

The 2019 invasion of Zefra into Daloon was a desperate attempt to unite Zefra's Bongo and Truscan ethnic groups under the umbrella of national pride, to crush the Zefran insurgents who established camps in Daloon and to seize critical resources in Daloon. Daloon's armed forces were able to halt the invasion, but at a considerable price in casualties and the Daloon ground forces were unable to expel all Zefran forces and fully reestablish the international border. Small pockets of Zefran forces remain inside Daloon territory.

The president of Zefra, having failed in his objective of seizing the resources of its southern neighbor and of unifying his nation to fight for a common purpose, stepped down and called for new presidential elections. In addition, Daloon appealed once more to the international community to assist it against the incursion and to deal with the internal Zefran issues that had led to the attempted invasion. The newly elected president of Zefra (April 2020) has been far subtler than his predecessors in his policies. Currently he seems to welcome a foreign military presence in his country as a means of quelling the insurrection.

ROLES

Order of Play
- President of Daloon
- President of Zefra
- Military Leader of the PLAM (Truscan)
- Commander of the IFF Battalion (Zefran)
- Head of Zefra Association (Bongo)
- Commander of CJTF-Z
- Capricornia Stability Index Update

Scales
- Each turn represents approximately one week (ranges from a few days to two weeks).
- A military counter is about one hundred men, a Protest counter represents about one hundred to two hundred civilians, a Police or Militia counter represents thirty to fifty men.

Commander of JTF-Z
The CJTF-Z has a United Nations (UN) mandate to restore stability to Zefra. The troop-contributing nations include Britain, Canada, Australia, and the Netherlands. While most of the military activity is expected to be land-based, CJTF-Z does have naval and air resources. The military leadership

in CJTF-Z believes it has a handle on the situation and is skeptical that any U.S. military action would be to the long-term benefit of CJTF-Z. However, the CJTF-Z commander has the ability to ask for and receive U.S. military assistance if necessary to achieve the CJTF-Z's objectives.

The IFF battalion is a direct military problem that will make the situation worse for you. They are militarily very capable and may be a match for you at the small unit level unless you use overwhelming force. The two insurgency groups (PLAM and Internal Security Bureau), while not a military match for you, will seek to disrupt stability and must be quickly brought under control.

Objectives
- Establish a sense of peace and stability within Zefra.
- Neutralize all forces that are creating instability, perpetrating acts of inhumanity, and generating the humanitarian catastrophe.
- Establish at least local cessation of hostilities and security as a prerequisite for other relief and development operations to take place.
- Reestablish the international boundary of Daloon and Zefra.
- Secure the safety of the displaced persons and refugees in Daloon.
- Cooperate as appropriate with any humanitarian operations in the area.

Setup (Blue Counters)
- Establish yourself in a port/airfield of your choice in Daloon.
- Place two military units anywhere in Daloon.
- Place one NGO anywhere on Capricornia.
- Retain all remaining CJTF-Z forces for future deployment on Capricornia.

Additional Events during Turn: none

Initial Units
Three heavy mobile military units; three light mobile military units; five infantry units; two artillery units; four naval units; four military police units; three air units (strike); three air units (lift); two drones (this is not intended to be all inclusive—player can designate additional units).

President of Zefra

The situation in Zefra is extremely fluid. Just a couple of months ago, you were elected president of Zefra and for the moment hold a narrow mandate for governing. The UN-backed coalition is moving into the area to deal with instability in Zefra, but you fear you will begin to lose your mandate and influence the longer they stay. You want to demonstrate to the world that you can administer Zefran affairs without outside interference. You would prefer to be subtle in your actions, but you are prepared to be fairly ruthless; after all, this approach has served the ruling Bongo class in the past. You are fortunate to have a very good relationship with the current regime in Beijing and may be able to call on them for needed support to stay in power.

The commander of the IFF battalion is a rogue and direct threat to the stability of Zefra and your power. You have fears that he may influence other senior military leaders and may plot to remove you from power.

The People's Liberation Armed Militia represents a political threat. You know they are responsible for much of the protests in the street calling for new elections. You realize that the longer they operate, the greater the likelihood that the CJTF will stay in Zefra.

The Zefra Association (ZA) provides a way to improve the situation for you in Zefra. They have the means to hobble any political or military gains of your opponents and could be a direct counter to the PLAM. The magic of your relationship with the ZA is "plausible deniability"—you can claim these are rogue elements that have no connection to your administration . . . as long as everyone keeps their mouths shut!

Objective

- Crush the Truscan (PLAM) insurgency.
- Get the UN-sponsored coalition force out of Zefra as soon as possible. Have Zefra return to the situation before the foreign interventions.
- Bring the IFF commander under your control or neutralize the group's ability to influence political and senior military leaders.
- Maintain "plausible deniability" for any covert action that might otherwise be attributable to the Zefran government.

- Appear in public to welcome foreign aid, especially funds. Offer to provide assistance to the UN-backed coalition (but keep them tied up so they do not cause trouble).
- Make sure you are still the president of Zefra at the end of the game.

Setup
- Place yourself in the presidential palace in the capital of Zefra.
- Place a military barracks and one military unit in any district of Zefra.
- Place one counter in any location in the Zefran capital.
- Retain all remaining counters for future deployment.

Additional Events during Turn

Once per turn you can use your presidential influence to focus and energize your administration to take a second action. Reduce your presidential influence by one on the presidential influence track.

Initial Units

Three police units; one Special Weapons and Tactics (SWAT) unit; four mobile military units; four infantry units; one military barracks (this is not intended to be all inclusive—player can designate additional units).

President of Daloon

You are a popular leader of your country, and the recent defeat of Zefra has given you the support of your people, but you are in a very difficult situation. The stability of Zefra keeps you awake at night. Unrest continues in the refugee camps in Daloon. Zefran military and paramilitary elements are sneaking across your border to attack refugees; the Zefran government argues that the refugee camps are providing shelter to insurgents who cross into Zefra to attack innocent Bongos.

The population of Daloon is currently still with you, but they are growing restless after more than a decade of border issues with Zefra. The inability to maintain a strong border is beginning to cause concerns among your supporters and is an easy topic for your political opponents.

As for the UN/coalition force moving into the area, it would be wise to give this force some support. However, the people of Daloon have always been suspicious of any foreign troops operating in their country.

Objectives
- Keep Daloon and its people safe.
- Secure the border. This applies to all Zefran elements crossing the border and to foreign troops of the UN-backed coalition.
- Encourage nongovernmental organizations to provide aid to the refugees in the camps; otherwise the Daloon government would have to fill the bill.
- Make sure you are still president at the end of the game.

Setup
- Place yourself in the capital of Daloon.
- Place one military unit in any district of Daloon.
- Retain all remaining counters for future deployment.

Additional Events during Turn
Once per turn you can use your presidential influence to focus and energize your administration to take a second action. Reduce your presidential influence by one on the presidential influence track.

Initial Units
One police unit; one medical care team; two mobile military units; two infantry units; one transportation unit (this is not intended to be all inclusive—player can designate additional units).

Military Leader of the PLAM

You are a very charismatic leader and loved and supported by the Truscans across Zefra. You know that the current president of Zefra gained power through an illegitimate election process. Truscan observers claimed that there was electoral fraud on a massive scale. Street protests are gaining international attention, especially when they are handled with a heavy hand by the current administration. You have a strong cadre of armed supporters you can call upon for direct action and the ability to call for more protests and riots in the country.

The last hope of the Truscan people is the UN-backed coalition moving into the area to deal with instability in Zefra. One way or another, you believe this coalition force must take action against the Bongo oppressors.

If needed to support your cause, you will foster more instability in the country to force the hand of the UN, even if you have to fabricate incidents to encourage this instability. You are hoping these incidents may even draw other international players into our conflict—particularly the United States. We are fighting for democracy in Zefra, and who better to have on our side than the leader of the free world.

The Zefra Association and its organization of secret police and spies represent the greatest threat to you and your cause.

Objectives
- Force an election where the majority (Truscans) can have the democratic government they deserve.
- Discredit the current president and show that he is an ineffective leader.
- Replace the president with someone who will support Truscans.

Setup
- Place yourself at the university in the Zefran capital.
- Establish a militia camp and one counter anywhere in Daloon.
- Place one refugee counter anywhere in Zefra.
- Place two protest counters anywhere in the capital of Zefra.
- Retain all remaining counters for future deployment.

Additional Events during Turn

Once per turn, if you are still alive and active (at least two ongoing events—protest, riot, or direct action) roll a six-sided dice and consult the Insurgency Results Table.

Initial Units

Three militia units; four protestor groups; one terrorist group; two refugee groups; one militia camp (this is not intended to be all inclusive—player can designate additional units).

Commander of the IFF Battalion

You are the commander of the Zefra's most effective fighting force consisting of a cadre of one thousand experienced fighters who are willing to die for you. You firmly believe that the only way to address the inequities your country has suffered at the hands of Daloon is through direct action. You believe the current president is too subtle and does not have the stomach to make the necessary hard decisions to secure a strong future for Zefra. You would not be unhappy if he was replaced by a stronger hard-liner, and you have even given thought to taking actions to remove him into your own hands.

The PLAM represents a direct threat, and you are growing tired of their ability to openly operate from their bases in Daloon. The current administration is too soft on eliminating this scourge on Zefra, and you are willing to take direct action to stop cross-border operations or eliminate insurgent camps in Daloon.

The head of the Zefra Association and his belief in taking a harder line on the insurgents may prove to be a great asset, especially if you decide to take actions to remove the president.

Objectives
- Drive the UN out of Zefra but avoid, if possible, being the first to take direct action.
- Eliminate the threat of the Zefran insurgents.
- Gain support from other Zefran military commanders for your cause.

Setup
- Place yourself in the city of Kabra.
- Place one counter in the Kabra district.
- Place one counter anywhere on Capricornia.
- Retain all other counters for future deployment.

Additional Events during Turn: none

Initial Units
Four mobile military units; four infantry units; two artillery units; two protestor groups; two refugee groups (this is not intended to be all inclusive—player can designate additional units).

Head of the Zefra Association (Bongo)

As one of the most respected and feared leaders of the Bongo community, you feel it is your duty to the Bongo tribes to defend them using any means at your disposal. The illegal rebellion of the Truscans and the continued existence of the PLAM against the lawfully elected administration in Zefra is a danger to public safety. You are concerned that the increased number of Truscan protests are a direct threat to the stability of Zefra and may draw unwanted international attention. A swift crackdown on these "street protests" by forces not attributable to the government is the right start. You are in control of the loyal Internal Security Bureau consisting of a cadre of special police, security forces, and spies that will do anything for you.

The rebel commander of the IFF battalion is a problem that may make the situation worse in the country. You are concerned that his attitude may spread to other military and political leaders, but you may be able to use him for your purposes.

Objectives
- Ensure that Zefra remains strongly in the hands of Bongos.
- Crush all insurgent resistance to Zefran rule, while ensuring you look good in the end.
- Ensure that fellow Bongos, especially old-time cronies, politicians, and senior military leaders, benefit financially and remain under your control.
- Support "plausible deniability" for the president's covert actions against Truscans.

Setup
- Place yourself in the intelligence directorate in the Zefran capital.
- Place one counter anywhere in the Zefran capital.
- Retain all remaining counters for future deployment.

Additional Events during Turn: none

Initial Units
Four police units; two SWAT units; three secret police units (this is not intended to be all inclusive—player can designate additional units).

NOTES

Introduction

1. William McCarty Little, "The Strategic Naval War Game or Chart Maneuver," *Proceedings* 38, no. 4 (1912): 1212–33.
2. There exist multiple versions of this story, with slight tweaks in the exact wording of the quote, but the theme and content are consistent across all sources. Peter P. Perla, *The Art of Wargaming: A Guide for Professionals and Hobbyists* (Annapolis, MD: Naval Institute Press, 1990), 100; Milan Vego, "German War Gaming," *Naval War College Review* 65, no. 4 (2012): 110, https://digital-commons.usnwc.edu/nwc-review/vol65/iss4/10.
3. Vego, 108.
4. Vego, 110.
5. Chairman of the Joint Chiefs of Staff (CJCS), Joint Publication (JP) 1-02, *Dictionary of Military and Associated Terms* (Washington, DC: CJCS, 2002).
6. Perla, 274.
7. Matthew Caffrey Jr., *On Wargaming: How Wargames Have Shaped History and How They May Shape the Future* (Newport, RI: Naval War College Press, 2019), 137–60.
8. Philip Pournelle, "U.S. Ongoing Wargaming Initiatives," presentation, Connections UK, London, 6 September 2016; CJCS, JP 5-0, *Joint Planning* (Washington, DC: CJCS, 2017), v-31.
9. JP 5-0, v-31.
10. Caffrey, 46.
11. JP 5-0, v-31.
12. Dean Takahashi, "Americans Spend $23.3B Each Year on Video Games," *Venturebeat.com*, 9 May 2010, https://venturebeat.com/2010/05/09/americans-spend-25-3b-each-year-on-video-games/; Ian Boudreau, "The Wargamer's Guide to Computer War Games 2018," *Wargamer* (blog), 31 December 2018, https://www.wargamer.com/articles/best-new-war-games-2018/.
13. Caffrey, 262.
14. Edward Miller, *War Plan Orange: The U.S. Strategy to Defeat Japan, 1897–1945* (Annapolis, MD: Naval Institute Press, 1991), 156.

15. James Lacey, "Wargaming in the Classroom: An Odyssey," *War on the Rocks* (blog), April 2016, https://warontherocks.com/2016/04/wargaming-in-the-classroom-an-odyssey/.
16. Brant Guillory, "Interview with Dr. James Sterrett, U.S. Army Command and General Staff College," *Grogheads* (blog), 5 October 2013, http://grogheads.com/interviews/2722. The division exercise is conducted by each seminar at the Command and General Staff College using the decisive action simulation in support.
17. Command post exercises with automation support are common experiential wargames.
18. JP 5-0, V-2.
19. Paul Edward Strong, "Wargaming the Atlantic War: Captain Gilbert Roberts and the Wrens of the Western Approaches Tactical Unit," *PAXsims* (blog), 12 December 2017, https://paxsims.files.wordpress.com/2017/12/2017-12-10-watu-mors.pdf.
20. Vego, 110.
21. Helmuth von Moltke, *Moltke's Tactical Problems from 1858–1882*, ed. Prussian Grand General Staff, trans. Karl von Donat (London: W. H. Allen & Co., 1894), 145.
22. Miller, 3.
23. Matthew Caffrey Jr., "Toward a History-Based Doctrine for Wargaming," *Aerospace Power Journal* 43 (Fall 2000): 33–56.
24. Caffrey, 45.
25. John M. Lillard, *Playing War: Wargaming and the U.S. Navy Preparations for World War II* (Omaha, NE: Potomac Books, 2016).

Chapter 1. Analytic Wargaming

1. Francis McHugh, *Fundamentals of War Gaming* (Newport, RI: Naval War College, 1966), 223.
2. Shawn Burns, "Annex A: Glossary of War Gaming Terms," in *War Gamers' Handbook: A Guide for Professional War Gamers*, ed. Shawn Burns (Newport, RI: Naval War College, 2015), https://www.usnwc.edu/Research-and-Wargaming/Wargaming/Publications-and-Journals
3. Jon Compton, "Toward an Epistemology of Wargaming—A Drunkard's Walk," PowerPoint Presentation, Military Operations Research Society, 18 March 2015.
4. Compton, 10.
5. Caffrey, *On Wargaming*, 79–84.
6. John Hanley, "Changing DoD's Analysis Paradigm," *Naval War College Review* 70, 1 (2017): 65–66, https://digital-commons.usnwc.edu/nwc-review/vol70/iss1/5.
7. Jeff Appleget and Fred Cameron, "Analytic Wargaming on the Rise," *Phalanx* 48, no. 1 (March 2015): 28–32.
8. Robert Washer, "Battle," in *Systems Analysis and Modeling in Defense*, ed. Reiner K. Huber (Boston: Springer, 1984), 807–27.
9. Edward Kerlin, "The IDA Tactical Warfare Model: A Theater-Level Model of Conventional, Nuclear, and Chemical Warfare," in *Systems Analysis and Modeling in Defense*, 357–73.
10. Appleget and Cameron, 3.
11. Caffrey, *On Wargaming*, 137.

12. William Scott, "Title 10 Games Shape Policies," *Aviation Week & Space Technology* (November 1998): 61–62.
13. Association of the United States Army, Torchbearer Special Report, "Unified Quest: Exploring the Nature of Warfare," April 2006, 1–4, https://www.ausa.org/sites/default/files/TBSR-2006-Unified-Quest-Exploring-the-Nature-of-Warfare.pdf; U.S. Army Training and Doctrine Command (TRADOC), Pamphlet 525-3-0, "The Army in Joint Operations: The Army's Future Force Capstone Concept 2015–2024" (Washington, DC: U.S. Army TRADOC, April 2005); David Johnson et al., *Joint Paths to the Future Force: A Report on Unified Quest 2004* (Santa Monica, CA: RAND, 2006), 1–9.
14. Caffrey, *On Wargaming*, 179–213.
15. Sam Bailey, interview with General David Petraeus, *Frontline*, 14 June 2011, https://www.pbs.org/wgbh/frontline/article/interview-general-david-petraeu/; Department of the Army, Field Manual 3-24, *Counterinsurgency* (Washington, DC: Headquarters Department of the Army, 15 December 2006).
16. Peter Perla, discussion with authors, September 2016.
17. Compton.

Chapter 2. Craft of Wargaming

1. Connections Wargaming Conference, https://connections-wargaming.com/.
2. Burns.
3. James Markley, *Strategic Wargaming Series Handbook* (Carlisle, PA: U.S. Army War College, 2015), https://ssi.armywarcollege.edu/PDFfiles/PCorner/WargameHandbook.pdf.
4. United Kingdom Ministry of Defence, *Wargaming Handbook* (Wiltshire, UK: Ministry of Defence, 2017).
5. "Art," Lexico.com, https://www.lexico.com/en/definition/art.
6. Perla, *Art of Wargaming*, 74.
7. Peter Perla and Ed McGrady, "Wargaming and Analysis," presentation at MORS Special Meeting, October 2007, https://www.cna.org/CNA_files/PDF/D0016966.a1.pdf.
8. "Scientific Method," Lexico.com, https://www.lexico.com/en/definition/scientific_method.
9. Compton.
10. "Craft," Lexico.com, https://www.lexico.com/en/definition/craft.
11. Stephen Downes-Martin, "How Not to Not Analyse Wargames," presentation at Connections UK, London, September 2015, www.professionalwargaming.co.uk/2016Analyse.pdf.
12. Malcolm Gladwell, *Outliers: The Story of Success* (New York: Back Bay Books, 2011), xx.
13. Modified from Pournelle, "U.S. Ongoing Wargaming Initiatives."
14. *Risk* (Parker Brothers, 1959).
15. Department of National Defence, "Designing Canada's Army of Tomorrow" (Kingston, ON: Directorate of Land Concepts and Designs, 2011), http://publications.gc.ca/collections/collection_2012/dn-nd/D2-282-2011-eng.pdf.
16. Andrew J. Rotherham and Daniel T. Willingham, "21st Century Skills: The Challenges Ahead," *Educational Leadership* 67, no. 1 (September 2009), http://www.ascd.org

/publications/educational-leadership/sept09/vol67/num01/21st-Century-Skills@-The-Challenges-Ahead.aspx.

Chapter 3. Wargaming Characteristics

1. James F. Dunnigan, *The Complete Wargames Handbook: How to Play, Design, and Find Them* (San Jose, CA: Writers Club Press, 2000), 110.
2. Perla, *Art of Wargaming*, 72.
3. UK Ministry of Defence, "Wargaming Handbook."
4. Perla, *Art of Wargaming*, 165.
5. McHugh, 9.
6. Brian Train, "Shining Path: The Struggle for Peru," BTR Games, 1999.
7. Rex Brynen, "Simulation and Gaming Miscellany," *PAXSims* (blog), 8 October 2018, https://paxsims.wordpress.com/2018/09/16/simulation-and-gaming-miscellany-16-september-2018/.
8. *Battleship* (Milton Bradley, 1967).
9. *Stratego* (Milton Bradley, 1960).
10. Authors' discussions at several Connections UK conferences.
11. Rex Brynen and Tom Mouat, "Matrix Games: An Introduction," *PAXSims* (blog), August 2017, https://paxsims.files.wordpress.com/2017/08/dstl-matrix.pdf.
12. John Curry and Tim Price, *Matrix Games for Modern Wargaming: Developments in Professional and Educational Wargames, Innovations in Wargaming* (History of Wargaming Project, 2014), 3.
13. Rex Brynen and Tom Mouat, "Engle: A Short History of Matrix Games," *PAXSims* (blog), 26 July 2016, https://paxsims.wordpress.com/2016/07/26/engle-a-short-history-of-matrix-games/.
14. Defence Science and Technology Lab, memorandum TL/WP100280, "Wargaming in Defence: A Thinkpiece for VCDS v2.0," 1 February 2017, 8; Perla, *Art of Wargaming*, 183; Philip Sabin, *Simulating War Studying Conflict Through Simulation Games* (London: Bloomsbury Academic, 2012), 67–101.

Chapter 4. Wargaming History

1. Dunnigan, 92–106.
2. Caffrey, *On Wargaming*, 219–57.
3. Perla, *Art of Wargaming*, 15–105.
4. McHugh, 27–56.
5. Vego, 106–19.
6. Perla, *Art of Wargaming*,16; Abe Greenberg, "An Outline of Wargaming," *Naval War College Review* (September-October 1981): 93–91; "A Brief History of Go," British Go Association, https://www.britgo.org/intro/history.
7. "Shadow_47," "Chaturanga . . . The Lost Game," *Chess* (blog), 8 October 2018, https://www.chess.com/blog/Shadow_47/chaturangahellipthe-lost-game.
8. Caffrey, "Toward a History-Based Doctrine for Wargaming," 34–35.

9. Caffrey, 35; Stephen Patrick, *Wargame Design* (New York: Simulations Publications, Inc., 1977), 4; John Young, *History and Bibliography of War Gaming* (Washington, DC: Department of the Army, 1957), 9.
10. Caffrey, "Toward a History-Based Doctrine for Wargaming," 35.
11. Caffrey, 36.
12. Caffrey, 37.
13. Caffrey, 36; Young, 16.
14. Miller, *War Plan Orange*, 45.
15. Miller, 45.
16. Donald C. Winter, remarks at Naval War College Current Strategy Forum, Newport, RI, 13 June 2006.
17. Caffrey, "Toward a History-Based Doctrine for Wargaming," 45.
18. Thomas Flemming. "Early Warning," *American Heritage* 52, no. 5 (2001), https://www.americanheritage.com/early-warning.
19. Capt. Wayne Hughes, USN (Ret.), and Capt. Jeff Kline, USN (Ret.), discussion with the authors about the Battle of Midway, January 2017.
20. McHugh, 40.
21. Perla, *Art of Wargaming*, 46–47.
22. Alan D. Zimm, *Attack on Pearl Harbor—Strategy, Combat, Myths, Deceptions* (Philadelphia: Casemate, 2011), 74.
23. Perla, *Art of Wargaming*, 48.
24. Caffrey, "Toward a History-Based Doctrine for Wargaming," 46.
25. Mark Herman and Mark Frost, *Wargaming for Leaders: Strategic Decision Making from the Battlefield to the Boardroom* (New York: McGraw-Hill, 2009).
26. Nicolaus Mills, "The General Who Understood Iraq from the Start," *Dissent* Magazine, 25 April 2008, https://www.dissentmagazine.org/online_articles/the-general-who-understood-iraq-from-the-start.
27. Thom Shanker, "New Strategy Vindicates Ex-Army Chief Shinseki," *New York Times*, 12 January 2007, https://www.nytimes.com/2007/01/12/washington/12shinseki.html.
28. Herman and Frost.
29. Murat Özçelik, "The Two Radical Sources of Instability in the Middle East," Council of Councils, 15 August 2014, https://www.cfr.org/councilofcouncils/global_memos/p33347.
30. Herman and Frost, 46–52.
31. Loveday Morris and Brian Murphy, "Ahmed Chalabi, Iraqi Exile Who Helped Spur the U.S. Invasion, Dies of Heart Attack," *Washington Post*, 3 November 2015, https://www.washingtonpost.com/world/ahmed-chalabi-iraqi-politician-who-pushed-for-us-invasion-dies-of-heart-attack/2015/11/03/07bd3a99-cd43-4f45-ab0f-5d37c9c6bbb5_story.html?noredirect=on&utm_term=.ca2218e3f8c4.
32. Herman and Frost, 46–52.
33. Jack Healy, "Arrest Order for Sunni Leader in Iraq Opens New Rift," *New York Times*, 19 December 2011, https://www.nytimes.com/2011/12/20/world/middleeast/iraqi-government-accuses-top-official-in-assassinations.html.
34. Roger Strother, "Post-Saddam Iraq: The War Game," National Security Archive Briefing Book no. 27, 2006, https://nsarchive2.gwu.edu/NSAEBB/NSAEBB207/index.htm.
35. Combatant command military staff officers in discussion with the authors, July 2016.

Chapter 5. Analytic Wargaming Fundamentals

1. Perla, discussion with the authors, 6 September 2016.

Chapter 6. Initiate

1. U.S. Army TRADOC Analysis Center, *Wargame Executive Summary*, 24 August 2018.
2. TRADOC Analysis Center.
3. TRADOC Analysis Center.
4. Jonathan Rosenhead, "What's the Problem? An Introduction to Problem Structuring Methods," *Interfaces* 26, no. 6 (November-December 1996): 11–31, https://doi.org/10.1287/inte.26.6.117; Chris Smith and Duncan Shaw, "The Characteristics of Problem Structuring Methods: A Literature Review," *European Journal of Operational Research* 24 (April 2019): 403–16.
5. Systems Thinking and Practice, http://systems.open.ac.uk/materials/T552/; "Art of Design Student Text, Version 2.0," Air University, https://community.apan.org/wg/aucoi/jadcc/m/mediagallery1/196938.
6. Authors' personal experience.
7. Christopher Morey, Michael F. Bauman, and Paul Works, *Constraints, Limitations, and Assumptions Code of Best Practice*, TRAC-TD-05-011 (rev. 1) (Fort Leavenworth, KS: TRADOC Analysis Center, June 2012), http://www.opanalytics.ca/MORS/pdf/TRAC%20CLA%20COBP%20(revised)%202012-06-25%20v3.pdf.
8. Burns, 17–18.

Chapter 7. Design

1. Perla, *Art of Wargaming*, 193.
2. Perla, 183.
3. Dunnigan, 109.
4. Curry and Price, 9–14; Rex Brynen, Tom Mouat, and Tom Fisher, "Matrix Game Construction Kit MaGCK," 2017, 7–13.
5. Curry and Price, 16–20; Brynen, Mouat, and Fisher, 16.
6. Dunnigan, 124–39.
7. *Midway* (Baltimore: The Avalon Hill Game Company, 1964).

Chapter 8. Development

1. Jonathan Kay, "The Invasion of the German Board Games," *The Atlantic*, 21 January 2018, https://www.theatlantic.com/business/archive/2018/01/german-board-games-catan/550826/.
2. Dunnigan, 122.
3. Dunnigan, 122.

Chapter 10. Analysis

1. "Synthesis," Lexico.com, https://www.lexico.com/en/synonym/synthesis.
2. Perla, *Art of Wargaming*, 287.
3. Peter Perla, "Operations Research, Systems Analysis, and Wargaming: Riding the Cycle of Research," in *Zones of Control: Perspective on Wargaming*, ed. Pat Harrigan (Boston: MIT Press, 2016), 176–77.

Chapter 12. Course of Action Wargaming

1. Gregory Fontenot, "Seeing Red: Creating a Red-Team Capability for the Blue Force," *Military Review* (September-October 2005): 4–8; Matthew Caffrey Jr., "Red Flag for Joint Campaigns: Building a More Effective Air and Joint Force through Better Operation and Strategic Wargaming," *Air & Space Power Chronicles Online* (2004), www.airpower.maxwell.af.mil/airchronicles/cc/Caffrey1.html.
2. Jim Dwyer, "A Nation at War: In the Field—V CORPS Commander; A Gulf Commander Sees a Longer Road," *New York Times*, 28 March 2003, https://www.nytimes.com/2003/03/28/world/nation-war-field-v-corps-commander-gulf-commander-sees-longer-road.html.
3. Roger Hill, "The Influence of War Gaming on the Schlieffen Plan," dissertation, Georgetown University, December 1968.
4. United Kingdom Ministry of Defence, Joint Doctrine Publication 5-00, *Campaign Planning*, 2nd ed. (Wiltshire, UK: Ministry of Defence, July 2013), 21–28.
5. Ministry of Defence.
6. CJCS, *Joint Planning*, xxv.
7. CJCS, V-34.
8. CJCS, xxv.
9. CJCS, V-32.
10. CJCS, V-32.
11. CJCS, V-33–34.
12. CJCS, V-39.
13. CJCS, V-34–35.
14. CJCS, V-41.
15. CJCS, V-32.
16. CJCS, V-32.
17. Matthew Hanson, "Improving Operational Wargaming: It's All Fun and Games Until Someone Loses a War" (Leavenworth, KS: School of Advanced Military Studies, U.S. Army Command and General Staff College, 2016), 32.
18. Hill, 57.
19. Fontenot, 4–8; Booz Allen Hamilton, "Think Like the Enemy with Red Teaming," https://www.boozallen.com/s/insight/blog/think-like-the-enemy-with-red-teaming.html.
20. Fontenot, 4–8; Tom Longland, "Red Teaming and Course of Action Wargaming," presentation at Connections UK, London, September 2016, http://www.professionalwargaming.co.uk/RedTeamingAndCOAGaming.pdf.

21. United Kingdom Ministry of Defence, *Red Teaming Guide* (Wiltshire, UK: Development, Concepts, and Doctrine Centre, January 2013).

Chapter 14. Educational and Experiential Wargames

1. U.S. Army Acquisition Support Center, "One Semi-Automated Forces (ONESAF)," https://asc.army.mil/web/portfolio-item/peo-stri-one-semi-automated-forces-pdm-onesaf/.
2. Department of the Army, TRADOC Army Regulation 350–28, "Army Exercises" (Washington, DC: HQDA, 9 December 1997), 26.
3. Lawrence Livermore National Laboratory, "Joint Conflict and Tactical Simulations (JCATS)," 30 May 2018, https://csl.llnl.gov/content/assets/docs/JCATS-LLNL-Brochure-30May2018.pdf.
4. Rob Riddell, "Doom Goes to War," *WIRED* (blog), 1 April 1997, https://www.wired.com/1997/04/ff-doom/.
5. Jeff Appleget and James Illingworth, "Land Warrior Training Initiative," *SimTecT 2001 Conference Proceedings* (May 2001): 319–23.
6. "Delta Force 2 Based Software to be Used at West Point," *Gamezone* (blog), 4 May 2012, https://www.gamezone.com/news/delta_force_2_based_software_to_be_used_at_west_point/.
7. James Vincent, "DeepMind's Go-playing AI Doesn't Need Human Help to Beat Us Anymore," *The Verge* (blog), 18 October 2017, https://www.theverge.com/2017/10/18/16495548/deepmind-ai-go-alphago-zero-self-taught.
8. U.S. Army Combined Arms Center, "Mission Command Training Program History," https://usacac.army.mil/sites/default/files/documents/cact/mctp/MCTP%20History.pdf.
9. U.S. Army Combined Arms Center.
10. Department of the Army, TRADOC Pamphlet 350-70-1, "Training Development in Support of Operational Training Domain" (Washington, DC: HQDA, February 2019).
11. Joint Chiefs of Staff, "Universal Joint Task List," accessed 5 July 2019, https://www.jcs.mil/Doctrine/Joint-Training/UJTL/.
12. Department of the Army, Field Manual 7-15, *The Army Universal Task List* (Washington, DC: HQDA, February 2009), https://usacac.army.mil/sites/default/files/misc/doctrine/CDG/cdg_resources/manuals/fm/fm7_15.pdf.
13. TRADOC Pamphlet 350-70-1, 63, 65.
14. ABCA Program Office, Publication 354, *Operational Assessment of ABCA Exercises and Experiments* (Rosslyn, VA: HQDA, 7 September 2004), 1-C-3.
15. Kevin Larrabee, email communication, 6 February–21 August 2018.
16. Perla, *Art of Wargaming*, 164.
17. Department of the Army, "Army Exercises," table 2-1, table 2-3, 8.
18. Department of the Army, 5.
19. Joint Publication 1-02, *Dictionary of Military and Associated Terms* (Washington, DC: Joint Staff, 8 November 2010, as amended through 15 February 2016), 41.
20. Department of the Army, Army Doctrine Publication 5-0, *The Operations Process* (Washington, DC: HQDA, May 2012), 12.

21. Department of the Army, "Army Exercises," table 2-1, 3.
22. Department of the Army, table 2-1, 10.
23. McCarty Little.

Chapter 15. Best and Worst Practices

1. Peter Perla, discussion with the authors, September 2107.
2. Donna Miles, "Strategy Groups Enhance PACOM's Regional Understanding, Engagement," American Forces Press Service, 30 July 2012, http://archive.defense.gov/news/newsarticle.aspx?id=117332.
3. John Grady, "U.S. European Command Emphasis Shifting to Russian Deterrence," U.S. Naval Institute News, 14 July 2016, https://news.usni.org/2016/07/14/u-s-european-command-shifting-russian-deterrence-missions.

Appendix 5. Case Studies in Wargaming Design

1. Brandon Daigle and Brian James, "Assessing the Strategic Utility of the High North: The Colder War," master's thesis, Naval Postgraduate School, 2016.
2. Mark Abdollahian et al., "Senturion: A Predictive Political Simulation Model" (Washington, DC: Center for Technology and National Security Policy, National Defense University, July 2006).

BIBLIOGRAPHY

ABCA Program Office. Publication 354, *Operational Assessment of ABCA Exercises and Experiments*. Rosslyn, VA: Headquarters Department of the Army, 7 September 2004, 1-C-3.

Abdollahian, Mark, et al. "Senturion: A Predictive Political Simulation Model." Washington, DC: Center for Technology and National Security Policy, National Defense University, July 2006.

Appleget, Jeff, and Fred Cameron. "Analytic Wargaming on the Rise." *Phalanx* 48, no. 1 (March 2015): 28–32.

Appleget, Jeff, and James Illingworth. "Land Warrior Training Initiative." *SimTecT 2001 Conference Proceedings* (May 2001): 319–23.

Association of the United States Army. Torchbearer Special Report, "Unified Quest: Exploring the Nature of Warfare," April 2006, 1–4, https://www.ausa.org/sites/default/files/TBSR-2006-Unified-Quest-Exploring-the-Nature-of-Warfare.pdf.

Bailey, Sam. Interview with General David Petraeus. *Frontline*, 14 June 2011, https://www.pbs.org/wgbh/frontline/article/interview-general-david-petraeu/.

Bartels, Elizabeth. "Getting the Most Out of Your Wargame: Practical Advice for Decisionmakers." *War on the Rocks* (blog), 26 January 2016, https://warontherocks.com/2016/01/getting-the-most-out-of-your-wargame-practical-advice-for-decision-makers/.

Booz Allen Hamilton. "Think Like the Enemy with Red Teaming," https://www.boozallen.com/s/insight/blog/think-like-the-enemy-with-red-teaming.html.

Boudreau, Ian. "The Wargamer's Guide to Computer War Games 2018." *Wargamer* (blog), 31 December 2018, https://www.wargamer.com/articles/best-new-war-games-2018/.

Brynen, Rex. "Simulation and Gaming Miscellany." *PAXSims* (blog), 8 October 2018, https://paxsims.wordpress.com/2018/09/16/simulation-and-gaming-miscellany-16-september-2018/.

Brynen, Rex, and Tom Fisher. "Matrix Game Construction Kit MaGCK." 2017.

Brynen, Rex, and Tom Mouat. "Engle: A Short History of Matrix Games." *PAXSims* (blog), 26 July 2016, https://paxsims.wordpress.com/2016/07/26/engle-a-short-history-of-matrix-games/.

———. "Matrix Games: An Introduction." *PAXSims* (blog), https://paxsims.files.wordpress.com/2017/08/dstl-matrix.pdf.

Burns, Shawn, ed. *War Gamers' Handbook: A Guide for Professional War Gamers*. Newport, RI: Naval War College, 2015, https://www.usnwc.edu/Research-and-Wargaming/Wargaming/Publications-and-Journals

Caffrey, Matthew, Jr. *On Wargaming: How Wargames Have Shaped History and How They May Shape the Future*. Newport, RI: Naval War College Press, 2019.

———. "Red Flag for Joint Campaigns: Building a More Effective Air and Joint Force through Better Operation and Strategic Wargaming." *Air & Space Power Chronicles Online Journal* (2004), https://www.airuniversity.af.edu/Portals/10/ASPJ/journals/Chronicles/Caffrey1.pdf.

———. "Toward a History-Based Doctrine for Wargaming." *Aerospace Power Journal* 43 (Fall 2000): 33–56.

Chairman of the Joint Chiefs of Staff. Joint Publication 1-02, *Dictionary of Military and Associated Terms*. Washington, DC: Chairman of the Joint Chiefs of Staff, 2002.

———. Joint Publication 5-0, *Joint Planning*. Washington, DC: Chairman of the Joint Chiefs of Staff, 2017.

Compton, Jon. "Toward an Epistemology of Wargaming—A Drunkard's Walk." PowerPoint Presentation, Military Operations Research Society, 18 March 2015.

Curry, John, and Tim Price. *Matrix Games for Modern Wargaming: Developments in Professional and Educational Wargames, Innovations in Wargaming*. History of Wargaming Project, 2014.

Daigle, Brandon, and Brian James. "Assessing the Strategic Utility of the High North: The Colder War." Master's Thesis, Naval Postgraduate School, 2016.

Defence Science and Technology Lab memorandum TL/WP100280, "Wargaming in Defence: A Thinkpiece for VCDS v2.0," 2017.

Department of the Army. Army Doctrine Publication 5-0, *The Operations Process*. Washington, DC: HQDA, May 2012.

———. Field Manual 3-24, *Counterinsurgency*. Washington, DC: HQDA, 15 December 2006.

———. Field Manual 7-15, *The Army Universal Task List*. Washington, DC: HQDA, February 2009.

———. TRADOC Army Regulation 350–28, "Army Exercises." Washington, DC: Headquarters Department of the Army (HQDA), 9 December 1997.

———. TRADOC Pamphlet 350-70-1, "Training Development in Support of the Operational Training Domain." Washington, DC: HQDA, February 2019.

Department of National Defence. "Designing Canada's Army of Tomorrow." Kingston, ON: Directorate of Land Concepts and Designs, 2011, http://publications.gc.ca/collections/collection_2012/dn-nd/D2-282-2011-eng.pdf.

Downes-Martin, Stephen. "How Not to Not Analyse Wargames." Presentation at Connections UK, London, September 2015, www.professionalwargaming.co.uk/2016Analyse.pdf.

———. "Wargame Players Don't Know that They Don't Know: What Is to Be Done?" Presentation at Roundtables on Innovation in Strategic Gaming, National Defense University, Washington, DC, 2009.

Dunnigan, James F. *The Complete Wargames Handbook: How to Play, Design, and Find Them*. San Jose, CA: Writers Club Press, 2000.
Dwyer, Jim. "A Nation at War: In the Field—V CORPS Commander; A Gulf Commander Sees a Longer Road." *New York Times*, 28 March 2003, https://www.nytimes.com/2003/03/28/world/nation-war-field-v-corps-commander-gulf-commander-sees-longer-road.html.
Flemming, Thomas. "Early Warning." *American Heritage* 52, no. 5 (2001), https://www.americanheritage.com/early-warning.
Fontenot, Gregory. "Seeing Red: Creating a Red-Team Capability for the Blue Force." *Military Review* (September-October 2005): 4–8.
Gladwell, Malcolm. *Outliers: The Story of Success*. New York: Back Bay Books, 2011.
Grady, John. "U.S. European Command Emphasis Shifting to Russian Deterrence." U.S. Naval Institute News, 14 July 2016, https://news.usni.org/2016/07/14/u-s-european-command-shifting-russian-deterrence-missions.
Guillory, Brant. "Interview with Dr. James Sterrett, U.S. Army Command and General Staff College." *Grogheads* (blog), 5 October 2013, http://grogheads.com/interviews/2722.
Haffa, Robert, and James Patton Jr. "Gaming the System of Systems." *Parameters* (Spring 1998): 110–21.
———. "The Need for Joint Wargaming: Combining Theory and Practice." *Parameters* (Autumn 1999): 106–17.
Hanley, John. "Changing DoD's Analysis Paradigm." *Naval War College Review* 70, no. 1 (2017), https://digital-commons.usnwc.edu/nwc-review/vol70/iss1/5.
Hanson, Matthew. "Improving Operational Wargaming: It's All Fun and Games Until Someone Loses a War." Leavenworth, KS: School of Advanced Military Studies, U.S. Army Command and General Staff College, 2016.
Healy, Jack. "Arrest Order for Sunni Leader in Iraq Opens New Rift." *New York Times*, 19 December 2011, https://www.nytimes.com/2011/12/20/world/middleeast/iraqi-government-accuses-top-official-in-assassinations.html.
Herman, Mark, and Mark Frost, *Wargaming for Leaders: Strategic Decision Making from the Battlefield to the Boardroom*. New York: McGraw-Hill, 2009.
Hill, Roger. "The Influence of War Gaming on the Schlieffen Plan." Dissertation, Georgetown University, December 1968.
Jensen, Benjamin M. *Forging the Sword Doctrinal Change in the U.S. Army*. Palo Alto, CA: Stanford Security Studies, 2016.
Johnson, David, et al. *Joint Paths to the Future Force: A Report on Unified Quest 2004*. Santa Monica, CA: RAND, 2006.
Kay, Jonathan. "The Invasion of the German Board Games." *The Atlantic*, 21 January 2018, https://www.theatlantic.com/business/archive/2018/01/german-board-games-catan/550826/.
Kerlin, Edward. "The IDA Tactical Warfare Model: A Theater-Level Model of Conventional, Nuclear, and Chemical Warfare." In *Systems Analysis and Modeling in Defense*, ed. Reiner K. Huber. Boston: Springer, 1984.
Lacey, James. "Wargaming in the Classroom: An Odyssey." *War on the Rocks* (blog), April 2016, https://warontherocks.com/2016/04/wargaming-in-the-classroom-an-odyssey/.

Lawrence Livermore National Laboratory. "Joint Conflict and Tactical Simulations (JCATS)," 30 May 2018, https://csl.llnl.gov/content/assets/docs/JCATS-LLNL-Brochure-30May2018.pdf.

Lillard, John M. *Playing War: Wargaming and the U.S. Navy Preparations for World War II*. Omaha, NE: Potomac Books, 2016.

Longland, Tom. "Red Teaming and Course of Action Wargaming." Presentation at Connections UK, London, September 2016, http://www.professionalwargaming.co.uk/RedTeamingAndCOAGaming.pdf.

Markley, James. *Strategic Wargaming Series Handbook*. Carlisle, PA: U.S. Army War College, 2015, https://ssi.armywarcollege.edu/PDFfiles/PCorner/WargameHandbook.pdf.

McCarty Little, William. "The Strategic Naval War Game or Chart Maneuver." *Proceedings* 38, no. 4 (1912): 1212–33.

McHugh, Francis. *Fundamentals of Wargaming*. Newport, RI: Naval War College, 1966.

Miles, Donna. "Strategy Groups Enhance PACOM's Regional Understanding, Engagement." American Forces Press Service, 30 July 2012, http://archive.defense.gov/news/newsarticle.aspx?id=117332.

Miller, Edward. *War Plan Orange: The U.S. Strategy to Defeat Japan, 1897–1945*. Annapolis, MD: Naval Institute Press, 1991.

Miller, James A. "Gaming the Interwar: How Naval War College Wargames Tilted the Playing Field for the U.S. Navy During World War II." Master's thesis, U.S. Army Command and General Staff College, 2013.

Mills, Nicolaus. "The General Who Understood Iraq from the Start." *Dissent Magazine*, 25 April 2008, https://www.dissentmagazine.org/online_articles/the-general-who-understood-iraq-from-the-start.

Morey, Christopher, Michael F. Bauman, and Paul Works. *Constraints, Limitations, and Assumptions Code of Best Practice*, TRAC-TD-05-011 (rev. 1). Fort Leavenworth, KS: TRADOC Analysis Center, June 2012, http://www.opanalytics.ca/MORS/pdf/TRAC%20CLA%20COBP%20(revised)%202012-06-25%20v3.pdf.

Morris, Loveday, and Brian Murphy. "Ahmed Chalabi, Iraqi Exile Who Helped Spur the U.S. Invasion, Dies of Heart Attack." *Washington Post*, 3 November 2015, https://www.washingtonpost.com/world/ahmed-chalabi-iraqi-politician-who-pushed-for-us-invasion-dies-of-heart-attack/2015/11/03/07bd3a99-cd43-4f45-ab0f-5d37c9c6bbb5_story.html?noredirect=on&utm_term=.ca2218e3f8c4.

North Atlantic Treaty Organization. Allied Joint Publication 5, *Allied Joint Doctrine for the Planning of Operations*, February 2019.

Özçelik, Murat. "The Two Radical Sources of Instability in the Middle East." Council of Councils, 15 August 2014, https://www.cfr.org/councilofcouncils/global_memos/p33347.

Papadopoulos, Sarandis. "Wargaming: Now More than Ever . . . ." *CHIPS*, 17 August 2015, https://www.doncio.navy.mil/chips/ArticleDetails.aspx?ID=6718.

Patrick, Stephen. *Wargame Design*. New York: Simulations Publications, Inc., 1977.

Perla, Peter P. *The Art of Wargaming: A Guide for Professionals and Hobbyists*. Annapolis, MD: Naval Institute Press, 1990.

———. "Operations Research, Systems Analysis, and Wargaming: Riding the Cycle of Research." In *Zones of Control: Perspective on Wargaming*. Edited by Pat Harrigan. Boston: MIT Press, 2016.

Perla, Peter P., and Ed McGrady. "Wargaming and Analysis." Presentation for MORS Special Meeting, October 2007, https://www.cna.org/CNA_files/PDF/D0016966.a1.pdf.
Pournelle, Philip. "U.S. Ongoing Wargaming Initiatives." Presentation at Connections UK, London, September 2016.
Riddell, Rob. "Doom Goes to War." *WIRED* (blog), 1 April 1997, https://www.wired.com/1997/04/ff-doom/.
Rosenhead, Jonathan, "What's the Problem? An Introduction to Problem Structuring Methods." *Interfaces* 26, no. 6 (November-December 1996): 117–31, https://www.jstor.org/stable/25062196.
Rotherham, Andrew, and Daniel T. Willingham. "21st Century Skills: The Challenges Ahead." *Educational Leadership* 67, no. 1 (September 2009): 16–21, http://www.ascd.org/publications/educational-leadership/sept09/vol67/num01/21st-Century-Skills@-The-Challenges-Ahead.aspx.
Sabin, Philip. *Simulating War Studying Conflict Through Simulation Games*. London: Bloomsbury Academic, 2012.
Scott, William. "Title 10 Games Shape Policies." *Aviation Week & Space Technology* (November 1998): 61–62.
"Shadow_47." "Chaturanga . . . The Lost Game." *Chess* (blog), 8 October 2018, https://www.chess.com/blog/Shadow_47/chaturangahellipthe-lost-game.
Shanker, Thom. "New Strategy Vindicates Ex-Army Chief Shinseki." *New York Times*, 12 January 2007, https://www.nytimes.com/2007/01/12/washington/12shinseki.html.
Smith, Chris, and Duncan Shaw. "The Characteristics of Problem Structuring Methods: A Literature Review." *European Journal of Operational Research* 274 (April 2019): 403–16, https://doi.org/10.1016/j.ejor.2018.05.003.
Strong, Paul Edward. "Wargaming the Atlantic War: Captain Gilbert Roberts and the Wrens of the Western Approaches Tactical Unit." *PAXsims* (blog), 12 December 2017, https://paxsims.wordpress.com/2017/12/20/wargaming-the-atlantic-war-captain-gilbert-roberts-and-the-wrens-of-the-western-approaches-tactical-unit/.
Strother, Roger. "Post-Saddam Iraq: The War Game," National Security Archive Briefing Book no. 207, https://nsarchive2.gwu.edu/NSAEBB/NSAEBB207/index.htm.
Takahashi, Dean. "Americans Spend $23.3B Each Year on Video Games." Venturebeat.com, 9 May 2010, https://venturebeat.com/2010/05/09/americans-spend-25-3b-each-year-on-video-games/.
Train, Brian. "Shining Path: The Struggle for Peru." BTR Games, 1999.
United Kingdom Ministry of Defence. Joint Doctrine Publication 5, *Campaign Planning*, 2nd ed. Wiltshire, UK: Ministry of Defence, July 2013.
———. *Red Teaming Guide*. Wiltshire, UK: Development, Concepts, and Doctrine Centre, January 2013.
———. *Wargaming Handbook*. Wiltshire, UK: Ministry of Defence, August 2017.
U.S. Army Combined Arms Center. "Mission Command Training Program History," https://usacac.army.mil/sites/default/files/documents/cact/mctp/MCTP%20History.pdf.
U.S. Army Training and Doctrine Command (TRADOC). Pamphlet 525-3-0, "The Army in Joint Operations: The Army's Future Force Capstone Concept 2015–2024." Washington, DC: U.S. Army TRADOC, April 2005.

Vego, Milan. "German War Gaming." *Naval War College Review* 65, no. 4 (2012): 106–47, https://digital-commons.usnwc.edu/nwc-review/vol65/iss4/10.

Vincent, James. "DeepMind's Go-playing AI Doesn't Need Human Help to Beat Us Anymore." *The Verge* (blog), 18 October 2017, https://www.theverge.com/2017/10/18/16495548/deepmind-ai-go-alphago-zero-self-taught.

von Moltke, Helmuth. *Moltke's Tactical Problems from 1858–1882*, ed. Prussian Grand General Staff, trans. Karl von Donat. London: W. H. Allen and Co., 1894.

Washer, Robert J. "Battle." In *Systems Analysis and Modeling in Defense*. Edited by Reiner K. Huber. Boston: Springer, 1984.

Winter, Donald. Remarks at the Naval War College Current Strategy Forum, Newport, RI, 13 June 2006.

Wintjes, Jorit. "Europe's Earliest Kriegsspiel? Book Seven of Reinhard Graf zu Solms' Kriegsregierung and the Prehistory of Professional War Gaming." *British Journal for Military History* 2, no. 1 (2015): 15–33.

Young, John. *History and Bibliography of War Gaming*. Washington, DC: Department of the Army, 1957.

Zimm, Alan D. *Attack on Pearl Harbor—Strategy, Combat, Myths, Deceptions*. Philadelphia: Casemate Publishers, 2011.

INDEX

AAR. *See* after action review
adjudication: in Kriegsspiel, 52–54; in matrix games, 46; in seminar games, 45; in system games, 45; using computer simulation support, 65–66, 114–15, 174; using expert panel, 49, 112–13, 173–74; using methods, models, and tools (MMT), 41, 49, 64, 111–15, 117, 201; using white cell, 43; using various methods, 49–50, 111–15, 172–74
administration: director for management of wargame, 204–5; testing of, 202; process developed for, 66
adversaries: benefits of competition, 160–65; opposing force (OPFOR), 162–65, 179, 184–85
after action review (AAR), 196, 202, 203, 207; over-reliance upon, 206
AI. *See* artificial intelligence
Air Force, U.S.: Global Engagement wargames, 18
American, British, Canadian, Australian, and New Zealand Armies' Program (ABCA): assessment procedures/handbook, 180
analysis: best and worst practices, 207–9; data collection and data collectors, 110–11, 135–37, 139–40, 153–55; design process and decisions about, 107–8, 110–11; elements of wargaming, 37, 42; essential questions and corresponding, 93–94; finalizing wargaming findings, 143–44; integrity of analysis, 207; linking findings to sponsor issues, 208; observations to insights to results, 141–43; obtaining missing data for, 136–37; personnel in the analysis group, 141; planning wargame analysis data, 160; player-feedback data as analysis data, 67, 94, 109, 111; play-testing data collection, 123–24, 125; post-game analysis data, 41, 67–68, 94, 95, 110–11, 140–43, 205–7; post-game development of findings, 141–43; practical exercises for, 145–48, 265–67; quick-look report as starting point for final analysis report, 67, 68, 136–37, 139; research and analysis process for future work, 143–44; seminar wargame data, 93–94, 169, 175; starting analysis, 139–40; subject matter experts (SME) assisting analysis team, 141, 155, 208–9; surveys and interviews for collection of, 110–11, 128–29, 136, 137, 140, 175, 180, 181, 206–7; synthesis of data, 140, 141–43, 170; time scheduling for analysis phase, 151–52; vetting the final report, 209; wargaming analysis treated as a project, 10, 62, 63, 67–68. *See also* analysis data
analysis data: adjudication associated with, 174; associated with "Player Info-Out" in DCMP, 94–95; best and worst practices, 207–9; caution on reliability of first-turn data, 135; collection outside of wargame framework,

128–29; collection using branches, sequels, injects, and vignettes, 126–28; defined, 41; deriving findings from data, 141–44; during design phase, 110–11; educational games, adapting to, 181; from a planning wargame, 160; last-move madness, 136, 207; obtaining missing data, 136–37; personnel needed, 110; player feedback data included in, 109; play-testing DCMP improves understanding of how analysis data will be collected, 124–25; post-game analysis, 140–41; practical exercise on analysis, 145–46; practical exercise on quick-look report, 146–47; requirements for analysis data lead to design of the measurement space, 117; scheduling time for analysis based on amount of, 151–52; tracking collection using DCMP, 139–40, 152–55; translating sponsor's issues into requirement for, 42; use contingencies to fill holes in data collection, 126, 136; used to answer essential questions (EQ), 93. *See also* data collection and management plan (DCMP)

analysis of alternatives (AoA), 103–4, 117

analysis phase of a wargame, 139–48

analysis planning. *See* planning for analysis

analytic organizations: combination wargaming and computer simulation in some, 18; need pipeline that produces wargamers, 29; shifting after 9/11 to counterinsurgency gaming, 18; using analysis of alternatives (AoA), 7; using wargaming, 4, 18; worst practice of not collocating sponsor and wargame team, 187

analytic wargames: best and worst practices, 186–209; defined, 15–16; focus on sponsor's objective, 5, 6–9; marginalized by computer-based simulations, 3, 16–20; Perla's seven elements of wargaming, 37–42; renaissance, 27; used in doctrine development, 19, 27–29; used in future concept development, 80, 289–92; used in planning, 158–62

AoA. *See* analysis of alternatives

apprentice wargamer: as baseline level of knowledge, 28; education of, 31–32; defined, 30; hierarchy of the craft, 30; lessons from history, 51; Wargaming Apprentice Certification Exam, 34

apprenticeship: as steps in the craft of wargaming, 2, 27, 30–32, 34, 51, 68. *See also* apprentice wargamer; journeyman wargamer; master wargamer; neophyte wargamer; novice wargamer

Army, U.S.: Army After Next wargame series, 18; collective training and task lists, 179–80; command post exercises, 6; Delta Force 2 (COTS wargame) investigated, 178; JANUS combat simulation, 177–78; main battle tank study using wargaming, 103–6; Mission Command Training Program (MCTP), 179; training exercises, 183–85; Unified Quest wargame series, 18–19, 85–86, 171, 187, 197; Vector-in-Command (VIC) combat simulation, 115

Art of Wargaming, The (Perla), 23, 27, 37, 183

artificial intelligence (AI), 179

assessment: of a wargame, 42; of operational effectiveness, 103; white cell responsibility for, 43

assumptions, 10, 41, 80, 82–83, 85–86, 90, 93–94, 96, 100, 103, 106, 116, 130, 135, 167, 175, 194; defined, 90. *See also* constraints, limitations, and assumptions

Australia: Connections conference, 21

Battleship (game), 43, 47

best and worst practices: analysis group skills, 141; in analysis phase, 207–9; collegial exchanges through Connections conferences, 21–22; in conduct phase, 202–7; constraints, limitations, and assumptions practices, 89–90; craft of wargaming and associated standards, 26–27; in design and development phases, 10, 192–202; in initiate phase, 186–92; reasons for wargame

failures, 186; successful wargame practices, 10, 20
Blue versus Red wargames, 3, 108–9, 110, 163–64, 192–93
branches and sequels, 126–28, 159
bunch of guys and gals sitting around the table (BOGGSAT), 46, 169–70, 189–90, 193

CAA. *See* Center for Army Analysis
Caffrey, Matt, 51
campaign analysis, 4, 7
Canada: army wargames, 33; Connections conference, 21; first on-site wargaming course, 35; High North case study (special operating forces in the Arctic), 306–10; matrix games, 47; naval boarding party case study, 283–87; origins of ZEFRA scenario, 33
carrier presence wargame (case study), 296–302
case studies: carrier presence wargame, 296–302; confrontation in the South China Sea in 2030, 279–83; fleet design for Baltic Sea operations, 289–92; High North operations (special operating forces in the Arctic), 306–10; Navy Special Warfare Command operations, 310–13; non-lethal weapons in naval boarding operations, 283–89; striking power and targeting capabilities in Eastern Mediterranean, 292–96; wargame set in South China Sea, 302–5
case study sponsors: Distributed Lethality Task Force, 279–83; Royal Canadian Navy (Maritime Command Pacific), 283–89; U.S. Fleet Forces Command (Fleet Design, Concepts, and Experiments Division), 289–92; U.S. Navy, 302–5; U.S. Navy (Naval Special Warfare Command), 310–13; U.S. Navy N96, 292–96; U.S. Navy N98, 296–302; U.S. Special Operations Command (SOCOM J-3I), 306–10
CENTCOM. *See* Central Command, U.S.
Center for Army Analysis (CAA), 18
Central Command, U.S. (CENTCOM), 58, 60

CGSC. *See* Command and General Staff College, U.S.
characteristics: of analytic games, 15; of closed games, 154; of closed planning/open execution, 44, 48, 169, 174; of current conflicts, 19; of educational games, by elements, 3, 37–42, 180–81; of experiential games, 177–80; of gaming facilities, 152; of hybrid format, 48; of open games, 43, 45, 167; of seminar format, 45–46; of system format, 45, 47–48; of systems used in wargaming, 64, 82–83; of wargames in general, 9, 36–50
Chaturanga (game), 52
checklists, 22, 26, 37, 117, 170
chess (game), 52
China: focus group within Indo-Pacific Command, 192–93
CLA. *See* constraints, limitations, and assumptions
closed format wargames, 43
closed planning/open execution wargames, 44, 48, 169, 276, 280
closed-loop simulations, 105, 111, 178
COA wargaming. *See* course of action (COA) wargaming
Cold War, 17, 18, 114
combat simulations. *See* computer simulations
command and control: case including command and control, 289; closed format better for problems associated with, 43; CPX type of wargames particularly good for training in, 179; Japanese wargaming found problems in, 162
Command and General Staff College, U.S. (CGSC), 6, 39
command post exercise, 5–6, 184
commercial wargame design and development, 120–21, 122–23
commercial-off-the-shelf (COTS) wargames, 178–79; Delta Force 2, 178; Doom, 178
communities of practice, 21, 27, 35. *See also* Connections conferences
Complete Wargames Handbook, The (Dunnigan), 37

352 INDEX

computer simulations, 1, 18, 24, 65, 105, 177, 180: akin to rigid Kreigsspiel, 2; Delta Force 2 commercial game (and first person shooter), 178; Doom commercial game (and first person shooter) adapted by the U.S. Marine Corps, 178; embracing of closed-loop combat simulation, 18; friction with wargamers over counterinsurgency operations, 19–20; grouped under M&S (modeling and simulation), 12; human in the loop (HITL), 177–79; JANUS, 177–78; OneSAF, 178; pressure to insert computer simulations into various processes, 18; "simulation" presumed to mean *computer* simulation, 12, 14; Vector-in-Command (VIC), 115

computer-based combat simulations. *See* computer simulations

conduct phase of a wargame: avoiding distractions during, 152; best and worst practices, 202–7; closing events, 140; ending the game, 205–7; execution of game, 134–37, 203–5; facilities for, 152; first turn can be practice run, 134–35, 203; gateway exam questions, 272–73; in-brief to players to start game, 134, 203; last-move madness, 136, 207; management of game (best/worst practice), 204–5; management required during, 66–67; practical exercise for, 137–38, 263–65; preparing for, 132–34, 202–4; read-ahead packet provided to players, 64, 108, 132–33, 134, 199, 203; responding to challenges and crises during, 137–38, 263–65; scheduling the wargame, 151–52; social events and mixers, value of, 134; timeline of daily activities, 136; tools, models, and formats for designing and conducting games, 28–29

confrontation in the South China Sea in 2030 (case study), 279–83

Connections conferences, 21–22, 26, 32

consensus: consensual adjudication, 49–50, 113, 172–73; on continuum of wargame spectrum, 45; and contrarians discovered through wargame participation, 46; consensus in SME panel, 112–13; consensus procedure in matrix games, 46; lack of consensus on definition of wargame, 3; wargame team consensus on sponsor's objective and issues, 82–83,

constraints, 16, 62, 87, 88, 89, 190. *See also* constraints, limitations, and assumptions

constraints, limitations, and assumptions (CLA), 80, 89, 99, 142, 190; assumptions during design and development processes, 86, 106, 116, 130; code of best practice, 89–90; essential questions (EQ) and, 93, 95, 142–43; exercise for, 99–100, 257; gateway exam questions, 275–76; initiate phase and discussions with sponsor about, 80, 86, 89–90

contrarians: discovered through wargame participation, 46

control cell. *See* white cell/control cell

COTS. *See* commercial-off-the-shelf (COTS) wargames

counterinsurgency. *See* irregular warfare

counterterrorism. *See* irregular warfare

course of action (COA) wargaming: best and worst practices, 192–93; combatant command COA analysis requirements, 158, 164; competition and adversaries in, 160–65; in doctrine, 6, 10, 48, 80, 107; focus and purpose of, 6, 157–58, 159; four methods according to degree of competition and available time, 161–62; full competitor representation, 160, 161, 164–65, 167; general, 156–67; issues addressed by, 159–60; joint doctrine on, 157, 182; limitations of, 156–57, 161–62; methods for depiction of actions of competitors, 160–62; narrative of actions of competitor, 160–62; outputs feed to other activities, 16; planning doctrine and framework for wargame construction, 158–62; planning function supported by wargames, 4–5, 6, 157–58, 182; rules and procedures of,

INDEX 353

160; sketch-note method of actions of competitor, 160–62; sophisticated level of actions of competitor, 160–61; value of free-thinking adversaries, 162–65; wargaming principles incorporation into planning process, 165–67

CPX. *See* command post exercise

craft of wargaming: from apprentice to journeyman, 2; characteristics as a skilled profession, 21–27; levels of membership in the craft, 30; practice craft by doing, 9–11; sidelined in DoD, 16

cycle of communications: communications skills needed in wargame team, 141; cycle between sponsor and wargame team, 62–63; failure of communications between sponsor and wargame team, 79

data: analysis data defined, 41; analysis data, general, 93–94; analysis data required, 42, 109; collecting analysis data, 132, 135–37, 139–44; collecting feedback data, 111, 140–41; feedback data defined, 40; feedback data during game play, 108, 109–10; feedback data produced by methods, models, and tools (MMT), 111–15; feedback data to keep players engaged, 94; initiate data, 108–9; initiate data, additional, 93; initiate data defined, 40; player information, 94; play-testing collection, 124–26, 130; practical exercise, 118–19. *See also* data collection and management plan (DCMP); qualitative data; quantitative data

data collection and management plan (DCMP): for analysis of alternatives (AoA), 103–4, 105–6; as basis for game design, 42, 63–64, 67, 91, 96, 152–53, 176–77; best and worst practices, 192, 193–94; core elements of, 94–96; development of, 91–96, 175; during game execution, 135–37; for a training exercise, 183–85; for an educational wargame, 176–77, 181; for an experiential wargame, 176–77, 180; essential questions (EQ) as component of, 88, 91–94, 95, 107, 117, 140–41, 153–54, 172, 194; foundational role and purpose of, 152–55, 193–94; initial DCMP as a challenging task, 64; matching analysis findings to sponsor issues, 208; monitoring completeness during game, 205; not sharing with sponsors, recommendation for, 283; play-testing, 124–25; post-game analysis role of, 140–41; revising during design and development, 65, 130, 194; scenario and drafting of, 107; scoping wargames and drafting of, 87–88, 91; specifying initiate, feedback, and analysis data, 40–41; spreadsheet template for, 94

DCMP. *See* data collection and management plan

decisionmaking: analytic wargames used to examine and assist in, 6–8, 15–16, 20, 25, 49–50; data collection of, 110–11, 135–37, 141–43, 153–54; impact of on military operations, 29; process for during combat, 3; quantitative basis for decisions, 20, 29; rationales behind including revisionist history, 175; response to action of adversary, 160–65; seminar wargame data, 93–94, 169, 175; study during exercises, 3, 4–5; study of, 2

definition: analytic wargame, 15–16; apprentice, 30; assumption, 90; constraint, 89; craft, 25–26; hybrid wargame, 40, 48; journeyman, 30; limitation, 90; master, 30; matrix wargame, 46; neophyte, 30; novice, 30; seminar wargame, 45; system wargame, 47; wargame, candidate definitions of, 2–4;

Delta Force 2 (game), 178–79

Department of Defense, U.S.: analytic organizations using wargames, 7; classified planning scenario requirements, 196–97; doctrine for planning wargames doctrine, 157, 182; need to expand community of wargamers, 28–29; planning activities similar to wargames, 5; planning doctrine for military operations, 279; professional

354 INDEX

military education (PME), 26, 27–28; use of "buzz words", 85; use of matrix games, 47; wargame-like activities, 5; wargaming education, 31–32; wargaming marginalized, 16; wargaming renaissance, 27; wargaming requirements, 27–29; wargaming use by, 4–5, 6; worst wargaming practices, 10

Desert Crossing wargame: implications for future operations in Iraq, 58–59; results overlooked when preparing to invade Iraq, 59; retrospective, 60, 156

design and development: balance realism and playability in design, 194–96; benefits of broad participation in, 28–29, 187–88; best and worst practices, 192–202; blend of art and science in, 22–25; borrowing from other wargames (Dunnigan said "plagiarize"), 102–3; communication during, 62; complexity of design, 198–99; contingencies planned for, 126–29, 135, 194; craft of, 25–27; creation process phases, 10, 62, 63, 64–66; creativity and imagination for, 23, 102; cyclical process of, 63, 64–66, 102, 120–22, 125–26, 130; design can be challenge, 102–3; design in educational wargames, 10; design in experiential wargames, 10; design process, 101–3; development process, 120–22, 129, 198–99; gateway exam questions, 270–72; limited tools may limit approaches in design, 28–29; players as wildcard in wargames, 126, 135; practical exercises for, 118–19, 130–31, 258–62; purpose and objective of wargame driving, 22–25, 82–90, 196–98; research before designing a wargame, 102–3; sources of success, 10, 26–27; tendency to use a familiar design, 117–18; transition from initiate phase to design phase, 63–64, 96. *See also* methods, models, and tools (MMT); play-testing

design phase of a wargame, 101–19. *See also* design and development

development phase of a wargame, 120–31. *See also* design and development

dice, 52, 113–14, 172

doctrine about wargaming: analysis results expected from a planning wargame, 160; reference to Joint Publication 5-0 *Joint Planning*, 4–5; respecting course of action wargaming, 157; various definitions of wargaming in U.S. doctrine, 3–4. *See also* handbooks

doctrine development: counterinsurgency doctrine developed through wargaming, 19; requires wargaming, 27–28; wargame designers need to understand doctrine white papers, 102; wargaming can support innovation in, 29

DoD. *See* Department of Defense

Doom (game), 178–79

Dunnigan, James: advice to "plagiarize" (reuse or borrow), 103; Drive on Metz game as example, 113–14; on history and hobby gaming, 51; on play-testing, 121; ten steps of wargame design, 37

education, training, or experience in wargaming: apprentice certification exam, 32, 34; apprentice wargamers, 2, 27, 30, 31–32, 35; competent uniformed wargamers, 30; education program for wargaming craftsmanship, 31–32; learning as means to develop wargaming craftsmanship, 25–29; levels of craftsmanship, 30; master wargamers, 26, 28, 32, 78; opportunities for planners, 165–67; participation and practice are critical component, 9, 10, 11, 26–27, 31–32, 68, 77, 97; requirement for, 193; senior leaders to be provided with executive education, 32; student-centered methods of, 35; wargaming program of Naval Postgraduate School (NPS), 32–35, 81–82

educational and experiential wargames, 6, 176–85

educational wargames: analytic wargames as, 7–8; computer simulations replaced wargaming, 180–81; data collection and management plan (DCMP) adapted to, 176–77, 181; focus and purpose of, 5–6, 8–9, 15, 176, 181;

foundation for, 177, 181; overlapping purposes in, 8–9; phases for construction of, 176–77; planning function of, 182; player surveys and interviews, 181; play-testing, 181–82; process for design of, 10; seminar wargames as, 169; waning and comeback of, 180–81
elements of wargaming, 3, 37–42
Engle, Chris: creation of the matrix wargaming format, 47
entertainment wargame: Delta Force 2, 178; Doom, 178; Dunnigan on history of hobby wargames, 37, 121
essential questions (EQ): adjudication and, 112, 172; constraints, limitations, and assumptions (CLA) associated with, 95, 142–43; data collected in response to, 140, 141–53; data collection and management plan (DCMP) to include, 88, 91–94, 95, 107, 117, 140–41, 153–54, 172, 194; developed from sponsor's issues, 88, 91–96, 175; identifying, 92–94; methods, models, and tools (MMT) and, 93, 112, 117, 172; player interactions and, 93; practical exercises for, 98–99, 256–57; scenario creation framed by, 93, 106–7, 117
exercises and experiments: DCMP application to, 183–85; excluded from definition of wargame, 3, 183; investigation of decision making during, 3, 4–5; planning could use combination of educational, analytic, and experiential wargames, 183–85; wargames, exercises, and analysis woven together, 144; Yarnell's 1932 exercise against Pearl Harbor, 55–56
experiential and training wargames, 183–85. *See also* education, training, or experience in wargaming
expert panel adjudication, 49, 112–13, 173–74

facilitation: in analysis process, 144; in seminar games and less structured games, 66, 168, 170–71; testing, 66, 202

facilitator: use of in free Kriegsspiel, 2; used for adjudication, 41, 45–46, 48, 49, 111, 112, 172, 173; using expert advice, 173
feedback data: defined, 40. *See also* data collection and management plan (DCMP)
field training exercise: conditions to conform to definition of wargame, 185
first-person shooter (FPS) games, 178–79. *See also* computer simulations
fleet design for Baltic Sea operations (case study), 289–92
free Kriegsspiel. *See* Kriegsspiel
FTX. *See* field training exercise
fundamentals (of analytic wargaming): cycle of communications, 62–63; five phases, 63–68
Fundamentals of War Gaming (McHugh), 38–39, 51

Germany: history of Prussian/German gaming, 51. *See also* Kriegsspiel
Gladwell, Malcolm, 30
Go (game), 52, 179
Great Britain. *See* United Kingdom

handbooks: ABCA's, 180; United Kingdom Ministry of Defence's, 37. *See also Complete Wargames Handbook, The*
Hegel, Georg, 47
High North operations (special operating forces in the Arctic) (case study), 306–10
HITL. *See* human-in-the-loop (HITL) computer simulation
hobby wargames. *See* entertainment wargame
human-in-the-loop (HITL) computer simulation, 177–79. *See also* computer simulations
hybrid wargame: blending seminar and system game formats, 48, 68; combination of open and closed structure, 43–44, 48, 68, 117; open, closed, seminar, and system formats, 152

India: 51–52. *See also Chaturanga*
initiate data: defined, 40. *See also* data collection and management plan (DCMP)

INDEX

initiate phase of a wargame: best and worst practices, 186–92; constraints, limitations, and assumptions (CLAs), 80, 89–90, 93, 95, 99–100, 257; creation process phase, 9–10, 62, 63–64, 77–78; data for, 40, 63–64, 93, 95, 107–9; essential questions (EQs) initially developed, 88, 91–96, 98–99, 256–57; objective and issues for wargame, 82–90, 97–98, 255; practical exercises for, 97–100, 253–57; preliminary research before sponsor engagement, 80; problem structuring methods, 83–85; sponsor engagements, 77, 78–90, 97–98, 253–55; transition to design phase from, 63–64, 96

International Security Assistance Force (of NATO), 169

interviews of players: best practice, 206–7; in conjunction with quick-look report, 67, 136; data collection forms used in, 154; must be scheduled in advance, 129, 140; part of contingency planning for data gaps, 128–29, 142; planned for in DCMP, 110–11; purpose, 137; scrambling for, 110–11, 137; in seminar wargames, 175. *See also* data collection and management plan (DCMP)

Iraq: planning operations using Desert Crossing wargame, 58–60, 156–57; retrospective, 60; wargaming for operations in, 18–19, 85–86, 156–57, 197.

irregular warfare (IW), 18–19, 85–86, 156–57, 187, 197

ISAF. *See* International Security Assistance Force

JANUS (simulation), 177–79. *See also* computer simulations

Japan: Midway battle gamed by, 56–57, 161–62; Plan Orange developed for war against, 6, 8–9, 54–55; wargaming for outcome of war against U.S., 57–58; Yarnell's 1932 exercise against Pearl Harbor provided inspiration, 55–56

JCATS (simulation). *See* Joint Conflict and Tactical Simulation system

Joint Conflict and Tactical Simulation system (JCATS), 178. *See also* computer simulations

journeyman wargamer: defined, 30; education of, 31; examples from other crafts, 26; hands-on learning, 35; hierarchy of the craft, 30; as a step in the craft of wargaming, 26

Kriegsspiel: 1–2, 52–54; free Kriegsspiel, 2, 36, 45–46, 47, 49, 53, 168, 172–73, 185; rigid Kriegsspiel, 36, 45, 47, 49, 53, 94

last-move madness, 136, 207

less structured wargames: adjudication methods used in, 172–74; analysis and deriving data from, 175; facilitating for, 66, 168, 170–71; focus and purpose of, 168–69

limitations: defined, 90. *See* constraints, limitations, and assumptions

Livermore, William R.: beginning of modern wargaming in the United States, 53

look-up tables, 24, 65, 115, 174, 196, 201

managing wargames, 204–5

map exercise, 184–85

Marine Corps, U.S.: case study sponsored by, 289–92; Doom commercial game modified by, 178; and impact of Plan Orange wargaming, 55; *Marine Corps Gazette* and tactical decision games, 31; Yarnell's 1932 simulated amphibious assault on Oahu, 55–56

Marine Corps War College, U.S., 6

master wargamer: defined, 30; as a step in the craft of wargaming, 21–35, 78

mathematical models for adjudication, 24, 174

matrix wargames: adjudicating, 49, 50; consensual adjudicating, 172; contingencies development for, 126; dice used in adjudicating, 113, 172; player engagement structure of, 45, 46–47; play-testing, 130–31, 261; popularity of, 46–47; wargaming principles incorporated into planning process, 165–67. *See also* Engle, Chris

McCarty Little, William, 1, 54, 185
McHugh, Francis, 51
McNamara, Robert: embracing operations research methods by Department of Defense, 16
measurement space: analysis of alternatives (AoA) example, 103–6; applied to educational and experiential games, 177; applied to training games, 180; assumptions associated with, 116; best and worst practice, 196–98; created during wargame design and development, 64, 103–15, 192; elements as foundation of wargame design, 63, 64, 106, 196; idealized and reality, 116–18; identification of, 64, 96; players a consideration in decisions about, 115–16; practical exercise for, 118–19, 258–61; realism and playability balance, 194–96; updating during design and development cycle, 130
methods, models, and tools (MMT): adjudication methods may rely upon, 49, 64, 111–15, 117, 201; analysis of alternatives (AoA) example, 103–4, 105; best and worst practices, 196–98; common adjudication MMTs, 112; computer-based MMTs, 65–66, 200–1; data needed to apply, 40; design and development phases include identifying, 64, 101–2, 111–15; essential questions (EQ) and, 93, 112, 117, 172; idealized and reality, 116–18; as one of seven wargame elements, 37–38, 41; as one of three elements of the measurement space, 37, 41, 64, 180; player engagement and, 45–48; play testing, 65–66, 124, 200–1; practical exercise, 118–19, 258–61; preferences of some game designers, 23; purpose to provide adjudication, 111–12; realism and playability balance, 194–96; seminar wargames, 172; unique MMTs for each wargame, 196–97
Midway (game), 118
Midway, battle of, 56–57, 161–62
Military Academy, U.S. (West Point), 178
mission creep, 91, 190

MMT. *See* methods, models, and tools
Moltke, Helmuth von (elder), 8, 53
Moltke, Helmuth von (younger), 157, 162–63
Mustin, Henry, 144

NATO. *See* North Atlantic Treaty Organization
Naval Postgraduate School (NPS) wargaming activity: curriculum design, 32–35; international courses, 35; mobile education wargaming course, 35, 60, 81, 102; student wargame designs for sponsors, 33, 34, 35, 81–82, 278–313; teaching philosophy, 32; team size decisions, 34–35, 102; Wargamers' Apprentice Certification Exam, 34; Wargaming Applications course, 33–34, 117–18, 278–79
Naval War College (U.S.): developing Plan Orange, 6, 9, 51, 54–55, 181; sponsor agreement (contract), 90–91; use of data collection and management plan, 96
Navy, U.S.: case study of carrier presence, 296–302; case study of Littoral Combat Ships in the South China Sea, 302–5; Global wargame series at Naval War College, 18; using Plan Orange wargames to counter Japan, 8–9, 51, 54–55; wargaming/chart maneuvers by, 54; Yarnell's 1932 exercise against Pearl Harbor, 55–56
Navy special warfare operations (case study), 310–13
Navy Special Warfare Command, U.S. (NAVSPECWARCOM or NSWC): case study to explore and identify support for theater commanders in 2030 maritime conflict, 310–13
NEO. *See* non-combatant evacuation operations
neophyte wargamer, 20, 22–23, 41: defined, 30; hierarchy of the craft, 30
Netherlands: Connections conference, 21
Nimitz, Chester, 8–9, 55
non-combatant evacuation operations (NEO), 158

non-lethal capabilities in naval boarding operations (case study) 283–89
North Atlantic Treaty Organization (NATO): case study for System Analysis Study SAS-094 on non-lethal capabilities, 283–89; future close air support for forces, 144; International Security Assistance Force (ISAF) seminar wargame, 169; NATO-Warsaw Pact engagement, wargaming for, 3, 17, 112, 114, 116, 197
novice wargamer, 22–23, 26–27: defined, 30; hierarchy of the craft, 30
NPS. *See* Naval Postgraduate School (NPS) wargaming activity
NSWC. *See* Naval Special Warfare Command, U.S.
NWC. *See* Naval War College

objective: construct game to meet sponsor's objective, 82–90, 97–98, 196–98, 255; one of seven elements of wargaming, 37, 38–39; purpose of wargames, 22–25
OneSAF (simulation), 178. *See also* computer simulations
open format wargames, 43
operations: decisionmaking within military operations, 29; planning wargames need thinking and competitive adversary, 160–65; wargames can examine future concepts for operations, 6–7, 8–9, 15–16, 25, 57, 144; wargaming as critical to planning and analysis research for, 10–11, 16, 18–20; wargaming for planning, 156–58; wargaming principles incorporation into planning process, 165–67; whole of government approach to, 2, 4, 18–20
opposing force (OPFOR): need for active and realistic, 184–85; value of free thinking in, 179
organizational learning opportunities, 21, 28

parking lot: technique in facilitation, 135, 171
Perla, Peter: *Art of Wargaming, The*, 27, 37, 183; continuous cycle of research, 144; creativity in wargaming, 23; definitions of wargaming, 3, 183; design phase, 101–2; elements of wargaming, 37–38; history of wargaming, 51; wargaming as act of communications, 61
Petraeus, David: development of U.S. doctrine for counterinsurgency, 19
phases of a wargame project, 63–67. *See* initiate phase of a wargame; design phase of a wargame; development phase of a wargame; conduct phase of a wargame; analysis phase of a wargame
Plan Orange wargames: planning for operations against Japan, 6, 8–9, 54–55. *See also* Naval War College
planning for analysis: finalizing findings, 143–44; from data to observations to insights to results, 141–43; post-game analysis, 140–41; practical exercise, 145–148; pre-game basic research, 139; schedule quicklook report, surveys, and interviews, 140; tracking progress, 139. *See also* data collection and management plan (DCMP)
planning organizations: course of action (COA) wargaming for planning, 157–58; need thinking adversary in games, 164; shortcoming in some combatant commands, 164; struggle with wargaming, 28. *See also* analytic organizations
planning wargames: best and worst practices, 192–93; combatant command wargames, 158, 164; competitive environment and adversaries in, 160–65; doctrinal wargaming framework for creation of, 10; focus and purpose of, 6, 157–58, 159; four methods according to degree of competition and available time, 161–62; free-thinking adversaries, 162–65; full competitor representation, 160, 161, 164–65, 167; issues addressed by, 159–60; joint doctrine on, 157, 182; limitations of, 156–57, 161–62; methods for depiction of actions of competitors, 160–62; narrative of actions of competitor, 160–62;

outputs feed to other activities, 16; in planning doctrine, 6, 10, 48, 80, 107; planning doctrine and framework for wargame construction, 158–62; planning function supported by wargames, 4–5, 6, 157–58, 182; planning within course of action (COA) wargames, 156–67; rules and procedures of, 160; sketch-note method of actions of competitor, 160–62; sophisticated level of actions of competitor, 160–61; wargaming principles incorporation into planning process, 165–67

players: anticipate arrival of unprepared players, 202–4; data for players to start gaming, 108–9; design process and decisions about, 101–2, 115–16; essential questions (EQ) and interactions of, 93; feedback data for, 40, 41, 94, 95, 107–8, 109–10, 111; guides for, 204; last-turn madness, 136, 207; measurement space and, 115–16; objectives for, 107; one of seven elements of wargaming, 37, 41–42; participation of, 134–37, 203–5; player engagement structure, 45–48; play-testing with players, 124, 200; practical exercise for, 118–19, 258–61; preparation to start gaming, 132–34, 202–4; read-ahead packet for, 64, 108, 132–33, 134, 199, 203; resources for during conduct of wargame, 107, 108–9; social event (mixer) to encourage engagement, 134; surveys and interviews of, 110–11, 128–29, 136, 137, 140, 175, 180, 181, 206–7; vetting the final report by, 209; as wild card in wargames (unexpected or unintended direction), 126, 135

play-testing: of adjudication methods, 66, 130–31, 202, 261–62; best practice, 194–96, 198–201; blind play-test, 122–23, 181, 194, 196, 198, 199–200; of data collection and management plan (DCMP), 124–26, 202; design-develop iterations and, 130; design-play-test cycle, 64, 87–88, 102, 121; dress rehearsal play-test, 66, 122, 123–24, 131, 177, 198, 199, 201–2, 262–63; during development phase, 121–26, 130–31, 137; of educational and experiential wargames, 181–82; of methods, models, and tools (MMT), 65–66, 124, 200–201; process for, 122–24; of training wargames, 180

political-military wargames, 169

practical exercises (for wargaming apprentices and journeymen): conduct of wargame, 137–38, 263–65; constraints, limitations, and assumptions (CLAs), 99–100, 257; essential questions (EQs), 98–99, 256–57; measurement space, 118–19, 258–61; play-testing, 130–31, 261–62; recommendation on completion of, 68; sponsor interaction, first, 97, 253–54; sponsor interaction, second, 97–98, 255

problem definition: initiate phase focused on, 77; methods for problem structuring and decomposition, 84–85; sponsor engagement and, 78–81; in a training wargame, 179–80; worst practice is failure to finalize and agree to, 186, 188–90

problem structuring methods and techniques, 83–85, 190

Prussia: *See* Germany

qualitative data: challenge converting to findings, 141; on human behavior, interactions, and decisions, 20; more from seminar games, 67–68, 175; and quantitative data, 48, 68, 98, 105, 141

quantitative data: from closed-loop simulation for system game, 111–12; data need not always be quantitative, 107–8; JANUS wargame, 178; massive amounts from computer simulation, 17, 20; may not need to be precise, 112; and measurement space, 103; more from system games, 94; and qualitative data, 48, 68, 98, 105, 141; relying less on, 113; in seminar games data not usually quantitative, 174; some sponsor issues may demand more, 96; sparse in study of

counterinsurgency operations due to unreliable computer simulations, 103
quick-look report: educational wargames, 177; facilitator to review with players, 67, 205–6; feedback for team from, 41, 67; finalizing wargaming findings, 143–44; format of and framework for, 65, 67, 68, 136–37; play-testing reports, 124; practical exercise for, 145–46, 265–66; presentation provided while players still available, 136; purpose of, 67, 136, 205–6; as starting point for analysis, 67; used to match analysis findings to sponsor issues, 208

random number generator and adjudication, 172–73
RCN. *See* Royal Canadian Navy
Red Teaming: UK's *Red Teaming Guide*, 164
Red versus Blue wargames. *See* Blue versus Red wargames
request for information (RFI): back to sponsor, 85, 91, 93; from players, 66–67; practical exercise, 262; tracking RFI in the data collection and management plan (DCMP), 95
RFI. *See* request for information
rigid Kriegsspiel. *See* Kriegsspiel
Risk (game), 33–34, 43–44, 47
Royal Canadian Navy: case study on non-lethal capabilities and boarding parties, 383–89
rules and procedures: applied during conduct of wargame, 134–35; best practice, 194; development of, 129–30; for planning wargames, 160; play-testing of, 122–24; provide wargame structure, 41

scenario: analysis of alternatives (AoA) example, 103–4; best and worst practices, 196–98; classified planning scenario requirements in defense analysis, 196, 197; design and development of, 64, 101–2, 106–7; as element of wargaming, 37, 39–40, 64; essential questions (EQ) and derivation of, 93, 106–7, 117; exercise for, 118–19, 258–61; fighting the scenario, 106–7; idealized and reality, 116–18; plausibility of, 106–7, 194–96; realism and playability balance, 194–96; road to war example, 107, 108–9
Schoof, Patrick, 39
scientific inquiry, 24
scientific method, 20, 24
scoping with sponsor, 79, 86, 87–90, 91, 190–92
seminar game format: adjudication methods for, 50, 172–74; analysis data from, 93–94, 169, 175; analysis of completed game, 67–68; BOGGSAT characteristics compared to, 169–70; challenges in creation of, 170; conduct of, 66; contingencies development for, 126, 128; creation of, 10; defined, 168; facilitation of, 66, 168, 170–71; focus and purpose of, 168–69; information structure of, 169; player engagement structure of, 45–46, 48; play-testing adjudication exercise, 130–31, 261; role players in, 168; wargaming principles incorporation into planning process, 165–67
sequels, 126–28, 160. *See also* branches and sequels
Settlers of Catan (game), 121
Sherman, William T., 54
Shinseki, Eric: estimate of force strength for invasion of Iraq, 58–59
SME. *See* subject matter experts
special operations, 38, 117, 309, 311, 312
sponsors: analytic wargames to assist sponsor's decisionmaking, 6–8, 15–16; best and worst practices for interacting, 186, 188–92; contract (signed agreement) between team and, 80, 90–91, 188–90; deadline for wargame delivery, 82, 151; engagements (initial, clarification, scoping), 79–87; engagements with, 77, 78–90; essential questions (EQ) from issues of, 88, 91–96, 175; example wargame designs incorporating, 33, 34, 35, 81–82, 278–313; exercises on interactions with, 97–98, 253–55; facilitator for engagements with, 80–81; initial engagement with,

INDEX

78–79, 81–82; interactions and communication with, 61–63, 79; matching analysis findings with sponsor's issues, 208; objectives and issues for wargames for, 22–25, 82–90, 97–98, 255; objectives of, 62–67, 78, 81; problem identification and understanding needs of, 77–78, 81–90, 97–99, 102, 188–90, 253–57; scoping engagement with, 79, 86, 87–90, 91, 190–92; scribe designated to record engagement process, 81; terms of reference agreement with team, 85–86; wargaming requirements from, 27–29, 61–63, 77–78, 188–90

Stratego (game), 44

striking power and targeting capabilities in Eastern Mediterranean (case study), 292–96

subject matter experts (SME): for adjudication, 49, 112–13, 173–74; for analysis support, 141, 155, 208–9

surveys, 67, 110–11, 128–29, 136, 137, 140, 175, 180, 181, 206–7. *See also* data collection and management plan (DCMP)

system game format: analysis data from, 94; analysis of completed game, 68; conduct of, 66–67; example of, 33; player engagement structure of, 45, 47–48; play-testing adjudication exercise, 130–31, 262; quantitative adjudication of, 48, 68, 111–12; rules and procedures for, 66–67

tabletop exercise (TTX), 167, 284

teams, wargaming: agreement (contract) between sponsor and, 80, 90–91, 188–90; benefits of team approach to wargame design, 78; communications cycle with sponsors, 61–63; consensus or lack of within team, 82–83; decision on team size, 34–35, 102; feedback for, 67; identification of a need or requirement to conduct a wargame, 77–78; networking with other wargamers, 103; size and composition of, 28–29, 62, 78, 96, 102, 187–88, 208–9; sponsor's needs and objectives, 81–90, 97–99, 102, 188–90, 253–57; subject matter experts on, 86, 90, 141, 155, 208–9; terms of reference agreement with sponsor, 85–86; value of book, 9; vetting the final report by, 209

technology: analysis of alternatives (AoA) acquisition study, 7; analytic wargames to examine, 6–7; innovative and creative thinkers develop new tactics and doctrine for new technology, 29; measurement space to assess, 196–98

Title 10 wargames, U.S. Code (wargames at service level): U.S. Air Force's Global Engagement, 18; U.S. Army's Unified Quest, 18–19, 85–86, 171, 187, 197; U.S. Navy's Global, 18

TRAC. *See* Training and Doctrine Command Analysis Center

TRADOC. *See* Training and Doctrine Command

Training and Doctrine Command (TRADOC), U.S., 179, 187, 197

Training and Doctrine Command Analysis Center (TRAC), U.S., 85, 115

TTX. *See* tabletop exercise

Ugaki, Matome, 56–57, 161

Unified Quest wargame, 18–19, 85–86, 171, 187, 197

United Kingdom: Connections conference, 21

United States: beginning of modern wargaming, 53; Connections conference, 21. *See also* Air Force, U.S.; Army, U.S.; Center for Army Analysis (CAA); Command and General Staff College (CGSC); Department of Defense, U.S.; Marine Corps, U.S.; Naval Postgraduate School (NPS); Naval War College; Navy, U.S.; Training and Doctrine Command Analysis Center (TRAC); Training and Doctrine Command (TRADOC)

Vego, Milan: history of Prussian and German wargaming, 51

Vector-in-Command (simulation): more complicated than necessary for a wargame, 115. *See* computer simulations

vetting reports, 67, 111, 151: best practice for, 209
VIC. *See* computer simulations
vignettes, 96, 104, 117, 125–26, 128, 136, 197, 199, 280, 311

wargame set in South China Sea (case study), 302–5
wargame teams. *See* teams, wargaming
Wei Hai (game), 51–52
white cell/control cell: function of, 154–55; information structure of wargames, 43, 48; management of, 204, 205; play-testing, 123–24; subject matter experts in and facilitator with advice for adjudication, 173–74; training and exercising staff for, 66, 202
worst practices. *See* best and worst practices

Yamamoto, Isoroku, 161–62
Yarnell, Harry, 55–56

Zefra scenario: adaptation from Canadian "Army of Tomorrow", 33–34; 265–67; attitudes and goals, 224–34; background and issues faced by, 10, 69–73, 210, 214–34; conduct of wargame exercise, 137–38, 263–65; Crisis in Zefra matrix wargame, 314–32; desired end states, 234–37; initiate phase exercises, 97–100, 253–57; location of, 10, 69, 214; player objectives, 237–52; practical exercise on design and development using, 118–19, 130–31, 258–62; practical exercises on quick-look report and analysis using, 145–48; tasking briefing, 210–13
Zimm, Alan, 57
Zinni, Anthony: sponsor of Desert Crossing wargame in 1999 at CENTCOM, 58; urging staff to use Desert Crossing results to plan invasion of Iraq, 60

ABOUT THE AUTHORS

Col. Jeff Appleget, USA (Ret.), raised in Vermont, graduated from West Point in 1979. He served as an artillery officer and an operations research analyst, providing analytic support for combat operations and acquisition programs. Upon his retirement from the Army in 2009, he joined the Naval Postgraduate School's Operations Research Department faculty, where he teaches wargaming and combat modeling.

Col. Robert Burks, USA (Ret.), raised as an Army brat, enlisted in the infantry in 1982 and spent more than thirty years serving the country. He retired from military service in 2013 and joined the Naval Postgraduate School, where he has focused on teaching quantitative methods and wargaming to Special Operations Forces students from around the world.

Fred Cameron served as a civilian analyst in the Canadian Department of National Defense for more than thirty-five years. For nearly a decade he has been teaching analytical wargaming in courses provided by the Naval Postgraduate School. He resides on Vancouver Island.

The Naval Institute Press is the book-publishing arm of the U.S. Naval Institute, a private, nonprofit, membership society for sea service professionals and others who share an interest in naval and maritime affairs. Established in 1873 at the U.S. Naval Academy in Annapolis, Maryland, where its offices remain today, the Naval Institute has members worldwide.

Members of the Naval Institute support the education programs of the society and receive the influential monthly magazine *Proceedings* or the colorful bimonthly magazine *Naval History* and discounts on fine nautical prints and on ship and aircraft photos. They also have access to the transcripts of the Institute's Oral History Program and get discounted admission to any of the Institute-sponsored seminars offered around the country.

The Naval Institute's book-publishing program, begun in 1898 with basic guides to naval practices, has broadened its scope to include books of more general interest. Now the Naval Institute Press publishes about seventy titles each year, ranging from how-to books on boating and navigation to battle histories, biographies, ship and aircraft guides, and novels. Institute members receive significant discounts on the Press' more than eight hundred books in print.

Full-time students are eligible for special half-price membership rates. Life memberships are also available.

For more information about Naval Institute Press books that are currently available, visit www.usni.org/press/books. To learn about joining the U.S. Naval Institute, please write to:

Member Services
U.S. Naval Institute
291 Wood Road
Annapolis, MD 21402-5034
Telephone: (800) 233-8764
Fax: (410) 571-1703
Web address: www.usni.org

www.ingramcontent.com/pod-product-compliance
Lightning Source LLC
Chambersburg PA
CBHW030226100526
44585CB00012BA/229